The Economics of Leisure and Tourism

The Economics of Leisure and Tourism

Second Edition

John Tribe

OXFORD   AUCKLAND   BOSTON   JOHANNESBURG   MELBOURNE   NEW DELHI

Butterworth-Heinemann
Linacre House, Jordan Hill, Oxford OX2 8DP
225 Wildwood Avenue, Woburn, MA 01801-2041
A division of Reed Educational and Professional Publishing Ltd

$\mathcal{R}$ A member of the Reed Elsevier plc group

First published 1995
Reprinted 1996, 1997, 1998
Second edition 1999
Reprinted 2000

British Library Cataloguing in Publication Data
Tribe, John
    Economics of leisure and tourism – 2nd ed.
    1. Tourist trade – Economic aspects   2. Leisure industry –
    Economic aspects
    I. Title
    338.4'791

ISBN 0 7506 4232 7

Composition by Genesis Typesetting, Laser Quay, Rochester, Kent
Printed and bound in Great Britain

Contents

Preface to the second edition

Leisure and tourism continues to provide a fascinating field of study for economists. The first edition of this text was written just after a period of intense recession in the UK economy. This revised second edition has been prepared during a period of growth in the economies of the UK, the USA and Europe. But elsewhere, the economies of Japan – the second largest in the world – Brazil, Russia, and what were once referred to as the Asian tiger economies have suffered decline. It is, of course, impossible to predict the economic conditions that will prevail in the year when, or the region where, this text will be read. But it is important to understand what has happened over the course of economic business cycles to prepare for what may happen in the future.

The change in fortunes of the economy are mapped out through the updated statistics which are a central feature of this second edition. The effects of these changes on the leisure sector are also evident in these statistics and more so in the many new and updated exhibits that illustrate the text. In some cases original exhibits have been retained so as to provide the reader with contrasting evidence and a sense of the dynamics of the economy. In terms of geographical coverage, this text uses the UK as its main focus, but incorporates examples from the European Union and the rest of the world.

The aim of this text remains that of offering those involved in the business of leisure and tourism an understanding of the practicalities of economics. To support this aim real-world examples continue to be emphasized in this text rather than economic theory for theory's sake. Thus in contrast to general economics introductory texts, the marginal productivity theory of labour theory is excluded, but pricing of externalities is included on the grounds that the latter is more useful to students of leisure and tourism than the former.

The key themes of the book focus on a series of questions:

● How is the provision of leisure and tourism determined?
● Could it be provided in a different way?
● What are the key opportunities and threats facing leisure and tourism?
● What are the economic impacts of leisure and tourism?
● What are the environmental impacts of leisure and tourism?
● How can economics be used to manage leisure and tourism?

The other key features of this text are:

- Visual mapping of the content of each chapter.
- Liberal use of press cuttings to illustrate points.
- Chapter objectives.
- Key points summarized.
- Data response questions.
- Short answer questions.
- Integrated case studies.
- Useful websites.

It is hoped that this text will create a lasting interest in the economics of leisure and tourism and generate a spirit of critical enquiry into leisure and tourism issues affecting consumers, producers and hosts.

Finally, students are encouraged to keep this textbook up to date. They should attempt to bring case studies and tables up to date, therefore space has been left in key tables to insert updated statistics.

John Tribe, 1999

Acknowledgements

The author extends sincere thanks to those organizations which have given permission to reproduce text and data. Articles from the *Independent*, *Guardian* and *Observer* newspapers have helped to illustrate many points as have guidelines from the World Travel and Tourism Council. Press releases have been used from Friends of the Earth and the World Tourism Organization and the Barclays Bank *Economics Review* maintains a generous policy in allowing reproduction of its material.

The author would also like to thank colleagues at Buckinghamshire Chilterns University College who have assisted in the preparation of this book. In particular, Nigel North and Anne Aichroth have both kindly provided case studies, while the director, Professor Bryan Mogford, and the Dean of the Faculty of Leisure and Tourism, Gill Fisher, have both provided much encouragement and support.

1 Introduction

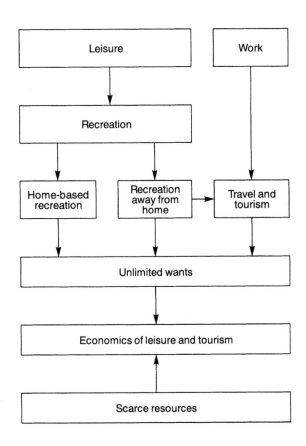

Objectives

- What is the globalization of leisure and tourism?
- Is passenger forecasting a load of old crystal balls?
- Are leisure and tourism shares good investments?
- Is the growth of leisure and tourism sustainable

This book will help you investigate these issues. The objectives of this chapter are to define and integrate the areas of study of this book. First the scope of leisure and tourism will be discussed, and second the scope and techniques of economics will be outlined. The final part of the chapter explains how the study area of leisure and tourism can be analysed using economic techniques.

By studying this chapter students will be able to:

- understand the scope of leisure and tourism and their interrelationship
- explain the basic economic concerns of scarcity, choice and opportunity costs
- outline the allocation of resources in different economic systems
- explain the methodology of economics
- understand the use of models in economics
- understand the use of economics to analyse issues in leisure and tourism
- access sources of information

Definition and scope of leisure and tourism

Defining leisure and tourism is like defining an orange. We all know an orange when we see one and we can generally distinguish it from a banana without too much difficulty. We could try a definition. 'An orange is a round citrus fruit, of orange colour and with orange taste'. But you can be sure that once a definition has been made, problems arise. Does a definition of an orange using the term 'orange' add to our understanding? If the object I am looking at seems to be an orange but is oval-shaped, is it an orange? Is a satsuma an orange? Questions such as these inevitably arise and are important, particularly where data collection or interpretation is concerned. For example, the number of oranges imported into the UK is a different number according to whether related fruit such as satsumas and clementines are included in the definition. Similar problems occur in using and measuring the term 'unemployment'. In 1999 UK unemployment was around 1.7 million. But are people on training schemes unemployed? Are those fraudulently claiming unemployment benefit unemployed? According to the definition used, unemployment can in fact range from around 1 million to around 2.5 million.

What then is leisure and tourism? A common element in many definitions of leisure is that of free time. Thus working, sleeping and household chores are excluded. However, should we then include people who are sick or recovering from illness? If the definition is extended to include doing things that one wants to do, this problem is avoided, but another arises. What about the parts of people's jobs that they enjoy, or things done to support their employment in their spare time? For example, is a computer programmer's use of computers in non-working time a leisure activity?

Similar questions arise in defining tourism. The common element in definitions of tourism is that of 'temporary visiting'. Questions of scope immediately arise. Are people who are engaged in study overseas tourists? Are people travelling on business tourists?

Aware of the problems involved, some working definitions of travel and tourism are now attempted.

Working definitions

- Leisure = discretionary time

  Discretionary time is the time remaining after working, commuting, sleeping and doing necessary household and personal chores which can be used in a chosen way.

- Recreation = pursuits undertaken in leisure time

  Recreational pursuits include home-based activities such as reading and watching television, and those outside the home including sports, theatre, cinema and tourism.

- Tourism = visiting for at least one night for leisure and holiday, business and professional or other tourism purposes.

  Visiting means a temporary movement to destinations outside the normal home and workplace.

- Leisure and tourism sector organizations = organizations producing goods and services for use in leisure time, organizations seeking to influence the use of leisure time and organizations supplying leisure and tourism organizations. Many organizations produce goods and services for leisure and non-leisure use, for example computer manufacturers.

Figure 1.1 shows the relationship between leisure and tourism and the constituent parts are discussed below.

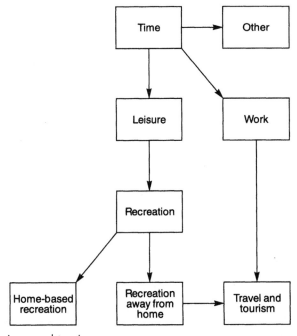

Figure 1.1 Leisure and tourism.

Home-based recreation

This includes:

- listening to music
- watching TV and videos
- listening to the radio
- reading
- DIY
- gardening
- playing games
- exercise
- hobbies
- leisure use of computers

Recreation away from home

This includes:

- sports participation
- watching entertainment
- hobbies
- visiting attractions
- eating and drinking
- betting and gaming

Travel and tourism

This includes:

- travelling to destination
- accommodation at destination
- recreation

Definition, scope and methodology of economics

The nature of economics

Resources and wants

Economics arises from a basic imbalance that is evident throughout the world. On the one side there are resources which can be used to make goods and services. These are classified by economists into land (raw materials), labour and capital (machines). On the other side we have people's wants.

The worldwide economic fact of life is that people's wants appear unlimited and exceed the resources available to satisfy these wants. This is true not just for people with low incomes, but for people with high incomes too. Clearly the basic needs of rich people are generally satisfied in terms of food, clothing and shelter, but it is evident that their material wants in terms of cars, property, holidays and recreation are rarely fully satisfied.

Scarcity and choice

The existence of limited resources and unlimited wants gives rise to the basic economic problem of scarcity. The existence of scarcity means that choices have to be made about resource use and allocation. Economics is concerned with the choice questions that arise from scarcity:

- What to produce?
- How to produce it?
- To whom will goods and services be allocated?

Opportunity cost

Since resources can be used in different ways to make different goods and services, and since they are limited in relation to wants, the concept of opportunity cost arises. This can be viewed at different levels.

At the individual level, consumers have limited income. So if they spend their income on a mountain bike, they can consider what else they could have bought with the money, such as 50 CDs. Individuals also have limited time. If an individual decides to work extra overtime, leisure time must be given up.

At a local or national government level the same choices can be analysed. Local councils have limited budgets. If they decide to build a leisure centre, that money could have been used to provide more home help to the elderly. Even if they raised local taxes to build the new leisure centre there would be an opportunity cost, since the taxpayers would have to give up something in order to pay the extra taxes. At a national government level, subsidizing the arts means less money available for student grants.

Opportunity cost can be defined as the alternatives or other opportunities that have to be foregone to achieve a particular thing. Figure 1.2 illustrates this concept by use of a production possibility frontier (PPF). It is assumed first that the economy only produces two types of goods (leisure goods, and other goods) and second, that it uses all its resources fully.

Curve PPF plots all the possible combinations of leisure goods and other goods that can be produced in this economy. It is drawn concave to the origin (bowed outwards) since, as more and more resources are concentrated on the production of one commodity, the resources available become less suitable for producing that commodity.

Curve PPF shows that if all resources were geared towards the production of leisure goods, 600 units could be produced with no production of other

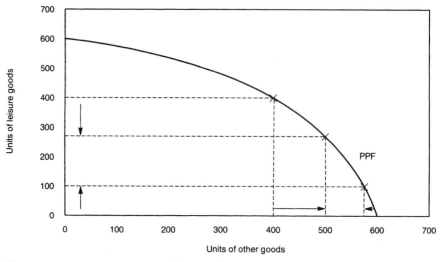

Figure 1.2   Opportunity cost and the production possibility frontier (PPF).

goods. At the other extreme, 600 units of other goods could be produced with no units of leisure goods. The PPF describes the opportunity cost of increasing production of either of these goods. For example, increasing production of leisure goods from 0 to 100 can only be done by diverting resources from the production of other goods, and production of these falls from 600 to 580 units. Thus the opportunity cost at this point of 100 units of leisure goods is the 20 units of other goods that must be foregone. Similarly, if all resources are being used to produce a combination of 400 units of leisure goods and 400 units of other goods, the opportunity cost of producing an extra 100 units of other goods would be 100 units of leisure goods.

Allocative mechanisms

The existence of scarcity of resources and unlimited wants means that any economy must have a system for determining what, how and for whom goods are produced. The main systems for achieving this are:

● free market economies
● centrally planned economies
● mixed economies

Free market economies work by allowing private ownership of firms. The owners of such firms produce goods and services by purchasing resources. The motive for production is profit and thus firms will tend to produce those goods and services which are in demand. Figure 1.3 shows the market mechanism in action.

Centrally planned economies do not allow the private ownership of firms which instead are state-owned. Production decisions are taken by state

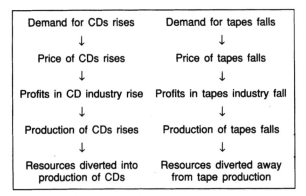

Figure 1.3 The price mechanism in action.

planning committees and resources are mobilized accordingly. Consumers generally have some choice of what to buy, but only from the range determined by state planners.

Mixed economies incorporate elements from each system. Private ownership of firms tends to predominate, but production and consumption of goods and services may be influenced by public ownership of some enterprises and by the use of taxes and government spending.

The allocative mechanism has important implications for leisure and tourism. The collapse of communism in the eastern bloc has meant that many economies are now in transition from centrally planned to market systems. Tourism facilities, such as hotels and restaurants, in these countries are having to revolutionize their organizational culture and become more customer-oriented. The economies of Cuba and China are still nominally centrally planned, but free enterprise is currently flourishing under the

---

Exhibit 1.1   Cuba allows limited private enterprise

Cuba took another cautious step towards establishing a mixed economy in 1993 when its communist government authorized limited private enterprise in a wide range of trades, crafts and services. The move, announced in a decree signed by President Fidel Castro, lifted a long-standing state monopoly of production, employment and sales. Ordinary Cubans welcomed the decision and predicted the return to city streets of the private vendors who disappeared in the late 1960s when state control was extended to all sectors of the economy.

Taxi drivers, mechanics, plumbers, carpenters, painters, hair dressers, cobblers, cooks, domestics, craftsmen, farm products salesmen and computer programmers are among those who will now be able to run their own businesses.

This move may have been prompted by visits of Cuban Officials to China and Vietnam where private enterprise has been introduced into state-run economies.

Source: Guardian, 10 September 1993 (adapted).

economic reforms in China, and a visit to the Great Wall is repaid by privately owned souvenir shops jostling for custom. Exhibit 1.1 illustrates the loosening of central planning restrictions in Cuba.

Equally, the mix of the British mixed economy is of direct importance to leisure and tourism provision. The 'Thatcher revolution', which involved 'rolling back the frontiers of the state', involved privatization of British Airways (BA) and the British Airports Authority (BAA), and also limited the spending powers of local government, thus reducing public provision in arts and leisure. Exhibit 1.2 illustrates the extension of this policy to the privatization of Britain's forests and considers views for and against this process.

The debate surrounding the mix of private versus public provision tends to centre on several key issues. Advocates of the free market argue that the system allows maximum consumer choice or sovereignty. They point to the efficiency of the system as firms compete to cut costs and improve products, the fact that the system does not need wastefully to employ officials to plan and monitor production, and lower taxes under free market systems. Their evidence is the one-way flow of human traffic observed across the Florida Straits from Cuba and past the former Iron Curtain from Eastern Europe in search of the free market.

Exhibit 1.2   Selling off the family tree

Although the government insists there are no plans 'at present' to private the Forestry Commission, with assets of £1.6 bn and 6300 employees, forestry unions are in no doubt that their organization has been subjected to 'creeping privatization' since 1981 when the government ordered the commission to begin a programme of 'asset sales'. By July 1992, it has sold 410 000 acres of plantations and prime forests and passed almost £170 m to the Treasury. Now with land prices depressed, it has been given a firm target: sell a further 247 000 acres by the end of this decade and aim to raise a further £150 m. And that could be just the start.

The commission was established in 1919 to provide a strategic timber reserve after 'the desperate timber shortages of the first world war'. The Countryside Acts of 1967 and 1968 formally recognized the importance of state forests for public recreation. The commission was then given new powers to provide campsites, picnic places and visitor centres. The Ramblers' Association is so concerned by the privatization threat to the commission's 'freedom to roam' policy that its main event this summer will be devoted to preserving access to the forests. Dave Beskine, the association's assistant director, say: 'While the commission has been a model landowner, private landlords often seem hostile to access'.

The radical right has long regarded the commission as a corporate anachronism at odds with the market economy. When the Adam Smith Institute launched a report, *Pining for Profit*, in the late 1980s, it undoubtedly struck a chord in government circles by calculating that the agency had been a drain on the Exchequer for more than 70 years, to the tune of £1 bn at today's prices.

Source: Guardian, 16 March 1993 (adapted).

Critics of the free market argue that choice is an illusion. Thus, although by day the shops in Oxford Street are full of every conceivable product, by night their doorways are full of homeless people. Only those with purchasing power can exercise choice and purchasing power is unequally distributed in free market economies. They also point to the free market chaos evident in post-communist Russia.

Macroeconomics and microeconomics

Economics is often subdivided into the separate areas of microeconomics and macroeconomics. Microeconomics studies individual consumer and household behaviour as well as the behaviour of firms. It analyses how these interact in particular markets to produce an equilibrium price and quantity sold. Thus microeconomics looks at the price of air travel, the output of running shoes and the choice between leisure and work.

Macroeconomics looks at the economy as a whole. The national economy is composed of all the individual market activities added together. Thus macroeconomics looks at aggregates such as national product and inflation.

Marginal analysis

The concept of 'the margin' is central to much economic analysis. Consumer, producer and social welfare theories are based on the idea that an equilibrium position can be achieved which represents the best possible solution. This position can theoretically be found by comparing the marginal benefit (MB) of doing something with the marginal cost (MC). For example, MC to a firm is the cost of producing one extra unit. MB is the revenue gained from selling one extra unit. Clearly a firm can increase its profit by producing more if $MB > MC$. It should not expand such that $MC > MB$, and thus profits are maximized, and the firm is in equilibrium, because it cannot better its position, where $MC = MB$.

The methodology of economics

Economics is a social science. As such it draws some of its methodology or way of working from other sciences such as physics or chemistry, but also has important differences.

The 'science' of social science

The science part of economics is that it is a discipline that attempts to develop a body of principles. Economic principles attempt to explain the behaviour of households and firms in the economy. It therefore shares some common methods with other sciences.

The first of these is the need to distinguish between positive and normative statements. Positive statements are those which can be tested by an appeal to the facts. They are statements of what is or what will be. 'Swimming cuts cholesterol' is a positive statement. It can be tested, and accepted or refuted. Normative statements are those which are statements of opinion, and therefore cannot be tested by an appeal to the facts. 'There should be a swimming pool in every town' is a normative statement.

Second, economics uses scientific method. The scientific method acts as a filter which determines which theories become part of the established body of principles of economics, and whether existing theories should maintain their place. Figure 1.4 illustrates the scientific testing of theories.

New and existing theories are subject to testing and are accepted, rejected, amended or superseded according to the results of testing. Thus the body of economic principles is, like that of other sciences, organic in the sense that knowledge is being extended and some theories are shown to be no longer valid.

This can be illustrated by considering the shape of the earth. Hundreds of years ago, people were in agreement that the earth was flat. This theory was

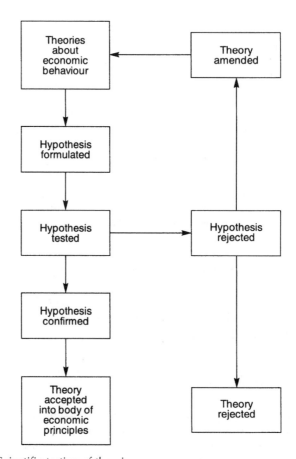

Figure 1.4   Scientific testing of theories.

confirmed by scholars who reasoned that if it was not flat people would fall off it. It was further reasoned that the stars were attached to a canopy above the earth and this fitted observations nicely. This then was the accepted set of principles until the theory no longer tested true. It was developments in geometry and astronomy that first led to serious questioning of the accepted principles and circumnavigation of the earth endorsed such findings. Modern space programmes continue to confirm our current belief in a round earth by providing supporting photographic evidence.

Academic journals in economics, leisure and tourism provide the arena for testing old and new hypotheses in this field.

The 'social' of social science

The difference between social sciences such as economics, sociology and psychology and natural sciences such as physics and chemistry is that the former study people rather than inanimate objects. This means first that their investigative methods are often different. It is difficult to perform laboratory experiments in economics and often data must be collected from historical records or from surveys. Second it means that economic 'laws' are different from physics laws. If interest rates increase it can be predicted that the demand for credit will fall but we cannot predict that will be true for every individual. The law of gravity, on the other hand, applies universally.

Economic models

Economic models are built to describe relationships between economic variables and predict the effects of changing these variables. They can be compared to models used elsewhere. For example, civil engineers build models of bridges and subject them to stress in a wind tunnel. The purpose of the model is to predict what will happen in the real world, and in the case of a bridge ensure that the design is safe in extreme conditions.

Models are generally simplified abstractions of the real world. They have two key components. First assumptions are made which build the foundations for the model. For example, the model of firms' behaviour under perfect competition assumes that firms maximize profits, that there are many buyers and sellers, and that the products bought and sold are identical. Second implications or outcomes are predicted by the working of the model. For example, theory predicts that firms operating under conditions of perfect competition will not be able to earn abnormally high profits in the long run. As the channel crossing becomes a more competitive environment, since the opening of the tunnel, the predictions of competition theory can be tested empirically, or in other words by making observations.

The term *ceteris paribus* is often used in economic analysis, meaning all other things remaining unchanged. This is important because in the real world several factors often occur at the same time, some exaggerating a particular effect, and some countering it. So for example it can be said that for most goods an increase in price will lead to a fall in demand *ceteris paribus*. Thus a rise in cinema ticket prices should cause a fall in demand. Clearly if other things are allowed to change this might not happen. For example, if incomes rose significantly this might more than offset the increase in price and we might observe demand for cinema tickets rising whilst prices rise.

The economics of leisure and tourism

The rest of this book uses economic analysis to explore issues in leisure and tourism, approaching the area in the following way:

Part One: Organizations and markets in leisure and tourism

This section analyses the demand for leisure and tourism goods and services and their supply in an attempt to understand the factors that influence which goods and services are supplied and what prices are charged for them.

Chapter 2: Leisure and tourism organizations

● What is the mission of British Airports Authority?
● How was finance raised for the Channel tunnel?
● What was the Thomson flotation?
● How does the Department of Culture, Media and Sport influence the leisure and tourism sector?

In order to analyse the supply of leisure and tourism goods and services, the motives, missions and structures of leisure and tourism organizations are scrutinized in this chapter.

Chapter 3: The market for leisure and tourism products

● What is the economic function of ticket touts?
● How do changes in the exchange rate affect the demand for foreign holidays?
● How are squash courts allocated at peak times?

In market economies the 'invisible hand' of the price mechanism performs an essential function. It signals consumer demands to producers. Producers wishing to maximize their profits will allocate resources into markets where demand and prices are rising and away from markets where demand and prices are falling.

Chapter 4: Choice, elasticity and demand forecasting

● If wages increase do people demand less leisure time?
● How do consumers choose between Eurostar and BA?
● How can we predict the demand for golf balls for the next five years?

This chapter examines how consumers behave in markets to maximize their personal satisfaction, and also considers techniques for forecasting demand.

Chapter 5: Supply and costs

● Why do ski holidays cost more during school holiday periods?
● What are the fixed costs of football?
● Why do students get cheap seats in West End theatres but have to pay full price for ice creams?
● Why do Thomson brochures get best rack space in Lunn Poly?

This chapter investigates production, the use of inputs and the behaviour of firms' costs. It also analyses the motives of mergers and takeovers.

Chapter 6: Price and market strategy in the real world

● How can the person sitting next to you on a flight to New York have paid twice your ticket price?
● Can you haggle at the Hilton?
● The Channel price war: who wins?

This chapter looks at the classic strategies for increasing profits and market share.

Chapter 7: Market intervention

● Are CD prices a rip-off?
● Why do we need OFFRAIL?
● Why do we subsidize opera but not rock?

This chapter investigates the problems of the unregulated free market and considers the arguments for intervention.

Part Two: Leisure and tourism organizations and the external environment

Things are changing fast. The operating environment within which organizations work is often characterized by the four Ds:

- Difficult.
- Dangerous.
- Dynamic.
- Diverse.

The aim of this section is to enable organizations to scan their environments and plan their futures, by using opportunities and threats analysis. Chapters 8 to 11 investigate different parts of the operating environment and the latter part of Chapter 11 summarizes the issues.

Chapter 8: The competitive environment

- UK holidays: unfair competition?
- Who will win the battle of the computer games?
- Is BSkyB good for Manchester United?

Current or potential threats from competitors or new products need to be monitored. This chapter provides a framework for auditing the competitive environment

Chapter 9: The economic environment

- When will the next recession start?
- Are interest rates going up or down?
- What levels of consumer spending are likely next year?

Chapter 9 analyses how leisure and tourism organizations are affected by changes in the national economy and investigates the trends in key macroeconomic variables.

Chapter 10: The political and sociocultural environment

- What is the green revolution?
- How will the grey revolution affect leisure demand?
- Politics: which party will be celebrating the new year in 2005?

This chapter investigates the political and sociocultural aspects of the organization's operating environment.

Chapter 11: The technological environment and opportunities and threats analysis

- Will leisure disappear into cyberspace?
- Are video cassettes yesterday's technology?
- The Internet: opportunity or threat?

Opportunities and threats analysis is often used in marketing and strategic planning. The key issues from the competitive and political, economic, sociocultural and technological (PEST) environments are highlighted as opportunities and threats to enable organizations to plan effective strategies to exploit opportunities and counter threats.

Part Three: Investing in leisure and tourism

This section analyses the trends in and factors affecting investment in the leisure and tourism sector, looking separately at the private sector and the public sector.

Chapter 12 Investment appraisal in the private sector

- Will the British Airports Authority suffer terminal failure?
- What is the relationship between the Asian economic crisis and Boeing and the city of Seattle?
- How accurate have Eurotunnel cash flow projections been?

Profit is the main motive for private sector investment in leisure and tourism capital. This chapter investigates the factors which determine the profitability of investments and considers techniques for appraising investment projects.

Chapter 13: Investment and the public sector

- Why does leisure provision differ so widely between local authorities?
- Can government investment in leisure contribute to urban regeneration?
- Should the BBC have different investment criteria from commercial broadcasters?

This chapter considers how decision making for investment projects in the public sector differs from practice in the private sector.

Part Four: Leisure and tourism impacts on the national economy

While Chapter 9 investigated the impact of the economy on leisure and tourism organizations, this section looks at this from the other direction and analyses the impacts of the leisure and tourism sector on the economy.

Chapter 14: Leisure and tourism; income, employment and inflation

- Which industry is the world's biggest employer?
- What is the cheapest holiday destination?

- Why are wages in the hospitality sector so low?
- How much of £100 tourist spending in the Hotel Beijing Toronto stays in China?

This chapter attempts to measure the contribution of the leisure and tourism sector to national economies. For example, travel and tourism is often cited as the world's biggest industry. Inflation, and price indices are also examined in this chapter with particular emphasis on comparing prices in tourism destinations.

Chapter 15: Leisure and tourism and economic growth

- Can tourism save Castro's Cuba?
- How has China cornered the toy market?
- Why do Japanese play golf overseas, but some locals think this to be a handicap?
- Can the UK's industrial heritage make up for its lost industry?

This chapter reviews the contribution that the leisure and tourism sector can make to the economic growth of national economies. It particularly looks at the potential the sector can contribute to growth strategies in developing countries.

Part Five: International aspects of leisure and tourism

This section considers the impact of leisure and tourism on foreign currency earnings, analyses the effects of exchange rates on leisure and tourism organizations and charts the growth of multinationals.

Chapter 16: Leisure and tourism; the balance of payments and exchange rates

- What can be done to turn around the UK's growing tourism deficit?
- How does EuroDisney contribute to the French balance of payments?
- Why is the low pound good for UK leisure but bad for UK tourists?
- How does the Euro affect leisure and tourism?

This chapter examines the contribution of the leisure and tourism sector to countries' balance of payments, and considers how the sector is affected by changes in the exchange rate.

Chapter 17: Multinational organizations

- Why is British Airways going global?
- Why are British-owned ferries registered in the Bahamas?
- MNEs – opportunity or threat to Zanzibar?

This chapter investigates the growth of the multinational enterprise and considers benefits and costs to parent and hosts economies.

Part Six: Leisure and tourism and environmental issues

This part is divided into two chapters. The first critically evaluates the contribution of leisure and tourism to human well-being. The second chapter suggests how economic analysis can be used to modify leisure and tourism developments to minimize the costs and maximize the benefits to society.

Chapter 18: Environmental impacts of leisure and tourism

- How does aircraft noise add to our GNP?
- Why do we pump raw sewage into the sea?
- How can successful tourism development self-destruct?
- Why has war been declared on mountain bikes?

This chapter looks beyond conventional economic analysis and casts a critical environmental economist's eye over the benefits that are claimed for development of leisure and tourism industries.

Chapter 19: Sustainability and 'green' leisure and tourism

- What are 'Surfers against Sewage' trying to achieve?
- What are the costs and benefits of Terminal 5 construction at London Airport, Heathrow?
- How are Forte's hotels going green, and reducing costs?
- How can we encourage green recreation and green tourism?

This chapter examines the meaning of green leisure and tourism, and considers how economics can help deliver a sustainable future for these industries.

Part Seven: Integrated case studies

Chapter 20: Integrated case studies

- Is Costa Rican tourism sustainable?
- What are the economic impacts of football?
- Tourism – prosperity for Cuba?
- Leisure tourism and taxation.

Real world issues are complex. They are not neatly divided into sections on costs, sections on competition and sections on exchange rates. This chapter contains integrated case studies which provide problems requiring analysis using tools developed throughout the book.

Sources of data

Sources of data for the economics of leisure and tourism can be found in newspapers, journals, magazines, reports and statistical publications as well as company annual reports and websites. Table 1.1 lists the main sources.

Table 1.1   Leisure and tourism sources

Publication	Publisher	Publication	Publisher
Journals		Magazines/reviews	
Annals of Tourism Research	Elsevier Science (UK/USA)	Barclays Economic Review	Barclays Bank
Tourism Management	Elsevier Science (UK)	Leisure Management	The Leisure Media Co. Ltd
International Journal of Hospitality Management	Elsevier Science (UK/USA)	Tourism Marketplace	AMS Publishing (UK)
		Travel GB	
Museums Journal	Museums Association (UK)	Travel Trade Gazette	
		Travel Weekly	
Journal of Sustainable Tourism	Channel View Books (UK)	Statistical sources	
Journal of Leisure Research	National Recreation and Parks Association (USA)	Annual Abstract of Statistics	Office for National Statistics (UK)
		Compendium of Tourist Statistics	World Tourism Organization (Spain)
Journal of Travel Research	Travel and Tourism Research Organization (USA)	Digest of Tourist Statistics	British Tourist Authority (UK)
Tourism Economics	In-Print-Publishing Ltd	Economic Trends	Office for National Statistics (UK)
		Employment Gazette	Office for National Statistics (UK)
Reports		Social Trends	Office for National Statistics (UK)
International Tourism Reports	Economist Publications (UK)		
Leisure Forecasts	Leisure Consultants (UK)	General Household Survey	Office for National Statistics (UK)
Leisure Futures	Henley Centre for Forecasting (UK)	Family Expenditure Survey	Office for National Statistics (UK)
International Tourism Reports	Travel and Tourism Intelligence (UK)	Tourism Intelligence Quarterly	British Tourist Authority/English Tourist Board

Review of key terms

- Leisure = discretionary time.
- Recreation = pursuits undertaken in leisure time.
- Tourism = visiting for at least one night for leisure and holiday, business and professional or other tourism purposes.
- Economic problem = scarcity and choice.
- Leisure and tourism sector organizations = organizations producing goods and services for use in leisure time, and organizations seeking to influence the use of leisure time.
- Opportunity cost = the alternatives or other opportunities that have to be foregone to achieve a particular thing.
- Free market economy = resources allocated through price system.
- Centrally planned economy = resources allocated by planning officials.
- Mixed economy = resources allocated through free market and planning authorities.
- Microeconomics = study of household and firm's behaviour.
- Macroeconomics = study of whole economy.
- Marginal analysis = study of effects of one extra unit.
- Positive statement = based on fact.
- Normative statement = based on opinion.
- *Ceteris paribus* = other things remaining unchanged.

Data questions

Task 1.1   The uses and misuses of economics

Economics is a discipline which can help to understand leisure and tourism and provides tools to help decision making. But it is only one of a number of ways of looking at leisure and tourism. For example, the disciplines of sociology, psychology, anthropology and philosophy each investigate different aspects of leisure and tourism and use different methods and theories in their investigations. So philosophy may look at meaning (what is the concept of leisure?), aesthetics (is a football stadium attractively designed?) and ethics (are violent video games good or bad?). Focusing on video games can help to see how different disciplines tackle different issues. Psychology might investigate human motivation for playing video games. Economics may forecast the demand for them. Sociology can help to understand the effects of video games on society.

A complex field of study such as leisure and tourism often requires a multidisciplinary approach. That is we may seek understanding not just from one discipline but from a number of disciplines. In addition, there are approaches which are interdisciplinary. Here a new set of methods, theories and language emerge from those working collaboratively across disciplines. Environmentalism, which uses economics, sociology, biology, physics and chemistry, is an example of an interdisciplinary approach.

Table 1.2   Differences between disciplinary and functional approaches to leisure and tourism

	Disciplinary	*Functional*
Knowledge	Knowing that	Knowing how
Site of knowledge creation	Universities	Industry
Interest	Is it true?	Does it work?
Emphasis	Theory	Practice

Then there are functional approaches to leisure and tourism. These have a more distant relationship to disciplines and their specific focus is on management. Examples here include accounting, law, marketing and human resource management. Whilst disciplines are nurtured in universities and concentrate on the development of theories, functional approaches are developed in the practising field. The main differences between disciplinary knowledge and functional knowledge are summarized in Table 1.2.

The importance of this discussion is that we live in a society of specialists with a highly developed division of labour. It is easy for people to become highly knowledgeable in one area while being ignorant of other significant aspects of a situation. It is therefore important to understand the limits of any single approach and the fact that most leisure and tourism issues are multi-faceted. It is always worth asking what kind of a question is being investigated (is it an economic, philosophical, psychological question, or one of law or marketing?). Of course, the wider the approach, the more difficult decision making can become.

Questions

1 What contribution can economics make to environmentalism?
2 What kinds of questions are each of the following?
   ● the level of a minimum wage for the hotel industry
   ● whether violent video games should be banned
   ● the effects of a rise in interest rates
   ● maximizing profits from the sales of video games
   ● imposing a tax on aviation fuel
   ● ending duty-free sales
   ● the location of the next Olympic Games
3 Is there a correct answer to any of these questions?
4 Frame two leisure and tourism questions which are exclusively economic.

Task 1.2   *Human-powered outdoor recreation in the US*

Human-powered outdoor recreation is that sector of leisure in which participants use the power of their own muscles. According to ORCA (The Outdoor Recreation Coalition of America) estimates, it contributes $35 billion to the US economy. These estimates are based on sales of manufacturers, suppliers, distributors, retailers, and guides, as well as related expenditures such as travel, accommodation and fees. It consists of two main parts, consumers and suppliers.

In terms of consumers, the four most popular activities are, in descending order, walking, running and jogging, bicycling and hiking. Other significant activities include rafting, backpacking canoeing, mountain climbing and Nordic skiing. Scuba diving is practised by a small proportion of the population but is economically significant because of its high expenditure per person. It is estimated that scuba divers spend an average of $400 each annually while mountaineers spend an annual average of $325.

Suppliers of directly related goods and services include manufacturers and retailers, providing items such as equipment, footwear, and clothing and services, providers offering tuition, guiding and accommodation and packaged activities.

ORCA estimates the total annual outdoor product and speciality retail sales to be approximately $10 billion. The most popular activities have an established market with steady growth, but newer sports activities such as mountain biking and in-line skating are big contributors to the value of the industry. Retail sales of in-line skates are estimated at $1200 million for 1995, while mountain bike sales reached $4.6 billion in the same year.

There is also a market for publications related to the outdoor recreation industry. These include magazines for participants, trade publications, and books. It is more difficult to measure related revenues accruing to accommodation, etc. Much of this contributes to the rural economies and provides employment. Some states have made estimates of the value of outdoor recreation. Colorado estimated that visitors to its state parks in 1992–1993 spent $692 million.

Questions

1 What kind of jobs are provided by human-powered outdoor recreation?
2 How might these activities affect US imports and exports?
3 What is the opportunity cost of scuba diving?
4 What aspects of microeconomics and macroeconomics are illustrated in this article?
5 Explain (a) how the US market economy works to produce changing patterns of output of human-powered outdoor recreation goods and services; (b) what are the main determinants of the level of outputs; (c) how the 'allocative mechanism' of the USA differs from that in Cuba.
6 Distinguish between the positive and negative economic impacts of these activities.

Task 1.3

Question

Table 1.3 lists organizations that operate in the leisure and tourism sector. Classify these organizations according to the industry structure illustrated in Figure 1.5, adding to or amending the structure where necessary.

Table 1.3   Leisure and tourism organizations

Arts Councils	Carlton	Eurotunnel	Eurodollar
English Tourist Board	Eurocamp	Department for National	Alton Towers
British Tourist Authority	Chrysalis	Heritage	British Rail
Lonrho	Forte	Tate Gallery	BSkyB
Council for the Protection of	First Choice	Sega	Camelot
Rural England	First Leisure	Virgin	CenterParcs
Bass	Reed Elsevier	Lunn Poly	Ladbrookes
Pearson	Touche Rosse	Sony	National Trust
British Airports Authority	Airtours	Boeing	Raleigh
Britannia	Qantas	P&O	SNCF
BBC	BTR plc	Air France	Sports Council
Capital Radio	Manchester Utd	Henley Centre	Thorpe Park
British Airways	Thomson	Going Places	Wembley
		Disneyland Paris	

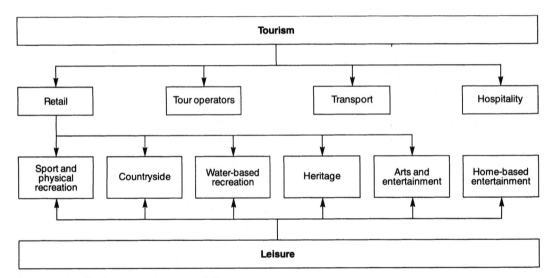

Figure 1.5   The leisure and tourism industry

Short questions

1 What is the opportunity cost of watching television?
2 Explain in terms of marginal analysis at what point you will turn off the television.
3 Formulate a hypothesis that links the level of unemployment to the demand for video rentals. How would you test this hypothesis and what problems might you encounter?
4 Explain how the market mechanism responds to a change in consumer tastes or demand using an example from the leisure or tourism sector.

5 Distinguish between the kinds of problems which physics, biology, psychology and economics might address in the area of sports. What similarities and differences in investigative methods are there between these disciplines?

Websites of interest

Leisure opportunities: daily news   www.leisureopportunities.co.uk
Institute of Leisure and Amenity Management   www.ilam.co.uk
World Tourism Organization   http://www.world-tourism.org/
World Travel and Tourism Council   www.wttc.org/
Learning help in economics and business studies   http://www.bized.ac.uk

Part One
Organizations and Markets in Leisure and Tourism

2 Leisure and tourism organizations

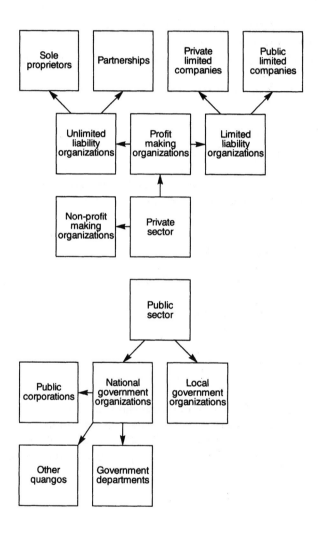

Objectives

In order to analyse and understand the behaviour of organizations in the leisure and tourism sector, we need to be able to clarify their aims and objectives. The National Trust for example will follow different policies to English Heritage which itself will have different policies to Alton Towers.

The similarity between these three is that they all have historic houses open to the public. The key difference is in their forms of ownership – the first being a voluntary organization, the second a government-funded organization and the third a private sector organization.

By studying this chapter students should be able to:

- distinguish between private sector and public sector organizations
- understand the differences in finance, control, structure and objectives of organizations
- understand ways in which capital can be raised
- analyse movements in share prices
- analyse the effects of different organizational structures on organizational behaviour
- distinguish between operational management and strategic management

Public sector organizations

Public sector organizations are those owned by the government. This can be national government or local government.

Local government organizations

Leisure and tourism provision in the local government sector includes:

- leisure centres and swimming pools
- libraries
- arts centres
- parks and recreation facilities
- tourism support

It should be noted that some provision occurs in the commercial marketplace. For example, customers of arts centres and leisure centres have to pay for the services provided. On the other hand facilities such as parks and children's playgrounds are generally provided without charge.

Sources of finance

The finance of these organizations comes from:

- charges for services where applicable
- central government grants
- grants from other sources (e.g. the Arts Council of Great Britain)
- local government taxation (the council tax)
- local government borrowing

The ability of local government to provide the level of services it wishes has been severely curbed by government legislation in recent years. Local government no longer has the power to set its own level of spending but is regulated through a system of central government-determined expenditure targets, council tax capping and financial penalties for exceeding central government spending targets. Chapter 9 analyses factors influencing the level of government spending.

Ownership and control

In essence local government organizations are owned by the local population. Policy decisions or decisions of strategic management are taken on their behalf by the local council. Each local government area elects councillors or members to represent them. The political party which holds the majority of seats on the council will generally be able to dictate policy and such policy will be determined through a series of committees such as:

- libraries and arts
- recreation and leisure
- planning and resources

The planning and resources committee is a particularly powerful one as it determines the medium- to long-term strategy of the council and thus provides the financial framework within which the other committees must operate.

The day-to-day or operational management of local government-run services depends on the nature of the service being provided. The council officers are responsible for overall management and services which are spread out across a local government area, such as parks, will be run from the council offices. Larger services such as leisure centres will have their own management which in turn will be responsible to a service director at the council offices (see Chapter 7 for details of compulsory competitive tendering – CCT).

Aims and missions

The aims of local government and its organizations are largely determined by the political party or coalition of parties who hold the majority. This often means that leisure provision for example will vary between neighbouring local authorities which have different political parties in power. Administrations to the right of the political spectrum favour lower local taxes and market-driven provision. Those to the left favour public provision and subsidized prices.

To determine the differing aims of political parties we need to consult their manifestos as well as review their actual provision. However, political parties do not operate in a vacuum. They will be influenced by:

- pressure groups
- trade unions
- local press
- national government

National government organizations

National government-owned organizations can be further subdivided into public corporations, other quangos and government departments.

Public corporations

There are few public corporations left after the Thatcher programme of privatization. Those privatized in the leisure and tourism sector included BA and BAA. The BBC remains in the public sector but it is increasingly being subjected to private sector objectives and management techniques.

Other quangos

There are a whole range of leisure and tourism organizations which are known as quangos – quasi autonomous non-governmental organizations. Their autonomy stems from the fact that they are not directly answerable to ministers or parliament. The 'non-governmental' description of them is only partially true as they are funded by government. They include organizations such as:

- the Sports Council
- the Arts Council of Great Britain
- the British Tourist Authority
- English Heritage
- the Forestry Commission
- the Countryside Commission

Government departments

There are a number of government departments which impinge on the leisure and tourism sector of the economy, including:

- the Department of Culture, Media and Sport (DCMS)
- the Department of Transport, Environment and the Regions

Of these, the DCMS is the most significant, having responsibility for:

- the British Tourist Authority
- the English, Welsh and Scottish Tourist Boards
- royal parks and palaces

- arts and libraries
- sport
- broadcasting and the press
- heritage sites

Exhibit 2.1 discusses the role of the Department of Culture, Media and Sport.

Aims and missions

Before the 'Thatcher revolution' of the 1980s there was a much clearer difference between public corporations such as the BBC and private sector organizations. Public corporations tended to aim for public service and without the discipline of the profit motive were able to provide services that were loss-making. The rigours of efficiency and private sector management styles were rarely apparent. The old stereotypes are less true today. Public corporations have been subjected to efficiency targets, performance indicators, target rates of return on investment and citizen's charters, all of which have made them more closely mimic private sector organizations. The aims of public corporations are contained within their charters or constitutions.

The aims of other quangos are specific to each organization. For example, the aim of the Countryside Commission is to promote the conservation and enhancement of landscape beauty and to encourage the provision and improvement in facilities in the countryside. The aim of the Sports Council is to promote the development of sport. In doing so it has developed a strategy which emphasizes participation and access. By its distribution of grants the Sports Council is able to encourage organizations which support its strategy. Both of these organizations support smaller, often voluntary organizations, and there is some tension between their government funding and their ability to support particular lobbies.

The aim of government departments is to carry out the policy of the government of the day and includes the planning, monitoring and reviewing of provision and legislation.

Sources of finance

National organizations in the public sector are financed in the main from:

- taxes
- trading income

There has been continuing pressure from the government for more contribution from sponsorship and trading activities. The dependence on tax funding makes public sector organizations subject not only to the whims of the government of the day but also to the state of the economy as a whole. Exhibit 2.2 shows the changing fortunes of public sector organizations.

Exhibit 2.1   A new approach to investment in culture

The Department for Culture, Media and Sport (DCMS) is the central UK government department responsible for government policy on the arts, sport and recreation, the National Lottery, libraries, museums and galleries, export licensing of cultural goods, broadcasting, film, press freedom and regulation, the built heritage, the royal estate and tourism. The aims and objectives of the department in 1998 were as follows:

● To improve the quality of life for all through cultural and sporting activites, and to strengthen the creative industries.
● The Department will work to bring quality and excellence in the fields of culture, media and sport; make these available to the many, not just the few; raise standards of cultural education and training; and help to develop the jobs of the future in the creative industries.

Objectives of DCMS
The Department, in partnership with others, works to:

● Create and efficient and competitive market by removing obstacles to growth and unnecessary regulation so as to promote Britain's success in the fields of culture, media, sport and tourism at home and abroad.
● Broaden access to a rich and varied cultural sporting life.
● Ensure that everyone has the opportunity to achieve excellence in the areas of culture, media and sport and to develop talent, innovation and good design.
● Maintain public support for the National Lottery and ensure that the objective of the Lottery Fund supports DCMS' and other national priorities.
● Promote the role of the Department's sectors in urban and rural regeneration and in combating social exclusion.
● Seek maximum value for money in using human and financial resources, through applying the principles for efficiency among and effectiveness in its sectors and in encouraging partnership with others.

In a review of its activities in 1998 entitle *A New Approach to Investment in Culture*, the department set the following priorities.

● The promotion of access for the many not just the few.
● The pursuit of excellence and innovation.
● The nurturing of educational opportunity.
● The fostering of the creative industries.

And set the following targets:

● 300 000 new opportunities to experience the arts, 200 000 new educational sessions.
● Visitor numbers increased substantially in the national museums as entry charges disappear.
● Increased access and enhanced education opportunities; measures to boost employment and combat social exclusion.

On the financial side the Secretary of State announced in December 1998 the investment of an extra £290 million over the next three years. This includes a planned increase in funding for the arts in England, from £199 million in 1998–1999 to £247 million in 2001–2002, and support for the library sector rising from £91 million to £97 million over the same period.

Organizational changes are also planned with reform of cultural institutions that including combining the Arts and Crafts Councils, merging English Heritage and the Royal Commission on the Historical Monuments of England, and the creation of a slimmer English strategic body for tourism. The department also announced the creation of a new watchdog body, 'QUEST', responsible for monitoring efficiency and financial management in the cultural sector.

Sources: Department for Culture, Media and Sport website (http://www.culture.gov.uk). Newspapers: *Guardian* and *The Independent*.

Exhibit 2.2   The ups and downs of the public sector

The English Tourist Board has seen staff levels severed since the government announced drastic cuts in funding in 1992. Funding of £15.4 million in 1992–1993. . . . will drop to £11.3 million in 1994–1995. In 1995–1996 funding will be down to £10 million – representing an investment of about 12p per domestic visitor.

Source: *Travel Trade Gazette*, March 1994.

Leading figures in the arts reacted with enthusiasm and relief to the distribution of £290 million in extra funding announced by the Culture Secretary, Chris Smith, yesterday. Although some cautioned that they wanted to see the fine print, most reflected that after years of feeling neglected by the Tories, the arts community should praise the Government for its spending commitments. Theatre director Sir Peter Hall, who has been outspoken in his criticism of the Government, said Labour had stopped a 20-year rot.

Source: *Guardian*, July 1998.

Ownership and control

National government organizations are owned by the government on behalf of the population at large. However, each type of organization is controlled in a different way.

Public corporations are given some autonomy and have a legal identity separate from the government. An act of parliament outlines aims, organization and control for each industry. The basic structure is one where a board is established responsible for day-to-day running of the industry. The chair of the board and its other members are appointed by an appropriate government minister. Strategic decisions will be taken by the minister in consultation with the government.

Despite their non-governmental status, the government exerts considerable control over other quangos by its power of appointment. The Sports Council, for example, which meets four times a year has its chair, vice chair and members appointed by Under Secretary of State for Culture, Media and Sport. Exhibit 2.3 shows the relationship between the Sports Council and the government.

Government departments are headed by a minister and staffed by civil servants. The degree of political control is thus more direct than for public corporations and other quangos.

Private sector organizations

Private sector organizations are those which are non-government-owned. They can be further sub-divided into profit-making organizations and non-profit-making organizations.

Exhibit 2.3   Tony Banks on Walker for Sports Council

UK sports minister Tony Banks has chosen Sir Rodney Walker, former rugby league forward and Yorkshire shot-put champion, as chairman of the Sports Council for a three-year period (1998–2001). The former chief executive, Howard Wells, reportedly found the organization unwieldy and virtually unworkable.

Sir Rodney describes his role as follows: 'At the end of the day I understand the relationship between a government and a quango, and my job is to deliver the policies laid down. It would only be if I fundamentally disagreed with the policies that I would personally have a problem. Fortunately, sport is probably the only thing discussed in parliament that doesn't have to be overtly party political. Tony Banks seems to have a philosophy that sport matters more than the party that is in power.'

He clearly thinks that the Sports Council can improve its effectiveness. '. . . the Arts Council have done tremendously well in the share-out of Government money. We have to establish better relationships with our Government and put ourselves about a bit more with those overseas.'

His agenda includes overseeing the completion of a new national stadium, setting up the UK Sports Institute, tackling drugs in sport and investing in potential future winners for UK sport. He concludes, 'I can't go to any sport and say: "Do this or else." But the Government have given us money and clout and told us to make a difference. We shall endeavour to do so.'

Source: The author, 1999

Profit-making organizations

Profit-making private sector organizations consist of sole proprietors, partnerships, private limited companies and public limited companies. There is an important distinction between these types of company in terms of the liability of investors.

Limited and unlimited liability

Sole proprietors and unlimited liability partners both operate under conditions of unlimited liability. Unlimited liability means that the owners of such companies face no limit to their contribution should the organization become indebted. Most of their personal assets can be used to settle debts should the business cease trading. This includes not only the value of anything saleable from the business, but also housing, cars, furniture, stereos – the only exceptions being a person's 'tools of the trade' and a small amount of bedding and clothes. In contrast to this, limited liability places a limit to the contribution by an investor in an organization to the amount of capital that has been contributed. This applies to private and public limited companies as well as some partners who enjoy limited liability. Should one of these organizations cease trading with debts, an investor may well lose the original investment, but liability would cease there and personal assets would not be at risk.

Sole proprietors

Because of the discipline that unlimited liability brings, there are very few formalities required to start trading as a sole proprietor. The main requirement dictated by the Business Names Act 1985 is that the name and address of the owner must be displayed at the business premises and on business stationery.

The advantages of the sole proprietor include:

- independence
- motivation
- personal supervision
- flexibility

The problems of the sole proprietor include:

- unlimited liability
- long hours of work
- lack of capital for expansion
- difficulties in case of illness

Partnerships

The usual maximum number of partners is 20. A Deed of Partnership is generally drawn up to determine contribution of capital and sharing of profits. The Limited Partnership Act 1907 permits the admission of partners with limited liability as long as they do not take part in the management of the firm and as long as at least one partner retains unlimited liability.

The advantages of partnerships include:

- more capital available
- more expertise available
- flexibility
- motivation

The problems of partnerships include:

- unlimited liability
- disagreements

Private and public limited companies

The main difference between these is that public limited companies must have a minimum share capital and that shares in the private limited companies can only be transferred with the consent of other shareholders. Shares in public limited companies can be freely traded on the stock market. The similarities between the company forms are that they are bound by closer rules and regulations than are unlimited liability organizations. Recent examples of leisure and tourism sector organizations that have been floated on the stock market (i.e. changed from private to public limited companies) include:

- Thistle Hotels (hotels) 1996
- Thomson (tour operator) 1998

Exhibit 2.4 illustrates some of the debate in the travel sector over moving from a private limited company to a public limited company. Airtours sees access to capital as being a key advantage of becoming a public limited company. On the other hand Eurocamp stresses the costs of flotation and Unijet voices concerns about the constant need to perform as a public limited company, and the possible loss of control. The extent of share ownership and lack of control on transfer of shares mean that it is more difficult to retain control of public than private limited companies.

To commence business, limited liability companies must obtain a Certificate of Incorporation and a Certificate of Trading from the Registrar of Companies.

The following must be provided:

- Memorandum of Association. The key points included in this are the name and address of the company, the objectives of the company, and details of share capital issued.
- Articles of Association. This details the internal affairs of the company including procedures for annual general meetings, and auditing of accounts.

Exhibit 2.4   trade weighs taking the plunge

Airtours profits rocketed from £2 m in 1987 to £45 m in 1993 – that could never have happened without Airtours floating on the stock market. Perhaps that explains why travel companies continue to make cash calls on the City either by going public or seek venture capital investment.

One person who believes more holiday companies should float did it himself – Inspirations managing director Vic Fatah. 'If you float on the stock exchange you give up less than if venture capitalists come in', said Mr Fatah. Companies could also consider raising private funds. 'The advantage of venture capitalists is that you can get people in at an earlier stage of your development.' Another advantage in taking the private route is that a company does not have to pay fees to advisors such as merchant bankers, brokers, lawyers and public relations firms.

Expense is one reason why former Eurocamp group sales and marketing director Julian Rawel advises caution before opting to float. Mr Rawel helped steer Eurocamp through its flotation in 1991.

The demands on a quoted company are always great, says Chris Parker, who has taken Unijet to the brink of floatation on two separate occasions: 'A quoted company always has to perform in the short term, which can be very difficult in a volatile industry'.

Source: Travel Trade Gazette, 9 March 1994 (adapted).

Incorporation confers separate legal identity on the company. This may be contrasted with the position of unlimited liability organizations where the owners and the organization are legally the same.

Sources of finance

Sources of finance available to sole proprietors and partnerships are limited to:

- capital contributed by the owners
- ploughed-back profits
- bank loans

This is a key reason why small firms remain small.
Companies are able to raise capital through the additional routes of:

- shares (equity)
- debentures

Shares can be seen from the shareholder and company perspective. From the company point of view, share capital is generally low-risk since if the company doesn't make any profits then no dividends are issued. Shareholders seek dividend payments as well as growth in the value of shares. Debentures can be seen as a form of loan as they carry a fixed rate of interest. Thus to the company they pose a problem when profits are low, but their fixed interest rate is attractive when profits are high. Debenture holders get a guaranteed rate of return.

Several points emerge from Table 2.1 on the financing of Eurotunnel. First, Eurotunnel's capital represents a mixture of loans from banks which carry interest payments until they are repaid, and share issues which will not pay dividends until profits are earned. If profits from the tunnel are insufficient

Table 2.1 Financing Eurotunnel

1986	Concession to build the Channel Tunnel awarded to Eurotunnel £46 m seed corn equity raised £206 m share placing with institutions
1987	£5 bn loan facility agreed with 200-bank syndicate £770 m equity funding from public offer in UK and France
1990	£1.8 bn additional debt from syndicate £300 m loan from European investment bank £650 m rights issue
1994	£700 m raised from banks £850 m rights issue, priced at 26 per cent discount and entirely underwritten

Source: *Guardian*, 27 May 1994 (adapted).

to repay loans and interest, the company may be forced into liquidation by the banks. The assets of the company would then be sold to repay the banks. Under this scenario, shareholders would get nothing. However because their liability is limited, neither would they stand to lose any personal assets. Under a more optimistic, high-profit scenario, payments to the banks are limited to previously negotiated rates, leaving substantial profits to be distributed in the form of high dividends to shareholders.

Second, three different forms of share issue are illustrated:

- A placing in 1986. This is where Eurotunnel's shares were placed directly with institutions such as pension funds and insurance companies.
- An offer for sale in 1987. This is where shares are advertised and offered to the public.
- A rights issue in 1990 and 1994. This is where existing shareholders are able to buy new shares at a discount.

Finally, the underwriting of share issues means that insurance has been taken out against the eventuality of shares remaining unsold.

Share prices and the stock market

Shares which are sold on the stock market are second-hand shares and thus their purchase doesn't provide new capital to companies. Prices of shares are determined by supply and demand. The stock market approximates to a perfect market (see Chapter 3) and thus prices are constantly changing to bring supply and demand into equilibrium. The demand for and the supply of shares depend upon the following:

- price of shares
- expectations of future price changes
- profitability of firm
- price of other assets
- interest rates
- government policy
- tax considerations

Aims and missions

Objectives in the private sector are generally to maximize profitability. Many organizations have elaborated their aims into mission statements, and exhibit 2.5 illustrates the mission statement of BAA.

Ownership and control

Understanding small business organization is straightforward. The owner is the manager. This may mean that profit maximization is subject to personal considerations such as environmental concerns or hours worked.

Exhibit 2.5   BAA's mission statement

'Our mission is to make BAA the most successful airport company in the world.'
This means:

- always focusing on our customers' needs and safety
- seeking continuous improvements in the costs and quality of our services
- enabling our employees to give of their best

Source: BAA

For companies, size of operations and number of shareholders make the picture more complex. Companies are run along standard lines: the managing director is responsible for directing managers in the day-to-day running of the organization. The board of directors is responsible for determining company policy and for reporting annually to the shareholders. This can lead to a division between ownership (shareholders) and control (managers) and a potential conflict of interests. Shareholders generally wish to see their dividends and capital gains, and thus company profits, maximized. Managers will generally have this as an important objective since they are ultimately answerable to shareholders. However, they may seek other objectives – in particular, maximizing personal benefit – which may include kudos from concluding deals, good pension prospects and a variety of perks such as foreign travel, well-appointed offices and high-specification company cars.

Non-profit-making organizations

Non-profit organizations in the private sector vary considerably in size and in purpose. They span national organizations with large turnovers, smaller special interest groups, professional associations and local clubs and societies, and include:

- the National Trust
- the Council for the Protection of Rural England
- the Ramblers Association
- the Tourism Society
- the Institute of Leisure and Amenity Management
- the British Amateur Gymnastics Association

The National Trust

The National Trust is a charity and independent from the government. It derives its funds from membership subscriptions, legacies and gifts, and trading income from entrance fees, shops and restaurants. It is governed by an act of parliament – the National Trust Act 1907. Its main aim is to safeguard places of historic interest and natural beauty.

Aims and missions

Aims and missions of voluntary groups include protection of special interests, promotion of ideas and ideals, regulation of sports and provision of goods and services which are not catered for by the free market.

Review of key terms

- Public sector = government-owned.
- Private sector = non-government-owned.
- Council member = elected councillor.
- Council officer = paid official.
- Private limited company = company with restrictions governing transfer of shares.
- Public limited company = company whose shares are freely transferable and quoted on stock market.
- Public corporation = public sector commercial-style organization.
- Dividend = the distribution of profits to shareholders.
- Limited liability = liability limited to amount of investment.
- Strategic management = long-term policy making.
- Operational management = day-to-day management.
- Flotation = floating a private limited company on the stock market, thus becoming a public limited company.

Task 2.1   New direction sought for Arts Council

In January 1998, Gerry Robinson was appointed as chairman of the Arts Council of Great Britain. His other job is chief executive of Granada plc. Granada plc is a private sector leisure company with interests in hotels, catering and the media. At Granada, Mr Robinson has a reputation for cost-cutting having reduced staff numbers at its headquarters to just 32.

Mr Peter Hewitt, is chief executive of the Arts Council. It is a quango acting on behalf of the Department of Culture, Media and Sport and responsible for around £400 million of grants to the arts.

Critics of the Arts Council have dismissed it as a 'bloated and over-centralized bureaucracy', but it is now going through a period of significant change. This is prompted by the government's wish to introduce a culture of commercial thinking into to arts funding organizations. The appointment of Gerry Robinson demonstrates the government's commitment to fulfil this wish.

In June 1998 Mr Robinson cut the Arts Council ruling body from twenty-three members to ten. Working with Peter Hewitt, he has reorganized the Arts Council into three directorates. These are communications, finance and operations, and arts and policy.

In September 1998 Mr Hewitt invited all 322 Arts Council staff to a meeting at the Mount Royal Hotel in central London where he announced proposals which include more than 170 job losses reducing the number of permanent staff to around 150. These proposals will need to be ratified by the ten-member of the ruling Council which determines policy. A spokesman for Mr Hewitt described the changes as being 'about changing mindsets and getting people to think less defensively'.

The attempts to reform the Arts Council have met with strong opposition, and one senior employee has described the proposed staffing cuts as a 'disgrace'.

Questions

1 Distinguish between the Arts Council, The Department of Culture, Media and Sport and Granada plc in terms of:
   ● aims and missions
   ● organization and control
   ● finance
2 Is the Arts Council more or less likely to be a 'bloated and over-centralized bureaucracy' than an organization such as Granada plc?
3 What is the argument for having an Arts Council at all, rather than leaving arts provision to private sector companies?
4 Write a mission statement that might be suitable for:
   ● The Arts Council
   ● Granada plc
5 Should the Arts Council run on different lines to a plc?

Source: The author, 1999.

Task 2.2   Post-flotation: Thomson shares sink

In May 1998, Thomson was floated by its Canadian parent company Thomson Corporation on the London stock exchange who want to concentrate on their core business of publishing in North America. It became the Thomson Travel Group (TTG) plc with an estimated value of £1.7 billion. The group's main brands include Thomson Holidays (the market leader in the UK), Lunn Poly Travel Agents, Britannia Airways and the Holiday Cottages Group, 1 billion shares were offered at a flotation price of 170p.

In the period immediately following flotation share prices rose to a peak of 195p, but by September 1998 prices had fallen to below 130p. This followed a fall in first-half profits in 1998 from £12.2 million to £5.5 million. As compensation for the poor results the company paid out an interim dividend of 0.75p a share.

Source: The author, 1999.

Questions

1 What are the main benefits for the Thomson Corporation of this flotation?
2 How does a flotation occur?
3 What are the benefits and problems to TTG of being a plc?
4 What is the current share price of Thomson? What are the main factors affecting its price and would you recommend buying Thomson shares?

Task 2.3   Leisure in a London borough

The London Borough of Hounslow is one of 32 London local government areas with responsibilities for a range of services including recreation and tourism. Table 2.2 shows income and expenditures for the major service committees over a two-year period.

The Leader of the Council (which is a labour majority council) stated that 1989–1999 was 'another difficult financial year for the council' but one where they had managed to allow for 'increased expenditure in our key pledge areas'. Table 2.3 shows the approximate sources of finance for its services for 1998–1999. The required level of council tax works out at an average of £2.43 per head of the council population.

Source: The author, 1999.

Questions

1 What kinds of recreation and tourism are provided by local councils?
2 What trends are evident in provision of recreation and tourism?

Table 2.2   Income and expenditure on services (£000s)

	1997–1998			1998–1999		
	Gross expenditure	Income	Net expenditure	Gross expenditure	Income	Net expenditure
Education	147 185	36 463	110 722	152 880	34 699	118 181
Social services	54 490	6 424	48 266	62 053	12 289	49 764
Highways and planning	21 689	15 308	6 381	29 285	22 069	7 216
Economic development	4 572	1 242	3 330	5 038	1 084	3 954
Recreation and tourism	21 178	4 885	16 293	20 522	4 402	16 120
Environmental health	1 480	56	1 424	2 040	205	1 835
Refuse	7 929	1 045	6 884	9 436	1 453	7 983
Housing	119 020	110 919	8 101	109 954	102 685	7 569
Other services	45 766	36 832	8 934	43 186	34 992	8 194
Total	423 309	213 174	210 135	434 394	213 878	220 516

Table 2.3   Budget requirement (£000s)

Total budget requirement*	202 000
Less Revenue support grant	105 000
Less Redistributed non-domestic rates	47 000
To be funded from council tax	50 000

*After adjustments.
Source: The author, 1999

3 What are the economic arguments for and against local government provision of such services as opposed to private enterprise provision?
4 What factors determine the level of provision of recreation and tourism?
5 What factors determine the level of local council tax?

Task 2.4   *Right to Roam*

While Finland has 'Everyman's Right' (the right to walk unheeded across any land), the UK equivalent 'The Right to Roam' has yet to become law (1999).The Ramblers Association has conducted an opinion poll which shows that 85 per cent of those questioned support such a right becoming law. The Ramblers Association commissioned the poll to exert pressure on the Department of Transport, the Environment and the Regions which is seen to be wavering on pre-election promises to legislate on the right to roam. The government has also come under a major campaign by the Country Landowners Association (CLA) to accept a voluntary code instead of legislation.

Source: The author, 1999.

Questions

1 Distinguish between the missions, finance and organization of a government department, the Ramblers Association and the CLA.
2 What other organizations might have an interest in this issue?
3 Evaluate 'The Right to Roam' from an economic perspective.

Task 2.5   *Wonders of creation: the record label that gave us the Jesus and Mary Chain – Ben Thompson*

Alan McGee – jet setting Glasgow exile, British Rail clerk turned indie-music mogul – sits in the corner of a London brasserie, sipping a cappuccino in the refined manner of his hero, Paul Weller.

 McGee is affable in the extreme. He has good reason to be. Creation Records, the Motown in leather trousers' he founded on a £1000 bank loan, has looked bankruptcy in the face on several occasions. But in 1994 it had an expected turnover of £8–10 m, and a complex and lucrative deal with Sony has brought new and unprecedented stability. Perhaps more importantly, all this has been achieved with no dilution of the label's mystique. 'We've always been brilliant at the music,' McGee observes modestly, 'but we've had to learn the business part as we've gone along.' McGee's sharp eyes and ears have always been the label's greatest assets.

The Cramps, Creation's offices, are still in less-than-salubrious E8 just south of London Fields, but they have expanded to take over another floor.

'We are never going to be too big,' McGee insists. 'We'll always be what the business calls a "boutique" independent, reflecting one man's tastes.' These range from Lynryd Skynryd to the Orb; from Miles Davis to Willie Nelson'. It was Creation's long overdue and patently drug-induced embrace of dance culture in 1989–90 that eased their way into the pop mainstream. Primal Scream, led by McGee's schoolfriend Bobby Gillespie, were the key players here – and their new album, already the subject of furious debate in the music press 2 months prior to release, will be the key to Creation's 11th year 'I took Bobby to his first concert,' McGee remembers, 'I was 2 or 3 years older than him and his dad wouldn't let him go to concerts.'

Which concert was it? 'Thin Lizzy in 1975.'

Source: *Independent on Sunday* 30 January 1994 (adapted)

Questions

1 Creation Records is a private limited company. How suitable do you think this type of business organization is for its purposes?
2 If you were setting up a record company today on £10 000, what form of business organization would be most appropriate?

Short questions

1 Distinguish between the public sector, public limited companies and public corporations.
2 What is the major benefit of incorporation?
3 Who determines strategic policy for:
    (a) local government organizations?
    (b) public limited companies?
    (c) public corporations?
4 What conflicts of aims might occur in:
    (a) public limited companies?
    (b) quangos?
5 Identify four public limited companies in the leisure and tourism sector.
    (a) Research and record movements in their share prices over the past 24 months as well as those of the *Financial Times*-Stock Exchange (FT-SE) index.
    (b) Suggest reasons for the movements in these share prices.

Websites of interest

British Tourist Authority　www.visitbritain.com
English Sports Council　http://www.english.sports.gov.uk/
Forestry Commission　http://www.forestry.gov.uk/
Adam Smith Institute　http://www.adamsmith.org.uk/
Department for Culture, Media and Sport　http://www.culture.gov.uk
English Nature　http://www.english-nature.org.uk
Eurostar (UK) Ltd　http://www.bized.ac.uk/compfact/euro/epsindex.htm
UK share prices　http://www.moneyworld.co.uk/stocks/
Virgin Atlantic　http://www.bized.ac.uk/compfact/vaa/vaaindex.htm
Time Warner Corporation　http://www.timewarner.com
Countryside Commission　http://www.countryside.gov.uk/
The National Trust　http://www.nationaltrust.org/
The Ramblers Association　http://www.ramblers.org.uk/
Department of Transport　www.open.gov.uk/dot
British Airways　www.british-airways.com
Furzefield Leisure Centre　www.hertsmere.gov.uk/leisure
Learning help in economics and business studies　http://www.bized.ac.uk

3 The market for leisure and tourism products

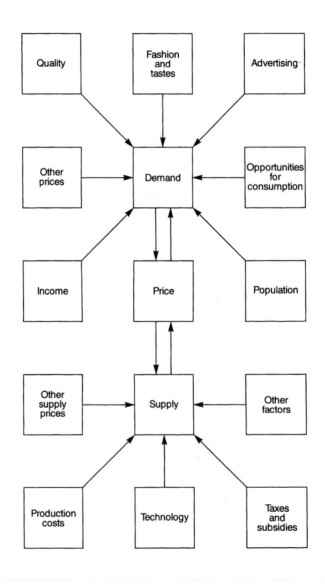

Objectives

Prices in a market economy are constantly on the move. For example, the price of package holidays has fallen considerably in real terms over the last decade, whilst the price of foreign currency changes many times in a single day. Price has a key function in the market economy. On the one hand it signals changes in demand patterns to producers, stimulating production of those products with increasing demand and depressing production of those products where demand is falling. At the same time price provides an incentive for producers to economize on their inputs. This chapter will investigate how price is formed in the market. It will investigate the factors which determine the demand for and the supply of a good or service and see how the forces of demand and supply interact to determine price.

After studying this chapter students will be able to:

- identify a market and define the attributes of a perfect market
- analyse the factors that affect the demand for a good or service
- analyse the factors that affect the supply of a good or service
- understand the concept of equilibrium price
- analyse the factors that cause changes in equilibrium price
- relate price theory to real world examples

Definitions

Effective demand

Effective demand is more than just the wanting of something, but is defined as 'demand backed by cash'.

Ceteris paribus

Ceteris paribus means 'all other things remaining unchanged'. In the real world there are a number of factors which affect the price of a good or service. These are constantly changing and in some instances they work in opposite directions. This makes it very difficult to study cause and effect. Economists use the term *ceteris paribus* to clarify thinking. For example, it might be said that a fall in the price of a commodity will cause a rise in demand, ceteris paribus. If this caveat were not stated then we might find that, despite the fact that the price of a commodity had fallen, we might observe a fall in demand, because some other factor might be changing at the same time – a significant rise in income tax, for example.

Perfect market assumption

A market is a place where buyers and sellers come into contact with one another. In the model of price determination discussed in this chapter we make a simplifying assumption that we are operating in a perfect market. The characteristics of a perfect market include:

● many buyers and sellers
● perfect knowledge of prices throughout the market
● rational consumers and producers basing decisions on prices
● no government intervention – e.g. price control

The stock exchange is an example of a perfect market – equilibrium price is constantly changing to reflect changes in demand and supply.

The demand for leisure and tourism products

Demand and own price

Generally, as the price of a good or a service increases, the demand for it falls, *ceteris paribus,* as illustrated in Table 3.1. This gives rise to the demand curve shown in Figure 3.1.

Table 3.1   The demand for Matashi 21″ colour televisions

Price (£)	220	200	180	160	140	120	100
Demand (per week)	2000	2400	2800	3200	3600	4000	4400

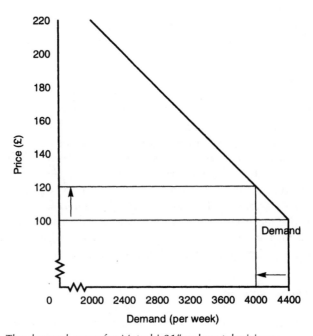

Figure 3.1   The demand curve for Matashi 21″ colour televisions.

The demand curve slopes downwards to the right and plots the relationship between a change in price and demand. The reason for this is that as prices rise consumers tend to economize on items and replace them with other ones if possible. Notice that as price changes we move along the demand curve to determine the effect on demand so that in Figure 3.1 as price rises from £100 to £120, demand falls from 4400 units a week to 4000 units a week.

The main exceptions to this are twofold. Some goods and services are bought because their high price lends exclusivity to them and thus they become more sought after at higher prices. Also, if consumers expect prices to rise in the future, they might buy goods even though their prices are rising.

Demand and other factors

The following factors also affect the demand for a good or service:

- income
- other prices
- comparative quality/value added
- fashion and tastes
- advertising
- opportunities for consumption (e.g. leisure time)
- population

Since the demand curve describes the relationship between demand and price, these other factors will affect the position of the demand curve and changes in these factors will cause the demand curve to shift its position to the left or the right.

Disposable income

Disposable income is defined as income less direct taxes but including government subsidies. The effect of a change in disposable income on the demand for a good or service depends on the type of good under consideration. First, for normal or superior goods, a disposable income rises, so does demand. This applies to holidays abroad, CDs and membership of leisure clubs. However some goods or services are bought as cheap substitutes for other ones. These are defined as inferior goods and examples might include domestic holidays, casse the tape players cheap-range hi-fi systems, or trainers without a leading brand name. As income rises the demand for these goods and services declines. Exhibit 3.1 shows that Morecombe can be classified as an 'inferior' destination in economic terms.

An income consumption curve shows the relationship between changes in income and changes in the demand for goods and services and Figure 3.2 shows the different income consumption curves for superior and inferior goods. As income rises from *A* to *B*, the demand for superior goods rises from *C* to *E*, whilst the demand for inferior goods falls from *C* to *D*.

Exhibit 3.1   UK seaside resorts: from superiority to inferiority

In Victorian England the place to be for the British monied, leisured classes was a British seaside resort. Queen Victoria herself had a residence at Osborne House near Cowes on the Isle of Wight and the Victorian boom brought railways, piers, promenades and seafront hotels to resorts such as Brighton, Ventnor and Eastbourne.

Today, piers have collapsed, accommodation has shrunk and resorts are in decline. Since 1970 long holidays taken abroad by UK residents have increased from 5 million to over 30 million and the number spent in the UK has shown a steep decline. The resort of Morecombe has suffered a severe reduction in visitor spending in real terms. In 1974 it was over 63 million Euros, but had fallen to 9 million Euros by 1990. Increased incomes made Spain the major destination for UK holidaymakers in the 1980s and 1990s, but as incomes continue to rise Spanish resorts are becoming inferior substitutes for more exotic, distant destinations.

Source: The author.

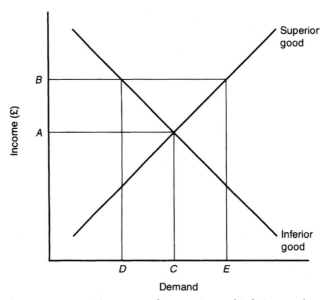

Figure 3.2   Income consumption curves for superior and inferior goods.

Price of other goods

Changes in the prices of other goods will also affect the demand for the good or service in question. In the case of goods or services which are substitutes, a rise in the price of one good will lead to a rise in the demand for the other. In the skiing market, for example, Verbier in Switzerland, Ellmau in Austria, and Courcheval in France are to some extent substitutes for each other and changes in relative prices will cause demand patterns to change.

Exhibit 3.2 shows how prices of other related goods differ between ski resorts.

Some goods and services are complements or in joint demand. In other words, they tend to be demanded in pairs or sets. In this case an increase in the price of one good will lead to a fall in the demand for the other. Examples of such goods include CDs and CD players, and exhibit 3.3 reports on the link between the demand for deckchairs and the weather and other factors.

Exhibit 3.2   Skiing: unpacking the price

The demand for skiing at different resorts is affected by a range of price factors. The price of accommodation in the resort (own price) will be a key factor. But other prices will also affect demand. Demand will be sensitive to substitute prices which includes prices in other resorts and prices of other alternative activities (e.g. diving holidays). Demand will also be affected by the price of other essential parts of a ski package (complementary goods and services). Lift pass prices, equipment hire and tuition are key factors here. Table 3.2 shows some of these for ski resorts in Europe. Of the three roughly comparable resorts of Ellmau, Courcheval and Verbier, Ellmau offers the best value in terms of a complete package.

Exhibit 3.3   Bad year for beach tourism

1998 was a bad year for beach tourism in the UK. Brighton beach reported a sharp downturn in deckchair and boat hire. Things were no better at Blackpool where Geoffrey Thompson, managing director of Blackpool Pleasure Beach, estimates that visitor numbers for 1998 were 20 per cent less than for 1997. Mr Thompson blamed three factors – bad weather, the World Cup keeping people in front of their TVs and higher mortgage rates cutting spending power.
Source: Adapted from *Financial Times*, July 1998.

Table 3.2   *Price comparisons for ski package elements, 1999 (Euros)*

Resort	Local lift pass (week)	Boot and ski hire	Ski school (adult)	Three-course meal	Bottle of house wine
Borovets, Bulgaria	82	60	90	8	6
Ellmau, Austria	110	52	86	10	14
Courcheval, France	140	92	106	30	12
Verbier, Switzerland	166	110	84	34	8

Source: The author, adapted from data collected by Thomas Cook.

Comparative quality/value added

Consumers do not just consider price when comparing goods and services – they also compare quality. Improvements in the quality of a good or service can be important factors in increasing demand and exhibit 3.4 describes how airlines are improving quality in business class.

This is an important consideration for airlines' strategies for increasing market share and is developed further in Chapter 6.

Fashion and tastes

Fashion and tastes affect demand for leisure goods and services as in other areas. For example, the demand for tennis facilities and accessories rises sharply during Wimbledon fortnight. Similarly, holiday destinations move in and out of fashion. In recent years Turkey, Florida, Spain and Greece have moved in and out of fashion. Goods and services are particularly prone to sudden changes in popularity in the age of mass, instantaneous communications. Florida has been affected by bad publicity surrounding the violent mugging of tourists and exhibit 3.5 shows how the fortunes of a destination can quickly change.

Exhibit 3.4   Food for thought in business class

Quality and added value are important factors which affect the demand for premium price air travel. The following review of airline food from the Aviation Health Institute uses a five-star classification system and shows how some airlines are excelling in the galleys:

- *Swissair* (*****) Food is of the highest quality – American beef, Australian lamb, Norwegian salmon.
- *Austrian Airlines* (*****) Succeeds where many fail in translating top dishes to the sky. These include roast venison medallions in mountain artemisia sauce with celery puré and cranberries.
- *SAS* (****) Combines classic Scandinavian dishes with those from other cultures. Salmon carpaccio with Vasterbotten cheese is a good example.
- *Lauda Air* (****) Offerings include poppy-seed cake and mushroom soup served in a black-bread pot.
- *Virgin Atlantic* (***) Features avant-garde menus, with sauces and accompaniments a special feature. Excellent cuisine.
- *Emirates* (***) One of the hottest flying restaurants, both figuratively and literally. Spicy Middle Eastern influences.
- *Air France* (***) Generally perceived to have some of the best food in the air. Employs special wine inspectors.
- *Lufthansa* (**) Although the service can deteriorate into stiff-necked formality, top-quality Champagne and caviar are offered on every table in first class.

Source: The author, adapted from report of the Aviation Health Institute.

Exhibit 3.5   From dreams to nightmares on a Greek island

'The half-forgotten island of Cephallonia rises improvidently and inadvisedly from the Ionian Sea,' writes Dr Iannis, a character in Louis de Bernière's best-selling novel *Captain Corelli's Mandolin*. The book has sold over half a million copies in the five-year period following its publication in 1994. The publication of the book coupled with a BBC holiday programme on the island and the strong pound prompted an increase of 62 per cent in the British holidaymakers in 1997, and 10 000 thousand tourists arrived at the island airport in May 1998 alone.

But this marketer's dream turned suddenly to a nightmare when the brutal murder of two pensioners who had retired to the island hit the newspaper headlines. Roy Eccles, a former RAF electrical engineer, and his wife Judith were murdered in their beds by burglars. Dicky Dawes, a retired computer programmer living on the island explains how things have changed. 'Even the Greeks are now putting up their shutters and locking doors when they go out, which they would never have done before.' Dawes had his life savings stolen by the murderers.

Source: The author from press cuttings, 1999.

Advertising

The aim of most advertising is to increase the demand for goods and services. The exception to this is advertising that is designed to inhibit the demand for some goods and services. For example, Health Education Council advertising includes campaigns to inhibit the demand for cigarettes and drugs. Exhibit 3.6 reports on how advertising affects demand for different leisure services.

Exhibit 3.6   Marketing moves

- The UK Conran group of restaurants ran a campaign with the *Evening Standard* newspaper to offer readers meals for £10 in top London restaurants such as Quaglinos during the off-peak months of January and February.
- The Hythe Imperial Hotel at Hythe in Kent (UK) received more than 1000 requests for further information after being featured on the TV travel programme *Wish You Were Here*.
- The budget airline easyJet took out full-page advertisements to promote its punctuality record to counter bad publicity arising from a TV documentary series which highlighted passenger delays.
- Warner Bros Movie World, Sea World and Wet'n'Wild Water World won the 1998 Queensland Tourism Award in Australia with its three-park superpass promotion. This helped to increase admissions by 20 per cent in the Christmas 1997 period.

Source: Adapted from Leisure Opportunities.

Opportunities for consumption

Unlike many sectors of the economy, many leisure and tourism pursuits require time to participate in them. Thus the amount of leisure time available will be an important enabling factor in demand. The two main components here are the average working week and the amount of paid holidays. The level of unemployment is also an important consideration, but the unemployed lack effective demand. Table 3.3 illustrates time use in the UK.

Table 3.3 Time use: UK adults, 1995
(hours and minutes/day)

Sleep	8:42
TV and radio	2:33
Cooking, routine housework	1:35
Personal care	1:01
Eating at home	0:44
Gardening and DIY	0:39
Care of children and adults	0:27
Other home leisure	1:08
Paid work	3:01
Travel	0:46
Socializing	1:03
Shopping	0:36
Eating or drinking out	0:31
Other out-of-home leisure	1:03

Source: Adapted from Office for National Statistics, *Social Trends*.

Population

Demand will also be influenced by the size of population as well as the composition of the population in terms of age, sex and geographical distribution. Population is discussed in more detail in Chapter 10.

The supply of leisure and tourism products

Supply and own price

Generally as the price of a good or a service increases, the supply of it rises, *ceteris paribus*. This gives rise to the supply curve which is illustrated in Table 3.4 and Figure 3.3.

The supply curve slopes upwards to the right and plots the relationship between a change in price and supply. The reason for this is that, as prices rise, the profit motive stimulates existing producers to increase supply and

Table 3.4　The supply of Matashi 21″ colour televisions

Price (£)	220	200	180	160	140	120	100
Supply (per week)	4400	4000	3600	3200	2800	2400	2000

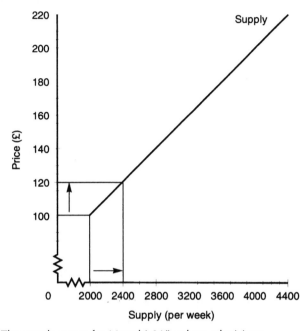

Figure 3.3　The supply curve for Matashi 21″ colour televisions.

induces new suppliers to enter the market. Notice that as price changes we move along the supply curve to determine the effect on supply so that in Figure 3.3, as price rises from £100 to £120, supply rises from 2000 units a week to 2400 units a week.

Supply and other factors

The following factors also affect the supply of a good or service:

- prices of other goods supplied
- changes in production costs
- technical improvements
- taxes and subsidies
- other factors (e.g. industrial relations)

Since the supply curve describes the relationship between supply and price, these other factors will affect the position of the supply curve and changes in these factors will cause the supply curve to shift its position to the left or the right.

Prices of other goods supplied

Where a producer can use factors of production to supply a range of goods or services, an increase in the price of a particular product will cause the producer to redeploy resources towards that particular product and away from other ones. For example, the owners of a flexible sports hall will be able to increase the supply of badminton courts at the expense of short tennis, if demand changes.

Changes in production costs

The main costs involved in production are labour costs, raw material costs and interest payments. A fall in these production costs will tend to stimulate supply, whereas a rise in production costs will shift the supply curve to the left.

Technical improvements

Changes in technology will affect the supply of goods and services in the leisure and tourism sector. An example of this is aircraft design: the development of jumbo jets has had a considerable impact on the supply curve for air travel. The supply curve has shifted to the right, signifying that more seats can now be supplied at the same price. Technology has had a large impact on the production of leisure goods such as TVs, video cassette recorders (VCRs), personal computers (PCs) and video cameras. The supply curve for these goods has shifted persistently to the right over recent years, leading to a reduction in prices after allowing for inflation.

Taxes and subsidies

The supply of goods and services is affected by indirect taxes such as VAT and excise duty, and also by subsidies. In the event of the imposition of taxes or subsidies, the price paid by the consumer is not the same as the price received by the supplier. For example, if the government were to impose a £20 tax on televisions at the price to the consumer of £200, the producer would now only receive £180, so the supply curve will shift to the left since the supplier will now interpret every original price as being less £20. Table 3.5 shows the effects of the imposition of a tax on the original supply data.

The effects of an imposition of a tax are illustrated in Figure 3.4, Notice that the supply curve has shifted to the left. In fact the vertical distance between the old (S0) and the new (S1) supply curves represents the amount of the tax.

Similarly, the effects of a subsidy will be to shift the supply curve to the right.

Table 3.5   The effects of the imposition of a tax on supply

Price (£)	220	200	180	160	140	120	100
Original supply (per week; S0)	4400	4000	3600	3200	2800	2400	2000
New supply (per week; S1)	4000	3600	3200	2800	2400	2000	

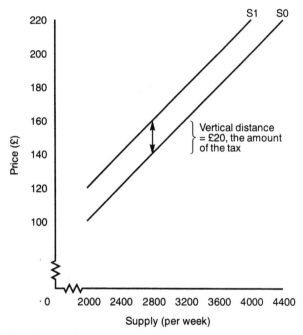

Figure 3.4   The effects of the imposition of a tax on supply.

Other factors

There are various other factors which can influence the supply of leisure and tourism goods and services, including strikes, wars and the weather.

Equilibrium price

Equilibrium is a key concept in economics. It means a state of balance or the position towards which something will naturally move. Equilibrium price comes about from the interaction between the forces of demand and supply. There is only one price at which the quantity that consumers want to demand is equal to the quantity that producers want to supply. This is the equilibrium price. Figure 3.5 uses the demand schedule from Table 3.1 and the supply schedule from Table 3.4. The equilibrium price in this case is

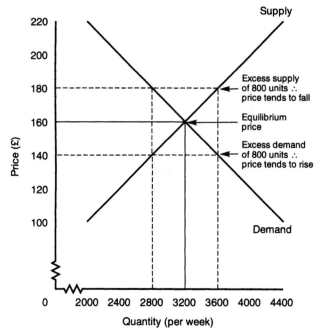

Figure 3.5 Equilibrium price in the market for Matashi 21″ colour televisions.

£160, since this is where demand equals supply, both of which are 3200 units per week.

It can be demonstrated that this is the equilibrium by considering other possible prices. At higher prices supply exceeds demand. In the example, at a price of £180 there is excess supply of 800 units a week. Excess supply will tend to cause the price to fall. On the other hand, at lower prices demand exceeds supply. At a price of £140 there is excess demand of 800 units a week. Excess demand causes the price to rise. Thus the equilibrium price is at £160, since no other price is sustainable and market forces will prevail, causing price to change until the equilibrium is established.

Changes in equilibrium price

Equilibrium does not mean that prices do not change. In fact, prices are constantly changing in markets to reflect changing conditions of demand and supply.

The effect of a change in demand

We have previously identified the factors that can cause the demand curve to shift its position. Table 3.6 reviews these factors, distinguishing what will cause the demand curve to shift to the right from that which will cause it to shift to the left.

Table 3.6 Shifts in the demand curve

Demand curve shifts to the left	*Demand curve shifts to the right*
Fall in income (normal goods)	Rise in income (normal goods)
Rise in income (inferior goods)	Fall in income (inferior goods)
Rise in price of complementary goods	Fall in price of complementary goods
Fall in price of substitutes	Rise in price of substitutes
Fall in quality	Rise in quality
Unfashionable	Fashionable
Less advertising	More advertising
Less leisure time	Increased leisure time
Fall in population	Rise in population

Table 3.7 A shift in demand for Matashi 21″ colour televisions

Price (£)	220	200	180	160	140	120	100
Original demand (per week; *D0*)	2000	2400	2800	3200	3600	4000	4400
New demand (per week; *D1*)		2000	2400	2800	3200	3600	4000
Supply (per week; *S0*)	4400	4000	3600	3200	2800	2400	2000

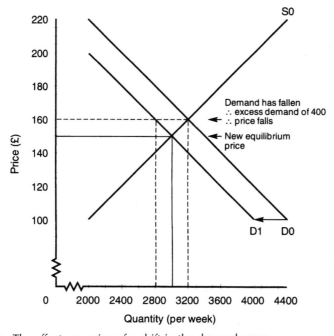

Figure 3.6 The effects on price of a shift in the demand curve.

In the example of Matashi TVs, a fall in the price of substitutes, for example Sony TVs, will cause the demand curve to shift to the left from $D0$ to $D1$. The supply curve will remain unchanged at $S0$. This is illustrated in Table 3.7.

Figure 3.6 shows the effect of this on equilibrium price. The original price of £160 will no longer be in equilibrium, since demand has now fallen to 2800 units a week at this price. There is now excess supply of 400 units per week, which will cause equilibrium price to fall until a new equilibrium is achieved at £150 where demand is equal to supply at 3000 units a week.

Similarly, if the demand curve were to shift to the right as a result of an effective advertising campaign, for example, the excess demand created at the original price would cause equilibrium price to rise.

The effect of a change in supply

The factors which cause a leftward or rightward shift in supply are reviewed in Table 3.8.

In the example of Matashi TVs, the effect of the imposition of a tax is shown in Table 3.9.

A tax will cause the supply curve to shift to the left from $S0$ to $S1$ but the demand curve will remain unchanged at $D0$, as illustrated in Figure 3.7.

Table 3.8 Shifts in the supply curve

Supply curve shifts to the left	Supply curve shifts to the right
Rise in price of other goods that could be supplied by producer	Fall in price of other goods that could be supplied by producer
Rise in production costs	Fall in production costs
Effects of taxes	Effects of subsidies
Effects of strikes	Technical improvements

Table 3.9 A shift in supply of Matashi 21″ colour televisions

Price (£)	220	200	180	160	140	120	100
Original demand (per week; $D0$)	2000	2400	2800	3200	3600	4000	4400
Original supply (per week; $S0$)	4400	4000	3600	3200	2800	2400	2000
New supply (per week; $S1$)	4000	3600	3200	2800	2400	2000	

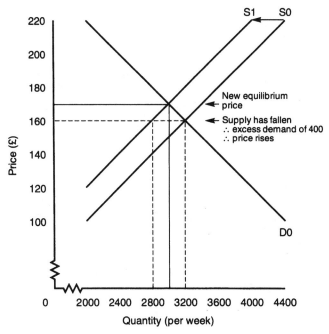

Figure 3.7   The effects on price of a shift in the supply curve.

The original price of £160 will no longer be in equilibrium, since supply has now fallen to 2800 units a week at this price. There is now excess demand of 400 units per week, which will cause equilibrium price to rise until a new equilibrium is achieved at £170 where demand is equal to supply at 3000 units a week.

Similarly, if the supply curve were to shift to the right as a result of an improvement in technology, for example, the excess supply created at the original price would cause equilibrium price to fall.

The price mechanism in action

Maximum prices and black markets

It is common in the leisure sector to interfere with free market pricing. The effects of this are particularly evident at prestige sports and music events where the capacity of the stadium is fixed, as illustrated in Figure 3.8.

The capacity of the Rugy Football Union (RFU) ground at Twickenham for example is about 70 000, and thus the supply curve (*S*) is fixed and vertical at this point. The demand curve for tickets is downward-sloping (*D*). The RFU fixes a price (*P0*) which is considerably below the equilibrium price (*P1*). At the RFU official price there is considerable excess demand (*a b*).

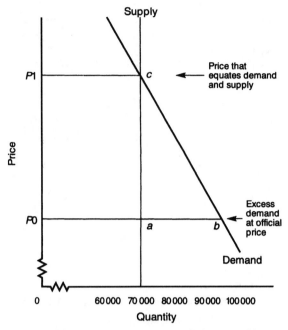

Figure 3.8   The effects of setting a maximum price below equilibrium price.

Equilibrium is restored through the activities of ticket touts in the black market. Prices charged by touts rise and the effects of this can be shown by moving along the demand curve (*b* to *c*) until demand falls sufficiently to match supply.

Exhibit 3.7 reports on how ticket touts are well aware of elementary economics.

Exhibit 3.7   Touts win at World Cup

Japan versus Argentina at Toulouse – a typical fixture in the 1998 World Cup in France. But even with games like this, where ticket demand is suppressed by the huge distances that fans have to travel to follow their home side, tickets are in short supply.

Driving up demand are the are estimated 30,000 Japanese football fans in France. Their presence is marked by their drums, painted faces and blue hats bedecked with miniature rising-sun flags. Their desperation to follow their team is evident from many T-shirts on which is written the hopeful Magic Marker slogan, 'I seek tickets for Japan games'. Chief among the attractions for Japanese fans is Hidetoshi Nakata, the 21-year-old player from Bellmare Hiratsuka.

But most are unlucky – even at games such as this which are on the fringes of the tournament, ticket touts are driving up prices in the black market to the Euro 500 mark.

Source: The author, from press reports, 1998.

Review of key terms

● Effective demand = demand backed by cash.
● Perfect market = many buyers and sellers, rational players, perfect knowledge, no interference.
● Normal good = demand rises as income rises (also called superior good).
● Inferior good = demand falls as income rises.
● Equilibrium price = where demand equals supply.

Data questions

Task 3.1

Questions on Figure 3.9

1 If a local authority decided to build OB tennis courts what would happen if they decided to make these free?
2 If the authority wished to create a market equilibrium, what price should they charge?
3 What problems arise from charging an equilibrium price?
4 How would the courts be allocated if they were provided free of charge?

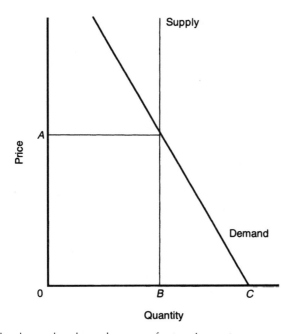

Figure 3.9 The demand and supply curves for tennis courts.

Task 3.2

Question

Discuss the factors that influence the figures given in Table 3.10.

Table 3.10   Audio-visual activities (% participation)

	1991	*1993*	*1996*
Watching TV (excluding video)	85	88	90
Listening to radio (not in car)	44	49	52
Playing records, tapes or CD (not in car)	37	41	46
Watching recorded TV on video	31	39	42
Watching hired/bought films on video	21	25	28
Using home computers for business	n/a	10	18
Using home computers to play computer games	n/a	8	10

Source: Adapted from Mintel.

Task 3.3   *What am I bid for a week in the sun?*

The reporter for a TV holiday programme was looking pleased with himself as he sipped a cocktail on a Caribbean beach. He'd managed to book a week in Cuba's winter sun for couple of hundred pounds, and he was keen to make a point.

It wasn't long before his camera crew had found a couple to gloat over. Gill and Tom had paid over £500 each for an identical holiday and they had booked several months before.

Enter camera left a man who stole the show £110 – *for two weeks.*

So how can the price of the same holiday go up and down like share prices and currencies? The answer lies back in the UK where the late bookings section of Airtours, the UK's second biggest tour operator, resembles a share dealing room with banks of flickering screens. Here analysts change holiday prices several times a day. They are not alone – Thomson, the industry number one and First Choice, the industry number three, change their holiday prices every day too.

Each uses the latest information on their competitors' prices to adjust their own prices to maximize profits. First Choice gets much of its information on competitors' prices through its ownership of Going Places.

When demand for their products is strong and supply is tight, the companies push up prices. However, faced with a half-empty plane departing in 2 days' time, prices plummet as the team tries to get bums on seats that would otherwise earn nothing at all.

The First Choice team have developed some ground rules for pricing. There's nothing like grey skies and rain at home to move prices up on the day.

Somehow in the face of all this Gill and Tom managed to keep their smiles fixed.

Source: The author, adapted from news cuttings, January 1995.

Questions

1 Illustrate, using demand and supply diagrams, how the Airtours late bookings section sets prices.
2 Why is it difficult to keep to the prices printed in brochures?
3 How does a plane with empty seats represent market disequilibrium and how does Airtours attempt to restore equilibrium?
4 What is the significance of information and knowledge to market prices?

Task 3.4   *The market for recorded music*

Table 3.11   Household penetration of audio hardware (UK, % of households)

	1982	1986	1990	1994	1998
Record player	84	86	84	78	72
Cassette player	75	84	90	93	94
CD player	0	3	24	56	80

Source: Adapted from British Phonographic Institute data.

Table 3.12   Retail prices for singles and albums (UK, £)

	1992	1993	1994	1995	1996
Full-price singles					
CD	4.49	4.49	4.49	4.49	4.49
Cassette	1.99	1.99	1.99	2.29	2.29
Full-price albums					
CD	12.99	13.49	13.49	13.99	14.99
Cassette	9.49	9.99	9.99	10.49	10.99

Source: Adapted from British Phonographic Institute data.

Table 3.13   Advertising expenditure on recorded music (UK, £000)

	1992	1993	1994	1995	1996
Expenditure	49 000	52 000	66 000	89 000	93 000

Sources: Various.

Table 3.14 Expenditures on recorded music formats 1997 (UK, £m)

	CD	Albums Cassette	Vinyl	CD	Singles Cassette	Vinyl
Expenditure	1385	200	15	150	30	20

Sources: Various.

Questions

1 Use demand and supply analysis to explain possible relationships between data shown in the tables.
2 What is the significance of *ceteris paribus* to your answer to Question 1?
3 Why have prices of CD albums increased during this period?
4 Account for the price differentials between CDs and cassettes.
5 What other data would be useful in analysing demand and supply?
6 Give a reasoned account of likely changes in the market for recorded music over the next 3 years.
7 In 1999, UK record companies sold some new singles at a discounted price of £0.99 for cassettes and £1.99 for CDs for the first week of their release only. Top-selling bands such as Boyzone are not discounted. What are the economics behind this?

Short questions

1 Distinguish between the factors which cause a movement along a demand curve, and those which cause a shift of the curve.
2 'An increase in the price of a good may arise from an increase in the price of its substitute, *ceteris paribus*'. Explain this statement.
3 Distinguish between a normal and an inferior good using examples from the leisure and tourism sector.
4 What is the likely effect of setting the maximum price of a good below its equilibrium price?

Websites of interest

Mintel International range of market intelligence
on the leisure sector   www.mintel.co.uk
Learning help in economics and business studies   http://www.bized.ac.uk

4 Demand: choice, elasticity and forecasting

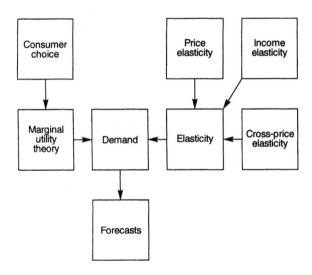

Objectives

This chapter looks in more detail at the demand curve. It considers consumer theory and the part it plays in explaining consumer behaviour, and the choice between leisure and work. Various concepts of demand elasticity are explained and the importance of these concepts to the leisure and tourism sector examined. Finally the chapter considers some techniques of demand forecasting, their uses and shortcomings.

By studying this chapter students will be able to:

- understand the concept of consumer equilibrium
- utilize marginal utility theory
- understand and apply the concept of price elasticity of demand
- understand and apply the concept of income elasticity of demand
- understand and apply the concept of crossprice elasticity of demand
- describe simple methods of demand forecasting
- evaluate techniques of demand forecasting

Consumer theory

Consumer theory attempts to explain consumer behaviour, and investigates consumer choice in consuming goods and services. It assumes first that consumers have limited income, second that consumers act in a rational manner, and third that consumers aim to maximize their total satisfaction, subject to the constraint of limited income.

Consumer equilibrium will occur when purchases are arranged so as to maximize a consumer's total satisfaction. In other words a consumer cannot rearrange purchases and be better off. Thus in order to analyse consumer equilibrium, the idea of satisfaction needs to be investigated.

Marginal utility theory

Utility is the term economists use to measure a person's satisfaction from consuming a good or service. In fact it is not possible to measure utility precisely, but predictions can be made about how utility changes with consumption. Marginal utility theory can be used to explain consumer choice in a simple model.

Assume a person has a monthly income of £60, and spends all of it on two services – visits to a fitness centre which cost £6 each and visits to the theatre which cost £12 each. To see how this person will divide income between the two services the concept of total utility must first be considered.

Total utility

Total utility is defined as the total benefit or satisfaction a person gets from the consumption of goods and services. Generally a person's total utility increases the more of a good or service they consume. Table 4.1 shows the

Table 4.1   Total utility and marginal utility from visits to theatre and fitness centre

Visits to fitness centre			Visits to theatre		
Quantity per month	*Total utility*	*Marginal utility*	*Quantity per month*	*Total utility*	*Marginal utility*
0	0	–	0	0	–
1	25	25	1	37	37
2	44	19	2	57	20
3	60	16	3	74	17
4	74	14	4	88	14
5	86	12	5	100	12
6	96	10	6	110	10
7	105	9	7	119	9
8	112	7	8	127	8
9	118	6	9	134	7
10	123	5	10	140	6

total utility associated with different levels of consumption of fitness centre and theatre visits.

Notice that where consumption is zero no utility is derived, but as consumption of each service increases, so does total utility. However, closer examination of the data reveals that total utility does not rise at a uniform rate, and this can be revealed by studying marginal utility.

Marginal utility

Marginal utility is defined as the utility gained from consuming one extra unit of a good or service. This can be calculated from the total utility data: for example, two visits to the fitness centre resulted in a total utility of 44 units and three visits resulted in 60 units, so the marginal utility of the third visit is 16 units. Table 4.1 also shows the marginal utility of visits to the theatre and fitness centre.

The information shows that marginal utility falls as consumption rises. This is known as the principle of diminishing marginal utility. The extra satisfaction consumers derive from successive consumption of a good or service tends to diminish. The freshness or novelty of a good or service wears off a little the more of it is consumed.

Maximizing utility (1)

In the above example, a person has a monthly income of £60 which is spent on consuming two services. Table 4.2 shows the various combinations of theatre and fitness centre visits that can be obtained from this income. In addition it shows the total utility obtained from each of the possible combinations of theatre and fitness centre visits.

The consumer will be in equilibrium when total utility is maximized. This occurs with a combination of six visits to the fitness centre (total utility = 96)

Table 4.2 Combinations of theatre and fitness centre visits possible from monthly income of £60, and total utilities of each combination

Visits to fitness centre (£6)			Visits to theatre (£12)			Combined total utility
Total utility	Expenditure	Quantity	Quantity	Expenditure	Total utility	
123	60	10	0	0	0	123
112	48	8	1	12	37	149
96	36	6	2	24	57	153
74	24	4	3	36	74	148
44	12	2	4	48	88	132
0	0	0	5	60	100	100

and two visits to the theatre per month (total utility = 57), giving a combined total utility of 153. The consumer cannot rearrange purchases and be better off.

Maximizing utility (2)

It is also possible to find the combination which maximizes utility by calculating and comparing the marginal utility per pound spent on different goods and services. Table 4.3 shows these calculations for the example under consideration, listing the possible combinations of visits to the fitness centre or theatre that could be purchased with a limited monthly income of £60.

The consumer can again be seen to be maximizing satisfaction by purchasing six visits to the fitness centre and two visits to the theatre, since this is where the marginal utility per pound spent is equal for each (MU/£ = 1.67). This can be seen to be maximizing satisfaction by looking at other possible choices.

Consider a choice with less fitness centre and more theatre visits. Four fitness centre visits (MU/£ = 2.33) and three theatre visits (MU/£ = 1.33) could be purchased. However, since the fitness centre visits are giving more marginal utility per pound spent than theatre visits, the consumer can increase satisfaction by switching spending away from theatre towards fitness. Similarly, eight fitness centre visits (MU/£ = 1.17) and one theatre visit (MU/£ = 3.08) could be purchased. However, since the fitness centre visits are giving less marginal utility per pound spent than theatre visits, the consumer can increase satisfaction by switching spending away from fitness towards theatre. Thus it is only where the consumer equates the marginal utility per pound spent for each good and service consumed that utility is maximized. This can be expressed for more general cases as:

$$\text{Consumer equilibrium} = MUa/Pa = MUb/Pb = MUn/Pn$$

where: MU = marginal utility; P = price; and a, b, n = individual goods and services.

Table 4.3 Marginal utility per pound spent on theatre and fitness centre visits

Visits to fitness centre (£6)			Visits to theatre (£12)		
Quantity	Marginal utility (MU)	MU/£ spent	Quantity	Marginal utility (MU)	MU/£ spent
10	5	0.83	0	–	
8	7	1.17	1	37	3.08
6	10	1.67	2	20	1.67
4	14	2.33	3	16	1.33
2	19	3.17	4	14	1.17
0	–		5	12	1.00

Free goods and maximizing utility

Some goods and services are provided free to consumers (for example, roads, parks and beaches). People will consume such goods and services to the point where their marginal utility equals zero. This is because consuming extra units has no cost in terms of other goods which could have been bought with limited income, but will add to total satisfaction as long as marginal utility is positive. This point has important implications for providers of such 'free' goods and services as national parks. There is considerable scope for extra consumption of these services since existing levels of consumption do not take many users to the point where MU = 0. Figure 4.1 illustrates this point.

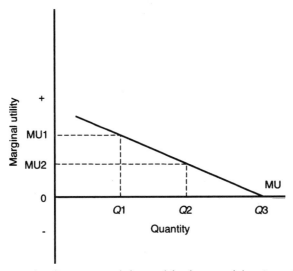

Figure 4.1   Marginal utility (MU) and demand for free goods/services. Q = Quantity.

Consumers of free services using quantity OQ1 derive positive marginal utility of OMU1 from this level of usage. However they may extend their usage to OQ2 and up to OQ3 at no extra cost to themselves whilst adding to their total satisfaction, since the marginal utility of using the service is positive throughout this range.

Utility: a postscript

The term utility raises many questions in considering consumer behaviour: what factors generate utility in a good or service for consumers? The answers to these questions may be found by using analysis from other disciplines, particularly psychology and sociology. Psychology, for example, investigates personal motivation in consumption, and considerable research has taken place in motivation of tourists.

Derivation of demand curve

Marginal utility theory confirms that demand curves slope downwards to the right and that as price falls demand rises. This can be shown using the data from Table 4.3 as a starting point. At the price of £12 per visit to a theatre, the consumer in our example will demand two visits per month. What happens if the price falls to £6 per visit? Table 4.4 shows the new possible combinations of fitness centre and theatre visits from a limited income of £60 monthly using data from the Tables 4.1–4.3.

Table 4.4 Effects of a fall in price on consumer choice

Visits to fitness centre (£6)				Visits to theatre (£6)		
Quantity	Marginal utility (MU)	MU/£ spent		Quantity	Marginal utility (MU)	MU/£ spent
10	5	0.83		0	–	
9	6	1.0		1	37	6.16
8	7	1.17		2	20	3.33
7	9	1.5		3	17	2.83
6	10	1.67		4	14	2.33
5	12	2.0		5	12	2.0
4	14	2.33		6	10	1.67
3	16	2.67		7	9	1.5
2	19	3.17		8	8	1.33
1	25	4.17		9	7	1.17
0	–	–		10	6	1.0

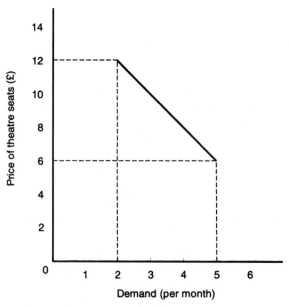

Figure 4.2 Demand curve for consumer for theatre seats

Examination of the new calculations of marginal utility per pound spent reveals that the consumer will maximize utility at the point of five theatre visits and five visits to the fitness centre since this is where the marginal utility per pound spent is equal for each (MU/£ = 2.00). Thus there are now two points that can be used to construct a demand curve for this consumer for theatre visits: at seat price £12, demand equals two seats per month and at seat prices £6, demand equals five seats per month. On this basis, the demand curve in Figure 4.2 is constructed.

Market demand

A market demand curve is found by adding together the individual demand curves for a particular good or service.

The demand for leisure

Leisure time represents an element in the choice set available to consumers, and maximization of consumer utility will therefore also involve choice about how much leisure time to take. Just as when choosing between other goods and services, consumers will consider the extra utility or satisfaction they derive from leisure time against the price or cost of leisure time.

Consumers face the problem of limited time. There are only 24 hours in a day, and thus the most fundamental choice that consumers face is whether to devote their limited time to leisure or work.

We can consider the cost or price of leisure time as its opportunity cost – what has to be given up in order to enjoy leisure time? The opportunity cost of leisure time is clearly earnings that are lost through not working. What will happen to the trade-off between work and leisure when prices change? The key 'price' in this case is wages, and if wages increase there are two potential effects on the demand for leisure time.

First, an increase in wages means an increase in the price of leisure time, in terms of loss of earnings. Therefore consumers will tend to demand less leisure time as its price has increased. This is a substitution effect. Consumers will tend to substitute work for leisure to reflect their new relative prices. But the increase in wages will also lead consumers to have more income and spending power. Leisure can be classed as a 'normal service', and in common with other 'normal' goods and services, as income increases more will be demanded. This is called the income effect. There are clearly a complex set of forces which will determine whether the income or substitution effect is greater. One consideration is that as income increases, consumers have the ability to get more satisfaction out of their leisure time, thus resulting in a strong income effect. The utility derived from labour is also influenced by psychological and social factors. Some individuals may favour long leisure hours which they can happily fill with cheap or free activities such as reading, watching television, sleeping or walking. Other individuals may have a low boredom threshold and thus have a low marginal utility from leisure time. Equally there are cultural influences at work. There appears to be a greater work ethic in countries such as Germany and Japan than in other countries, particularly those with warmer climates.

Choice or rigidity?

The extent to which choice can actually be exercised in the work/leisure trade-off depends on flexibility in the labour market. When choosing between most goods and services, consumers can readily vary the amounts consumed in response to changing relative prices. Consumers generally have less choice in their participation in labour markets. Many jobs have standardized hours where individuals cannot choose to add or subtract hours in response to changes in wages. However workers can express their general preferences through trade unions and staff associations and these may be taken into account in determining the overall work package of pay, hours and holiday benefits.

Some jobs offer flexibility in offering overtime provision, and some individuals may have extra employment in addition to their main job. In these cases individuals will be in a position to exercise more precisely their choice between work and leisure.

Finally the unemployed are generally not acting out of choice but by lack of opportunity in their allocation of leisure time. However there has been considerable debate regarding social security benefits and incentives to work. Right-wing economists argue that benefit levels are distorting the labour market so that some unemployed maximize their total utility by remaining unemployed rather than entering the labour market.

Trends in work and leisure

There are several ways of examining these trends including analysis of:

● unemployment data
● holiday entitlement
● hours worked

Unemployment data

Recent data and trends in unemployment are discussed fully in Chapter 9.

Holiday entitlement

There has been a steady increase in paid holiday entitlement in the post-war period. For example, for manual workers the average holiday period has risen from 2 weeks in 1951 to 4–5 weeks by 1999.

Hours worked

Table 4.5 shows data for average working hours in European Union countries. It can be seen that the UK total is close to the European Union average, with Portugal having the highest number of hours.

Table 4.5 Average hours usually worked per week in European Union countries, 1992–1996 (excludes meal breaks, includes overtime)

Country	Hours per week	
	1992	*1996*
Portugal	40.6	37.8
Greece	40.0	37.9
Spain	39.5	36.0
Luxembourg	38.4	34.5
Irish Republic	38.2	33.8
Italy	37.8	34.7
France	37.4	34.0
UK	37.1	30.6
Germany	35.7	32.8
Belgium	34.1	31.7
Denmark	32.1	31.9
EU average	37.2	32.8

Source: Adapted from Office for National Statistics, *Social Trends*.

Price elasticity of demand

Price elasticity of demand measures the responsiveness of demand to a change in price. This relationship can be expressed as a formula, and exhibit 4.1 shows a worked example for calculating price elasticity of demand.

$$\frac{\text{Percentage change in quantity demanded}}{\text{Percentage change in price}}$$

Where demand is inelastic it means that demand is unresponsive to a change in price, whereas elastic demand is more sensitive to price changes. The range of possible outcomes is summarized in Figure 4.3. It should be noted that, since a rise in the price of a good causes a fall in demand, the figure calculated for price elasticity of demand will always be negative. Economists generally ignore the minus sign.

Note that the demand curve, which has elasticity of demand of 1 throughout its length, is a rectangular hyperbola.

Exhibit 4.1   Price elasticity of demand: a worked example

When the price of Matashi 21" colour TVs rose from £160 to £180, demand fell from 3200 to 2800 sets per week. Calculate elasticity of demand:

1 To calculate percentage change in quantity demanded, divide the change in demand ($\Delta Q = 400$) by the original demand ($D0 = 3200$) and multiply by 100:
2 $400 \div 3200 \times 100 = 12.5$
3 To calculate percentage change in price, divide the change in price ($\Delta P = 20$) by the original price ($P0 = 160$) and multiply by 100:
4 $20 \div 160 \times 100 = 12.5$
5 Elasticity of demand = $12.5 \div 12.5 = 1$

Numerical value	Graph	Explanation	Term
0		Demand is unresponsive to a change in price	Perfectly inelastic
> 0< 1		Demand changes by a smaller proportion than price	Inelastic
1		Demand changes by the same proportion as price	Unit elasticity
> 1< ∞		Demand changes by a larger proportion than price	Elastic
∞		Any increase in price causes demand to fall to zero	Perfectly elastic

Figure 4.3   Elasticity of demand.

Factors affecting price elasticity of demand

The following are the main factors which influence price elasticity of demand:

- necessity of good or service
- number of substitutes
- addictiveness
- price and usefulness
- time period
- consumer awareness

Necessity of good or service

Goods and services which are necessities generally have a lower price elasticity of demand than goods which are luxuries.

Number of substitutes

Goods and services which are provided in conditions of near monopoly tend to have inelastic demand, since the consumer cannot shop elsewhere should prices increase. Competition in a market makes demand more elastic.

Addictiveness

Goods such as cigarettes which are addictive tend to have inelastic demand.

Price and usefulness

Cheap and very useful goods and services tend to have inelastic demand since an increase in a low price will have little impact on consumers' purchasing power.

Time period

Demand elasticity generally increases the more time is allowed to elapse between the change in price and the measurement of the change in demand. This is because consumers may not be able to change their plans in the short run. For example, many holiday-makers book holidays 6 months in advance. Thus a fall in the value of the US dollar might have limited effect on the demand for US holidays in the short run since consumers have committed holiday plans. It may not be until the next year that the full effects of such a devaluation on demand can be measured.

Consumer awareness

Package holidays represent a bundle of complementary goods and services which are bought by consumers, and consumers may be attracted to the bottom-line price of a holiday. Consumers may be unaware of destination prices. For this reason, elasticity of demand for services such as ski passes may be inelastic for UK holiday-makers due to lack of information.

Elasticity of demand and total revenue

The concept of price elasticity of demand is useful for firms to forecast the effects of price changes on total revenue received from selling goods and services, as well as for governments wishing to maximize their tax receipts. Total revenue is defined as:

Total revenue = price × quantity sold

Consider a rise in the price of a good by 10 per cent. If demand is elastic, quantity sold will fall by more than 10 per cent and thus total revenue will fall. However, if demand is inelastic it will fall by less than 10 per cent and thus total revenue will rise.

Similarly, a fall in the price of a good will lead to a rise in total revenue in the case of elastic demand and a fall in total revenue where demand is inelastic. Exhibit 4.2 illustrates the application of these principles to the pricing of admission charges to royal palaces.

Exhibit 4.2 implies that market research was used to estimate elasticity of demand for royal palaces, and since it was found to be inelastic, prices were increased. Several other studies have been made into price elasticity of demand in the leisure and tourism sector of the economy. Boviard and

---

Exhibit 4.2   Polishing the crown jewels – David Bowen

In 1994 the Queen opened the new Jewel House. The new Jewel House, which cost £10 m, is run by Historic Royal Palaces (HRP), HRP was set up as a 'next steps' agency to look after the Tower, Hampton Court Palace, Kensington Palace state apartments, the Banqueting House, Whitehall and Kew Palace. The agency's staff are civil servants but are not supposed to behave like them.

In 1989, the palaces were generating £11 m in revenue, which was topped up with £10 m from the tax-payer. In 1994 despite the recession, turnover was £26 m and only £6 m came from taxes. The trick has been to apply modern management methods to what is, after all, a substantial business. The first stage was market research. This revealed that tourists were not going to boycott the palaces for the sake of a couple of quid, so HRP increased entrance fees by 50 per cent.

Source: Independent on Sunday, 20 March 1994 (adapted).

colleagues (1984) researched elasticity values for National Trust sites. Time series analysis was used and changes in visitor numbers were compared with changes in admission prices, with account being taken of other factors such as changes in the weather, travel costs, unemployment and inflation. Using data from 1970 to 1980, estimates for price elasticity varied from 0.25 at Wallington to 1.05 at Hidcote, but with most results lying in the inelastic range.

Income elasticity of demand

Income elasticity of demand measures the responsiveness of demand to a change in income. This relationship can be expressed as a formula:

$$\frac{\text{Percentage change in quantity demanded}}{\text{Percentage change in income}}$$

Calculation of income elasticity of demand enables an organization to determine whether its goods and services are normal or inferior.

Normal or superior goods are defined as goods whose demand increases as income increases. Therefore their income elasticity of demand is positive (+/+ = +). The higher the number, the more an increase in income will stimulate demand.

Inferior goods are defined as goods whose demand falls as income rises. Therefore their income elasticity of demand is negative (−/+ = −).

Knowledge of income elasticity of demand is useful in predicting future demand in the leisure and tourism sector. It also helps to explain some merger and take-over activity as organizations in industries with low or negative income elasticity of demand attempt to benefit from economic growth by expanding into industries with high positive income elasticity of demand. Such industries show market growth as the economy expands. Examples of this include Pearson plc. Pearson owns the Financial Times Group Ltd. (low income elasticity of demand), and has bought into BSkyB Ltd. (high income elasticity of demand). Similarly, First Choice has bought into the cruise market, which promises high income elasticity of demand.

Cross-price elasticity of demand

Cross-price elasticity of demand measures the responsiveness of demand for one good to a change in the price of another good. This relationship can be expressed as a formula:

$$\frac{\text{Percentage change in quantity demanded of good A}}{\text{Percentage change in price of good B}}$$

Cross-price elasticity of demand measures the relationship between different goods and services. It therefore reveals whether goods are substitutes, complements or unrelated.

An increase in price of good B will lead to an increase in demand for good A if the two goods are substitutes. Thus substitute goods have a positive cross-price elasticity of demand (+/+ = +).

For goods which are complements or in joint demand, an increase in the price of good B will lead to a fall in demand for a complementary good, good A. Therefore complementary goods have negative cross-price elasticity of demand (−/+ = −).

An increase in the price of good B will have no effect on the demand for an unrelated good, good A. Unrelated goods have cross-price elasticity of demand of zero (0/+ = 0).

Demand forecasting

The supply of leisure goods and services cannot generally be changed without some planning. The supply of capital goods such as aircraft requires long planning cycles. Tour operations require considerable planning to book airport slots and hotel accommodation. Equally, leisure and tourism services are highly perishable. It is not possible to keep stocks of unsold hotel rooms, aircraft and theatre seats, or squash courts. Whilst the supply of some leisure goods, such as golf balls and tennis rackets, can be more readily changed, and stocks of unsold goods held over, there is clearly a need for forecasting of demand for leisure and tourism goods and services.

Exhibit 4.3 reports on forecasts from Airbns Industrie for aircraft demand.

Methods for forecasting demand include:

- naïve forecasting
- qualitative forecasts
- time-series extrapolation
- surveys
- Delphi technique
- models

Naïve forecasts

Naïve forecasting makes simple assumptions about the future. At its simplest, naïve forecasting assumes that the future level of demand will be the same as the current level. Naïve forecasting may also introduce a fixed percentage by which demand is assumed to increase, for example 3 per cent per annum.

Qualitative forecasts

Qualitative forecasts consider the range of factors which influence the demand for a good or service, as discussed in Chapter 3. These factors are then ranked in order of importance and each of them is in turn analysed to

---

Exhibit 4.3   Aircraft set to for take off

In a review and forecast of the airline business, the European plane manufacturer – Airbus Industrie has forecast a doubling in the number of passenger aircraft. This is set to rise from 9700 to 17 900 between 2000 and 2020.

Airbus is a consortium of plane manufacturers from Britain, France, Germany and Spain and Mr Adam Brown, its vice-chairman for strategic planning, has explained how the company plans to meet this demand for aircraft which is linked to a predicted 5 per cent growth of annual passengers. First, Airbus is focusing production on large 650-seater aircraft. The Airbus A3XX will be launched in 2004. This is a Euros 8.4 billion project in a plane which will allow passengers to sleep in their own private cabins on long-haul flights.

This optimistic forecast is made despite the poor performance of the Asian economies in 1998–2000. John Leahy, Airbus's commercial vice-president, said: 'Our latest forecast confirms that, despite the Asian crisis, this business will enjoy sustained growth.' In fact the projected world's biggest growth area is the Far East and China. Here, 25 new airports are planned in the period 2000 to 2010. The region is forecast to account for 33 per cent of the world's fleet by 2020, compared with 25 per cent in 2000.

The increased demand for air travel will have knock-on effects on airports, demand for fuel and airspace. According to Mr Brown, airlines would be making 88 per cent more flights between 2000 and 2020. 'This will present a major challenge to airports and air-traffic control capacity. Those involved realize the urgency of the situation. Huge investment will be needed.'

Source: The author, from Airbus Industrie reports and forecasts

---

reveal future trends. Although statistical data may be consulted at this stage, no attempt is made to construct a mathematical formula to describe precise relationships between demand and its determinants. Such forecasts rely on a large measure of common sense and are likely to be couched in general terms such as 'small increase in demand' or 'no change in demand envisaged'.

Time-series analysis

A time series is a set of data collected regularly over a period of time. An example of such data is given in Table 4.6.

First this data can be seen to exhibit seasonal features. Sales of this product rise within each year to a peak in the fourth quarter and drop back sharply in the first quarter of the next year. Second there seems to be a trend. The figures for each quarter and the yearly totals nearly all display an upward movement. Third, the figure for the first quarter in year 3 does not fit in with the rest of the data and appears as an unusual figure. This may well have been caused by a random variation such as a strike or war or natural disaster.

Table 4.6 Time series of sales of a product

Year	Q1	Q2	Q3	Q4	Total
1	112	205	319	421	1057
2	124	220	350	460	1154
3	90	245	383	503	1221
4	138	267	412	548	1365
5	160	285	450	595	1490

Note: Q1, Q2, etc. = year quarters.

Forecasting using time-series data first averages seasonal and random variations from the data, to reveal the underlying pattern or trend. The trend can then be used to predict future data, for general yearly totals and adjusted to indicate future seasonal totals. This is illustrated in Figure 4.4 and is a process known as extrapolation.

Time-series forecasting is useful in predicting future seasonal demand and adjusting supply to anticipate seasonal fluctuations. This is particularly important in the leisure and tourism sector where demand tends to be very seasonal (tennis equipment in early summer, leisure centre use after work and at weekends, and holiday demand).

However, care must be taken in using time-series data. Planning ski holiday capacity using time-series data may be useful in predicting market growth, but seasonal fluctuations due to school holidays are not best predicted from past events (which would give the average date) but by looking to see when Easter falls to find the precise date. Equally it is random

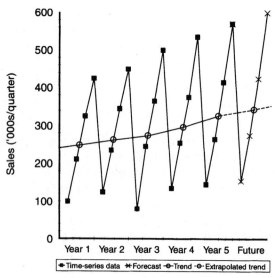

Figure 4.4 Time-series data, trend and forecast.

events that can cause significant changes in the demand for ski holidays. Clearly snowfall and exchange rates are two key factors that cannot be forecast using time-series analysis. It is important therefore that time-series analysis should be used as part of a package of forecasting techniques.

Surveys

Surveys may be carried out by the organization itself or contracted out to a specialist market research organization. Alternatively use may be made of published forecasts constructed using surveys. Surveys can be useful ways of forecasting demand for new or revised products where no time-series data exist. However, survey results are only as valid as their underlying methodology, so care must be taken to ensure that the sample used for the survey is a true reflection of an organization's potential customers, and is of a large enough size to be valid. Additionally a pilot survey needs to be conducted and analysed to iron out any problems of interpretation of words or leading questions. In fact, surveys turn out to be more useful for testing ideas such as advertising campaigns or design, where respondents are asked to choose between real and concrete alternatives. Hypothetical questions are generally used in demand forecasting, and respondents' answers may not necessarily reflect what they would actually do if they had to spend money.

Delphi technique

The Delphi technique is a method of forecasting which attempts to harness expert opinion on the subject. Questionnaires are used to discover opinions of experts in a particular field. The results of the forecasts are then fed back to the participants with the aim of reaching a consensus view of the group.

Modelling

More complex forecasting methods attempt to describe accurately the relationship between demand for a product and the factors determining that demand. They consider a number of variables, and use statistical techniques of correlation and regression analysis to test relationships and construct formulae. Some include econometric techniques which forecast key economic variables such as growth rates, interest rates and inflation rates to construct a comprehensive model which relates general economic conditions to the factors affecting demand for a particular product to the demand forecasts for that product.

Problems with forecasts

There are several problems which arise from using forecasts. First the forecasts are only as good as the assumptions of the model being used.

For example, the assumption that the past is a good guide to the future limits the validity of extrapolation using time-series analysis. However, there are equally questionable assumptions included in some very complex models. It is important to know what these assumptions are so that should any of these assumptions prove to be incorrect, forecasts can be re-evaluated.

The major problem, however, is the unpredictability of economic trends and outside events such as wars or strikes or disasters. For example, the recession of the late 1980s undermined the accuracy of many forecasts and caused severe financial problems to those who had relied on overly optimistic predictions of future levels of demand. This does not mean that forecasts are useless, but that those who use them should be constantly monitoring their operating environment to detect any factors which will upset the forecasts they are using.

Sources of forecasts

The following list gives an idea of the range and content of specialist and general sources of forecasts.

Barclays Economic Review *(Barclays Bank)*

This quarterly review offers a concise forecast for general economic conditions. It contains an economic outlook for the UK, and an international outlook, with forecasts of key economic variables such as exchange rates, income levels, inflation and interest rates for the next 2 years.

Leisure Futures *(the Henley Centre for Forecasting)*

The Henley Centre provides forecasting services, making particular use of market research. For example, in a 1998 report it highlights the increasing importance of brands, and the rise of 'time-poor, money-rich consumers' for the leisure industry.

Retail Business *(Corporate Intelligence in Retailing)*

Retail Business, published monthly, conducts market surveys, including those in the leisure and tourism sector. For example, its 1999 forecast for sales of books to UK consumers predicts static sales with figures for 2001 (£2000 m) being the same as those for 1998.

Tourist Intelligence Quarterly *(British Tourist Authority/English Tourist Board (BTA/ETB) Research Services)*

Tourism Intelligence Quarterly provides data and comment on trends in tourism in the UK as well as forecasts. Its estimates for tourist visits to the

Table 4.7 Forecasts of local entertainment visits (UK adults, millions)

	1998	*1999*	*2000*	*2001*	*2002*
Cinema	139	144	150	157	165
Dances/discos	240	239	241	242	244

Source: Leisure Forecasts 1998–2002.

UK for example are based on a mixed method. Firstly, time-series data are analysed and extrapolated. These are then adapted in the light of the wider knowledge of BTA research staff.

Leisure Forecasts *(Leisure Industries Research Center/Leisure Consultants)*

Leisure Forecasts is an annual two-volume publication which reviews changes in the leisure sector and makes 4-year forecasts with recommendations for action in each market. Table 4.7 illustrates forecasts for cinema and disco visits.

Other Sources

- *Mintel Leisure Reports* (Mintel)
- *Keynote Market Review* (Key Note)
- *New Leisure Markets* (Marketscope)
- *Travel and Tourism Analyst* (Travel and Tourism Intelligence)
- *International Tourism Reports* (Travel and Tourism Intelligence)

Review of key terms

- Consumer equilibrium = when a consumer's purchases are arranged so as to maximize a consumer's total satisfaction.
- Utility = satisfaction.
- Diminishing marginal utility = the extra satisfaction consumers derive from successive consumption of a good or service tends to diminish.
- Market demand = sum of individual consumers' demand.
- Income effect = change in demand caused by change in income.
- Substitution effect = change in demand caused by change in relative prices.
- Price elasticity of demand = the responsiveness of demand to a change in price.
- Inelastic demand = demand is unresponsive to a change in price.
- Elastic demand = demand is responsive to a change in price.

- Income elasticity of demand = the responsiveness of demand to a change in income.
- Cross-price elasticity of demand = the responsiveness of demand for one good to a change in the price of another good.
- Time series = a set of data collected regularly over a period of time.
- Seasonal variation = regular pattern of demand changes apparent at different times of year.
- Extrapolation = extending time-series data into the future based on trend.
- Delphi technique = finding consensus view of experts.

Data questions

Task 4.1 Teleworking

An office worker who works for 48 weeks a year and has a 90 minute journey to and from work clocks up some alarming statistics. An average of 720 hours each year are spent on commuting. That's 30 whole days.

Over the last decade, commuting has reached new heights, largely because of high inner-city house prices and motorways. Cheaper house prices in out of city locations, together with the development of a comprehensive network of motorways, have encouraged people to increase their time spent on commuting and to cast a wider net in search of well-paid employment.

It may be, though, that we are nearing the peak of commuting. The technological revolution in the office means that the possibility for people to work from home is becoming a reality. Why spend a fortune in time and money sending people to the office, when the office can be sent to the people? The fax, digitalization of information, the telephone network, PCs, modems and video-conferencing are all enabling the spread of teleworking. Meanwhile environmental concerns have encouraged the government to increase taxes to curb the use of car journeys.

Almost half of major UK companies are experimenting with teleworking schemes. This has resulted in the creation of a new class of over half a million full-time teleworkers.

British Telecoms (BT) is a major potential benefactor of increased teleworking, since teleworking means more use of datalinks. However, BT also uses the scheme itself. Directory enquiries operators can now work at home where they have databases with telephone numbers installed on PCs and calls rerouted. To the customer there is no apparent change in service.

The Henley Centre for Forecasting has estimated that more than 15 per cent of hours worked in the UK was worked from home in the mid 1990s, which translates into a figure of over 3 million people.

The choice for workers looks fairly straight-forward. It has been estimated that the overall benefit to a $25 000-a-year employee who is able to work at home for 4 days a week and cut commuting to 1 day a week is of the order of $7080 a year. This is calculated mainly in terms of increased leisure time, period at £6335.

To these benefits employees can add more flexibility in terms of house location and hours worked, and less commuting stress. On the other hand some psychologists have pointed out the important functions that a place of work may fulfil, particularly pointing to the friendship factor, and the benefits of a physical separation of work and home.

A key question posed by the release of commuting time is how it will be spent. Will people choose to use it as leisure time or might they instead seek to increase their earnings by working more hours?

Source: The author, from news cuttings.

Questions

1 Consumer choice theory assumes people act rationally and maximize their total utility. Explain this proposition and discuss whether people who spend 30 days a year commuting fulfil these assumptions.
2 'For individuals, the advantages of teleworking are usually believed to have more to do with quality of life than with economics.' Does consumer choice theory consider the quality of life?
3 The value of the extra leisure time made available to the employee cited above is $6335.
   (a) How might this calculation be made?
   (b) What factors will determine what the person will do with the extra leisure time?
4 If the benefit to individuals of teleworking is so clear, why do not more people telework?
5 How might teleworking affect the leisure sector?

Task 4.2   Elasticity

Jensen (1998) estimated income and price elasticities for tourist visitors to Denmark. He found considerable variation in results for different nationalities. His key finding was 'For German tourists, who account for the largest share in Danish tourism, the estimates for price elasticity with respect to the prices in Denmark is close to –1.5 and the long-run income elasticity is found to be near 2' (1998:101).

Questions

1 Classify German tourism demand in Denmark as elastic/inelastic/inferior/normal
2 Comment on these findings.
3 What implications do these figures have for policy-makers and tourist organizations in Denmark?
4 Devise a method of estimating price and income elasticity of demand for cinema attendance, explaining any problems foreseen.

Task 4.3   1995 Forecasts predict strong growth in the UK cruise market to the year 2000

New forecasts talk of 'revolutionary' growth in the cruise market, with passenger numbers and revenues soaring in the next 5 years while prices and holiday-makers' ages drop. Deck quoits are out, discos are in.

Only 80 000 Britons took a cruise 10 years ago, a figure which according to new estimates is set to quadruple to 320 000 this year and more than double again by the year 2000. Figure 4.5 illustrates these trends and forecasts.

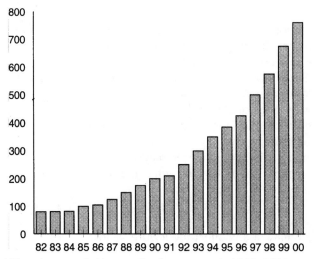

Figure 4.5   UK cruise growth (thousands of passengers), 1982–2000.
Source: Lunn Poly.

The average age of the cruise passenger has already dipped. Forty-somethings are replacing over-60s as the main age range and new ships are being designed with the family in mind. It is the new, younger cruise fans who are putting capacity and revenue projections on full steam ahead.

High-street travel agent Lunn Poly predicts that if, as expected, more than 750 000 UK holiday-makers set sail in 2000, at an average price of $1500 cruising will generate around $1.12 bn in revenue. That exceeds the entire non-ski winter overseas holiday market from the UK, which is 2 million strong and generates $1.08 bn in revenue.

Cruise giants P&O and Cunard enjoy around 30 per cent UK market share each. The UK's second largest tour operator, Airtours [First Choice] bought a ship from Kloster Cruises earlier this year and has a competitive 1995 cruise brochure.

Source: *Observer*, 28 August 1994 (adapted).

Questions

1 What additional information would you like before trusting 'new estimates' on cruise market growth?
2 What factors would be taken into account in preparing demand forecasts for the cruise industry?
3 Which organizations will use the above forecasts, and why?
4 Evaluate the accuracy of these forecasts in the light of events which have occurred since 1995.

Task 4.4   Cinemas: 2001 and beyond

Mintel has produced forecasts of the cinema market in the UK to 2002. Its method is to 'correlate historic market size data with key economic and demographic determinants (independent variables), identifying those factors having most influence on the market. Using forward projections of these factors, a market size forecast is produced.' Mintel points out that the impact of blockbusters such as *2001: A Space Odyssey*, or *Titanic* is difficult to predict. Key factors identified as highly correlated to attendance by Mintel are personal disposable income and the size of the ABC1 socio-economic group.

Table 4.8   Forecast of the cinema market, 1998–2002 (1998 prices)

	Admissions (tickets)	Admissions (£m)
1998	160	616
1999	173	665
2000	181	691
2001	188	712
2002	198	737

Source: Adapted from *Mintel Report on Cinemas*, 1998.

Questions

1 Evaluate the method used by Mintel by comparison with other possible methods for forecasting.
2 To what extent is it true that forecasts are 'a load of old crystal balls' ?
3 What factors might cause these forecasts to be inaccurate?
4 Which organizations will find cinemas forecasts useful?
5 The Rank Group plc owned Odeon cinemas (UK) in 1999 as well as other leisure interests. Its share price on 12 February 1999 was 199p. Would you recommend its shares on the basis of the above forecasts?

Short questions

1 What is meant by consumer equilibrium?
2 What is diminishing marginal utility? Are there any exceptions to this?
3 When will a consumer no longer demand a free good?
4 What degree of income elasticity of demand would you expect for summer holiday breaks in Bognor?
5 What cross-price elasticity of demand would you expect to find between:
   (a) price of pesetas/holidays in Spain?
   (b) holidays in Spain/holidays in Greece?
   (c) Nintendo games consoles/Nintendo games cartridges?
6 What is meant by extrapolation?

References

Boviard, A., Tricker, M. and Stoakes, R. (1984) *Recreation Management and Pricing*, Gower.
Jensen, T., Income and price inelasticities by nationality for tourists in Denmark, *Tourism Economics*, **4**(2), 1998.

Websites of interest

Mintel International: a wide range of market intelligence on the leisure sector   www.mintel.co.uk
Learning help in economics and business studies   http://www.bized.ac.uk

5 Supply and costs

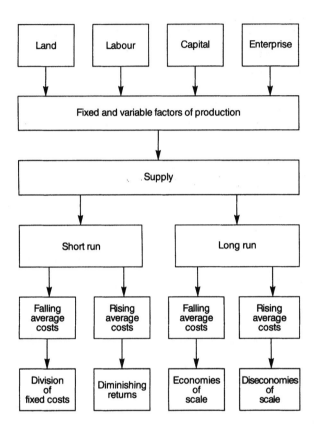

Objectives

Shuttle services such as BA's London to Belfast service operate on a turn-up-and-fly principle, so BA's operations division has to be able to provide a flexible service in order to meet sudden changes in demand. Air traffic control routes across Europe on the other hand are fairly inflexible – they are sometimes unable to cope with sudden surges in demand and this can lead to long delays in peak times of the year. This chapter looks behind the supply curve at issues such as these. It investigates how easily the supply of leisure and tourism products is able to respond to changes in demand, using models of elasticity. It also considers how an organization's costs respond to changes in output and distinguishes between private costs and social or external costs.

By studying this chapter students will be able to:

- understand and utilize the concept of elasticity of supply
- identify the factors of production
- distinguish between fixed and variable factors of production
- analyse the relationship between costs and output in the short run and long run
- establish the relationship between costs and the supply curve
- understand the reasons for economies of scale
- identify methods and rationale for growth
- distinguish between social and private costs

Price elasticity of supply

Elasticity of supply measures the responsiveness of supply to a change in price. This relationship may be expressed as a formula:

$$\frac{\text{Percentage change in quantity supplied}}{\text{Percentage change in price}}$$

Exhibit 5.1 shows a worked example of how to calculate elasticity of supply.

Exhibit 5.1   A worked example

When the price of Matashi 21″ colour TVs rose from £160 to £180, supply rose from 3200 to 3600 sets per week. Calculate elasticity of supply:

1 To calculate percentage change in quantity supplied, divide the change in supply ($\Delta Q = 400$) by the original supply ($S0 = 3200$) and multiply by 100:
2 $400 \div 3200 \times 100 = 12.5$
3 To calculate percentage change in price, divide the change in price ($\Delta P = 20$) by the original price ($P0 = 160$) and multiply by 100:
4 $20 \div 160 \times 100 = 12.5$
5 Elasticity of supply = $12.5 \div 12.5 = 1$

Where supply is inelastic it means that supply cannot easily be changed, whereas elastic supply is more flexible. The range of possible outcomes is summarized in Figure 5.1.

Note that any straight line supply curve passing through the origin has supply elasticity of 1.

Numerical value	Graph	Explanation	Term
0		Supply is unresponsive to a change in price	Perfectly inelastic
> 0< 1		Supply changes by a smaller proportion than price	Inelastic
1		Supply changes by the same proportion as price	Unit elasticity
> 1< ∞		Supply changes by a larger proportion than price	Elastic
∞		Suppliers can supply any amount at the current price but none if price falls	Perfectly elastic

Figure 5.1   Elasticity of supply.

Factors affecting price elasticity of supply

The following are the main factors which influence price elasticity of supply:

- time period
- availability of stocks
- spare capacity
- flexibility of capacity/resource mobility

Time period

Generally the longer the time period allowed, the easier it is for supply to be changed. This is illustrated in Figure 5.2. In the immediate time scale, it is difficult to change supply and thus supply is relatively inelastic, and a change in price of $P0$ to $P1$ results in supply being unchanged at $Q0$ on curve $S0$. In the short run it may be possible to divert production or capacity

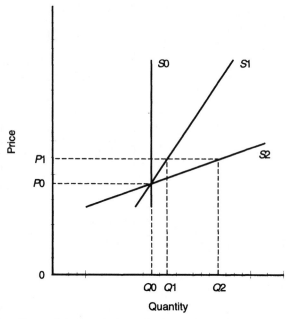

Figure 5.2 The effects of time period on elasticity of supply.

from another use and thus supply becomes more elastic. This is shown by supply curve $S1$, where a rise in price from $P0$ to $P1$ results in a small rise in supply from $Q0$ to $Q1$. In the long run it is possible to vary fixed factors of production and increase capacity. Supply is thus more elastic during this time period, as shown by curve S2, where a rise in price from $P0$ to $P1$ results in a rise in supply from $Q0$ to $Q2$.

Availability of stocks

For manufactured goods the availability of stocks of goods will enable supply to be more flexible and more elastic. Modern 'just-in-time' methods of production are geared towards enabling manufacturing to be more sensitive to market needs without recourse to large stocks.

Spare capacity

The existence of spare capacity either in terms of service capacity or manufacturing capacity will make supply more elastic.

Flexibility of capacity/resource mobility

Flexibility of capacity means that resources can easily be shifted from provision of one good or service to another. Flexible sports halls, for example, enable capacity to be shifted from one leisure service to another to reflect market conditions and thus make supply more elastic. Flexibility of the labour force is also a key factor here.

Changing the supply of specialist goods or services may require the use of specialist skills or machines. These may be difficult or expensive to hire in the short period and hence will tend to make supply inelastic.

Significance of price elasticity of supply to leisure sector

The supply of some tourist attractions is totally inelastic. For example, there is only one tomb of Chairman Mao in Beijing, there is only one Sistine Chapel, and there is only one home of Sir Winston Churchill at Chartwell. It clearly is not possible to replicate these sites as it is for other popular attractions such as Disneyworld.

Considerable thought therefore has to be given to managing such sites. The market could establish an equilibrium if prices were allowed to fluctuate, but the heritage aspect of such sites generally precludes such a solution since they are generally meant to be universally accessible. Inevitably, then, there is excess demand for these sites at the given price and this problem is managed differently at each site. At Mao's tomb, capacity is raised substantially by having the queue divide into two to pass each side of Mao's body. White-gloved attendants furiously wave people by and thus queuing is kept to a minimum despite free admission. At the Sistine Chapel large queues do form, but they are accommodated in an imaginative way by making the detour, through the Vatican museum, to the Sistine Chapel progressively more and more circuitous. The problem of inelastic supply and excess demand at Chartwell is addressed by issuing timed tickets to visitors.

In general terms, price elasticity of supply determines the extent to which a rise in demand will cause either a change in price or shortage. Tour operators generally have relatively fixed capacity in ski resorts, and thus the supply curve is inelastic. When demand rises, for example, during school holiday periods, supply is unable to expand to meet the increased demand and so price changes considerably.

Supply and costs

Leisure and tourism outputs

We need to distinguish between different forms of output in the leisure and tourism sector. Where manufacturing of a product takes place, for example in the production of sports clothing, then output is measured in terms of physical product. Where the provision of a service takes place, output is measured in terms of capacity.

Leisure and tourism inputs

Inputs are classified in economics under the following general headings.

- Land – includes natural resources such as minerals, and land itself and can be divided into renewable and non-renewable resources. Land is a significant resource for tourism.
- Labour – includes skilled and unskilled human effort.
- Capital – includes buildings, machines and tools.
- Enterprise – is the factor which brings together the other factors of production to produce goods and services.

Factors of production are further classified as:

- fixed factors
- variable factors

Fixed factors of production are defined as those factors which cannot be easily varied in the short run. Examples of fixed factors of production in the provision of leisure and tourism services include the actual buildings of theatres and hotels, whilst factories and complex machinery are examples in leisure manufacturing.

Variable factors of production on the other hand can be changed in the short run and include unskilled labour, energy (e.g. electricity, gas, oil) and readily available raw materials. The existence of fixed and variable factors of production means that changes in output will be achieved by different means in the short run and the long run.

Production

Entrepreneurs bring together factors of production in order to supply goods and services in the market and maximize their profits. There are generally several possible ways to produce a given level of output or to provide a service. Profit maximization implies cost minimization and thus entrepreneurs will seek to combine inputs to produce the least-cost method of production.

Input prices themselves are constantly changing to reflect changing conditions in their markets. As input prices change, entrepreneurs will adapt production methods to maintain lowest costs, substituting where possible factors of production which are rising in price with cheaper ones.

Short-run costs

Fixed costs

The existence of fixed factors of production means that the costs associated with that factor will also be fixed in the short run. Such costs are sometimes called indirect costs or overheads since they have to be paid irrespective of

---

Exhibit 5.2   High fixed costs for art galleries

The demand for art fluctuates according to the state of the economy. When economic growth is strong, galleries can be full of buyers, but these soon disappear when economic times are hard. During the recession in the early 1990s one commentator reported that 'buyers had gone into hibernation' and many art galleries were forced out of business.

A major factor in this is the high fixed costs that galleries face which can be easily accommodated when sales are strong. But the point about fixed costs is that they cannot be changed in the short term. If demand falls suddenly they can force a gallery into bankruptcy since they must still be paid even when there are few or no customers. Galleries are located in prime locations and so their major fixed costs are rent and property taxes. In addition, galleries typically produce three or four catalogues a year with an average cost of Euros 18 000 per edition.

Source: The author, based on article from *The Independent*.

---

the level of production. So, for example, whether a plane flies to New York empty or full, its fixed costs or overheads are the same. Exhibit 5.2 illustrates fixed costs for art galleries.

Variable costs

Variable costs are those costs which vary directly with output. They are sometimes called direct costs. For the production of leisure goods they would include raw materials, energy and unskilled labour costs, but for the provision of services such as air transport they are proportionately small and would include such items as meals and passenger handling charges.

Total costs

Total costs are defined as total fixed costs plus total variable costs. This distinction is an important one when deciding whether to continue to operate facilities out of season. A firm which is not covering its costs is making a loss and in the long term will go out of business. However, in the short run a firm which is covering its variable costs and making some contribution to its fixed costs may stay in business. This is because it has to pay for its fixed costs anyway in the short run and thus some contribution to their costs is better than none at all.

Average costs

Average costs are defined as total costs divided by output.

Marginal costs

Marginal costs are defined as the cost of supplying one extra unit of output.

Relationship between output and costs in the short run (production)

Figure 5.3 shows a typical short-run average cost curve for the production of goods in the short run.

If a manufacturer has planned for a level of output $OQ0$, then $OC0$ represents the average costs of production. These will represent the least-cost method of production and combination of factors of production, since profit maximization is assumed. However, if the level of output should subsequently be changed in the short run, then by definition only variable factors of production can be changed and fixed factors remain constant. Average costs will therefore rise as the mix of inputs resulting in the least-cost method of production cannot be maintained.

Consider first a fall in output to $OQ1$. Average costs (AC) will rise to $OC1$. This is because the fixed costs will now be borne by a smaller level of output. Similarly, if output rises to $OQ2$, average costs rise to $OC1$. The fixed factors of production become overcrowded and production less efficient. This is related to the law of eventual diminishing returns. The marginal cost curve MC is drawn to fit the above analysis. For mathematical reasons AC is always falling when $MC < AC$; AC is always rising when $MC > AC$, and thus the MC curve always cuts the minimum point of the AC curve.

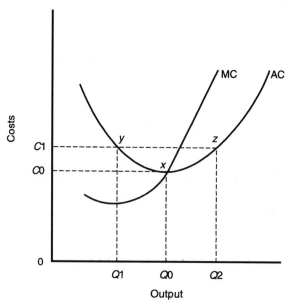

Figure 5.3   Short-run average costs (AC) and marginal costs (MC) for typical manufacturing firm.

Relationship between output and costs in the short run (services)

The provision of services often involves different cost relationships from the provision of goods. For a hotel, a theme park or a theatre, for example, fixed costs represent a large proportion of costs in the short run. There also exist some costs which can be termed semivariable costs. These represent capacity that is available only in blocks, such as putting on an extra plane. Variable costs for extra visitors to a theme park or a theatre are negligible up to the capacity level.

Figure 5.4 illustrates typical cost curves for the provision of a service with high fixed costs. Notice that the average cost curve falls all the way to short-run capacity and that for much of its range the marginal cost is low and constant. The existence of low or sometimes zero marginal costs explains some marketing activity for the service sector. Theatres sell standby seats to students at low prices but students still have to pay full prices for ice creams.

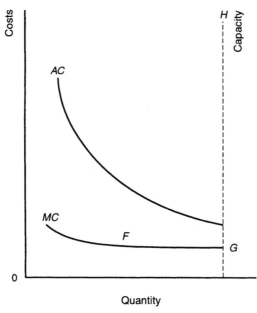

Figure 5.4 Costs for a firm providing a service with high fixed costs. AC = Average costs; MC = marginal costs.

The short-run supply curve under perfect competition

Firms in the private sector will seek to produce at a level of output where profit is maximized. Knowledge of marginal costs and marginal revenue informs this decision. We have already derived a short-run marginal cost curve. Under perfect competition the marginal revenue curve is easily deduced.

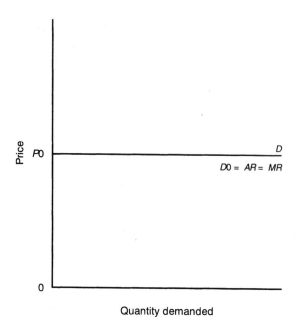

Figure 5.5   Revenue curves under conditions of perfect competition. AR = Average revenue; MR = marginal revenue.

A competitive firm will face a perfectly elastic demand curve. This is because, if the firm raised prices, consumers would make their purchases from competing firms. A perfectly elastic demand curve, $D0$, is illustrated in Figure 5.5.

This shows that the firm can sell as much as it wants at the prevailing market price of $P0$. This also derives from the fact that, under perfect competition, there are many small firms, none of which are big enough significantly to affect total supply. Therefore if one of these firms increases supply there will be no impact on market price.

Table 5.1 calculates revenue data for a typical firm under perfect competition. As explained above, price remains the same irrespective of output. Recapping, total revenue equals price multiplied by quantity sold,

Table 5.1   Revenue for competitive firm (£)

Output	Price	Total revenue	Average revenue	Marginal revenue
0	10	0	0	–
1	10	10	10	10
2	10	20	10	10
3	10	30	10	10
4	10	40	10	10
5	10	50	10	10

average revenue equals total revenue divided by output and marginal revenue equals the revenue earned from selling one extra unit of output. Thus, if price is £10 per unit, the total revenue from selling three units is £30 and for selling four units is £40, and both average revenue and marginal revenue for selling the fourth unit are £10. It can be calculated that average revenue equals marginal revenue at all levels of output.

Thus, in Figure 5.5, the demand curve *D0* is the same as the average revenue curve *AR* and the marginal revenue curve *MR*.

Figure 5.6 shows the cost and revenue curves for a typical manufacturing firm operating under conditions of perfect competition. We can now deduce where a profit-maximizing firm will seek to operate. *MR0* represents marginal revenue at price *P0* and *MC* represents marginal costs. At any level of output below *OQ0*, marginal revenue will exceed marginal cost and thus the firm can increase profit by increasing output since extra output is profitable. However, if output is increased beyond *OQ0*, marginal costs exceed marginal revenue, so the firm is making a loss on extra units produced and sold. Thus the profit-maximizing level of output will be at *OQ0* where marginal costs equal marginal revenue (*MC = MR*).

We can now derive the firm's supply curve. At *P0*, the marginal revenue curve is at *MR0* and the firm will produce at *Q0* (*MC = MR0*). At *P1*, the marginal revenue curve rises to *MR1* and the firm will produce at *Q1* (*MC = MR1*). At *P2*, the marginal revenue curve rises to *MR2* and the firm will produce at *Q2* (*MC = MR2*). Thus the supply curve for a firm operating under conditions of perfect competition is the upward sloping part of its marginal cost curve – SS in Figure 5.6.

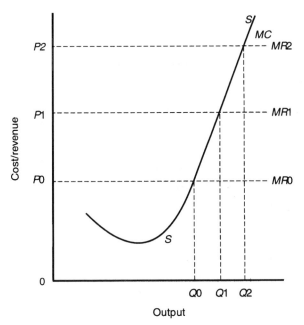

Figure 5.6   Profit-maximizing level of output and supply curve for typical manufacturing firm.

Similarly, in Figure 5.4, the curve *FGH* represents a typical supply curve for a firm providing a service with high fixed costs. The supply curve is elastic up to the point of capacity, when it becomes totally inelastic.

Long-run costs

In the long run all factors of production are variable and so organizations are not faced with the problems of fixed factors or diminishing returns. Output can be satisfied by the most suitable combination of factors of production. Figure 5.7 illustrates three possible ways in which average costs of production may vary with output in the long run.

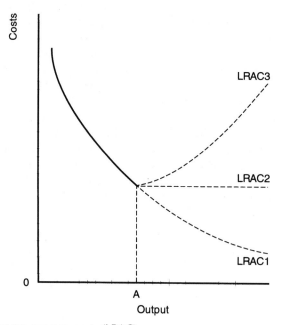

Figure 5.7   Long-run average costs (LRAC).

In curve LRAC1, average costs fall for the entire range as output rises, illustrating economies of scale. In the case of LRAC2, the curve flattens out after point *A* when constant returns of scale are achieved. For the curve LRAC3, average costs begin to rise again after point *A* where diseconomies of scale begin to set in.

Internal economies of scale

Economies of scale arise from increases in the size of an organization and can be summarized as follows:

● financial
● buying and selling

- managerial/specialization
- technical
- economies of increased dimensions
- risk-bearing

Financial

Large organizations tend to have bigger assets. When they borrow money, they often raise large amounts and these two factors lead to financial economies. Borrowing from banks is likely to be at preferential rates of interest reflecting the security offered by large organizations and the amount borrowed. Additionally, larger organizations have the option of raising funds directly from capital markets by, for example, a rights issue of shares which can be an economical method of financing large projects.

Buying and selling

Buying and selling economies arise from buying and selling in bulk. On the buying side this leads to bulk purchase discounts, and on the selling side costs such as advertising are spread out over a large number of sales.

Managerial/specialization

As firms grow the potential for managerial and specialization economies becomes greater. The proprietor of an independent travel agency, for example, will have to act across a range of managerial functions and may lack specialist knowledge. Large travel agency chains such as Going Places, however, will have the scope for employing experts in functional areas such as accounting marketing and personnel.

Technical

Technical economies are also possible as firms grow. These relate in particular to the utilization of complex and expensive technology and machinery. A large hotel may employ a computerized reservations and accounting system since the cost per guest per year will be relatively insignificant. A small boarding house however may have insufficient business to justify the capital outlay.

Economies of increased dimensions

Economies of increased dimensions are well-illustrated by the example of jumbo jets. Although these have the capacity of perhaps three conventional jets, they do not cost three times as much to buy, or staff, or run. Thus the cost per seat of a jumbo jet is less than that in a conventional jet – costs rise proportionately less than capacity.

Risk-bearing

Risk-bearing economies derive from the ability of large organizations to weather setbacks. This arises from two factors. First many large organizations have diversified interests and thus a fall in demand in one area can be compensated for by business elsewhere. Second, large organizations with substantial assets are able to sustain short term losses from their reserves.

External economies of scale

External economies of scale result not from the size of an organization but from the concentration of similar organizations in a particular location. For example, hotels in a particular resort benefit from resort as well as their own advertising, and may attract visitors on the strength of complementary attractions supplied by neighbouring organizations.

Diseconomies of scale

Internal diseconomies

The main reason for the occurrence of diseconomies of scale is managerial capacity. For some organizations, it becomes difficult to manage efficiently beyond a certain size and problems of control, delegation and communications arise. These may become significant enough to outweigh economies of scale generated in other ways. Diseconomies of scale may also arise from growth due to mergers when the two firms find that there is insufficient fit between themselves in terms of systems of management or organizational culture. Exhibit 5.3 illustrates economies and diseconomies of scale at work in the restaurant and hotels sector.

External diseconomies

The negative side of concentration of organizations in a particular area can be overcrowding and the associated congestion costs.

How firms grow

The main methods by which firms grow are by:

- internal growth
- mergers and take-overs

Exhibit 5.3   Perfect pizzas, synergies Chez Gerard and a marriage made in hell?

1998 was a good year for the pizza and pasta sector in the UK which is estimated to be worth approximately Euros 1170 million a year. Pizza Express moved ahead in the sector when it acquired the Café Pasta chain. The *Guardian* business correspondent described this move as underlining 'the trend towards creating branded chains of restaurants which benefit from economies of scale in financing and property costs'. Pizza Express currently has 175 outlets with expansion plans for an extra 125 outlets. It paid Euros 8.5 million in cash for the Café Pasta chain.

Advertising and branding are becoming increasingly important in the mid-range restaurant sector with names such as Café Rouge and All-Bar-One and a recent Mintel report concludes that branded chains now account for more than a half of all outlets in the pasta and pizza markets This move by Pizza Express helps bring down the average costs of marketing. David Page of Pizza Express also notes that costs tend to be higher in general for smaller independent companies.

In a similar move, Groupe Chez Gerard has also announced plans to buy the Richoux group of restaurants. Chez Gerard explained that expected marketing, purchasing and head office synergies are a key motive for the acquisition. Commentators have also noted that the move strengthens the position of Chez Gerard in the case of a possible downturn in expenditure since the Richoux group effectively covers the lower end of the market.

Of course there are potential downsides to mergers. One is a possible conflict of personalities between directors. In early 1999 The Ladbroke Group (owners of the non-US Hilton hotels) took over the Stakis hotel chain. This has led the *Guardian* financial corespondent to describe the new partnership between Mr Peter George (Ladbroke) and Mr David Michels (Stakis) as 'potentially a marriage made in hell'.

Source: Adapted from the *Guardian* and *Financial Times* by the author.

Internal growth is often a slow process and firms can accelerate their growth by mergers and take-overs. The difference between these is that mergers are a joint agreement for two organizations to join together whereas a take-over does not necessarily have the agreement of the target firm.

It is also useful to identify different types of integration:

● vertical integration
● horizontal integration
● conglomerate merger

Table 5.2 shows the structure of the package holiday industry in matrix form. The vertical part of the matrix represents the different stages of the industry moving from suppliers at the top, through operators to retailers at the bottom. Note that Thomson and Airtours represent fully vertically integrated groups. The horizontal part of the matrix represents competing firms at each stage of the industry.

Table 5.2   The structure of the package holiday industry

Airline	Britannia	Airtours Intl	Caledonian	Air 2000
Tour operator	Thomson	Airtours	Thomas Cook	First Choice
Retail	Lunn Poly	Going Places	Thomas Cook	

Vertical integration

This occurs when a firm takes over or merges with another firm in the same industry but at a different stage of production. It is termed backward integration when the merger is in the direction of suppliers, and forward integration when it is towards the consumer. Thomson Holidays demonstrates a vertically integrated organization with its ownership of a charter airline, Britannia, and travel agency chain, Lunn Poly.

Airtours purchased Pickfords retail travel in 1992 and the Hogg Robinson travel agency chain in June 1993 (see exhibit 5.4), subsequently renaming its acquisitions Going Places.

The key motive in forward vertical integration is in ensuring a market for an operators product. This may be offensive – selling your product at the expense of your rivals – or defensive – making sure your rivals do not monopolize retail outlets and thus block the selling of your product. Backward integration gives your organization control over suppliers, and means that you have better control over quality.

Horizontal integration

This occurs when a firm merges with another firm in the same industry and at the same stage. For example, in 1998 Thomas Cook merged with Carlson and the Thomson Travel Group bought ski operator Crystal. In 1999, the

---

Exhibit 5.4   Airtours to buy Hogg agencies – Gail Counsel

Airtours is buying Hogg Robinson's leisure arm for £25 m cash in a move that will create the UK's second largest travel agency. Last September the tour operator paid £16 m for the 334-branch Pickfords travel division.

With 548 outlets Airtours-owned travel agencies will be within a whisker of Lunn Poly, the UK's largest travel agency network, which has more than 600 branches, and considerably larger than Thomas Cook, with only about 350 outlets.

Economies of scale, plus the advantages of being able to sell its own packages through the network, should mean Airtours will be able to boost profitability significantly.

Source: The Independent, 15 June 1993 (adapted).

Exhibit 5.5   Thomson Travel: stalking the stalker

The *Travel Trade Gazette* (3 March 1999) reported 'Thomson continued its spending spree this week by buying one of the UK's leading upmarket brands as well as the top operator in Poland'. Recent acquisitions include:

- Simply Travel and Headwater Holidays (£22.5 million).
- Scan Holidays (£6.2 million).
- Callers Pegasus (£17 million).
- Magic Travel Group (£20 million).

The purchase of Scan Holidays has bought Thomson an immediate 38 per cent share of the Polish travel market which is seen as having a strong potential for growth.

However in the same week Thomson shares rose 13p to £1.68 amidst rumours that Thomson itself might be the target of a take-over from a German travel company.

Sources: *Travel Trade Gazette* and *Financial Times*, adapted by the author.

Ladbroke Group owners of The Hilton chain outside of the USA bought up Thistle Hotels.

Economies of scale is a prime motive for horizontal integration. For example, advertising costs per holiday fall, and bulk purchase discounts can be maximized. Market share and market domination are also key motives. Horizontal acquisition can also occur to purchase firms operating in complementary areas. The interest of the Thomson Travel Group in companies such as Headwater and Blakes Cottages is to extend its portfolio beyond the ski and sun markets. There is also scope for cost savings through rationalization of activity and closing down of sites which duplicate work. This has certainly been the case for the Going Places travel agency chain formed from Airtours' acquisitions of Hogg Robinson and Pickfords. Horizontal integration also buys into an existing market and its customers and can be an effective way of reducing competition. One of the arguments made by Stenna Sealink and P&O for merging was the potential for service improvement.

Merger

A conglomerate merger or diversification occurs when a firm takes over another firm in a completely different industry. The motives for such activity may include first a desire to spread risks. Second growth prospects in a particular industry may be poor, reflecting a low or negative income elasticity of demand. In such circumstances diversification into an industry with high income elasticity of demand may generate faster growth. Third it may be possible to get benefits of synergy, where the benefits of two firms joining exceed the benefits of remaining separate. For example, the Rank

Group plc is a conglomerate organization with interests across the leisure sector. Its divisions include:

- Deluxe (film and entertainment services).
- Hard Rock (restaurants).
- Holidays (Haven, Oasis, Warner and Butlins).
- Leisure (Mecca Bingo, Grosvenor Casinos, Odeon Cinemas and Tom Cobleigh pubs).
- Universal (Theme Parks).

Exhibit 5.6 illustrates diversification in the defence industries.

Exhibit 5.6   War games

With the demise of the cold war and the move of military action away from battlefields to computer screens there have been moves towards diversification by companies in the military hardware sector. The military aerospace company Lockheed Martin has set up its own games division. Real 3D is based in Florida, and has developed arcade games with Sega. There is a clear profit basis for the move into military-entertainment with the games industry being worth around $5 billion with war-based games representing an important segment of the market.

Lockheed's new fighter plane the F-22 Raptor (real) now has a virtual cousin in the hangar. A deal with the software company Novalogic has resulted in the release of *F-22 Raptor* (Novalogic, PC 16Mb RAM). 'As a game, it's adequate, better than Microsoft's ropey Flight Sim series . . . but not up there with Sabre Ace' is the verdict of the *Guardian's* reviewer, Campbell Stevenson.

Source: adapted from the *Guardian* by the author.

Declutter

A problem that may occur from diversification is that an organization may lose sight of its aims and objectives and find strategic management difficult. Under such circumstances 'decluttering' may take place, whereby an organization disposes of its fringe activities and concentrates on its core business.

Social and private costs

Private costs of production are those costs which an organization has to pay for its inputs. They are also known as accounting costs since they appear in an organization's accounts. However the production of many goods and services may result in side-effects. Violent videos may for example result in more violent and antisocial behaviour. A night-club may result in noise pollution. These are classed as external or social costs. They do not appear in an organization's accounts and do not affect its profitability, although they may well affect the well-being of society at large. These issues are discussed more fully in Chapters 7 and 18.

Review of key terms

- Price elasticity of supply = responsiveness of supply to a change in price.
- Factors of production = land, labour, capital and enterprise.
- Fixed factor = one that cannot be varied in the short run.
- Variable factor = one that can be varied in the short run.
- Average cost = total cost divided by output.
- Marginal cost = the cost of producing one extra unit of output.
- Vertical integration = merger at different stage within same industry.
- Horizontal integration = merger at same stage in same industry.
- Conglomerate merger = merger into different industry.
- Private costs = costs which a firm has to pay.
- Social costs = costs which result from output but which accrue to society.

Data questions

Task 5.1   Changes in brewing

Whitbread is the UK's third biggest brewer and markets brands such as Heineken, Boddingtons and Stella Artois. In early 1998 reports emerged of plans to close two of its five breweries in an attempt to cut costs and reduce overcapacity. The likely targets for closure are and the Castle Eden brewery in County Durham and the Flowers brewery in Cheltenham. About 300 staff are employed in these breweries, with just under 50 per cent involved on the production side. In late 1997, Bass, the UK's second biggest brewer, announced the closures of its Sheffield and Cardiff breweries where 180 staff were employed. These closures are in addition to eight other breweries that have been shut down by the top four brewers since 1993.

The main reason for this is a steady decline in beer sales in the UK. In 1970, annual beer consumption in Britain was more than 42 million barrels, but this had declined to around 36 million barrels by 1997. Industry analysts point to changing lifestyles, competing leisure activities, bootlegging (the importation of duty-free beer), a reduction in leisure time spent in pubs and a rise in drinking at home as key factors contributing to the decline in beer sales.

This has given rise to a programme of diversification by the major beer companies who are now expanding into other leisure businesses, like hotels and restaurants. Bass has grown into the world's biggest hotel owner and continues to enlarge its portfolio. For example, it announced in early 1998 the purchase of four hotels in Australia in a deal worth £48 million. These hotels will be converted to fit into the company's Holiday Inn brand.

Bass has also diversified into restaurants although not as successfully as its rival Whitbread, which boasts a substantial holding of restaurant chains. In a bid to catch up on its rival, Bass has purchased Browns, a UK restaurant chain with seven upmarket outlets for £35 million.

Questions

1 Distinguish between fixed and variable costs and the short and long run in the brewing industry.
2 What is overcapacity?
   ● What are its likely causes?
   ● What does it imply about the mix between fixed and variable costs?
3 Sales of beer in UK pubs has declined over the past decade.
   ● Suggest reasons for this using economic terms and analysis.
   ● Explain how this affects short-run and long-run costs using cost curves.
4 What is meant by diversification? What factors are driving diversification in this sector?
5 What is the relationship between branding and economies of scale?
6 What synergies exist between brewing, restaurants and hotels?
7 Distinguish between fixed and variable costs for:
   ● a single restaurant
   ● a chain of restaurants.

Task 5.2   Hotels: no reservations about growth

Americans corporations dominate the hotel sector with nine of the top fifteen positions in the global league table of companies. In Europe, UK hotel companies dominate the sector where firms that used to make their profits in beer have recently expanded into the hotel marketplace.

For example, Bass is second in the world-wide league table of hotels – ranked by number of rooms rather than number of hotels – compiled annually by the trade magazine *Hotels*. Bass owns the Holiday Inn and Crown Plaza brands. It has recently added InterContinental hotels to its portfolio. Whitbread has also embarked on a strategy of expansion and rebranding with its Travel Inn brand. Ladbroke, owner of the Hilton brand outside the United States, made a successful bid for Stakis hotels in 1999. There have been several rumours of an eventual merger with Hilton in America.

Melvin Gold, consultant with Pannell Kerr Forster, stresses the importance of branding. 'It is particularly important in some locations. If you are going to Moscow on business, you are more likely to choose a hotel whose name you recognize. You are more likely to choose something that you can be fairly sure will give you a break from the hustle and bustle of Moscow life.'

Other factors such as centralized reservations are also significant in the growth of hotel chains. These allow travellers to make bookings through any

Table 5.3 Major corporate hotel acquisitions 1995–1999

Year	Hotel	Purchaser	Cost (million)
1995	Westin Hotels	Starwood	$561
1995	Meridien Hotels (Air France)	Forte	$338
1996	Forte Hotels	Granada	£3870
1996	Metropole Group	Stakis Hotels	
1997	Renaissance Hotels	Marriott Int	$1000
1997	Wyndham American	Patriot	$1100
1997	Promus	Doubletree	$4700
1997	Westin Hotels & Resorts	Starwood	$1570
1997	ITT (ITT Sheraton)	Starwood	
1998	InterContinental Hotels (Saison Group)	Bass	£1780
1998	Arctia	Scandic	$100
1999	Stakis	Ladbroke	

Source: Pannell Kerr Foster.

Table 5.4 The ten largest hotel companies in the UK (1998)

Company	Hotels	Rooms
Forte Hotels (Granada)	161	22 203
Thistle Hotels	97	13 329
Whitbread	206	12 458
Hilton (UK) (Ladbroke)	40	8536
Stakis Hotels	55	8302
Queens Moat Houses UK Ltd	51	7103
Granada Travelodge	155	6621
Holiday Hospitality (Bass)	46	6399
Regal Hotel Group plc	102	5568
Jarvis Hotels	64	5447

Source: Deloitte & Touche.

Table 5.5 Concentration in UK hotel sector

	1991	1996
Number of hotels		
Top 15	15 834	21 039
16–200	6694	8422
Number of rooms		
Top 15	2 155 154	2 698 398
16–200	1 238 090	1 336 237

Source: *Hotels* magazine.

same-brand hotel in any location, and therefore represent an important marketing opportunity.

Elsewhere in Europe, France leads in the budget branded sector where Accor, the fourth largest hotel corporation in the world, owns Formule 1 and Ibis. Other European countries, particularly Germany, Spain, and Italy, are still relatively underdeveloped in terms of branded chains.

The benefits of economies of scale in the hotel sector mean that medium-sized hotel chains such as Jarvis, Thistle and Swallow are likely candidates for future acquisitions particularly by US corporations such as Starwood and Patriot and UK conglomerates such as Bass and Whitbread.

Questions

1 Distinguish between horizontal and vertical integration:
   ● What type of integration is occurring in the hotel sector?
   ● What form would other types of integration take and what would be its advantages?
2 What economic factors explain the increase in merger activity and concentration of hotel ownership in this sector?
3 What problems might prevent growth of US- or UK-branded hotels into Spain, Germany or Italy?
4 What economic factors determine the limits to the size of hotel chains?
5 Discuss the factors that determine the elasticity of supply of hotel accommodation.
6 Discuss the relationship between fixed costs, average costs and marginal costs for hotels. What are the implications of your analysis for pricing?

Task 5.3   Record companies: sharks and minnows swim side by side

Six record companies dominate the UK record industry with the top four accounting for over 55 per cent of sales. But at the same time there still exist a significant number of independent labels. So, on the one hand, the record industry demonstrates a trend towards globalization, larger companies, and less competition. In addition, there is a tendency towards global entertainment companies encompassing music, film and the press. But, on the other hand, the creative nature of the industry and the need to be responsive to changes in the market means that there is still an important place for small labels.

Eventually independent labels which are successful are often bought up by larger companies or are linked to them by distribution agreements. Creation Records, an independent famous for signing Oasis, is now 49 per cent owned by Sony having started life in 1984 with a £1000 bank loan (see Task 2.5). The big six are:

● UK market leader PolyGram incorporating labels such as A&M Island, Mercury and Polydor. PolyGram is part of part of the Dutch conglomerate Philips Corporation, and has recently been diversifying into films.

- EMI is second in size in the UK to PolyGram and also owns Virgin Music, which it purchased for £510 million in 1992.
- Sony Music is part of the Sony Corporation of Japan. Sony, originally known for its music hardware, entered the recording sector by its purchase of the CBS company. It also owns Colombia and Epic.
- BMG Entertainment International, UK & Ireland is part of Bertelsmann AG, the third largest media company in the world.
- Warner is part of Time-Warner Corporation. This US Corporation has interests in film making, television as well as recorded music.

Distribution is key to the success of recorded music and in the UK record stores are also dominated by a few large chains accounting for 65 per cent of sales. These include:

- Virgin Our Price, a group which includes 55 Virgin Megastores and the Our Price chain.
- Woolworths which is part of the Kingfisher Group.
- HMV which is part of the EMI group and operates over 1200 HMV outlets.
- WH Smith Retail which operates a chain of 549 shops selling books, magazines, stationery and greeting cards as well as records.
- The major supermarket chains, particularly Asda, are also increasingly important outlets for CDs and tapes.

Source: Adapted from the *Mintel Report* on records CDs and tapes (1998).

Questions

1 Illustrate examples of horizontal, vertical and conglomerate integration in the article.
2 Analyse the benefits to a record company of
   - horizontal integration
   - vertical integration
   - conglomerate integration
3 What evidence is there of potential diseconomies of scale existing in the record industry?
4 What is the significance of the terms *elasticity of supply* and *marginal costs* to the record industry?

Short questions

1 Why may an organization's average costs of production rise as output rises in the short run, but fall in the long run?
2 What is the marginal cost of selling an empty seat on a scheduled flight?

3 Distinguish between private costs and social costs in the provision of air travel.
4 How elastic is the supply of:
   (a) CDs?
   (b) Theatre seats?
   (c) Package holidays?
5 Distinguish between vertical and horizontal integration.
6 Why does an organization maximize profits when $MC = MR$?
7 Distinguish between fixed costs, variable costs, the short run and the long run.

Websites of interest

Granada Group plc   http://www.granada.co.uk
Marriott International   http://www.marriott.com
McDonald's Corp.   http://www.mcdonalds.com
Nintendo of America Inc.   http://nintendo.com
Scottish and Newcastle plc   http://scottish-newcastle.com
Sony Corporation   http://sony.com
Time Warner Corporation   http://timewarner.com
Trump Hotels & Casinos Resorts Inc.   http://trump.com
Wilson Sporting Goods Co.   http://www.wilsonsports.com/
Virgin Atlantic   http://www.bized.ac.uk/compfact/vaa/vaaindex.htm
Learning help in economics and business studies   http://www.bized.ac.uk

6 Pricing and marketing strategy in the real world

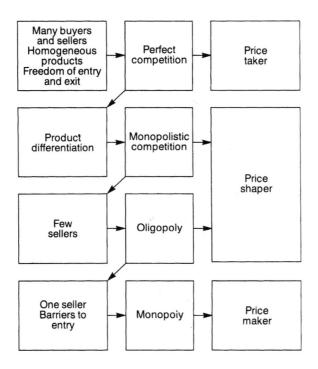

Objectives

In the real world it is often difficult to relate prices to the simple demand and supply analysis presented in Chapter 3.

For example, we find leisure centres and fitness centres offering similar services at vastly different prices. It has been said that an airline running a jumbo jet carrying 350 passengers will charge 350 different prices. Newspapers have been waging a price war that have dragged prices below production costs. Some shops have as many sale and offer days as normal trading days. This chapter investigates how prices are determined in the real world.

By studying this chapter students will be able to:

- understand how and why firms come to be price takers, price makers or price shapers
- analyse the pricing strategies that result from different market situations

Pricing in the private sector

Private sector organizations which seek to maximize profits will attempt to minimize their costs and maximize their revenue.

Revenue is composed of price multiplied by quantity sold, and the price that an organization can charge for its product depends largely on the type of market within which it is operating.

Price takers

Perfect competition

At one extreme, economic theory describes the model of perfect competition. In this model there are many buyers, many sellers, identical products, freedom of entry and exit in the market, and perfect knowledge about prices and products in the market. Here firms have to accept the market price, since any attempt to increase their own price over and above market price will lead to consumers purchasing identical goods or services from competitor firms. This is illustrated in Figure 6.1.

Figure 6.1 (a) shows the market demand curve *DM*, the market supply curve *SM* and the equilibrium price *P0*. Figure 6.1(b) shows the demand curve faced by an individual firm, *DF*, which is perfectly elastic. What do firms get for their labours in such markets? They get normal profits, defined as that level of return which is just sufficient incentive for a firm to remain in its present business. Any excess profits will lead new firms into the industry and this extra supply will drive prices down to the level where normal profits are restored.

However, whilst free market prices and normal profits are good for consumers, profit-maximizing producers will aim to increase and protect profits. Thus there are few examples in the real world of price takers, and if firms are not in the fortunate position of being price makers they will generally take steps to become price shapers.

Price makers

At the other extreme from perfect competition, some firms exist in conditions of monopoly or near monopoly and thus have considerable control over prices.

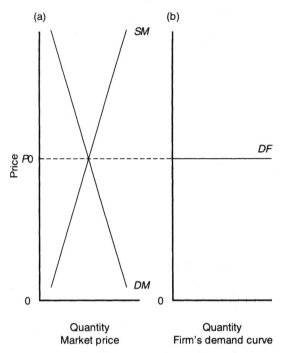

Figure 6.1 (a) The market and (b) the firm under perfect competition. See text for details.

Monopoly pricing

A monopoly is literally defined as one seller, and monopoly power is maintained by barriers to entry into the industry. Therefore the firm's demand curve is the same as the industry demand curve. Because of this, the monopolist is in a position to be a price maker.

There are examples of near-monopolies in the leisure and tourism sector. For example, there are only two car ferry services to the Isle of Wight and these operate on different routes, thus giving each operator some control over price. Unique tourist attractions also have some degree of monopoly power. There is no similar attraction to Madame Tussauds in London, although to some extent the main visitor attractions in London all compete with each other. Table 6.1 shows typical demand data for a unique attraction. It demonstrates the trade-off that a monopoly producer faces – the higher the price, the less the demand.

The price that maximizes total revenue for this organization is one of £5 when a total revenue of £250 per hour is generated. This is illustrated in Figure 6.2. In Figure 6.2(a), *D* represents the firm's demand curve, whilst in Figure 6.2(b), *TR* represents the firm's total revenue curve, found by multiplying quantity sold at each price. Price £5 generates total revenue of £250 per hour, whilst a higher price of £8 or a lower price of £2 causes total revenue to fall to £160.

This confirms the relationship between changes in price, changes in total revenue and elasticity of demand discussed in Chapter 4. Where demand is inelastic a rise in price will cause an increase in total revenue. Where demand is elastic, a fall in price will cause an increase in total revenue. Profit maximization therefore occurs where demand elasticity is (–)1. In Figure 6.2 the demand curve is elastic in the range X to Y, inelastic in the range Y to Z and has unit elasticity at point Y.

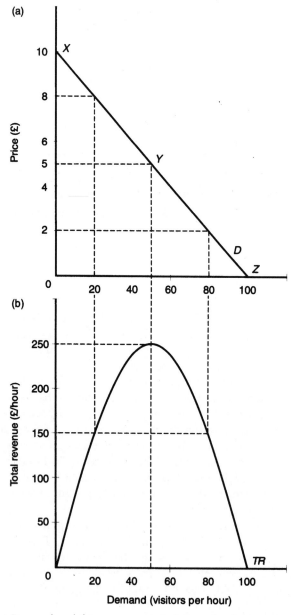

Figure 6.2   (a) Demand and (b) revenue-maximizing price for monopolist.

Table 6.1 Monopoly attraction demand data

Price (£)	Quantity demanded (visitors/hour)	Total revenue	Marginal revenue
10	0	0	
9	10	90	9
8	20	160	7
7	30	210	5
6	40	240	3
5	50	250	1
4	60	240	−1
3	70	210	−3
2	80	160	−5
1	90	90	−7
0	100	0	−9

Notes:
1 Total revenue = price × quantity sold.
2 Marginal revenue = the extra revenue gained from attracting one extra customer ($\Delta TR + \Delta Q$), where TR = total revenue, and Q = quantity.

To summarize, monopolists can choose a price resulting in high profits, without fear of loss of market share to competitors. The actual price chosen will reflect both demand conditions and the firm's cost conditions.

Exhibit 6.1 shows how top football clubs are exploiting their market position.

Exhibit 6.1   Chelsea fans: sold out

Price increases for season tickets at Chelsea Football Club for the 1998–1999 season are in some cases as high as 47 per cent as against inflation of around 2.5 per cent in the UK economy. This means that the cheapest season ticket for supporters is now £525, while the most expensive is £1250.

Top premier clubs find themselves in monopoly positions. Stadiums are full to capacity and price increases don't lead fans to chose alternative products elsewhere. Nearby Fulham or Arsenal do not offer alternative football for Chelsea fans, in the way that different brands of beer can be seen as substitutes.

At a meeting with the UK sports minister a Chelsea fan complained 'I'm an old age pensioner and have been following Chelsea since 1923. . . a season ticket now costs £1250. Me and my five pals have decided to join, but last season we had reduced tickets in the same seats for £600.' The minister replied, 'A number of clubs know that if they put up prices, they will sell them anyway. Football is a drug. But I am increasingly drawn to the conclusion that, sooner or later, a degree of regulation might be necessary.'

Source: The author, adapted from the *Guardian*.

Price discriminating monopolist/yield management

Some firms sell the same good or service at different prices to different groups of people. For example, BA return fares from London to New York (summer 1999) are: £5446 (first class), £3213 (club class), £828 (standard economy 1, £417. (APEX), £82.80 (staff 10 per cent standby) and £0 (staff yearly free standby/holders of airmiles or frequent flyer miles).

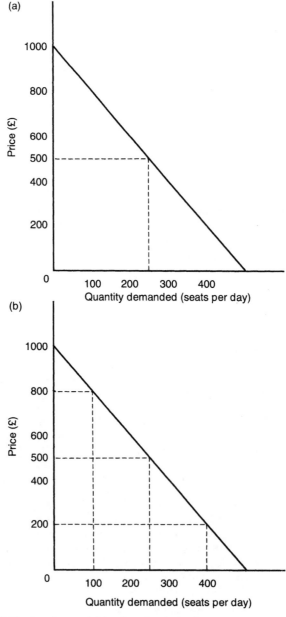

Figure 6.3   (a) Single price and (b) price discrimination.

In fact BA is not a monopolist since there is much competition on this route, but most fares are subject to International Air Transport Association (IATA) regulation and thus many firms are able to act as monopolists. It should also be recognized that the fare differential for club and first-class passengers is not strictly price discrimination since these represent different services with different costs. But since all economy-class passengers receive an identical service, why should BA charge different prices and why do passengers accept different prices?

The conditions for price discrimination to take place are:

● The product cannot be resold. If this were not the case, customers buying at the low price would sell to customers at the high price and the system would break down. Services therefore provide good conditions for price discrimination.
● There must be market imperfections (otherwise firms would all compete to the lowest price).
● The seller must be able to identify different market segments with different demand elasticities (for example, age groups, different times of use).

Figure 6.3 illustrates a typical demand curve for economy-class travel. If a single price of £500 is charged as in Figure 6.3(a), then 250 seats are sold and total revenue is £125 000. Figure 6.3(b) shows a situation in which three prices are charged. One hundred seats are sold at £800, the next 150 seats are sold at £500 and the next 150 seats are sold at £200, producing a total revenue of £185 000, an increase of £60 000 over the singleprice situation.

Airlines must consider the behaviour of costs when price-discriminating. Once the decision has been taken to run a scheduled service, marginal costs are low up until the aircraft capacity, when there is a sudden large jump. Airlines are able to discriminate by applying travel restrictions to differently priced tickets. So, for example, fullfare economy tickets are fully refundable and flights may be changed at no cost. Cheaper tickets are non-refundable and have advance purchase and travel duration restrictions. Exhibit 6.2 describes price discrimination in the supply of leisure goods and services.

Exhibit 6.2   Prices adrift

Prices of a whole range of leisure goods vary considerably between countries with tennis balls, trainers and CDs being prime examples. The UK Treasury has produced research which shows that audio cassettes are around 15 per cent cheaper in the USA than the UK and hand-held computer games such as a Game Boy are 4 per cent cheaper in the USA.

But it is in the market for cars where manufacturers charge the most widely varying prices. For 72 of the EU's best-selling models, the UK is the most expensive market for 61 of them. A glaring example of differential pricing is the VW Polo, which costs 50 per cent more in the UK than in Portugal.

Source: The author, from UK Treasury Reports, 1999.

Yield management is a sophisticated form of price discrimination. Computer technology is able to identify patterns of demand for a particular product with its supply. A request for a hotel reservation or an airline ticket will result in the system suggesting a price that will maximize the yield for a particular flight or day's reservations.

Price shapers

Whilst firms operating under conditions of perfect competition are price takers and those operating under conditions of monopoly are price makers, firms operating in markets between these two extremes can exert some influence on price. The two main market types which will be examined are:

- oligopoly
- monopolistic competition

Oligopoly pricing

An oligopoly is a market dominated by a few large firms. An example of this is the cross-channel travel market. Oligopoly makes pricing policy more difficult to analyse since firms are interdependent, but not to the extent as in the perfectly competitive model. The actions of firm A may cause reaction by firms B and C, leading firm A to reassess its pricing policy and thus perpetuating a chain of action and reaction. For these reasons firms operating in oligopolistic markets often face a kinked demand curve. This is illustrated in Figure 6.4.

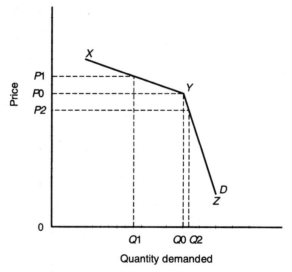

Figure 6.4 The kinked demand curve.

Consider the demand curve D, which might illustrate the demand curve for a cross-channel car ferry firm. The prevailing price is P0. Notice that the demand curve is elastic in the range X to Y. This is because, if a firm decides to increase its price, for example from P0 to P1, it will lose customers to its competitors and demand will fall sharply from Q0 to Q1 and the firm will suffer a fall in total revenue. On the other hand, if it should decide to reduce its price from P0 to P2, it is likely that its competitors will match the reduction in price to protect their market share, and there will be only a small increase in demand from Q0 to Q2, resulting in a fall in the firm's revenue. Thus the demand curve is inelastic in the range Y to Z, and the demand curve is kinked at point Y. In this situation it is clearly not in the interests of individual firms to cut prices, and thus such markets tend to be characterized by price rigidities.

Marketing and competition under oligopoly conditions are often based around:

- advertising
- free gifts and offers
- quality of service or value added
- follow-the-leader pricing – pricing is based on the decisions of the largest firm
- price wars occasionally break out if one firm thinks it can effectively undercut the opposition

Monopolistic competition

This is a common type of market structure, exhibiting some features of perfect competition and some features of monopoly. The competitive features are freedom of entry and exit and a large number of firms. However, firms which are operating in essentially competitive environments may attempt to create market imperfections in order to have more control over pricing, market share and profits.

It is competition from other sellers with homogeneous products that forces market prices down, and thus firms will often concentrate on these two issues in order to exert more market power. The more inelastic a firm is able to make its demand curve, the more influence it will have on price, and thus firms will attempt to minimize competition by:

- product differentiation
- acquisitions and mergers
- cost and price leadership

Product differentiation

The rationale for product differentiation is to make the demand for a good or service less elastic, giving the producer more scope to increase prices and/or sales and profits. There are a number of routes to product differentiation.

The first is by advertising. One of the aims of persuasive advertising is to create and increase brand loyalty even if there are no major differences between a firm's product and that of its competitors.

The second route to product differentiation is through adding value to a good or service. This may include, for example, making improvements to a good or service or adding value somewhere along the value chain. The value chain can be thought of as all the interconnecting activities that make up the whole consumer experience of a good or service. Table 6.2 demonstrates aspects of the value chain for BA Club World. Exhibit 6.3 shows how Virgin trains are bringing product differentiation to their services.

Exhibit 6.3 shows how Virgin trains are bringing product differentiation to their services.

The point of adding value and differentiating product is that it enables firms to charge a premium price but still retain customers.

Exhibit 6.3   Seven types of Virgin

Richard Branson, who introduced new standards of service to his Virgin Airlines with his 'Upper Class' service, is now attempting a similar exercise on his trains. While rival rail networks still operate a two-class system, Virgin has introduced no less than seven different classes of ticket: These are:

- *First Class* (*not pre-booked*): here you may sit in a first class compartment and enjoy free tea, coffee and alcoholic drinks.
- *Virgin Business Class* (*pre-booked*): with free drinks plus a free meal, parking and a London underground pass
- *Virgin Value First* (*pre-booked, off-peak trains only*): this also allows you to sit in first class but there is no free food or alcohol.
- *Standard Full Fare*: accommodation in standard compartment, free tea and coffee, and the possibility of upgrade to first (space permitting).

Then there are three types of bargain tickets:

- Saver.
- Super Saver.
- Virgin Value.

These all come with restrictions relating to pre-booking times, period of travel and time of travel. They are also colour coded so that bargain passengers wait at a different colour-coded zones of the platform, and sit in colour-coded seats. The seats are in fact identical to each other.

Product differentiation is such a money-spinner that even the Heathrow to Paddington rail link, owned by British Airports Authority, provides first and second class, although the journey takes only 15 minutes.

Source: The author.

Table 6.2 Value chain for BA Club World

Pre-sales	Pre-check-in	Check-in	Flight	Arrival	Post-flight
Advertising	Valet parking	Dedicated check-in	Dedicated cabin	Rapid transit arranged to city centre	Frequent-flyer awards
		Express security/ passport route	Luxury meal		Complaints procedure
		Dedicated lounge	Seat size		
			Increased staff ratio		

Acquisitions and mergers

These are discussed in detail in Chapter 5, but they are an important consideration in pricing strategy as they can:

● reduce competition (and thus reduce downward pressure on prices)
● lead to economies of scale (which can underpin price leadership strategies)

Cost and price leadership

Another key strategic move to increase market share and profitability is through cost and price leadership. Cost leadership involves cutting costs through the supply chain – squeezing margins from suppliers, and economizing where possible in the production of goods or provision of services by stripping out unnecessary frills. The aim of cost leadership may be to increase margins but this is unlikely to be achieved since consumers are likely to resist lower quality of goods or services without any compensation in price.

Exhibit 6.4 Thomson promises to remain cheapest until 21st century

There is keen rivalry between the Thomson Travel Group and its rival Airtours for market leadership in the package holiday market. Thomson have declared their intention to use price to keep ahead of their competitors.

Commenting on a recent campaign based on low prices, Thomson's managing director made this promise:

'To those competitors which think that Thomson's low prices are just a short term measure and the umbrella of high prices will return, think again. Thomson's low prices are here to stay. We intend to be the number one choice well into the 21st century'.

Source: The author.

Equally it is difficult to maintain cost leadership since other firms will attempt to achieve similar cost reductions. However, where cost leadership is translated into low prices it may be possible to increase market share. This can then lead to the creation of a virtuous circle where increased market share leads to economies of scale which enable lower costs and thus lower prices to be maintained ahead of rival firms. There has been a considerable battle for market share in the package holiday industry, as illustrated in exhibit 6.4.

Exhibit 6.5 describes a recent campaign for British Airways to beat its rivals on prices.

Exhibit 6.5   Air wars: BA cuts prices of 2 million seats

British Airways held a high profile summer sale in 1998 in a bid to attack its low-fare rivals on prices. The clearance sale which ran over a two-day period is viewed by analysts as a response to strong competition from no-frills airlines which has left BA with empty seats. Many of the biggest discounts were made on routes flown by low-cost rivals, although BA's marketing director attributed the sale to the stay-at-home factor caused by the World Cup.

Competition is particularly strong on flights to Nice where EasyJet, Debonair, AB Airlines, and a British Midland/Air France joint operation are all in direct competition with BA.

Seats for Nice were reduced by up to £150 to start at £79 and long-haul bargains to £199 to Bermuda and £299 to Cape Town.

Source: The author, from BA press release, 1998.

Pricing in the public sector

Prices of public sector goods and services will depend upon the market situation which prevails in a particular industry as well as the objectives set for a particular organization. These might be:

- profit maximization
- break-even pricing
- social cost/benefit pricing

Profit maximization

In the case of profit-maximizing aims, an organization's pricing policy will follow the pattern set out earlier in this chapter.

Break-even pricing

Break-even pricing aims at a price which is just sufficient to cover production costs rather than one which might take advantage of market

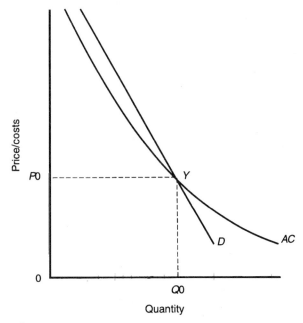

Figure 6.5   Break-even pricing.

imperfections and maximize profit. Figure 6.5 illustrates a firm with average costs of *AC* and a demand curve *D*. At price *P0* total revenue is $0 - P0 \times 0 - Q0$, and total cost is $0 - P0 \times 0 - Q0$ and thus the firm is breaking even. Any price higher than *P0* would result in extra profit and any price below *P0* would result in losses.

Social cost/benefit pricing

Where the aim of public provision is to take fuller account of public costs and benefits, the supply will be subsidized to produce a price either lower than market price (partial subsidy) or at zero price (total subsidy). More detailed analysis of this can be found in Chapter 7.

Pricing and the macroeconomy

The condition of the economy at large also has an influence on firms' pricing policy. If the demand in the economy is growing quickly, there may be temporary shortages of supply in the economy and firms will take advantage of boom conditions to increase prices and profits. Similarly, during a recession there may well be over-capacity in the economy and demand may be static or falling. These conditions will force firms to have much more competitive pricing policies to attract consumers.

Review of key terms

- Price taker = a firm in a perfectly competitive market which cannot directly influence price.
- Price maker = a firm in a monopoly market which sets its desired price.
- Price shaper = a firm in an oligopoly or imperfectly competitive market which may seek to influence price.
- Perfect competition = many buyers and sellers, homogeneous products, freedom of entry and exit to market.
- Monopoly = one seller, barriers to entry.
- Oligopoly = a small number of powerful sellers.
- Monopolistic competition = many buyers and sellers, freedom of entry and exit, products differentiated.
- Product differentiation = real or notional differences between products of competing firms.
- Price discrimination = selling the same product at different prices to different market segments.

Data questions

Task 6.1 Customers win in Channel wars

1994: The fares for Le Shuttle, the train that will ferry motorists and their cars under the Channel, have been set higher than expected. They range from £125 return for a carload in winter to a peak price of £310. Most are a little higher than the equivalent ferry fare.

There was an almost audible sigh of relief from the Channel ports as Christopher Garnett, Eurotunnel's commercial director, outlined the structure; at least the tunnel was not trying to undercut the ferries. Asked by the *Independent on Sunday* whether Eurotunnel would respond if the ferries cut their fares, Mr Garnett said: 'We would not be following. We're not going to get involved with price wars. We're not going to get involved in discounting.'

Richard Hannah, an analyst with UBS and a close follower of Eurotunnel, is sceptical: 'I'm convinced there will have to be a price war because of the excess capacity created by the tunnel.' He said fares would have to come down sharply to generate the extra volumes needed to meet Eurotunnel's ambitious revenue targets. 'Even if Eurotunnel captured the entire existing cross-Channel business from the ferry companies, it would still not generate enough revenues even to cover its costs.' He argued that Eurotunnel had to create a fresh wave of demand for cross-Channel travel, and it could only do that by cutting prices.

Mr Garnett sees Le Shuttle's advantages over ferries as speed, convenience and reliability. But the other unknown quantity in the calculation is the response of the ferry companies and the ports. According to chairman, Mr Dunlop, P&O has spent £400m over the past five years modernizing its fleet.

'We've revolutionized the ferry industry in the last five years, creating an attractive product.' Certainly its newer vessels, such as the *Pride of Dover* and the *Pride of Calais*, are a far cry from the shabby, vomit-smelling, beer-soaked, cramped, crowded tubs that used to ply their trade across the Channel. 'The ferry crossing is now part of the holiday,' said Mr Dunlop.

Source: The *Independent on Sunday*, 16 January 1994 (adapted).

1999: No one pays £310 to cross the channel any more. The opening of Eurotunnel gave rise to a period of intense competition and the 'Channel war' was a consumer's dream. The competition has seen the merger between the two ferry companies, P&O and Stena, but even so there continue to be good deals.

- Le Shuttle: A 35-minute crossing. A five-day return costs £95 per car with four departures an hour during the day and three an hour at night. Few facilities but weatherproof.
- British Airways: APEX tickets from £91 per person. Journey time is between 65 and 90 minutes.
- British Midland: APEX fares are from £69 per person.
- Sally Line: Ferry from Ramsgate to Ostend, from £25 for a car and two passengers. Smorgasbord restaurant, cafeteria facilities and a supervised crèche.
- P&O Stena Line: Car and passengers £95, for a five-day return and £159 for a standard return. Restaurants, games arcade, cinema and club class available.
- Hoverspeed: Standard return on the Hovercraft for a car and passengers is £158. Crossing time 35 minutes. Same price but 50-minute crossing on SeaCat.
- Eurostar: Three-hour, high-speed train service from London to Paris. Fares from £79 for a weekend return. City centre to city centre service. Buffet and bar. First and second class.

Questions

1 What degree of competition exists in the cross-Channel market?
2 Explain why the Channel Tunnel's initial strategy was not price based.
3 What elements of product differentiation strategy are illustrated?
4 What have been the key factors affecting price in the cross-Channel market between 1994 and 1999?
5 What pricing strategies would you recommend to P&P Stena Line to maximize revenue?

Task 6.2   *Researching prices and markets*

Conduct local research in one of the following areas:

1 Air travel suppliers and prices.
2 Hotel accommodation suppliers and prices.

3 Restaurant suppliers and prices.
4 Package holiday suppliers and prices.
5 Cinema suppliers and prices.
6 CD suppliers and prices.
7 Other leisure markets in your locality.

Your research should concentrate on a specific product or service (e.g. return air fare from Auckland to New York) and identify the main suppliers, prices and product differences.

Questions

1 Identify the market conditions which operate in your chosen market.
2 Account for the patterns of pricing which emerge from your research.
3 To what extent and why does your chosen market deviate from the model of perfect competition?
4 Is there any evidence of price discrimination or price leadership in your chosen market?
   ● If so, explain the reasons and consequences.
   ● If not, explain the reasons and consequences.
5 Compare and contrast your results with those of obtained in a different market.

Task 6.3   *Fidelity can equal free flights – Simon Calder*

My bank account may not be healthy, but I am heavily in credit with several organizations, reports Simon Calder. I have 52 593 Continental one pass miles, four United 5000-mile award cheques, 1100 Virgin freeway points and 1648 BA air miles. Frequent flyer miles are a simple concept. The more you travel with a particular carrier, the more you are rewarded for your loyalty. Usually the award is another flight. As far as the carrier is concerned, the idea is that you will fill a seat which would otherwise be empty.

The bottom line, for the passenger and the airline, is – do the schemes work? For passengers, the answer is a resounding 'yes'; you can get something for nothing, though it might not be a flight at the ideal time. For the airlines, the rewards are harder to define. Now that most carriers operate a frequent flyer scheme, passengers just take whatever is offered by each carrier and travellers are becoming more fickle.

Source: *The Independent*, 23 April 1993 (adapted).

Questions

1 What are the short-run and long-run benefits to airlines of operating frequent flyer miles incentives?

2 What are the costs to airlines of operating such schemes?
3 Evaluate frequent flyer incentive schemes in relation to other marketing techniques for increasing airlines' profits.
4 Why was the Hoover free flights scheme a fiasco?

Task 6.4   *Go ploy to stop competition?*

May 1998: British Airways launches its new cut price airline 'Go' which operates out of London's fourth airport – Stanstead. The first destinations include Rome, Milan and Copenhagen from 5 June with introductory fares of £100 return as opposed to BA's standard return fare to Rome of around £300. Industry sources expect Go to maintain some £100 flights beyond the launch period as a loss leader to attract attention.

In launching Go, BA is attempting to meet the challenge posed by a number of new cheap operators who have been highly successful in attracting passengers. These include Ryanair, Debonair and easyJet. These are so-called 'no-frill' airlines where passengers forgo free meals and drinks and are to be seated on a first-come first-served basis. Flights operate out of cheaper, secondary out-of-town airports and tickets are non-transferable and non-refundable. Go has initially avoided direct competition with these airlines by not duplicating their routes.

BA has assured its critics that Go is a completely separate business and it will not be cross-subsidized from the main airline. But opponents claim that Go represents a strategy to drive other no-frills airlines out of business and that in the long term prices will rise again as the competition is reduced through predatory pricing.

However, there are also critics of the easyJet set. They point to the limited availability of the cheapest seats and the fact that the small scale of the airline's operations mean that delays and cancellations are common. US experience suggests that the period of low air fares sweeping the UK in the late 1990s may be short-lived. No-frills flying was invented in the US by Peoples Express which has long since gone out of business as have most of its imitators as the big airlines have fought to maintain their domination in the market.

Questions

1 What kind of market type is evident in the UK for airlines and how has the market changed?
2 Are airlines price makers or price takers? Use diagrams to explain your answers.
3 Why are the continued prospects for low fares poor?
4 How does 'loss leadership' and 'cross subsidization' affect prices. Are these activities beneficial to customers?
5 How is BA able to charge different fares for similar flights to Rome?

Short questions

1 What kind of market structures do the following operate in:
  (a) Package tour operators?
  (b) London five-star hotels?
  (c) Brewers?
  (d) McDonalds?
2 Explain the elasticity of demand of a kinked demand curve.
3 Why will a monopolist choose not to produce in the inelastic range of its demand curve?
4 Why are there so few examples of perfectly competitive markets?
5 Under what circumstances is price leadership likely to lead to increased profits?

Websites of interest

British Airways   www.british-airways.com
Air Ticket Prices   http://www.cheapflights.co.uk/
EasyJet   www.easyjet.com
Learning help in economics and business studies   http://www.bized.ac.uk

7 Market intervention

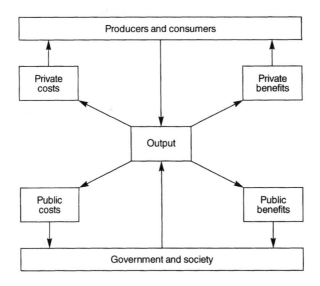

Objectives

The price mechanism as described in Chapter 3 seems to offer a simple yet effective system of signalling consumer demands to producers. It is often contrasted with systems of state planning – particularly as practised in former communist eastern Europe. Many commentators noted that the Berlin Wall was built to stop people escaping from eastern Europe to western Europe, not the other way round. The economic landscape of eastern Europe was characterized by queues for goods and services, empty shops, shoddy goods and service sector workers who exhibited indifference to their customers. Exhibit 7.1 illustrates some of the problems encountered by tourists to communist Cuba.

Free market economies, on the other hand, boast shops full of attractive consumer goods, few queues and a world of slick advertising. However critical analysis of the market mechanism raises issues of concern. Sex tourists to Thailand signal an effective demand for prostitution which suppliers satisfy. Similarly, the demand for snuff, and child pornography videos, and for addictive drugs is met by the operation of market forces. The market has also created the tower blocks of Benidorm.

Exhibit 7.1   Game for a fistful of dollars

With their sandals, shorts and insect repellent, Ann and Tony Crossley booked into the E1 Paradiso hotel, in Cuba's premier resort. 'As a tourist, it's all right if you don't expect too much' said Tony, and since the British tour group arrived their Airtours representative had been filing complaints.

First the swimming pool was closed for 5 days. Then a pack of dogs invaded the dance floor and then there was the smell of rotten eggs – the byproduct of nearby oil exploration.

Source: *The Observer*, 26 June 1994 (adapted).

The objectives of this chapter are first to examine whether leisure and tourism provision should be left to the free market, and second to consider reasons for, and forms of, market intervention.

After studying this chapter students will be able to:

- evaluate the benefits of the free market
- evaluate the problems of the free market
- understand the methods of market intervention
- justify market intervention
- understand recent developments in public sector provision

The free market

The benefits of free markets

Adam Smith wrote in *The Wealth of Nations* of the main benefits of the free market. He drew attention to the fact that people exercising choice in the market in pursuit of their own self-interest led to the best economic outcome for society as a whole. The concept that 'the market knows best' was also a central plank of the economic philosophy of the Thatcher government, post 1979. Indeed, Chancellor Nigel Lawson summed up this thinking as:

'The business of government is not the government of business'

In particular, free markets have the potential to deliver:

- economic efficiency
- allocative efficiency
- consumer sovereignty
- economic growth

Economic efficiency

Economic efficiency means having the maximum output for the minimum input. Profit maximization and competition between firms both result in firms choosing least-cost methods of production and economizing on inputs, as well as using the best technological mix of inputs. Exhibit 7.2 illustrates how competition in the market place stimulates organizations such as BA into a drive for economic efficiency.

Allocative efficiency

Allocative efficiency is related to the concept of Pareto optimality and means that it is not possible to reallocate resources, for example by producing more of one thing and less of another, without making somebody worse off. It results first from economic efficiency and second from consumers maximizing their own satisfaction and implies maximum output from given inputs and maximum consumer satisfaction from that output.

Consumer sovereignty

Consumer sovereignty means that consumers are able to exercise power in the market place. It implies that production will be driven by consumer demand rather than by government decisions. In a free market system, firms which survive and grow will be those which make profits by being sensitive to consumer demand.

Economic growth

Economic growth will be encouraged by the free market since those firms which are the most profitable will survive and flourish. Under conditions of

---

Exhibit 7.2   Intense competition forces more efficiency gains at BA

BA is emerging from a difficult period in an increasingly competitive market for airlines. Profits in the late 1990s have fallen partially as a result of a strike by cabin staff over BA's attempts to cut costs. Although the strike affected short-term profits, BA feels that the efficiency gains that caused the strike will benefit the company in the longer term.

Chief Executive of BA, Mr Bob Ayling, said that competition was driving prices lower as the industry deregulated. But he was optimistic about the future for BA saying that more efficient companies would have improved long-term prospects. He said that the company review of its wage structures was a key part of its efficiency programme and this would be continued through negotiations with Boeing and Airbus Industrie over orders for new aircraft.

BA's cost-cutting exercise had brought savings of £500 million in 1998 and these were due to increase to £700 million by 2001. Mr Ayling said that no other European airlines had achieved similar savings. In many cases this is due to lack of competition in other European airlines.

competition, firms will compete to increase productivity and thus in the market system resources will be allocated away from unprofitable and inefficient firms towards those which are profitable and efficient, thus generating economic growth.

In summary, under a competitive free market system consumers will get the goods and services they want at the lowest possible prices.

Criticisms of the market solution

Criticisms of the free market focus on the following:

- the inappropriateness of the perfect market assumption
- reservations about consumer sovereignty
- externalities
- public goods
- realities of economic growth
- equity

Perfect market assumption

For free markets to deliver economic and allocative efficiency, perfect markets as outlined in Chapter 3 are assumed, i.e. many buyers and sellers, homogeneous products, perfect knowledge, freedom of entry and exit in markets, and no government interference. The existence of market imperfections will reduce the efficiency of the free market system. The Thatcher government in fact devoted considerable legislation to the removal of market imperfections, particularly in the labor markets.

However, in practice markets are far from perfect. Many markets are dominated by a few suppliers and considerable product differentiation occurs by producers attempting to make their goods or services different from the competition in order to minimize price competition. These factors mean that consumers may not get the benefits of lowest prices afforded by perfect markets.

Consumer sovereignty

There are a number of at work in market economies that undermine the concept of consumer sovereignty. The first is lack of information. In the complex world of competing goods and services – particularly for technical products – consumers may not have enough information about the range of goods available and may find it difficult to make comparisons beyond the superficial. Second consumers are subject to persuasive advertising from producers, the aim of which is to interfere with the consumers' exercise of free choice.

Externalities

It is also evident that free markets fail in their signalling function in some areas. For example there are some missing markets. There is no market for the ozone layer. There is no market for peace and quiet. There is no market for views and landscapes. It is difficult therefore for people to register their preferences in these areas.

Equally markets do not always consider the full range of costs and benefits associated with production, or consumption of certain goods and services. The selling of alcohol is associated with the private benefit of feeling happy but has the unwanted public cost of fighting and accidents.

Missing markets and externalities are closely linked. Consider a plan for a development of holiday apartments on a piece of farmland adjacent to the sea. In a free market situation the developer will have to consider the costs of the land, materials and labour. However the development will clearly have an impact on the landscape, the view and the tranquillity of the area. But no one owns these rights, so there is no market in them and there is no price associated with the using up of them to develop the site. In this case there is a clear difference between the private costs of development and the public or social costs of development.

In Figure 7.1, *MPC* is the marginal private costs of the development. This shows the additional private costs of supplying extra units and represents the supply curve, *S*. The demand curve, *D*, shows the quantity demanded at different prices and the marginal private benefit, *MPB*. In this case it is

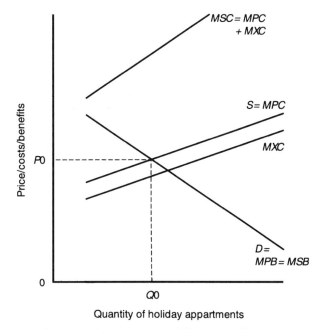

Figure 7.1 External costs and private costs: different equilibrium solutions. See text for details.

assumed that there are no external benefits to consumption and thus this
curve also represents the marginal social benefit (*MSB*). A market
equilibrium price is achieved at price *P0* and the development will go ahead
with a quantity of *Q0*.

However, *MXC* represents marginal external costs, i.e. the costs in terms
of amenities lost such as views and tranquillity. Adding *MPX* to *MPC* gives
the marginal social cost curve *MSC*. In this case it can be seen that the
external costs are such that no equilibrium is achieved in the market, since
the marginal social costs exceed the marginal social benefits at all prices.
Thus we can see that the free market overproduces goods and services
which have significant external costs.

A similar argument may be deployed to demonstrate that the free market
underproduces goods and services which provide external benefits to
society over and above the private benefits enjoyed by the consumer.

In Figure 7.2, *MPB* is the marginal private benefit derived from the use of
tennis courts and represents the demand curve, *D. S* is the supply curve
which shows the quantity supplied at different prices and the marginal
private costs, *MPC*. In this case it is assumed that there are no external costs
to provision and thus this curve also represents the marginal social cost
MSC. A market equilibrium quantity is achieved at *Q0*. *MXB*, however,
represents external benefits, i.e. the benefits to the community at large of the
use of tennis courts which might include a fitter and more productive
workforce and a reduction in petty juvenile crime. Adding *MXB* to *MPB*
gives the marginal social benefit curve *MSB*. In this case it can be seen that
the equilibrium quantity rises to *Q1*.

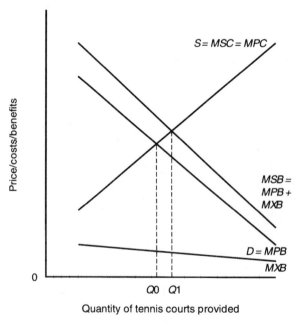

Figure 7.2 External benefits and private benefits: different equilibrium solutions. See
text for details.

Goods which include substantial external costs are sometimes termed demerit goods and goods which include substantial social benefits are sometimes termed merit goods.

Public goods

The market has an incentive to produce private goods or services because it can charge for them and make profits. It is very difficult to charge consumers for public goods and services and thus they are not provided in free markets. Signposts to tourist attractions are an example of a public good since:

- they are non-excludable (you cannot exclude people who do not want to pay for them from seeing them)
- consumption is non-rival (if I use the sign it does not prevent anyone else from using it – unlike a tennis court)

Economic growth

There is considerable debate as to whether the free market left alone will provide the fastest route to economic growth. Whilst it is true that the free market will naturally select profitable industries for survival, the free market is also subject to economic upswings and downswings which may hinder growth prospects.

Equity

Consumer sovereignty does not exist for those with insufficient purchasing power to influence a market.

Market intervention

The following forms of market intervention are often proposed in order to address the problems inherent in a pure free market economy:

- central planning
- legislation and control
- taxes and subsidies
- public provision

Methods and benefits of market intervention

Central planning

The most drastic solution to market failures is the adoption of state or central planning of production. In this model, production decisions are made by state planning teams rather than in response to consumer demand and profitability. This is the main way in which resources are allocated in China and Cuba.

Legislation and control

There are a variety of ways in which the government exerts control over the market including:

- monopolies and mergers legislation
- laws, planning controls and permits

One of the aims of monopolies and mergers legislation is to protect the consumer from higher prices an the reduction in choice that may result from concentration of ownership in an industry. The key milestones of monopolies and mergers legislation have included the following:

- 1948 UK Monopolies and Restrictive Practices Act. This set up the Monopolies and Restrictive Practices Commission which could investigate any industry referred to it that had a market share of more than 30 per cent, and investigate whether the public interest was being served.
- 1956 UK Restrictive Trade Practices Act. This banned formal restrictive practices (e.g. price agreements between firms) that were not in the public interest.
- 1965 UK Monopolies and Mergers Act. This instigated a name change to the Monopolies and Mergers Commission and allowed examination of proposed mergers that might create a monopoly. Such mergers could be blocked.
- 1973 UK Fair Trading Act. This reduced the definition of monopoly to 25 per cent of market share.
- 1980 UK Competition Act. This widened the terms of reference of the Monopolies and Mergers Commission to include public corporations.
- European Union Article 85. This bans agreements and restrictive practices which prevent, restrict or distort competition within the European Union and affect trade between member states.
- European Union Article 86. This prohibits a firm from abusing a dominant position in the European Union which affects competition and trade between member states.
- 1990 European Union Merger Control Regulation. This gave the European Union Commission (as opposed to national government regulators) responsibility for control over large-scale mergers which have a significant European Union dimension.

The European Commission is able to fine firms up to 10 per cent of their turnover if they are found to be in contravention of Articles 85 or 86. The Commission recently exercised its powers to prevent mergers which would be detrimental to competition, by blocking the proposed take-over in 1991 by

Aérospatiale of France and Alenia of Italy, of the Canadian aircraft manufacturer de Havilland. It was argued that the proposed new company would force up prices of certain aircraft, where it would control 76 per cent of the world market and 75 per cent of the European Commission market.

Investigations conducted by the UK Monopolies and Mergers Commission into firms in the leisure and tourism sector have included;

● the Ladbroke Takeover of Coral
● P & O/Stenna Sealink merger
● the supply of package holidays
● Isle of Wight ferry services
● the price of CDs
● the brewing industry
● vertical integration in the package tour industry

Exhibit 7.3 reports on the UK government ruling against the Ladbroke takeover of Coral, whilst exhibit 7.4 reports that the UK government is satisfied that CD prices are not excessively priced.

The government often uses laws, planning controls and permits to prevent the free market from operation in some areas. For example, licensing laws limit the hours that licensed premises may open. Betting and gaming are regulated by the law. Similarly, some goods and services are banned outright. Possession of a whole range of drugs is illegal. Interestingly, legislating against something is not sufficient to prevent a market emerging and so black markets have arisen for the supply of drugs. Because of the risk involved in supplying drugs the market price reflects considerable profit.

Exhibit 7.3   Ladbroke loses bet on MMC

In January 1998 the UK leisure conglomerate Ladbroke paid £363 million for 833 Coral betting shops. The result of this was to give Ladbroke 2600 shops representing 36.4 per cent of the market. The Monopolies and Mergers Commission took an immediate interest in the takeover and in order to placate them Ladbroke sold off 133 shops. They had hoped that the MMC would recommend the takeover if they sold off perhaps another 200 betting shops.

But the then Trade Secretary, Mr. Peter Mandelson ruled that the take-over of Coral could not go ahead. Commenting on the MMC decision, Mr. Peter George, chief executive of Ladbroke, said: 'We offered a number of potential remedies during the MMC process which we believed would ensure that any public interest concerns would have been allayed. We strongly believe this transaction should have been allowed to proceed.'

But Mr John Brown, managing director of William Hill a competing firm of bookmakers supported the MMC. He said: 'For strong, powerful competition in the industry it is essential to have three major companies. It can only be to the ultimate benefit of the punter.'

Source: The author 1999, based on report in the *Guardian*.

Exhibit 7.4   CD prices ruling infuriates consumer group

Record companies and shops were yesterday cleared by the Monopolies and Mergers Commission (MMC) of allegations that they charge too much for CDs.

The Commission's report was condemned as 'astonishingly complacent and misguided' by the Consumers' Association.

The Office of Fair Trading ordered the Commission to investigate in May 1993, days after the high price of CDs was condemned in a report from the Commons National Heritage committee.

Graeme Odgers, the MMC chairman, said that the UK profits of EMI, Polygram Sony, Warner and BMG, which control 70 per cent of sales, were not excessive, even though CD prices are higher in the UK than in the USA. 'Excessive profits are not being made', he said. 'They are not ripping the consumer off – it is a highly competitive industry'.

Source: *Guardian*, 24 June 1994 (adapted).

Planning control affects new buildings and change of use and is largely the function of local government with the right of appeal to the Department of Transport, the Environment and the Regions.

Taxes and subsidies

Taxes and subsidies may be used to encourage the consumption of merit goods and discourage the consumption of demerit goods.

Cigarette smoking, for example, is subject to large taxes although it is not entirely clear whether the main purpost of taxation is to collect revenue, or to cut consumption.

The effect on the market is illustrated in Figure 7.3. Originally, equilibrium price is established at $P0$ where demand equals supply at $Q0$. The effects of the imposition of a tax of TX is to shift the supply curve to the left, the vertical distance between the two supply curves representing the amount of the tax. Equilibrium price rises to $P1$ and cigarette consumption has been reduced to $Q1$. Notice that the demand curve has been drawn to reflect the relative demand inelasticity for cigarettes and thus the effect of a tax on quantity bought and sold is relatively modest.

If it were possible to measure marginal external costs of provision of a good or service, it would be possible to restore an optimum level of output in a market by the imposition of a tax. This is illustrated in Figure 7.4. The equilibrium price is at $P0$ with an equilibrium quantity of $Q0$. However the existence of external costs MXC establishes the marginal social cost curve MSC to the left of the supply curve S, which only reflects marginal private costs. This would suggest an optimal price of $P1$ and quantity of $Q1$, but since the marginal external costs are purely national and do not actually affect the supply curve, overproduction of $Q0–Q1$ occurs. This could be remedied by the imposition of a tax which would shift the supply curve to STX and result in an equilibrium quantity of $Q1$.

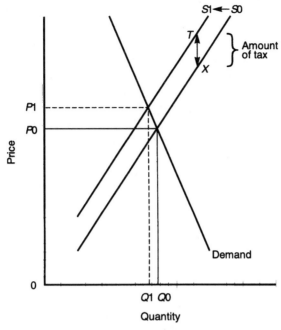

Figure 7.3   The effects of imposition of a tax on the market for cigarettes. See text for details.

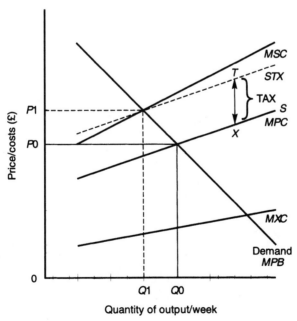

Figure 7.4   The use of taxation to restore optimal provision of goods with externalities. See text for details.

An example of a tax on airlines to reduce the amount of noise pollution demonstrates that, whilst the problem can be addressed from an overall perspective (i.e. marginal social benefit equals marginal social cost), it is likely to be the government which benefits from the tax and not those who are directly affected by the noise.

Similarly, where there are significant marginal social benefits involved in the supply of a good or a service, a subsidy could be used to ensure that the market equilibrium occurred where marginal social costs equal marginal social benefits, rather than where marginal private benefits equal marginal private costs. This is the economic justification for the subsidy of arts and recreation, much of which is done via the Arts and Sports Councils, and such a policy results in more provision than would result from free market activity alone.

As exhibit 7.5 argues, there is a strong economic case for subsidies for public goods.

Public provision

Public provision consists of supply through public corporations and local government ownership. The rationale for public ownership has included a mixture of political and economic aims. In the leisure and tourism sector, at a national level, BAA and BA have both been privatized whilst the BBC remains in public ownership. Around the world there are still many examples of nationalized airlines, Air France being a prime example. At a

---

Exhibit 7.5   Underground in need of an overhaul

The London Underground carries two and a half million passengers every day. But passengers are suffering from a chronic lack of investment. The trains are often overcrowded, prices are high, delays caused by system malfunctions are frequent and with one or two exceptions it is squalid.

The London Underground receives no government subsidy towards its operating cost, unlike other systems throughout the world. This means that metro users in Brussels, Madrid, Paris, and Berlin get better quality and cheaper fares.

Professor John Whitelegg of the School of the Built Environment at Liverpool John Moores University argues that government support is needed. He notes that benefits of a better underground are much more than just passenger satisfaction. Key benefits include incentives to tourists and firms considering inward investment. Additionally, a reduction in road congestion together with improvements in air quality and health represent significant social benefits.

He cites research report from London Transport in 1982 which demonstrated that investment in the London Underground would produce a 40 per cent rate of return and a social-benefit to cost ratio of 1:4. This is greater than the ratio associated with most road schemes.

Source: The author, based on an article by Professor John Whitelegg.

local level arts centres and leisure centres are commonly publicly owned. Economic arguments for public ownership have included first:

- economies of scale
- rationalization
- avoidance of competitive costs

These arguments all stem from government ownership of a whole industry. The resulting size of operation leads to economies of scale including bulk purchasing. Rationalization – making processes and products uniform and cutting waste – is also then possible, and competitive costs such as advertising can be eliminated. These arguments were powerful reasons for maintaining state monopolies in water, gas and electricity production.

The second group of arguments in support of public ownership includes:

- control of monopoly power and excess prices
- consideration of externalities
- provision of merit and public goods
- employment provision

Under private ownership monopoly industries are able to charge high prices in the absence of competition, and profit maximization will encourage such industries to do so. State ownership enables non-profit-maximizing pricing strategies to be adopted. Price may be set for example to ensure that the industry breaks even to protect consumers from excess prices.

In the case of an industry supplying merit goods or public goods, price may be set below market price where marginal social costs equals marginal social benefit. Such a pricing strategy would involve the industry making an accounting loss (since total private revenue would be less than total private costs) and thus require government subsidy. The use of public sector industries to provide employment would also be based on wider economic considerations, including social costs and benefits, rather than the narrow considerations of private costs and benefits.

Problems of market intervention

Resource allocation in disequilibrium

Where goods and services are provided free of charge – changing the guard, roads, and children's playgrounds, for example – price is not able to bring demand and supply into equilibrium. The problem of excess demand often arises and therefore allocation of goods and services occurs in some other way. Queuing, first come first served, and ability to push are methods in which goods and services may then be allocated.

Public ownership: efficiency and culture

The profit motive engenders an organizational culture of efficiency and customer service. A ctiticism of public ownership is that lack of incentive leads to waste and poor service.

Side-effects of subsidies and taxes

The provision of subsidies to industry has to be paid for. Subsidies are financed from increasing taxes or from reducing government spending elsewhere, or from government borrowing. Increasing the level of taxes can reduce incentives in the economy an it is rarely prudent to pay for current expenditure by borrowing since this merely postpones the raising of taxes.

Loss of consumer sovereignty

In the extreme case of total state planning, consumer sovereignty is replace by decision making by state officials, often leading to a mismatch between what consumers want and what the state provides. Government subsidies or ownership also reduce consumer sovereignty. Consumers' spending power is reduced by taxes, and government then makes decisions about how taxes will be spent.

Measurement of external costs and benefits

Private costs and benefits are easily measured since they all have market prices. On the other hand it is very difficult to measure social costs and benefits which are not directly priced – what is the cost of the loss of a view for example?

Government interference and changing objectives

A fundamental problem of state ownership of industry has been the lack of consistency of aims. As government policy and, indeed, as governments themselves change so public corporations are given different aims. Governments sometimes interfere in purchasing decisions for political reasons. Public corporations are also hypersensitive to the condition of the general economy. Governments may interfere with public sector pay to control inflation, and investment funds may suddenly disappear when public sector borrowing becomes to high.

Trends in public sector provision

Central planning

This has been abandoned by Eastern bloc countries and the two remaining significant examples of this – Cuba and China – are allowing the free market an increasing role in their economies.

Privatization

Since 1979, the scale of public ownership has been drastically reduced. Public corporations have been privatized, their shares floated on the stock exchange an their aims have become those of profit maximization. Examples include Lufthansa in Germany and the railways in the UK. Those organizations remaining in the public sector have been subject to greater accountability. Exhibit 7.6 demonstrates privatization in Russia.

Exhibit 7.6   Privatization of leisure in Russia

The city government of Moscow has extended its privatization programme by putting 200 hotels up for sale for an expected price of about $1 billion. The portfolio on offer is a mixed one. It includes the five-star National near to Red Square but also a number in a poor state of repair which require substantial refurbishment and in some cases reconstruction. The city has already been actively promoting joint ventures with foreign companies and currently has an equity stake in at least 80 hotels and restaurants.

The privatization will be subject to two conditions. First, the freeholds of the hotels, some of which are on prime sites will not be sold, but instead renewable leases of up to 49 years will be offered. Second, the city will retain a 25 per cent interest in the joint stock companies that are sold.

The main advantages to the city of Moscow are an immediate income from the asset sales and the inflow of foreign investment that is needed to bring the hotels up to international standards. Transfers of management expertise will also be beneficial as will the spreading of a service culture mentality from incoming multinational firms such as Hilton International and Marriott. Hotel management will be freed from the bureaucracy of local government ownership and control and uncertainties about finance and policy.

However, in the longer term, income will be lost to the city and profits in many cases will be repatriated to foreign multinational organizations. Employment prospects are mixed. Efficiency requirements will mean a loss of jobs and some jobs may be taken by foreign employees. However, the long-term development of the hotels may provide new jobs in the future. In terms of state planning, another small part of the economy will be lost to city control. Pricing policy, employment levels and the future development of these hotels will all be transferred to the free market.

Source: The author, from press cuttings, 1997.

Citizens' charters

These have defined the rights, complaints procedures and compensation provision for customers.

Performance targets and indicators

Public sector organizations are increasingly required to define their provision in terms of measurable outcomes. These outcomes are often subject to interorganizational comparison – 'league tables' and targets for improvement from year to year.

Compulsory competitive tendering (CCT)

Leisure centre management, in common with a range of local government services, was subject to CCT in 1993. The idea of CCT was an attempt to bring competitive market forces into areas of provision which were previously provided by government employees. The Thatcher government was convinced that local government provision of many services was subject to waste and inefficiency and that wage rates paid were uncompetitive and that restrictive work practices had arisen.

Bids are invited, by a process of open tender, to manage centres in line with a detailed contract. The sucessful bid is the one with the lowest cost. This is not privatization, since the buildings and policy objectives remain in local government hands. In many cases the local authority's own Direct Service Organization (DSO) bids for contracts, and in some cases they are the only bidder. In reality DSO contracts still form the majority of CCT contracts.

There are several advantages claimed for CCT. First, since the lowest-cost bid wins the contract, there is an inbuilt pressure to deliver services more efficiently. Inputs are used more economically, and cost-saving practices and technologies are encouraged. Second, the actual management of a facility gains autonomy and is not subject to interference from the local authority. Third, standards and performance indicators have to be established in order to monitor the effectiveness of services provided by third parties. This encourages more emphasis on quality than might otherwise have occurred. Fourth, savings generated by lower costs of services subject to CCT can result in lower taxes or more expenditure on services elsewhere. Fifth, the bureaucracy of local government is reduced and thus it has more time to devote to its core services and policies. Finally, firms which are successful in CCT and which win multiple contracts can achieve economies of scale and develop their expertise.

However, there are also some robust criticisms of CCT. Perhaps one of the key points is the hidden costs of CCT. A range of extra costs arise out of the process which were not necessary under direct provision. These costs include contract specification, and negotiation, regular monitoring of performance and any legal costs arising from disputes. Second, the drive to reduce costs leads to a deterioration of working conditions and wages of those employed. Third there arises an undue obsession with performance targets, since these are the measures by which contractors will be judged. In reality a service is greater than a collection of performance targets and contains a range of intangibles. Fourth there have been some conflicts of interest where persons with a direct link to councils have also acted on behalf of private sector tendering firms. Finally, services contracted to external suppliers must necessarily include a profit element that was not previously necessary. If the effects of CCT allow this profit to be met by increased efficiency of provision, there is a likely net gain, but it may be that the profit margin has to be met by shaving parts of the service.

Best value

Best value management replaces CCT legislation in January 2000. Best value requires local authorities to secure continuous improvements in the way functions are exercised. Reviews (local performance plans) must be carried out to:

1 Challenge why and how a service is being provided.
2 Invite comparisons with other councils' performance across a range of indicators.
3 Consult with local taxpayers, service users and the wider business community in the setting of new performance targets.
4 Embrace fair competition as a means of securing efficient and effective services.

Best value legislaiton includes powers for the Secretary of State to set performance standards for local authorities and to intervene if these standards are not met.

Review of key terms

- Consumer sovereignty = goods and services produced according to consumer demand.
- Economic efficiency = maximum output from minimum input.
- Allocative efficiency = maximum output from given inputs and maximum consumer satisfaction from that output.
- Externalities = costs or benefits which have social significance.
- Merit goods = goods with external benefits.
- Demerit goods = goods with external benefits.
- Public goods = goods which are non-excludable and non-rival.

Data questions

Task 7.1   *Peacock proposes privatization of the arts*

Sir Alan Peacock has recently made a plea for more public scrutiny over public arts expenditure even though, as he notes, government expenditure on creative performing and visual arts is a small part – less than 1 per cent – of total expenditure.

His argument is that those in receipt of public subsidy are loath to accept any objective measure of their success of failure. Theatre directors prefer to take the money without any strings, and where they are forced to account for subsidies their instinct is to judge success themselves.

The danger that Sir Alan sees in this approach is that those who are paying for the subsidies, the taxpayer, have little or no say in how their money is spent and often see little benefit from their contributions.

A major defense of public subsidy to the arts is that they deliver external benefits and that, if left to market forces, much arts provision would disappear, since it rarely makes a commercial profit, and these external benefits would be also be lost. Sir Alan questions the size of such benefits, noting that only a minority of people comprise the audience for the arts and that it is difficult to ascertain what benefits are received by the vast majority who do not attend concerts, plays and opera. He also points out that there is a disproportionate expenditure on the arts in London, which leads to a further narrowing of its effects.

Some right-wing politicians favour a pure market approach to the arts and favour an immediate withdrawal of state support. Why support opera and not football? Let those who want to see opera pay the full costs of it. If Covent Garden can't turn in a profit, let its assets be released for a purpose that can. So run the arguments of the free marketeers.

Sir Alan does not propose the immediate cutting of state subsidy. His long-term goal is for the arts to be self-supporting, and responsive to consumer demand. What he therefore proposes is 'investment in life-time education in the arts' so that an improved public appreciation of the arts would create bigger audiences who are prepared to pay for what they want, rather than the present position where a majority pay for what they don't care about. In effect this seems a proposal for consumer re-education.

Source: The author.

Questions

1 Where in the article are the marginal social benefits of the arts considered, and what are Peacock's views on the likely size of these benefits?
2 List what you consider to be possible social benefits of the arts. How would you seek to quantify these?
3 How does state subsidy of the arts affect consumer sovereignty?
4 Consider the case for privatizing the arts.

Task 7.2 Regulating the railways

Since the railways were privatized in the UK, the government has faced two problems: first how to stop them exploiting their monopoly position; and, second, how to maintain a good level of service. Classical economic theory suggests that a private sector monopoly will increase prices and have little incentive to improve services – since the customer cannot go elsewhere.

The initial response to this was the provision of a rail regulator – OFFRAIL – to protect consumer interests. The regulator has now come up with a new plan to increase competition in the industry. Under the new scheme, rail companies will be able to offer services on tracks run by other companies. Railways have traditionally been thought of as natural monopolies where competition between different firms on the same lines is not possible. The idea of this scheme is to introduce competition and stimulate innovation, improve customer service and produce cheaper fares.

The regulator, Mr Swift, said 'Passengers can reasonably expect to see the emergence of more attractive fares packages, higher frequency of service on popular routes and new direct services. It is my role to ensure that competition is in the public interest.'

The national secretary of the Save our Railways campaign group, Keith Bill, said: 'It will be cash from chaos, as companies take each other on, running services in direct competition on the most profitable routes. Commuters are losing out as companies switch their commuter trains to more lucrative routes like London to Birmingham and Gatwick. Mr Swift's proposals will turn these battles into full-scale rail wars, in which passengers will be the loser.'

Source: The author 1999, based on an article from the *Guardian*.

Questions

1 What are the economic arguments in favour of privatization of the railways?
2 What are the economic arguments against privatization of the railways?
3 Evaluate the economic success of the privatization of the railways.
4 Why is rail transport thought to be a natural monopoly?
5 Why does the government intervene in the rail travel market but not in the air travel market?
6 Evaluate the likely success of this scheme in comparison with other methods for controlling monopolies.

Task 7.3 Tour operators' cover blown

The Director-General of Fair Trading, Mr John Bridgeman, is continuing talks with the major travel companies about the problems for consumers of vertical integration. Many consumers are unaware of the links between retail travel agents and tour operators, and may not be given the impartial advice they expect when entering the major agency chains.

However, in the meantime the government has now banned a widespread practice where travel agents insist that customers buy their insurance as part of a complete package or give discounts where customers take the insurance they offer. This follows a Monopolies and Merger Commission report on malpractice in the selling of insurance cover for travel.

The Minister for Competition and Consumer Affairs, Mr Kim Howells, said: 'Consumers should not be forced to take out insurance which may not be competitively priced. Nor should they have to pay more for holidays because travel agents are discouraged by tour operators from offering discounts they would otherwise be prepared to offer.'

Customers who have bought insurance cover through travel agents can pay up to 60 per cent more than similar cover provided by direct insurers. For instance, cover for a two-week break in Europe costs around Euros 67 from Lunn Poly, while a comparable policy from an independent insurer costs just Euros 26.

The MMC found that agents were taking advantage of their size on insurance sales. Commission on travel insurance earned the top four travel agents Euros 186 million, a figure that was significantly more than the profits derived from selling holidays.

Source: The author, 1999, from MMC reports.

Questions

1 Why and how does the government seek to intervene in the activities of tour operators and travel agents?
2 One method of government control of the markets is by state ownership. Assess the economic arguments for public ownership of tour operators and travel agents.
3 Assess the degree of consumer sovereignty in relation to the main tour operators and travel agencies.

Task 7.4   *Council performance standards*

The Observer newspaper has produced an overall comparison of council performance. It finds that South Tyneside is the best-performing council whilst the London Borough of Lambeth is the worst. Council services are difficult to judge. Many are provided with a mix of public funding and private spending and different councils mix these parts differently. So it is difficult to compare services even across neighbouring councils.

In 1994 the Conservative Government required local authorities to conform to performance indicators. These included the speed with which council offices answer the phone and the time taken to reply to letters. Specific indicators were also required over a range of services such as education, libraries, parks and leisure services.

The Observer found that swimming produces good figures for comparison. Its report stated, 'Most councils have a swimming pool or leisure centre where the average cost per swim/visit – what each visit costs the local taxpayer – is around £1. But the cost of each swim at the Pondsforge International Sports Centre is £10.48. Sheffield Council admitted this was a hangover from the huge costs incurred when they hosted the World Students Games in 1990.The actual cost to the swimmer at Pondsforge is £3.10. By contrast, South Derbyshire District Council emerges as a model of swimming pool financial management: the cost per visit is 34p.'

Source: The author, based on report in *The Observer*, 3 May 1998.

Questions

1 What kinds of leisure services are provided by local councils?
2 Why are these services not left to provision by the free market?
3 Distinguish between merit goods and public goods in leisure services provided by councils.
4 Assess the contribution of CCT and Best Value to the provision of council services.
5 How might: (a) the government; (b) a local council; (c) a local resident use data such as that in the above article?

Short questions

1 Why might leaving provision of the arts entirely to the private sector lead to suboptimal resource allocation? Use a diagram to show how provision of a public subsidy to the Arts Council might restore optimal allocation and explain why achieving this aim might be difficult in practice.
2 Should children's playgrounds be provided free of charge?
3 Should opera be subsidized?
4 Should football admission be subsidized?
5 Should local authorities provide arts centres and what should their pricing policy be?
6 What problems arise from providing merit goods additional to those provided in the market?

Reference

Smith, A (1937) *The Wealth of Nations*, Modern Library Random House.

Websites of interest

Business organizations, tax, employment, government regulation, business incentives   www.foxwilliams.co.uk/doingbus.htm
UK Office of Fair Trading   www.oft.gov.uk/
Railway regulating body in the UK   www.rail-reg.gov.uk/
UK Monopolies and Mergers Commission   http://www.mmc.gov.uk/
Learning help in economics and business studies   http://www.bized.ac.uk

Part Two
Leisure and Tourism Organizations and the External Environment

Part Two

8 *The competitive environment*

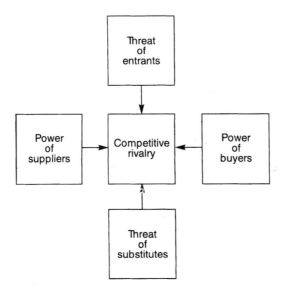

Objectives

The environment in which organizations operate is often now characterized by the four Ds:

- difficult
- dangerous
- dynamic
- diverse

In other words, the environment is constantly changing. It is this constant change that makes environment scanning important for leisure, tourism and other organizations. Organizations that remain static in a dynamic environment experience strategic drift and are likely to fail. Figure 8.1 illustrates the concept of strategic drift.

Between period *t*0 and *t*1, the operating environment is static, and the organization illustrated makes no policy change, so that by the end of the period, at *t*1, organizational policy at *B* is in tune with the environment at *A*.

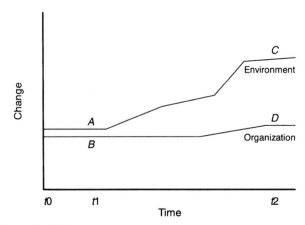

Figure 8.1 Strategic drift.

However, the period *t*1 to *t*2 represents a period of dynamic change in the operating environment. The organization, however, undertakes only marginal policy change so that by the end of the period it is experiencing strategic drift, represented by the distance *CD*.

Chapters 8–11 analyse the nature of the operating environment. This chapter considers the competitive environment, whilst Chapters 9–11 consider the political, economic, sociocultural and technological (PEST) environment, enabling a comprehensive opportunities and threats analysis to be undertaken in the second part of Chapter 11.

In his book *Competitive Strategy* (1980), Porter proposes the following model ('the five forces') for investigating the competitive environment:

1 the threat of entrants
2 the power of suppliers
3 the power of consumers
4 the threat of substitutes
5 competitive rivalry

Porter's model is used in this chapter to analyse the competitive environment.

By studying this chapter students will be able to:

● analyse an organization's competitive environment using 'five forces' analysis
● utilize strategic group analysis to identify competitive groupings

The threat of entrants

The threat of new entrants into an industry will have a significant effect on a leisure and tourism organization. New entrants may stimulate more price competition or more investment in product differentiation as they attempt to win market share and profits and existing firms seek to defend market share and profits. Chapter 6 analysed these effects of competition on pricing policy and strategy.

The extent of the threat of new entrants will depend upon barriers to entry such as:

● economies of scale
● capital and experience barriers to entry
● advertising barriers to entry
● availability of distribution channels (vertical integration)
● anticipated entry wars
● natural monopoly conditions
● product differentiation barriers

Clearly barriers to entry will represent a hurdle to be surmounted for organizations wishing to enter an industry or defences to be maintained and strengthened in the case of established organizations. Exhibit 8.1 reports the threat of new entrants in the holiday industry.

Economies of scale

Economies of scale, discussed in more detail in Chapter 5, result in reductions in average costs of production as the scale of production increases. Figure 8.2 illustrates the long-run average cost curve (LRAC) of an organization experiencing economies of scale.

Exhibit 8.1   Challenge CenterParcs

CenterParcs brought the concept of woodland holiday villages to the UK and very successfully too. Their occupancy rates are over 90 per cent year round. The CenterParcs concept is based around an all-weather indoor leisure dome with restaurants, bars, shops, but most importantly a leisure pool and sports facilities. So whilst most UK holiday attractions are seasonal, CenterParcs, in beating the weather, is a year-round attraction.

No doubt the success of CenterParcs has attracted the rival Rank Leisure Group to imitate – it has introduced Oasis Holiday Villages. The first village in Whinfell, Cumbria, has close similarities with CenterParcs. It is set in a forest, and up to 3500 guests stay in waterside villas and forest lodges. At the centre of things is an indoor waterworld, with shops, restaurants and sports facilities. Guests are encouraged to use the cycleways to move about the site.

The managing director of Rank said of similarities with CenterParcs, 'Although there will be some specific differences the two will be broadly similar'. But Sir Peter Moore, managing director of CenterParcs, retorted: 'It doesn't surprise us that Rank, no doubt prompted by our own success, are dipping a toe in the water but they won't find it easy. We are market leader and we intend to remain market leader.'

Source: The author, 1999.

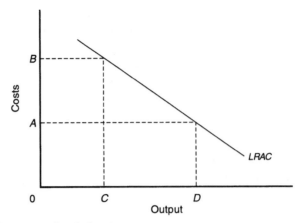

Figure 8.2   Economy of scale barriers to entry.

An established organization producing at level of output $0D$ will experience significant economies of scale with long-run average costs at $0A$. A new entrant to the industry will initially produce a low level of output, for example at $0C$ and lack of scale economies will result in high average costs of $0B$. The established organization can therefore often outcompete the new entrant by passing these lower costs on in the form of lower prices or use higher profit margins to finance more added value of the product.

Capital and experience barriers to entry

For some areas of business the capital costs of entry are fairly modest. This is true for example for video rental stores, for dance and fitness classes, small hotels and guest houses and for tour guiding. Entry into such areas is thus relatively easy. On the other hand there are substantial capital costs in entering the airline or theme park industry and thus entry barriers are stronger in such industries. Exhibit 8.2 ascribes the lack of competition in domestic air travel to high costs and lack of access to distribution channels – in this case 'slots'.

Similarly, an experience curve can be envisaged for the supply of complex goods and services. Established firms, having travelled along their experience curve, develop expertise that delivers lower costs and better service. Potential entrants will find themselves disadvantaged by being at the start of their experience curve.

Advertising barriers to entry

Advertising may be used to create an artificial barrier to entry. Successful brands can be underpinned by extensive advertising which makes it difficult for newcomers to break into the market. For example, extensive

---

Exhibit 8.2 Grandfather rights keep the competition grounded

Potential new entrants to the airline business in the UK have to surmount a formidable hurdle in gaining access to take-off and landing slots at major airports. These landing rights give established airlines a big advantage over potential rivals. For example, there are around 430 000 slots at Heathrow, the world's busiest airport and BA owns the rights to a large percentage of these. Airlines are able to build up their holdings of slots by so-called grandfathering rights, a system under which its slots are automatically renewed the following year.

But BA is not alone in squeezing out competition through control of access through ownership of slots. Swissair holds 37 per cent of the slots at Zurich Airport, KLM has 39 per cent at Amsterdam, Austrian Airlines owns 43 per cent at Vienna, Sabena has 56 per cent at Brussels, and Lufthansa has 55 per cent at Frankfurt Airport.

Even when slots are traded, new operators find it difficult to gain access to them since prime slots command premium prices, which means new entrants with limited capital are excluded.

Source: The author, 1999.

---

advertising on lager brands has the effect of minimizing the threat of new entrants.

Availability of distribution channels

Entry into some markets may be prevented or limited by access to distribution channels. There are many examples of this in the leisure and tourism sector. Many airlines would like to expand their operations into London Heathrow airport but are unable to do so because take-off and landing slots are either unavailable or are at inconvenient times. BA is able to maintain some of its market power because of its allocation of slots.

One of the motives for vertical integration may be to discriminate against other suppliers by ownership of distribution channels, as discussed in Chapter 5. Thus Thomson's ownership of the Lunn Poly travel agency and Airtours' ownership of Going Places may represent a strategy to prevent competitors from increasing their market share.

The Monopolies Commission report on the brewing industry in 1989 found that vertical integration in the brewing industry was stifling competition and as a result brewers were set limits as to the number of pubs they could own and pub tenants were allowed to sell beer from an alternative brewery.

Ownership of distribution channels has led to similar debates about fair access to markets in the film and cinema, and satellite TV industries. In the video games market, Nintendo and Sega had cornered 70 per cent of world sales by 1994. This is because, having bought a particular game console, customers have then been forced to purchase games from Sega or Nintendo.

Exhibit 8.3   Controlling the airwaves

The BSkyB (satellite TV) bid to take over Manchester United has raised a number of issues about competition, in a game where competition is part of the product. Gerald Holtham, Director of the Institute of Public Policy Research, notes that the proposed takeover is an example of vertical integration, in this case between a supplier of broadcast material and the broadcaster. He said: 'It raises the possibility that it could distort competition among clubs and among broadcasters. You have to resist the tendency to concentration.'

The takeover could enable both BSkyB and Manchester United to gain a strong competitive advantage over rivals. Manchester United could gain through being a favoured club for broadcasting, thus increasing its revenue. BSkyB could use ownership of Manchester United to steer negotiations over broadcast rights in its favour.

There are strong parallels with other industries where vertical integration has occurred, for example in the brewing and the travel industries. Here ownership by brewers of pubs and tour operators of travel agents allows them to use their distribution channels to gain a strong competitive advantage over other suppliers.

Source: The author, 1999.

However, with the price of PCs falling and their specifications rising, Nintendo sales are being threatened by games using floppy disk or CD-ROM technology.

Anticipated entry wars

Where entry into a market is likely to precipitate a strong reaction from established organizations, potential new entrants may be dissuaded from market entry. The example of SkyTrain is still a potent one. The arrival of this new service on transatlantic air routes led to price wars from BA and American carriers that were so intense that Laker Airways went out of business. The established companies had the financial muscle to cut prices deeper and for longer than Laker.

The arrival of Virgin Atlantic instigated similar entry wars that culminated in the infamous BA 'dirty tricks' campaign that allegedly poached Virgin customers by devious means. Exhibit 8.4 illustrates aspects of this entry war.

Natural monopoly conditions

A natural monopoly exists where it is not technically feasible or desirable to have many competing services. For example, it is only feasible to have one water pipe connecting each house, otherwise streets would be a tangle of competing pipes.

Exhibit 8.4   More BA 'dirty tricks' claims

Allegations of more 'dirty tricks' tactics have been made against BA. Virgin is currently engaged in a $1 bn lawsuit against BA in the USA, based on allegations of poaching passengers, and smears. One tactic used in the USA was to telephone Virgin passengers and offer them upgrades on BA flights. In the UK private detectives were hired to provide information for a disinformation campaign against Virgin.

New allegations involve American Airlines, Air France and Lufthansa whose passengers were poached by 'the ambush'. This involved business travelers arriving at Gatwick, who would be approached, often by young women, and offered a range of incentives to change their booking to BA. These teams, who were coordinated by radio handsets, were nicknamed 'Maude's marauders', after a Heathrow sales manager, Chris Maude. The reward for a successful maraud was a £5 gift voucher.

These allegations have called into question the notion of good faith and confidentiality, since many competing airlines have hired space on BA computers, and are now suspicious that BA may have used their passenger lists as a way of pirating passengers.

Source: The author, from news cuttings, March 1994.

Telecommunications were also held to be a natural monopoly for similar reasons, but there is now increasing competition to provide datalinks. Thus, although BT still owns most of the local lines into residential properties, cable has now established an alternative service and other companies such as Mercury have been given access to the telephone network, and the mobile phone networks are providing serious competition. Technology thus allows competition into an area that was previously a natural monopoly. This has led to strong price competition in telecommunications.

The power of suppliers

Supplier power is another important aspect of the competitive environment. Suppliers of inputs have a key impact on prices and quality and the greater the power of suppliers, the lower margins will be. Supplier power is increased by the degree of monopoly or oligopoly in the supplying industry, and if there are high costs of switching suppliers. Supplier power is diminished where the organization buying inputs has large purchasing power.

Credit card companies supply credit facilities in an oligopolistic market. There is little competition between the key players, Visa, Mastercard and American Express. This has led to considerable battles over their charges. Large organizations such as Holiday Inn International, BA and Lunn Poly can negotiate favorable deals because of the size of their turnover, but smaller organizations face an unequal struggle and supplier power forces them to accept high commission rates.

Similarly, centralized reservation systems such as SABRE and Amadeus supply a booking service for hotels, airlines and car hire companies. A similar picture emerges of strong supplier power that is resisted most successfully by large users of the services.

Backward vertical integration is a route to avoiding supplier power by take-over of the supplying organization. Thomson's ownership of its carrier Britannia and Airtour's ownership of Airtours International mean that they can dictate the level of service and its price. The latter is particularly important when demand is buoyant and airlines find their bargaining position enhanced.

Similar issues of supplier/buyer power can be found between Eurotunnel and its customers Eurostar and Le Shuttle, Railtrack and rail operators, and owners of the information superhighways and their commercial users.

The power of buyers

Where the buyer is a monopsonist (single buyer) or a near monopsonist, considerable power can be exerted over the selling organization. For example, in Spanish resorts where hoteliers have become dependent upon one or two UK tour operators, room rates are negotiated with very slim margins for the hoteliers.

Competition between suppliers is a key factor that increases buyer power. This is evident for air travel where there is intense competition on routes, for example London–New York fares are very competitive, but where a route is served by a single operator price per kilometre flown increases sharply.

The level of buyer knowledge is another important factor. In order to exercise buyer power, customers need information about goods and services on offer and prices of competitors. In some areas of leisure and tourism this is difficult. Customers do not always have full information when booking a hotel room for example and it is often a transaction undertaken sight unseen. National and international hotel chains often standardize their product to remove this kind of consumer uncertainty. Similar uncertainty exists for customers of restaurants. For standardized, mass-produced goods and services, buyer power is sometimes increased by the existence of specialist publications such as *What Hi Fi?* and *What PC?* which compare quality and prices.

Finally, the overall state of the market is important in determining the relative balance of buyer and supplier power. When the economy is growing strongly, there may be shortages of supply and supplier power becomes stronger. In conditions of recession there is often a shortage of customers and buyer power increases.

The threat of substitutes

Substitutes can take several forms. First a new product or service may make a current one obsolete. Word processors and CD players have made the typewriter and the turntable obsolete. Second a substitute may result in a

---

Exhibit 8.5   On-line travel treat to high street agents

The technical revolution in retailing continues with more on-line travel booking services available on the Internet. These services offer a serious potential threat to established high street travel agents since their costs are so much lower. For example, STA travel (http://www.sta-travel.co.uk) allows you to access prices for flights to over fifty destinations in an instant – a service which is very time consuming in a travel agent. Airline Network (http://www.airnet. co.uk/) offers no-frills airline tickets at bargain prices and provides both prices and the ability to buy tickets.

Source: The author, 1999.

---

new product or service competing closely with existing ones. Exhibit 8.5 reports on the arrival of on-line travel agents.

Similarly, the national lottery has resulted in increased competition for pools firms, bingo and betting shops.

Finally, to some extent all goods and services compete for consumers' limited incomes and thus new products even in distant markets may have some impact on a variety of unrelated organizations.

Organizations faced with the threat of substitutes may react in several ways. These include:

- price leadership strategies
- differentiation strategies
- withdrawal or diversification strategies
- creating switching costs to prevent loss of customers

Exhibit 8.6 examines the impact of substitutes on the demand for cinemas, and considers strategies to combat competition.

Similarly, Eurostar provides a close substitute for London–Paris air services. Different responses to the threat can be detected. BA has differentiated its product by adding more value to its Club Europe business class. British Midland has diversified into services not directly affected by the tunnel. Virgin, however, is in a affected by the tunnel. Virgin, however, is in a different position since it does not have an air route from London to Paris and is thus seeking to provide its own trains on the London–Paris route.

The degree of competitive rivalry

Competitive rivalry within an industry is increased by the threat of new entrants and the threat of substitutes, but it is also influenced by current conditions in the industry. These include:

- whether competitors can cross-subsidize
- degree of market leadership and number of competitors
- changes in capacity
- high storage costs/perishability

Exhibit 8.6   Gloomy projections fail to darken silver screens

The 1990s were meant to be the time when cinemas went into decline. The scenario was one of an industry squeezed by substitutes. The list of alternatives to the cinema grew longer and longer – videos, video on demand, widescreen TV, home surround sound, satellite TV, cable TV, playstations, megadrives. People, it was predicted, would just stay at home.

But in the late 1990s, cinema audiences have reached high numbers. Data from the Office of National Statistics show that cinema admissions recovered from a low of around 50 million in 1984 to around 80 million in 1990 and 112 million in 1996.

Industry analysts point to the power of the blockbuster movie such as *Titanic* to attract audiences. But cinemas themselves have responded with clear strategies to maintain their audiences in the face of strong competition from substitutes.

The building of multiplexes has been a central plank in the UK cinema industry's expansion. In 1993, there were 70 multiplexes in the UK with 625 screens. This had risen to 123 multiplexes with 1157 screens by 1998. Multiplexes are large multi-screen cinema complexes. They are generally built on out-of-town sites, have easy access by car, free parking, large foyers and offer fast food. Sally Beckett, director of publicity at Warner Village, explained the significance of this strategy: 'Multiplexes don't take audiences away from existing cinemas. They build new audiences instead.' Existing town-centre sites have also been upgraded with better seats and computerized booking.

But the industry is not standing still. The megaplex seems to be the next step. These have up to 30 screens and house a whole range of leisure activities with restaurants, bars and shops. Warner Village will open the UK's first megaplex in Birmingham in 2000, and in London there are plans to convert Battersea power station into one.

Leisure analyst Jane Anscombe, from Henderson Crosthwaite, said: 'A number of these have developed in the States. They offer staggered starts to a number of movies. So a big film can be showing on four or five different screens at different times. The megaplex is a leisure destination in its own right. You know that you can turn up whenever you like and see whatever you want to see.'

Source: The author, 1999, based on report in the *Guardian*.

Whether competitors can cross-subsidize?

Cross-subsidization occurs where an organization uses profits from one sector of its business to subsidize prices in another sector. This can lead to intense competition in the markets for some goods and services. For example, Task 6.4 in Chapter 6 illustrates the potential for British Airways to cross-subsidize its budget airline Go. The potential here is for Go to charge cheaper prices than other no-frills airlines in an attempt to regain market share and possibly put these new entrants out of business. The huge financial resources of British Airways can enable this to take place. The motive behind cross-subsidization is to win market share by low prices, and for airlines this leads to economies of scale and big increases in profits.

Degree of market leadership and number of competitors

Clearly monopoly or near monopoly supply means little competitive rivalry. Oligopoly conditions can lead to competitive rivalry, but since, as Chapter 6 explains, rivalry reduces profits all round, organizations may choose to follow the lead of the dominant firms in such circumstances. Competitive conditions of supply are likely to lead to a state of constant rivalry. Firms may attempt to insulate themselves from such rivalry by differentiating their product from other products.

Changes in capacity

Where the supply of a good or service is subject to large increases in capacity, competitive rivalry is likely to become more intense. For example, the opening of the channel tunnel has led to a sudden increase in the capacity for cross-channel traffic. Exhibit 8.7 illustrates the effects of an increase in local capacity of hotel accommodation in Glasgow.

Exhibit 8.7   £3 m investment despite tough competition

The 21-year-old Forte Crest Hotel is surrounded by newly built rivals: the Marriot, the Hospitality Inn, Moat House International and the most recent arrival, the £42 m Hilton International.

The opening of the Hilton led to a difficult time last year. A price war broke out in an attempt to fill empty rooms. The result was evident more in terms of lost revenue than in extra reservations, and Alberto Laidlaw, the manager of the Forte Crest, lost his job. A Forte spokesperson explained his sacking in terms of 'changes in the competitive environment'.

Despite this temporary blip in the hotel's fortunes, it has generally survived the ravages of the recession. A new manager, John Millar, has been appointed and profitability has been improved. The price war has been replaced with marketing-led competitive strategies to fill spare capacity.

Forte have confirmed their faith in the hotel's future by announcing a £3 m investment programme over the next 3 years.

Source: The author, from news cuttings, May 1994.

Similarly, some firms face substantial exit costs to leave an industry. These might be redundancy costs or a low scrap value of specialized buildings, machinery or equipment. In such cases, firms may stay in an industry despite falling demand, adding to overcapacity. Such conditions will often create the conditions for competitive rivalry. There is often overcapacity of rooms in resorts facing falling demand. This can be recognized in many UK seaside resorts and some of the older resorts in Spain.

High storage costs/perishability

Some goods and services have high storage costs or are highly perishable. Aircraft seats, hotel rooms, hire cars and theatre seats are highly perishable. There is always the prospect of intense last-minute competition to sell such services, but in reality competition here is carefully orchestrated so that an organization's main market is not disrupted. For example, tour operators want to encourage advance bookings at brochure prices and therefore do not make big advertising capital over the last-minute bargains that can be obtained.

Strategic group analysis

The notion of 'an industry' or 'an organization' may be too generalized and blurred to allow useful analysis of competition. For example, it is difficult to determine the competitive position of Pearson plc because it is an organization with diverse interests in newspapers, books, television and leisure. Instead it is necessary to look at competition in a particular area of operations such as newspapers. Similarly, the package tour industry is a diverse industry comprising, for example, domestic tours, coach tours, air tours, ski packages, winter sun, specialist and summer sun.

Table 8.1   Checklist of characteristics for identifying strategic groups (adapted from Porter, 1980)

Geographical coverage	Financial strength	Market segment served	Product range
Extent of branding	Vertical integration	Cost position	Size
Ownership	Quality	Marketing strategy	Technological position
Distribution channels used	Pricing policy	Research and development position	

The concept of strategic grouping has been developed to define areas of competition. Analysis of characteristic groupings will identify firms competing in similar areas, and Table 8.1 illustrates a checklist developed by Porter.

Key characteristics are defined for a particular market and the competitive structure of that market can then be identified. For the newspaper industry, for example, the key characteristics include quality and geographic coverage. Figure 8.3 maps strategic groups using these criteria and this enables close competition to be identified.

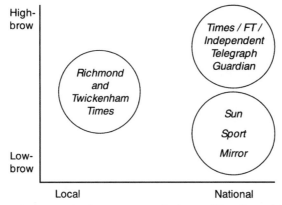

Figure 8.3   Strategic groups in the newspaper industry. *FT = Financial Times.*

Review of key terms

- Environment scanning = monitoring of operating environment.
- Strategic drift = failure of business strategy to keep abreast of environment change.
- Operating environment = competitive and PEST environment.
- PEST = political, economic, sociocultural, and technical environment.
- Barriers to entry = factors making entry into industry difficult.
- Monopsonist = single buyer.
- Cross-subsidization = using profits from one division to subsidize prices in another division.
- Strategic group analysis = determination of groups of competitors for a particular market.

Data questions

Task 8.1   Skywars

1995: A 14-day APEX return flight between London Heathrow and Glasgow costs £138. It is about the same distance as Los Angeles–San Francisco which costs only £51. That's not the worst comparison. Stanstead to Aberdeen is the same distance as Chicago to Kansas but at £192 costs three times as much. Why?

Some of the difference lies in costs. It costs more to run an airline in the UK than in the USA. But the main difference must lie in the competitive environment. People's Express, the now-defunct US carrier, started the ball rolling with its $49 New York–Miami fare. Recently there has been a huge growth in imitators of this service on the busy short-haul routes such as Los Angeles–San Francisco and Washington–New York. They offer no frills but low fares. You might have to lug your own bags to the far side of the runway (cheap aircraft parking), pack your own sandwiches and fly a propeller museum piece, but you won't have to dig too deep into your pocket.

Competition in Britain's domestic air travel market is much more limited. Since the collapse of Dan-Air in 1992 there are only three major players: BA, British Midland and Air UK. A major problem for potential entrants is the UK's crowded skies and airports. There are few slots available for competitors at London.

1999: London to Glasgow from £68 return (British Midland and easyJet) London to Inverness from £68 return (easyJet). 'Frills included' boasts British Midland in a swipe at its rival easyJet. Suddenly the UK skies are criss-crossed with competing airlines – KLM UK, Ryanair, Debonair, British Airways, EasyJet, Go, Virgin Express and British Midland. They are still airborne despite doubts that they could ever start up or that they wouldn't last. But although passenger numbers are booming profits are not. The new entrants have mainly logged losses.

Sir Michael Bishop, managing director of British Midland, predicts that not all the current airlines can survive. He points to cut-throat competition which has forced prices down to uneconomic levels, unsustainable losses being borne by some airlines, rising airport charges, and the planned abolition of duty-free sales. He also notes that few of the budget airlines that started in the USA have survived bankruptcy or takeover.

Several factors have helped the new airlines to gain a competitive advantage over their older-established competitors. For example, some of the new entrants managed to secure cheap use of secondary airports such as Stanstead, but these are now coming up for renegotiation, and slots at main airports remain heavily oversubscribed. Their cost-cutting 'no frills' have been undermined by the established carriers competing on price but maintaining frills. Also, duty-free sales have contributed to their revenues and these have been abolished after a ruling by the European Commission.

Sir Michael sums up the prospects saying: 'There will be some natural consolidation at some stage. The same thing has happened in the US, where there was a huge initial launch of low-cost airlines but then many disappeared. Five went bust last year.' He singled out Debonair as a likely victim.

Source: The author, 1995 and 1999.

Questions

1 Analyse the changes in the competitive environment of UK air travel using Porter's five forces analysis.
2 Examine the possible responses of BA to new entrants under the following headings:
   ● price leadership strategies
   ● differentiation strategies
   ● withdrawal or diversification strategies
   ● creation of switching costs

3 How have new entrants managed to penetrate the entry barriers found in the airline business?

4 What are the future prospects for the competitive environment of UK air travel?

Task 8.2   Hidden links

A prospective holidaymaker walks down a high street in search of a dream vacation. The competition looks good. There are plenty of different agents and inside each shop competing brochures fight for attention.

But the chances of ending up with a Thomson holiday are given an extra helping hand by the way the industry is organized. Walk into a Lunn Poly shop and you might expect to see Thomson brochures given best rack space and the travel consultants to be well versed in the Thomson product. After all they are owned by Thomson.

But Thomson has recently extended its incentives to other travel agents. A report in the *Guardian* of 22 August 1998 reports that 'Thomson Holidays has recently told agents who sell fewer Thomson holidays that they will get 5 per cent less commission. Agents who make 25 per cent of their sales through Thomson will get 12 per cent commission and access to improved technology to help them sell. Other agencies will get between 7 and 10 per cent, depending on factors including sales levels and the space they give Thomson on their shelves.'

Thomson see this as a legitimate way of defending market share but critics point out that the customer is unlikely to get impartial advice when the incentives to sell one particular company's products are so strong.

Source: The author, adapted from the *Guardian*.

Questions

1 Evaluate the relative power of suppliers and consumers in the market for travel.

2 To what extent will the introduction of Internet booking services change the competitive conditions in the travel market?

3 How easy is it for new tour operators to enter the travel market?

4 What strategies can Thomson take to improve its market position based on Porter's five forces analysis?

Task 8.3   Sonic the Hedgehog flattened

1994: Could it be that Sonic the Hedgehog will end up as a nasty squashed mess in the middle of the road of progress, flattened by the juggernaut of technology? Behind this gory vision lie some puzzling trading figures from Sega whose profit forecasts for the first quarter of this year are down from £423 million to £113 million.

Table 8.2

Product	Sony PlayStation	Nintendo N64	Sega Saturn
Launch	1994	1996	1994
Price (£)	129.99	99.00	99.99
Global sales to 1998	23 m	8.5 m	8.2 m
UK sales to 1998	1.2 m	600 000	90 000

What is going on? Has the games' boom bust? The answer is no, but Sega realize that it won't keep them going for ever so the company has been investing heavily in leisure for the future. Hence the blip in the figures.

Sega is advancing its leisure empire on several fronts. On the one hand, it has its sights set on Disney-style leisure parks. But while theme parks have traditionally involved large sites, sunny climates and bigger and better engineered rides, the Sega plan is for small, indoor settings for 'virtual' adventures.

Sega's other developing front? Enter Sega Channel TV. This is Sega's response to the communications revolution, which begins transmissions to American homes in the summer and will shortly be available in the UK. The concept is simple. The use of cartridges, discs and CDs for computer games are already yesterday's technology. Why not cut out the visit to the shops and download the game directly into your console from satellite or cable TV?

1999: The computer games market is estimated to be worth around $15 billion in 1999. But Sega, one of the leading Japanese games corporations, has been squeezed by its two main competitors – Sony and Nintendo. The battle for market share in the games market has been as intense as the on-screen battles fought on the rivals' consoles.

The scale of Sega's problems is revealed by a sharp turnaround in its financial fortunes Instead of an expected 15 billion yen profit for the year ending March 1998, Sega has posted a loss of around 39 billion yen. Scramble for market share has left the Japanese giant showing its first-ever loss. This has been mainly attributed to its games division responsible for losses of 47 billion yen.

The losses have arisen from a losing fight for market share where Sega's Saturn games console has been outplayed by Sony's PlayStation and the Nintendo N64. The figures above show the extent to which the market has been dominated by Sony. Mr Shoichiro Irimajiri, Sega's president, admitted 'We've got hurt and we'll apply the lessons we've learned as we develop our replacement.'

But the market for games is a fast-moving one and there is no guarantee that Sony will be able to maintain its market domination into the twenty-first century. Sega is working on new projects with Microsoft where there are possibilities of using Windows CE as an operating system for the next generation of games machines. Sony meanwhile plans continuing innovation in its game titles.

Source: The author, 1994, 1999.

Questions

1 To what extent can Sega be said to be suffering from strategic drift?
2 Evaluate the competitive environment for games.
3 Account for the success of the PlayStation.
4 What strategies could Sony use to maintain its dominant market position?

Short questions

1 How does strategic drift occur?
2 Which sectors of the leisure and tourism industry are currently secure from new entrants?
3 Where is supplier power high in the leisure and tourism industry?
4 What are barriers to entry? Identify entry barriers for airlines and hotels.
5 What factors tend to create a high degree of competitive rivalry?
6 Identify strategic groups in the hotel industry.

Reference

Porter, M. (1980) *Competitive Strategy: Techniques for Analysing Industries and Competitors*, Free Press.

Websites of interest

Granada Group plc   http://www.granada.co.uk
Marriott International   http://www.marriott.com
Scottish and Newcastle plc   http://www.scottish-newcastle.com
Trump Hotels & Casinos Resorts Inc.   http://www.trump.com
Virgin Atlantic   http://www.bized.ac.uk/compfact/vaa/vaaindex.htm

9 The economic environment

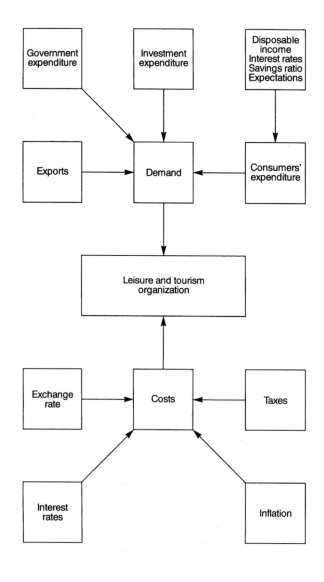

Objectives

The UK economy has a history of ups and downs. Recent years have witnessed the boom years of the mid 1980s – characterized by rising profits – as well as the profound recession of the early 1990s – characterized by rising bankruptcies. The period 1994 to 1999 saw the economy performing well, ending with some fears of another recession.

Figure 9.1 charts the path of the UK economy over recent years. It is clearly important for organizations to monitor their economic environment carefully. Managers who read the rapid growth of the UK economy between points *A* and *B* as being normal and sustainable may well have instigated optimistic and expansionary strategic plans. These plans may have proved ruinous as the economy nose-dived between points *B* and *C*. This squeezed organizations from two directions as sales revenue fell, and increasing interest rates added to costs.

Exhibit 9.1 illustrates the effects of changes in the economy on key tourism attractions.

This chapter considers the variables in the economy that affect leisure and tourism organizations and the causes of changes in these variables. It also peers tentatively into the future. It will equip you with the skills to perform the 'E' part of PEST analysis.

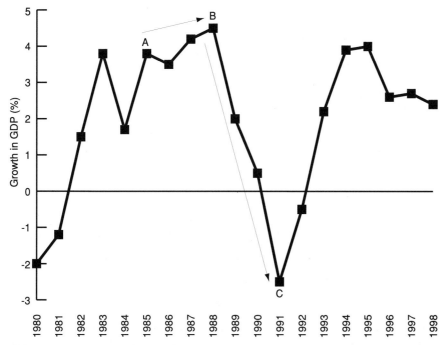

Figure 9.1 UK economic growth.
Source: Office for National Statistics, *Economic Trends*. GDP = Gross domestic product.
*Estimate.

Exhibit 9.1   Leisure ups and downs

Tourism recession

The Tower of London and other leading attractions are suffering in the recession, the English Tourist Board reported. The tower was visited by 1.9 million people last year [1991], 16% fewer than in 1990.

Source: *The Independent*, 10 August 1992.

Pearson PLC: annual reports 1991–1993

1991: Tussauds Group had a tough trading year. The Gulf War, and the recession affected visits to tourist attractions and the spending of those who did visit was less than 1990 levels. For the group as a whole, attendances were therefore lower than in the previous year, and profits down 44 per cent to £8 m.

   1993: Attendances, turnover and operating profits of the Tussauds Group reached new heights in 1993. Operating profits reached £14.1 m, an increase of 34 per cent. Attendances at Alton towers reached an all time high and there were improved attendances at Madame Tussauds in London. With continuing improvement in the UK economy, trading prospects for 1994 and beyond are encouraging.

Source: *Pearson Group Annual Reports*, 1991–1993.

Airtours: Annual Report 1998

In the UK, bookings for winter 1998–1999 are currently 6 per cent ahead of the previous year. To date the overall bookings taken in the UK for the next summer is 5 per cent ahead of the position achieved at the same time last year.

Source: *Airtours Annual Report*, 1999.

By studying this chapter students will be able to:

- identify the key variables in the economy which affect leisure and tourism organizations
- identify and utilize information sources
- explain the impact of changes in economic variables on leisure and tourism organizations
- explain the interrelationship between key economic variables
- understand the causes of change in the economic environment
- understand government economic policy and the significance of the budget
- understand the global economic environment
- utilize economic forecasts with due caution

What are the key variables?

The economic environment affects organizations in the leisure and tourism sector in two main ways. First changes in the economic environment can affect the demand for an organization's products and second changes may affect an organization's costs. Additionally background factors such as property prices may affect organizations, particularly those in the accommodation sector. These three areas will be discussed in turn.

The economic environment and demand

The key macroeconomic factors affecting demand for leisure and tourism products are:

- consumers' expenditure
- export demand
- investment demand
- government expenditure

Consumers' expenditure

Consumers' expenditure can be defined as the total expenditure on goods and services for immediate consumption. Thus the level of consumers' expenditure is a key element in determining the demand for goods and services in the leisure and tourism sector.

Care needs to be taken in interpreting consumers' expenditure statistics. Table 9.1 shows two series for consumers' expenditure. The top row shows consumers' expenditure at current prices (sometimes referred to as 'money consumers' expenditure'), whilst the bottom row shows consumers' expenditure at 1995, or constant prices (sometimes referred to as 'real consumers' expenditure'). Notice that the data for consumers' expenditure at current prices rise throughout the recession of the early 1990s.

An organization basing its business planning on such data would draw false and overly optimistic conclusions about the state of the economy. This is because consumers' expenditure at current prices includes the effects of inflation on consumer spending. However, consumers' expenditure at constant prices has had the inflationary element removed and is therefore a more useful guide.

It can be seen from Table 9.1 that consumers' expenditure at constant prices rose strongly between 1987 and 1989 and then fell in 1991. This burst of activity, followed by an abrupt halt, encouraged some organizations to expand recklessly only to suffer difficulties when the recession started to bite.

Table 9.1 Consumers' expenditure (£bn)

Consumers' expenditure	1987	1988	1989	1990	1991	1992	1993	1994	1995	1996	1997	1998*	1999
Current prices	251	238	310	336	358	377	399	419	438	468	501	524	
1995 prices	373	400	413	416	408	410	420	431	438	455	475	490	

Source: Adapted from Office for National Statistics, *Economic Trends*.
*Estimate

To understand fully movements in consumers' expenditure we need to consider its determinants. The main determinants of consumers' expenditure include:

- real disposable income
- interest rates
- expectations
- savings ratio

Real disposable income

The main determinant of consumers' expenditure is the amount of income earned. Figures for national income can be an important source here, but real disposable income provides a more useful guide.

To understand real disposable income we need to consider the meaning of the terms 'real' and 'disposable'. First, we are generally more interested in real income rather than money income since the former has had the effects of inflation removed.

Second, disposable income can be defined as the amount of income left after deduction of direct taxes (such as income tax and national insurance contributions), and the addition of state benefits (such as child benefit and unemployment benefit). In other words, it is the amount of income available for spending. Table 9.2 records recent data for personal disposable income.

Table 9.2 Gross household disposable income (£bn)

	1987	1988	1989	1990	1991	1992	1993	1994	1995	1996	1997	1998*	1999
Gross household disposable income (current prices)	260	287	319	356	390	424	452	468	494	521	555	567	
Real gross household disposable income (1995 prices)	385	405	423	438	445	461	475	481	494	505	525	536	

Source: Adapted from Office for National Statistics, *Economic Trends*.

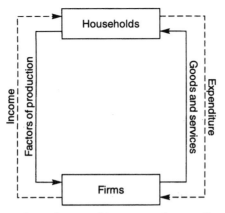

Figure 9.2 The circular flow of national income and expenditure.

The change in the income component of disposable income is determined by a number of factors. First income is related to the level of economic activity. Figure 9.2 illustrates the relationship between income and expenditure.

Households obtain income from selling factors of production (for example, labour) to firms. Firms use these factors of production to produce the goods and services that they sell. Thus as expenditure increases, more goods and services are sold which in turn creates demand for more factors of production such as labour. This in turn generates more income.

Changes in taxes and benefits can cause significant changes to the disposable element of disposable income. Such changes are often used by the government to manage the economy. For example, in 1987, Chancellor Lawson cut the basic rate of income tax from 29 to 27 per cent. He followed this in 1988 with a further cut to 25 per cent and reduced the top rate of income tax to 40 per cent. The effects of these measures can be seen in Table 9.2. Real personal disposable income rose by 5.97 per cent between 1987 and 1988 and by a further 4.78 per cent by 1989. In 1993, however, the government was forced to raise tax levels in order to reduce its own borrowing requirement. National insurance contributions were raised by 1 per cent from April 1994, personal allowances were frozen and mortgage tax relief reduced.

Real disposable income shows how much consumers have at their disposal for potential spending. How much they actually spend depends on the following factors:

- interest rates
- expectations
- the savings ratio

Interest rates

Interest rates have an important effect on consumers' expenditure. In general, higher interest rates tend to depress consumers' expenditure for two reasons. First, at higher interest rates borrowing becomes more costly

Table 9.3 Bank base rates (%)

	1987	1988	1989	1990	1991	1992	1993	1994	1995	1996	1997	1998*	1999
Bank base rates	11	13	15	14	10.5	7.0	5.5	6.25	6.50	6.00	7.25	7.25*	

*Estimate
Source: Adapted from Office for National Statistics, *Economic Trends*.

and thus consumer spending that is financed by credit is curbed. At the same time households with mortgages find their monthly repayments increasing, thus leaving less money available for spending. Second, high interest rates make savings more attractive and the savings ratio will tend to rise.

Table 9.3 illustrates recent changes in interest rates. It can be seen that in recent years interest rates peaked in 1989 and troughed in 1993. The impact of these changes on consumers' expenditure can be traced in Table 9.1. The growth in consumers' expenditure slowed dramatically in 1990 and went into reverse in 1991, whilst some growth was recorded again from 1993. Exhibit 9.2 illustrates the impact of lower interest rates on demand, and hence share prices in the leisure sector.

Exhibit 9.2   Stock market report

Amongst the market's best recent performers were leisure stocks as dealers pointed to the recovery potential of the sector amid speculation of further cuts in interest rates.

Source: author/FTSE index, first quarter 1994.

The term 'interest rates' can be misleading since there are many interest rates in the economy. The bank base rate which is quoted in Table 9.3 is the rate to which many other interest rates are referenced. Taking 1993 as an example, bank base rate averaged 5.5 per cent. Rates paid to savers in building society ordinary share accounts would be around 2 per cent. Mortgage rates would be around 8 per cent, whilst interest charges on credit cards would be about 23 per cent. A change in the bank base rate will trigger a change in the whole structure of interest rates. The reasons behind changes in interest rates are discussed later in this chapter.

Expectations

Expectations refers to the degree of optimism or pessimism with which consumers and business people view the future. Expectations have a profound effect on the economy because they tend to deliver self-fulfilling prophecies. When consumers feel good about the economy they tend to spend more and they thus cause the economy to grow. Conversely, when they feel bad about the economy they tend to spend less and thus they may prolong the recession that is causing their pessimism. Expectations tend to be influenced by recent experience, by the mass media, and by the level of unemployment. Measuring expectations is often done by way of surveys, as illustrated in exhibit 9.3.

Exhibit 9.3   Low expectations

1994: The most pessimistic level of confidence since April 1990 was revealed by a Gallup survey conducted in March 1994. Forty-two per cent of those questioned felt that their financial position would deteriorate over the next year.

Source: The author from Gallup data.

1998: The Dun & Bradstreet survey on business confidence questioned 1400 finance and managing directors in June 1998. It showed business confidence has hit its lowest level since the end of the last recession. Senior analyst Mr Philip Mellor said: 'As more firms expect further increases in interest rates, so gloom has spread from exporters into the domestic economy. For the first time in years the survey has shown a severe drop in confidence among the service, retail and wholesale sectors.'

Source: The author from Dun & Bradstreet survey.

Savings ratio

The savings ratio is defined as that proportion of personal disposable income that is saved. The savings ratio is important to firms since, when it increases, consumers are saving more of their disposable income and consuming less of it. The main factors which affect the savings ratio are the rate of interest and expectations. As interest rates rise, *ceteris paribus* consumers will generally wish to save more and consume less, since savings will be more profitable and borrowing more costly. When consumers' expectations about the future are pessimistic they will generally increase their savings.

Table 9.4 shows that the savings ratio rose considerably between 1989 and 1992. The high savings ratio of 1991 certainly fuelled the recession.

Export demand

The economic environment will affect an organization's export demand in two main ways. First, the exchange rate will affect the overseas price of

Table 9.4 Households savings ratio

	1989	1990	1991	1992	1993	1994	1995	1996	1997
Personal savings ratio	7.2	8.6	10.1	12.3	11.5	10.4	10.3	9.5	9.5

*Estimate
Source: adapted from Office for National Statistics, *Economic Trends*.

exports and this is discussed in detail in Chapter 16. Second, analysis of the international economic environment can provide information on the level of economic growth in countries which are markets for an organization's products. The major banks publish regular reviews of economic prospects for our major trading partners and exhibit 9.4 shows how sudden changes in economic regions of the world can affect the projects of trading partners.

Investment

Some organizations do not supply goods and services to consumers, but specialize in supplying capital goods to other firms. Thus the aircraft

---

Exhibit 9.4   Prospects uncertain for global economy

While 1997 saw the global economy performing well across the continents, 1998 saw the world edge nearer to a global recession. Japan and the tiger economies of Asia, for years the envy of the world, finally saw their economies suffer major downturns.

   The domino effect was started when Thailand devalued its currency in 1997 and, one by one, neighbouring countries and trading partners have dragged one another down. By 1998 Japan, the world's second largest economy, was in recession. Elsewhere, Russia has defaulted on its debts and Brazil suffered a major devaluation in its currency.

   The effects of this on the leisure and tourism industry have been mixed. In the countries suffering from recession, domestic demand for leisure and tourism has diminished considerably as real disposable incomes have fallen. For some countries, devaluation has caused an increase in the inflow of tourists who seek better value for money. Leisure and tourism outside of these countries is affected mainly by the Japanese recession. Japan traditionally has been a high-spending country on tourism abroad. So destinations which have previously been dependent on visitors from Japan have been affected.

   More serious consequences would result were the economic effects of economic problems in Asia, Russia and South America to cause a recession in Europe and the USA. The leisure and tourism industries would be early casualties of a global recession.

Source: The author, 1999.

Table 9.5 Gross domestic fixed capital formation (business investment; £bn at constant 1995 prices)

	1987	1988	1989	1990	1991	1992	1993	1994	1995	1996	1997	1998*	1999
Gross domestic fixed capital formation	102	121	125	118	105	107	110	118	121	124	132	136	

*Estimate
Source: Adapted from Office for National Statistics, *Economic Trends*.

manufacturer Boeing, selling to airlines and tour operators, finds demand for its products is sensitive to the level of investment in the economy.

Table 9.5 shows recent changes in gross domestic fixed capital formation. This refers to the total amount of investment in new capital goods. The term 'gross' means that it covers all capital investment including the replacement of worn-out machines. The term 'net' would cover only investment over and above the replacement of worn-out machines.

Table 9.5 shows a considerable fall in investment from 1990 to 1993. The main determinants of investment demand are:

- consumers' expenditure
- expectations
- amount of spare capacity
- interest rates

It is therefore changes in the above factors that should be examined for an explanation of the fall in investment evident from Table 9.5 in 1990. In fact, all four factors contributed to the fall in investment. High interest rates had the double effect of reducing consumers' expenditure and increasing the cost of borrowing for investment projects. The fall in consumers' expenditure meant that suppliers were left with spare capacity in the form of empty planes, unused accommodation and idle machinery and thus there was little need for additional or replacement investment. Finally, as the recession deepened, people's expectations became more pessimistic and investment depends on optimistic expectations about future levels of income and expenditure.

It should be noted that lower interest rates will not necessarily, single-handedly, stimulate investment demand in a recession since there may already be spare capacity in the organization and expectations may remain pessimistic. Thus there was no immediate recovery of investment in 1992 when interest rates fell.

Exhibit 9.5 describes how the early 1990s recession affected aircraft manufacturers. The demand for aircraft depends upon the demand for air travel and this was hit by the recession. Note that it is the prospect of rises in disposable income that is likely to stimulate the demand for travel and thus in turn the investment demand for new aircraft.

Exhibit 9.5   £270 bn dilemma for jet set: the aviation industry is banking on a tourism revival to help pay for new aircraft – David Black

A troubled aviation industry is pinning hopes on a massive upturn in the world tourist trade to ensure airline customers can continue to buy new jets.

Some 3200 jet airliners are on order from the big three plane makers – Boeing, Airbus and McDonnell Douglas. However, the recession and the aftermath of the Gulf War have conspired to knock the bottom out of the airline's biggest earner, the business traveller market. Tourist travel has also been hit. As a result, the huge backlog of airliners on order is under threat. The gravity of this situation has been slowly sinking in for the aircraft makers and the airlines over the past few months as the grim airline performance figures have filtered through. In November [1991], Boeing announced plans to cut production of 737 jets from 21 to 17 a month, and American Airlines said it was cancelling or deferring options on 93 aircraft worth $5.2 bn.

Overall the number of passengers carried by airlines between January and September [1991] was a mere 67 per cent of 1990's figure according to the International Air Transport Association, which represents most of the world's airlines. The airlines desperately need traffic growth to recover their profitability. That profitability is vital to repay the debts they must incur to take delivery of their new generation of jets.

All is not doom and gloom according to the IBA, the International Bureau of Aviation, which specializes in advising financial institutions on all aspects of the aviation industry. Its view is distinctly upbeat.

So on what factors do the financiers base their optimism? Tourism, says the IBA. And it is not alone. The World Travel and Tourism Council calculated that 11.4 per cent of global consumer spending is on personal travel. As a result, the IBA concludes: 'Rises in disposable income will reinforce the trend towards the growth of tourism, which will increasingly become the largest revenue earner for the airline industry'.

Source: *The Independent*, 10 January 1992 (adapted).

Reference to exhibit 4.3 in Chapter 4 shows that prospects for 2000 and beyond appear to be favorable for aircraft manufacturers.

Government expenditure

Leisure and tourism organizations which are sensitive to changes in government expenditure include the BBC, the Arts and Sports Councils, the BTA, and those organizations which depend on local government support.

The level and detail of government expenditure tend to reflect two things – the state of the economy (discussed later in this chapter) and the political party in power. The overall policy of Conservative governments between 1979 and 1997 was to reduce the level of government spending. Table 9.6 records data for overall government spending between 1994 and 1999. These are at current prices and have not been adjusted for inflation. It can be seen

Table 9.6   Selected public spending (1994–1999) (£m)

	1994–1995	1996–1997	1998–1999*
Department for Culture, Media and Sport			
Museums and galleries (England)	225	214	207
The arts (England)	195	195	193
Sport (UK)	53	52	50
Historic buildings and sites (England)	162	161	146
Tourism (UK)	44	46	45
Broadcasting and media (UK)	93	98	99
Total Central Government spending (including privatization proceeds)	264 919	286 412	304 421

* Estimates.
Source: Adapted from Office for National Statistics, *Monthly Digest of Statistics/Annual Abstract of Statistics*.

that many areas of government spending have suffered from real cuts in public spending. Overall government spending is likely to increase under the Labour Government, particularly after the year 2000.

The economic environment and costs

The key macroeconomic factors affecting costs of leisure and tourism products are:

- interest rates
- inflation
- the exchange rate
- indirect taxes

The rate of interest

The effects of changes in interest rates have been discussed above with reference to consumers' expenditure and investment. However interest rates also affect firms' costs, particularly those with significant borrowings such as Eurotunnel, as illustrated by exhibit 9.6.

It is reported that around half of Eurotunnel's borrowing is exposed to variable interest rates. The variations in interest rates illustrated in Table 9.3 show how risky exposure to variable interest rates can be. Assuming borrowing rates of base rate +2%, the interest payments without any capital repayment would be £75 000 per year per £1 m borrowed at 1993 interest rates. However, interest payments would rise to £170 000 per year per £1 m borrowed at 1989 rates of interest.

Exhibit 9.6   Debt floods the Chunnel

Yesterday's rescue package announced for the channel tunnel means that a total of nearly £10.6 bn has been raised to fund the massive project – more than double the amount that was originally projected. Eurotunnel said that £1.5 bn further projected cash requirements after May 6th [1994] mostly represented interest costs on the increased debt not covered by cash flow until the expected break-even of the project in 1998. Although this is the last cash call, there are numerous financial 'variables' which Graham Corbett, Eurotunnel's chief financial officer, set out, including the fact that around half of Eurotunnel's sterling borrowings are exposed to variable interest rates.

Source: *Guardian*, 27 May 1994 (adapted).

Inflation

Inflation will affect the price of a firm's inputs. Table 9.7 shows the varying rates of inflation on leisure and tourism-related items and the importance of inflation is discussed more fully in Chapter 14.

The exchange rate

Where imports form a substantial component of a good or service, changes in the exchange rate can have an effect on production costs. A fall in the exchange rate of the pound against foreign currencies will make imports more expensive. For example, component costs for tour operators such as Thomson include foreign hotel costs, and a fall in the exchange rate will increase such costs. This issue is discussed more fully in Chapter 16.

Indirect taxes

Indirect taxes are taxes paid indirectly to the government. They are paid first to a third party – generally a retailer. VAT is a key indirect tax and indirect taxes have a direct effect on prices.

Table 9.7   Retail prices in the UK leisure and tourism-related items, July 1998

Item	Percentage change over last year
Restaurant meals	4
Beer	4
Audiovisual equipment	−14
Entertainment	5
Tapes and discs	1
Toys, photographic and sports goods	−1
Foreign holidays	5

Source: Adapted from Office for National Statistics, *Labour Market Trends*.

Exhibit 9.7   Excerpt from 1993 budget speech

'This will be set at £5 for departures to anywhere within the UK and the European Union and £10 for departures to other destinations. The new duty will come into force next October [1994] and will raise some £330 million in a full year'.

Source: Kenneth Clarke's Budget speech to the House of Commons, 30 November 1993.

Exhibit 9.7 records the introduction of a tax on air travel which was announced by the chancellor in the autumn 1993 budget. There has been considerable protest from the airline industry over this new tax. In particular they fear that, since surface transport is not subject to such a tax, this may cause a loss of passengers. This is particularly likely on routes such as London to Paris, where Eurostar offers a close substitute to air travel.

The provision of some goods and services in the leisure and tourism sector is currently zero-rated for VAT. This includes books and magazines, travel and overseas package holidays. However there is no guarantee that the government will not extend VAT to these items.

Background features in the economic environment

The labour market

The level of unemployment has several effects on firms in the leisure and tourism sector. High unemployment has a detrimental effect on consumer spending and confidence. Ironically, it provides individuals with more leisure time, but with reduced spending power to enter leisure markets. On the other hand, in terms of hiring labour, high unemployment means greater availability of labour at competitive wage levels. The extent of membership and power of trade unions also affects wage rates.

Property prices

The volatility of property prices in recent years has had a profound effect on many organizations in the leisure and tourism sector. During the property boom of the mid 1980s organizations such as Brent Walker, with substantial property holdings, were able to use the increased valuation of these assets as security for increased borrowing. On the other hand, firms which made large property acquisitions at the top of the property boom often found themselves in terminal difficulties as property prices fell sharply and interest payments rose.

Government and the economy

It is impossible to understand changes in the external economic environment without consideration of the government's role in the economy. This in turn can be understood in terms of aims and policies.

Government economic aims

The following aims are followed by most governments:

- low inflation
- low unemployment
- balance between government spending and income over the medium term
- balance between overseas earnings and expenditure
- economic growth

However, different governments have different priorities among these objectives. The Thatcher, Major and Blair government, for example put control of inflation and a balanced budget at the top of the list. It must also be recognized that these aims are sometimes conflicting and also that as elections occur, policy aims are generally distorted towards reducing taxation.

Government economic policy

Economic policy refers to a set of measures designed to affect the economy. The budget, in late autumn, is the traditional time for making changes to economic policy. Policies can be divided into:

- Fiscal policy. This uses changes in the level of taxation or government spending to influence the economy.
- Monetary policy. This uses changes in interest rates, and thus the cost of borrowing, to influence the economy.

Recent economic policy

Table 9.8 shows changes in the main indicators for the UK economy in recent years, and four distinct phases can be identified.

1985–1988: Boom

It can be seen that the UK economy grew strongly in the period 1985 to 1988, and unemployment fell. This was despite the fact that monetary policy was

Table 9.8 The UK economy: selected indicators

	1985	1986	1987	1988	1989	1990	1991	1992	1993	1994	1995	1996	1997	1998*	1999	2000
Growth (percentage change)	3.8	3.6	4.4	4.5	1.9	0.6	-2.5	-0.5	2.0	3.9	4.0	2.6	2.7	2.4		
Inflation (percentage change)	6.1	3.4	4.1	4.9	7.8	9.5	5.9	3.9	1.9	2.5	3.5	2.4	3.1	3.1		
Current balance (£bn)	2.2	-0.8	-5	-16	-22	-18	-7	-11	-10	-0.1	-3.7	-0.6	8.0	-5.6		
Unemployment (m)	3.2	3.2	2.9	2.4	1.8	1.6	2.2	2.7	2.8	2.5	2.3	2.1	1.6	1.4		
Rate of interest (%)	15	13	11	13	15	14	10.5	7.0	5.4	6.25	6.5	6.0	7.25	7.25		
Public sector net cash requirement (£bn)	7.4	2.4	-1	-12	-9	-2	13	37	46	39	35	25	12	0		
£/$	1.3	1.5	1.6	1.8	1.6	1.8	1.8	1.8	1.5	1.5	1.6	1.6	1.6	1.6		
£/DM	3.8	3.2	2.9	3.1	3.1	2.9	2.9	2.5	2.6	2.5	2.3	2.4	2.8	2.7		

Note:
1 Rate of interest = three-month interbank.
Sources: Adapted from Office for National Statistics, *Economic Trends*, and *Barclays Bank Review*.
*Estimate

generally quite tight during this period. The purpose of tight monetary policy and high interest rates was to suppress inflation. The rationale behind this policy was first that high interest rates reduced consumer demand by making credit expensive, and second that import prices were kept low as high interest rates stimulated the demand for sterling and kept the exchange rate high.

However the chancellor reduced interest rates in 1987 and also made some adjustments to fiscal policy. The 1987 budget cut the basic rate of income tax to 27 per cent and the 1988 budget made a further cut in income tax to 25 per cent and scrapped higher rates of income tax from 60 to 40 per cent.

The result of this loosening of monetary and fiscal policy was that economic growth became unsustainable. By 1989 inflation had risen rapidly to nearly 8 per cent, and the UK's overseas trading account showed a deficit of £22 bn.

1989–1992: Bust

The rapid deterioration in inflation and foreign currency earnings meant that the government had to apply the brakes to the economy. Monetary policy was designated for this task, and interest rates were progressively increased to 15 per cent in 1989. John Major, as chancellor of the exchequer, used the famous phrase, 'if it's not hurting it's not working' to explain the policy. What he meant was that interest rates were going to be used by the government to slow down consumers' expenditure – mainly by making credit expensive – and that rates would continue to rise until consumers' expenditure was curbed.

Eventually the government's policy did work, but perhaps too successfully, since the economy slowed down and went into reverse, economic growth being a negative figure for both 1991 and 1992. As the recession took hold, unemployment rose quickly to reach 2.8 million by 1993.

During this period government policy got into a mess. The recession, and the consequent rise in unemployment, meant less tax receipts for the government and more spending on state benefits. Thus the public sector borrowing requirement (PSBR) increased sharply and the government had to borrow £37 bn in 1992. The high PSBR meant that it was difficult to stimulate the economy by reducing taxes.

At the same time, the government had taken sterling into the exchange rate mechanism (ERM) of the European monetary system (EMS). Monetary policy was used to maintain sterling's agreed rate of exchange against European currencies. High interest rates were used to make sterling an attractive currency and thus maintain its value.

Thus the recession was prolonged by high interest rates, and tax cuts could not be used to stimulate consumer spending because of the high PSBR. Monetary policy and fiscal policy were both tight.

1992–1994: a lucky escape

Despite all the government's efforts (interest rates were raised from 10 to 15 per cent in one day), sterling was forced to leave the ERM in September

1992. This enabled the government to relax its monetary policy and interest rates were lowered in a series of moves from 10.5 per cent in 1991 to 7 per cent in 1992. This allowed the economy to recover, led by a rise in consumers' expenditure.

However, PSBR was still high, reflecting the effects of the recession in reducing government tax income and increasing benefit payments and in 1993 the government had to borrow £46 bn. The budgets of 1993 and 1994 thus contained a series of measures to increase taxes (including the extension of VAT to fuels) to reduce government borrowing. They also maintained tight control on government expenditure and the £3.2 m cut in the Arts Council of Great Britain's grant for 1994 can be seen in this light.

1994–1999: sustainable growth?

The period between 1994 and 1999 has been a period of modest economic growth and stability in the British economy. Unusually there have been no significant crises in any of the main economic indicators. The economy has entered a period of low inflation. This has been helped by the recession in Japan which has caused a fall in input prices such as oil which had dropped to under $10 a barrel by 1999. The economic policy of the incoming Labour government in 1997 was to keep to existing public spending plans and to set up an independent monetary policy committee of the Bank of England whose task is to use interest rates to keep inflation at 2.5 per cent. This led to rises in interest rates in 1997 and 1998. The 1998 rises coincided with worries about a world recession and caused alarm amongst some policy analysts. But rates were reduced rapidly again in 1999 as inflation steadied. So as this text went to press in Spring 1999, the economic picture was one of:

● Low inflation.
● Falling unemployment.
● Modest economic growth.
● Balance of payments in medium term equilibrium.
● Falling interest rates.
● Balanced government budget.
● Overvalued sterling.

... a rosy picture but with warnings of a recession from some commentators.

The future

An eminent professor of economics, the Lord Maurice Peston of Mile End, cautioned against blind faith in economic forecasting, suggesting that random typing of a monkey at a keyboard would result in equally useful

Exhibit 9.8   Three views of the future

Accidental birth of a very British recovery

The British economic recovery at the macro level is a fact of life – or at least of the best statistics we have. From the point of view of the Treasury's Panel of Independent forecasters:

'The economy has continued to evolve favourably since . . . May, with robust growth, low inflation, falling unemployment and a much reduced trade deficit. We expect growth to continue at a healthy rate next year . . . inflation to remain within the Government's target range in the short term. In the very long term, with appropriate policies we think it should be possible for the economy to return to a low level of unemployment.'

Source: *Observer*, 13 November 1994.

UK economy

This year's overall economic performance is set to be much better than expected. Overall output should record an increase of at least 3.5 per cent, while inflation is now likely to end the year at around 2.5 per cent. At the same time, the balance of payments deficit, often viewed as a potential barrier to a sustainable recovery, has been on a clear downward trend.

[There] appears to be a healthy medium-term outlook, encompassing both a relatively strong and well-balanced recovery with low inflation and the restoration of sound public finances.

Source: *Barclays Economic Review* fourth quarter 1994.

World recession

As the (Asian) crisis has continued to spread and deepen, economists have been rapidly and repeatedly downgrading their forecasts. Roger Bootle, chief economist of HSBC, said: 'I do think it's going to get a lot worse. The chances of a global recession are significant.'

Source: *The Observer*, 23 August 1998.

forecasts as those produced by complex mathematical models. Equally, the 'flying by the seat of the pants' technique exercised by many in the late 1980s boom led to overly optimistic business decisions which, as Keynes said of the 1920s boom, 'discounted not only the future but the hereafter'. Economic forecasts are an essential part of business planning, but must be used with extreme caution, and the assumptions upon which they are made must be constantly monitored. Exhibit 9.8 illustrates how forecasts for the UK economy made by commentators in *The Observer* and from *Barclays Bank* were fairly accurate. But a commentator from HSBC is pessimistic about avoiding a global recession in 1999–2000.

Review of key terms

- Real consumers' expenditure = money consumer expenditure adjusted for inflation.
- Disposable income = income − direct taxes + government benefits.
- Recession = two consecutive quarters of falling output.
- Savings ratio = proportion of income saved.
- PSBR = public sector borrowing requirement (excess of government spending over taxes).
- Gross investment = net (new) investment + depreciation (replacement investment).
- Final goods = goods bought by consumers.
- Capital goods = goods bought by firms to assist production, e.g. machines.
- GDP = gross domestic product = total value of output of an economy in a year.
- Fiscal policy = use of tax and government spending levels to influence the economy.
- Monetary policy = use of interest rates to influence the economy.

Data questions

Task 9.1 *International economic outlook*

The Russian crisis has increased the level of uncertainty about the world economic outlook and triggered a downward revision of predictions for world growth over the coming year.

Our own forecasts now show world growth of 1.8% in both 1998 and 1999. This would make the current downturn broadly comparable to the last two global recessions in the early 1980s and the early 1990s. The regional pattern is, however, very different this time around. In the last two downturns the developed regions of North America and West Europe suffered outright falls in output whereas the Asian economy continued to expand strongly. The current world downturn is being led by very sharp falls in output for developing countries in Asia and elsewhere, whereas for North America and West Europe our view remains that there will be fairly modest slowdowns in growth.

This relatively benign assessment is based on three assumptions. First, that there will be no further shock to the world economy from developing countries on the scale of the Russian crisis. Second, that in Japan the combination of a massive fiscal stimulus and the bank support package will stabilize the Japanese economy in 1999. Third, that the authorities in North America and Europe will respond to any signs of pronounced weakening of growth by relaxing economic policy.

Concern over emerging markets currently centres on Brazil. The fear is that lack of investor confidence will force either a devaluation of the currency or debt default. Recent news has been favourable. The recently re-elected President is

Table 9.9   Key international forecasts

Indicator	Area	1990–1994 Average	1996 Outturn	1997 Outturn	1998 Forecast	1999 Forecast	1998 or 1999 Outturn
Growth (%)	USA	1.7	3.4	3.9	3.2	1.5	
	Japan	2.2	4.1	1.0	−2.2	1.0	
	Germany	2.9	1.3	2.3	2.4	2.2	
	EMU 11	1.8	1.6	2.5	2.7	2.6	
	Asia	7.5	7.8	6.1	1.1	3.4	
	Latin America	2.8	3.5	5.0	2.5	0.9	
	World	2.5	3.6	3.7	1.8	1.8	
Inflation (%)	USA	3.6	2.9	2.3	1.7	2.5	
	Japan	1.6	0.1	1.8	0.5	0.0	
	Germany	3.7	1.5	1.8	1.1	1.0	
	EMU 11	3.9	2.4	1.7	1.3	1.5	
	Asia	8.9	7.5	4.8	10.8	7.6	
	Latin America	817	16.5	10.2	7.5	8.6	
Interest rates (%)	US	5.2	5.4	5.7	5.4	4.4	
	Japan	4.9	0.5	0.5	0.5	0.5	
	Germany	7.9	3.2	3.3	3.5	3.5	

committed to implementing a tough fiscal policy and the IMF is expected to provide financial support. The tightening of policy will almost certainly mean a recession in Brazil next year, and low growth for Latin America as a whole, but this would not represent a large negative shock to the world economy.

Recent developments in Japan have been a mixture of good and bad. The bad news has been the release of figures which show the economy contracting sharply and the continuing gradual disclosure of the true health of the Japanese financial system. The good news has been the announcement of policy measures which stand a chance of being sufficient to start solving these problems.

The third reason for optimism is that the two major world economic blocs of North America and West Europe are not in recession – the EU grew at a 3 per cent rate during the first part of the year and the US economy by around 4 per cent. Exports from both regions are being affected by the recession in developing countries and this trend is likely to continue for some time yet. But the importance of these trade flows can be over-exaggerated. For both NAFTA and the EU, exports to the rest of the world account for only 6 to 7 per cent of GNP, and much of this trade is with each other. Even more importantly, the authorities in both regions have the scope to respond to signs of slower economic growth, from whatever cause, by relaxing economic policy.

The US authorities have already reduced interest rates and appear to be prepared to take further action as necessary.

Source: *Barclays Bank* (Fourth Quarter 1998).

Questions

1 Explain the significance of the terms 'recession', 'economic shock', 'fiscal stimulus' and 'GNP' to leisure and tourism.
2 Describe and account for the trends in the above table.
3 To what extent are the EU and USA affected by the global economic downturn evident in this report?
4 Explain and evaluate the assertion that 'authorities [in the US and EU] have the scope to respond to signs of slower economic growth . . . by relaxing economic policy'.
5 Choose a leisure/tourism organization with global links. The year is 1997 and your organization has commissioned the above report. Use it to compile a briefing which identifies the global economic opportunities and threats facing your organization. Include recommendations for action.
6 Fill in the final column of the table and account for deviations between forecasts and outcomes.

Task 9.2   The UK recession 1990–92

A widely used definition of a recession, adopted in this article, is that of 'two or more consecutive quarters of falling output'. The latest recession was spread over seven quarters. Recessions can be caused by many different factors. The 1990–1992 recession in the UK followed a period of unsustainably fast growth during the late 1980s.

The anatomy of the 1990–1992 recession was as follows: manufacturing output fell by 7.5 per cent and output in the services sector fell by 2 per cent. The services sector includes retailing and wholesaling, hotels and catering transport and communications, and business and financial services. The services sector amounted to over 60 per cent of gross domestic product (GDP) in 1990, whereas manufacturing only accounted for about 25 per cent, so its impact on total GDP is significant. Consumers' expenditure fell steeply in the 1990–1992 recession. Households built up debt rapidly during the boom years of the late 1980s; this led to a sharp retrenchment in their spending in 1990 and 1991 as they acted to reduce their debt in the face of high interest rates.

The initial impetus to recovery came mainly from consumer spending and exports. The substantial cut in interest rates over the past 3 years, and strong growth in real personal disposable income, boosted personal sector spending power. By the third quarter of 1993 most of the fall in consumer spending during the recession had been reversed.

As the recovery becomes more firmly established, businesses are likely to increase their spending as they become more confident that the pick-up in demand is sustained. The improvement in company finances and a modest increase in capacity utilization will also encourage investment in new and replacement stocks. These developments will help to broaden the recovery and strengthen growth.

Source: HM Treasury: *Economic Briefing* February 1994 (adapted)

Questions

1 What evidence is there to support the assertion of 'unsustainably fast growth during the late 1980s'?
2 Why did 'unsustainably fast growth during the late 1980s' lead to a recession?
3 'The initial impetus to recovery came mainly from consumer spending . . .' Explain this statement by reference to the determinants of consumer spending.
4 'As the recovery becomes more firmly established, businesses are likely to increase their spending . . . and a modest increase in capacity utilization will also encourage investment in new and replacement stocks'. Explain which industries in the leisure and tourism sector are likely to benefit from this and what other factors are likely to encourage investment.

Task 9.3 Scenario planning

Organizations increasingly use the method of scenario planning to anticipate changes in the external environment. This enables them to plan considered responses.

Questions

1 Choose two firms in the leisure and tourism sector and analyse how they might be affected by the following scenarios:
   (a) a rise in interest rates of 6 per cent
   (b) a fall in unemployment of 500 000
   (c) a fall in the savings ratio
   (d) a fall in investment
2 Which two of these represent the most likely scenario for the next 2 years?

Task 9.4 Leisure profiles, 1998

The following are extracts from the 1998 annual reports of leading UK leisure companies:

Eurocamp

	1994	1996	1998
Turnover (Euros m)	100	150	129
Pre-tax profit (Euros m)	12.4	13.2	20

- UK market: The recovery in demand experienced in 1997 after the 1996 low point continued apace.
- 1999 Trading: bookings for 1999 have started well in all sections of the camping division. Continued sterling strength promises to underpin demand in the UK market.

Airtours

	1994	1996	1998
Turnover (Euros m)	1430	2502	3289
Pre-tax profit (Euros m)	103	120	200

Results: in the 12 months to 30 September 1998, Airtours had another highly successful year with both profit before tax and earnings per share increasing by 17 per cent . . . This increase was driven by strong performance in our businesses in the UK and from our joint venture Costa Cruises.

Rank

- Hard Rock: at constant currency, turnover for the year was up 28 per cent.
- Holidays: Rank's UK holiday business performed well and improved profit by 18 per cent.
- Gaming: Mecca bingo had a good year with turnover up 15 per cent . . . In Casinos, profit for the year was flat.
- Entertainment: Odeon performed particularly well with turnover increasing by over 30 per cent.
- Universal Studios Resort: Universal Studios Florida had a good year and turnover increased by 6 per cent.

Sources: Company Annual Reports, 1998.

Questions

1 How would you expect the performance of Airtours and Eurocamp to be affected by changes in:
   - interest rates
   - inflation
   - consumers' expenditure
   - public sector net cash requirement
   - exchange rate?
2 Evaluate the affects of changes in each of these economic variables against turnover and profits, 1994–1998.
3 Evaluate the opportunities and threats in the economic environment as they relate to the above organizations.

Short questions

1 Consumers' expenditure at current prices rises from £100 bn in year 1 to £110 bn in year 2. Over the same period inflation is 10 per cent. What is the level of consumers' expenditure at constant (year 1) prices in year 2?
2 What is the definition and what are the characteristics of a recession?
3 What is the definition and what are the characteristics of a recovery?
4 Distinguish between fiscal and monetary policy.
5 What type of fiscal and monetary policy could be used to stimulate the economy in a recession?
6 What is the relationship between PSBR, taxation and government revenue?
7 What is the present outlook for the UK economy?
8 Explain the significance of the following to a named leisure or tourism sector organization:
   (a) Interest rates
   (b) Exchange rates
   (c) Real disposable income
   (d) Expectations

Websites of interest

Economic model of the economy   www.bized.ac.uk
USA: statistics   http://www.stat.usa.gov/
Global economic outlook   www.merrilllynch.com
Organization for Economic Development and Cooperation: statistics and commentary   www.oecd.org
European Union: statistics   http://europa.eu.int
Australian Bureau of statistics   http://www.abs.gov.au
Brazil: statistics   http://ibge.gov.br
Canada: statistics   http://www.statcan.ca
New Zealand: statistics   http://www.stats.govt.nz/statsweb.nsf
Office for National Statistics   http://www.emap.com
Learning help in economics and business studies   http://www.bized.ac.uk

10   The political and sociocultural environment

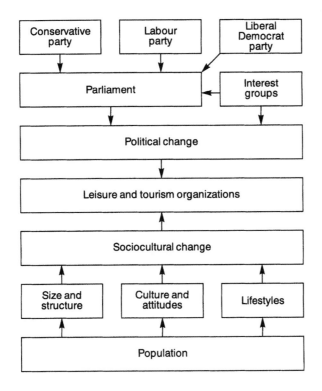

Objectives

This chapter continues the analysis of the operating environment focusing on the political and sociocultural parts of PEST analysis. It discusses the effects of political change on organizations and considers for example how leisure and tourism organizations might be affected by the results of the next election. The population is also undergoing change in its size, structure and attitudes, each of which may affect leisure and tourism organizations.

The fox-hunting debate illustrates points of a political and cultural nature. In terms of cultural change, the League Against Cruel Sports has influenced public attitudes against the sport and its campaigns of hunt sabotage have affected hunts. In the political arena however, the Criminal Justice Bill has outlawed demonstrations which involve trespass and thus hunting may well expand again.

By studying this chapter students should be able to:

● define the scope of the political environment
● identify sources of information for the political environment
● identify political opportunities and threats to leisure and tourism organizations
● define the scope of the sociocultural environment
● identify information sources for the sociocultural environment
● identify sociocultural opportunities and threats to leisure and tourism organizations

The political environment

The political environment is shaped by those with political power, or the ability to influence events. A key player in this is the party in government for the immediate period until the next election. Longer-term political trends are clearly difficult to predict since they depend largely upon which political party wins the next election. Although opinion polls give some indication of current party popularity they are likely to change considerably by the pre-election period and in any case do not have a good record of accuracy. The government itself will be subject to its own operating environment and thus policy will be shaped by the EU, the economy, international relations and interest group activity.

Given the range of possible directions of policy, scenario planning is likely to be used by organizations wishing to incorporate the political environment into their strategic planning. This involves analysing the impact of a range of possible political outcomes on an organization. Sources of information on changes in the political environment include:

● the Queen's speech
● government reports
● party manifestos
● interest groups
● changes in the law

The Queen's speech

The Queen's speech sets out the government's parliamentary agenda for the coming year. It is read on behalf of the government by the Queen at the state opening of parliament each autumn.

Government reports

Government reports are a useful guide to policy. They set out detailed points which can affect specific organizations (for example, the Taylor report on football) and give clues about the general direction of government policy. The 1988 White Paper on broadcasting supports a liberalization of the sector with the introduction of new channels and providers. However, the 1994 report on environmental pollution takes a much stronger interventionist line. The tone of the 1998 Green Paper on countryside access suggests that the government favours voluntary agreement.

The 1988 White Paper: broadcasting in the 1990s

This set out government policy for the 1990s as being one of encouraging competition and choice in broadcasting whilst maintaining quality. Its main proposals included:

● maintenance of publicly funded BBC
● ITV franchises to be sold to the highest bidder subject to minimum quality standards
● authorization for channels 5 and 6 for terrestrial TV
● expansion of commercial satellite and cable TV
● new radio franchises

   The results of this policy are likely to be a rapid expansion of TV and radio stations in the 1990s, but with a question mark over the quality of output.

The 1990 Taylor report

The Taylor report on football concluded the public inquiry set up after the 1989 Hillsborough disaster. It recommendations included:

● halting the proposed national identity scheme for football spectators
● football grounds to be converted to all-seat stadia by 1994 for top-division clubs and 1999 for the remainder of the league.
● making pitch invasions and the shouting of racial abuse a criminal offence

The 1994 Royal Commission on Environmental Pollution

This report concluded that current growth rates in road traffic, which are forecast to lead to a doubling in road traffic between 1995 and 2025, are neither socially nor environmentally acceptable. It made 110 recommendations to encourage 'a gradual shift away from lifestyles which depend on high mobility and intensive use of cars'. These included:

- a doubling of petrol prices in real terms between 1994 and 2004
- higher parking charges
- road pricing
- residential, commercial and leisure developments to be located to minimize car use
- switching investment from roads to public transport
- banning of super unleaded petrol
- ending of zero-rating of tax on aviation fuel

1998: A new cultural framework

This is the strategy document published by the Department of Culture, Media and Sport (DCMS) in 1998. Its key contents are:

- an increase in funding
- a commitment to widening access
- a commitment to the future of the English Tourist Board
- better management.

Better management is to be achieved by the merging of the museum and libraries commissions, and the arts and crafts councils. Additionaly a new body – QUEST – will be set up to monitor the performance of bodies which spend money on behalf of the DCMS.

1998 Green paper: access to the open countryside

While they were in opposition, the Labour Party had promised to introduce a 'John Smith Memorial Bill'. This was seen by pro-ramblers groups as legislation to introduce 'the right to roam' or complete freedom of access to the countryside.

In government, the Labour Party has wavered a little on this promise. In 1998 it published a consultation paper, Access to the Open Countryside which contains two key proposals. First, walkers are not being offered a complete right to roam over farmland, but only access to mountain, moor, heath and down. Second, the government would like to reach voluntary agreement and landowners will be given two years to reach this.

Prime Minister Tony Blair told the House of Commons, 'If voluntary means fail, we are prepared to legislate. But it is also right that if we can by voluntary means establish greater access to the countryside, then we can obviously have that access far quicker and far more easily.'

Part of the problem for the government is a logjam of new legislation passing through the House of Commons. Forty-five bills are in progress for the year which would make it difficult to include new legislation on countryside access.

1998: Low pay commission report on the minimum wage

One of the manifesto commitments of the Labour Government, elected to power in 1997 was the introduction of a statutory minimum wage. Leisure and tourism will be an industry where the introduction of a minimum wage has a significant effect since low wages are characteristic across much of the sector. Over a long period there have been two key interest groups fighting the battle for the minimum wage. On the one hand, the trade union movement has long supported a minimum wage since many of its members or potential members stand to gain by it. For example, Unison General Secretary Rodney Bickerstaffe has spent 35 years campaigning for a minimum wage. Opposed to this have been industrial groups such as the CBI (Confederation of British Industry).

It was the responsibility of the Low Pay Commission to recommend a figure for the minimum wage to the Treasury. The eventual recommendation was reached after a meeting where different interests were brought together. At the meeting, Professor Bain of Queen's University Belfast brought together the two opposing sides.

Bill Callaghan from the Trades Union Congress, Bill Gates, General Secretary of the Knitwear Union, and Rita Donaghy, from the public sector union Unison, represented union interests. Unison was committed to a target minimum wage of around £4.50 an hour. Employers' interests were represented by John Cridland, human resources director of the Confederation of British Industry, and Stephanie Monk, human resources director at Granada. Granada, a leisure company would be particularly affected by a minimum wage.

The eventual recommendation was for £3.60 an hour in 1999, rising to £3.70 in 2000. This represented a compromise between the TUC, which lobbied strongly for a rate of more than £4.00 an hour, and the CBI submission which favoured a lower rate of £3.20

Party manifestos

These identify policies which political parties will follow if elected to government. They are generally available in the period preceding a general election, and reflect the main differences between political groupings shown in Exhibit 10.1.

Other interest groups

The following examples demonstrate different approaches to policy from the right-wing thinking of the Adam Smith Institute, to the left-wing Trades Union Congress.

The Adam Smith Institute

This right-wing pressure group has produced numerous reports, including those advising on more privatization in leisure and tourism. For example,

---

Exhibit 10.1   Key differences between political parties

Left-wing (e.g. Labour/Democrat parties)	*Right-wing (e.g. Conservative/ Republican parties)*
● need to control the free market ● pro trade unions ● some state ownership of industry ● progressive taxation ● regulation of industry ● higher government spending and taxes ● reduce inequality of incomes ● pro minimum wage ● provision of jobs a priority ● comprehensive welfare state	● belief in supremacy of the free market ● anti-trade unions ● private ownership of industry ● proportional taxation ● minimal state interference ● low taxes and government spending ● inequality of income as incentive ● anti-minimum wage ● control of inflation a priority ● minimal welfare state

---

Exhibit 10.2   Privatize 'smug' BBC call

The BBC should be privatized through a stock market flotation and the licence fee phased out over 10 years with advertising and sponsorship making up its funding, the free-market Adam Smith Institute proposes today.

The report – *What Price Public Service?* – is highly critical of the licence fee, saying: 'The mentality of the bottomless purse allows new finance to be sought by asking for increases in the licence fee. The BBC, with that guaranteed source of income, is not liable to any penalty for failure to provide what the general public wants to see; nor for that matter to reap the rewards'.

It dismisses a suggestion in the government's green paper on the future of the BBC that advertising might alter the range and quality of programmes, arguing that there is little difference between the output of BBC and ITV. The report says: 'Members of the public would jump at the chance to become part owners of the corporation, and it would make good sense to set aside about 10 per cent of the shares for the BBC's employees, at attractive prices'.

A new industry-wide regulatory body, called Ofcast, would promote competition, protect consumers and monitor standards, while competition would make BBC programmes 'more adventurous and more innovative', shaking the corporation out of its 'smug complacency', the institute says.

Source: *Guardian*, 9 February 1993 (adapted).

Expounding the Arts (1987) advocates the phasing-out of government subsidies to the arts, and that museums should be encouraged to become more commercially oriented. *Pining for Profit* argued for the privatization of the Forestry Commission. Exhibit 10.2 illustrates the main points from its report on the BBC, *What Price Public Service?*

Exhibit 10.3   Unions pledge to raise the minimum

The 1998 Trades Union Congress (TUC) in Blackpool witnessed pleasure at finally achieving a statutory minimum wage but also signalled a determination to raise the minimum rate substantially. It supported a campaign to raise the rate from £3.60 to £4.61 an hour.

The leader of Unison, Britain's largest union, Rodney Bickerstaffe, said 'A rate of £3.60 before stoppages cannot be fair. It cannot be an acceptable level. It is not enough for food, clothing, rent. Not enough for a night out or to give the kids a treat. I defy Tony and Cherie [Prime minister and his wife], John Edmonds [TUC president] or me, anyone in this room to live for a lifetime on the rate of £3.60 and be happy and content.' The general secretary of the Transport & General Workers' Union [TGWU], Bill Morris, stated that the TGWU's target for a minimum wage would be £5.

The Trades Union Congress

This is a group representing a coalition of trade unions in the UK. One of its key campaigning issues has been to introduce the minimum wage, and Exhibit 10.3 demonstrates its continuing campaigning in this area.

Changes in the law

The 1994 Sunday Trading Act

The passing of this act made lawful what had already been widely practised. Although large stores have their opening hours restricted to 6 hours, the act enables leisure and travel retailers to trade lawfully. DIY stores have a long track record for Sunday opening, and the Sunday Trading Act has meant that a Sunday is now indistinguishable from any other day in many UK high streets.

The 1994 Criminal Justice Act

This wide-ranging act included some new offences which are of direct relevance to the leisure and tourism sector. These include:

- the banning of ticket touts
- aggravated trespass
- public disorder

The banning of ticket touts is unlikely to stop the practice completely, as the underlying economic disequilibrium that allows touts to operate will not be removed. Touts are likely to operate more discreetly.

Aggravated trespass will make it a criminal offence to trespass with intent to disrupt anyone from engaging in a lawful activity, and is thus likely to limit the actions of hunt saboteurs.

Unlicensed raves are liable to more focused police action as a result of the tightening of the law on public disorder.

The 1998 Working Time Directive

The 1998 Working Time Directive gives an employee the right the refuse to work more than 48 hours per week, although the limit may be exceeded in a given week, provided the 48-hour limit is an average over a 17-week period. The directive states that no one can be dismissed or discriminated against for claiming their rights. The EU is moving towards a reduction in working hours and for example France restricts working hours to 35 a week

1999: Minimum Wage Act

The government estimates two million people will have wage increases as a result of the new legal minimum wage of £3.60 per hour (£3 an hour for 18- to 21-year-olds). Employers who fail to pay the minimum wage will be fined £7.20 per worker – twice the amount of the new legal rate – every day they fail to comply. Enforcement will be carried out by the Inland Revenue-Contributions Agency.

The sociocultural environment

Sociocultural factors include the make-up of society, for example in terms of its population structure, levels of education, social class and attitudes.

Demographics

Demography is the study of population, and population trends are important for the leisure and tourism sector for two key reasons. First the population is an important factor in determining demand. So, for example, the leisure requirements of a country are likely to change considerably as the average age of the population increases. Football pitches may need to give way to bowling greens. The location of leisure facilities similarly needs to be tailored to the migration trends of the population. Tourism marketing also needs to be informed by relevant population data. The dramatic growth in extended winter sun breaks reflects the demands of an ageing population.

Second the population provides the labour force. Where there is a constant stream of school leavers entering the job market, recruitment and training are relatively straightforward. But when the proportion of the population in the working age group is shrinking, firms have to operate more worker-centred policies. Retention of the labour force (for example, by providing crèche facilities for working parents) and retraining of mature workers are likely to be important. Third an ageing population is likely to have a less progressive culture and adapt to change less easily.

It is therefore useful to have information about trends in the total population and its structure in terms of age, sex, geographic, and socioeconomic distribution.

Population: growth, age and sex structure

Table 10.1 details the age, sex structure and totals of the UK population.

The rate of growth of the population is determined by the birth rate, the death rate and net migration. The birth and death rates are generally expressed as crude rates, for example:

Crude birth rate = number of births per thousand population

The UK, in common with many developed countries, has a relatively stable population and Table 10.1 confirms that its population has only risen from 55.9 to 57.8 million in the period 1971 to 1991. This is because the birth rate and the death rate for the UK have both stabilized at similar levels.

Birth rates are linked with economic development and high per capita income countries tend to have low rates since women are more likely to want to be active in the labour market, the cost of upkeep of children is high,

Table 10.1 Age and sex structure of the UK population (percentage and millions)

Year	Percentage of total in each age group					Millions All ages
	<16	*16–39*	*40–64*	*65–79*	*>80*	
1961	24.9	31.4	32.0	9.8	1.9	52.8
1971	25.5	31.3	29.9	10.9	2.3	55.9
1981	22.3	34.9	27.8	12.2	2.8	56.4
1991	20.3	35.3	28.6	12.0	3.7	57.8
Males	21.4	36.7	29.0	10.6	2.3	28.2
Females	19.3	34.0	28.2	13.3	5.2	29.6
2001F	21.0	32.8	30.5	11.4	4.2	59.7
2011F	19.5	30.3	33.7	11.9	4.7	61.1
2021F	18.5	30.0	32.3	14.0	5.2	62.0
2031F	18.4	28.7	30.3	15.6	6.9	62.1
Males	19.0	29.7	30.9	14.9	5.5	30.7
Females	17.7	27.8	29.8	16.4	8.3	31.4

F = Forecast.
Source: The Office for National Statistics: *Social Trends*.

and birth control is widely practised. High birth rates in low per capita income countries need less explanation. In these countries there are fewer factors reducing the higher crude birth rate that is natural in humans. Children are seen as natural, as extra help and as an insurance in old age, and birth control is less widely adopted. Figure 10.1 illustrates the consequences of this for population sizes and growth rates in different countries.

Economic development tends to a lowering of death rates (which are partially determined by nutrition, hygiene and medical technology) earlier than birth rates, which are dependent on attitudes. Thus many countries are still witnessing rapid population growth. The population of India is forecast to grow by more than a third over the next 30 years, whilst that of Mali will more than double. The one important exception to this is China, where a strict one-child policy is enforced.

Analysis of the age structure of the UK population from Table 10.1 reveals an ageing population which is typical of many developed countries. In 1961, less than 12 per cent of the population were aged over 65. This proportion had risen to around 16 per cent by 1991, and is projected to rise to over 22 per cent by the year 2031. In contrast, the proportion of the population under 16 years is falling from 25 per cent in 1961 to a projected 18 per cent by 2031. Countries which are still experiencing rapid population growth have a much lower average age of their population.

Differing age groups of the population can be identified as having distinct demands for leisure and tourism. Table 10.2 illustrates characteristics and demands of distinct age groups.

Table 10.2   Age characteristics

Life stage	Characteristics	Leisure income	Leisure time
Child	Leisure decisions generally taken by parent	Low	High
Single	High propensity for leisure pursuits and travel. Independence asserted, budget travel popular, social aspects sought	Medium	Medium
Partnered	High leisure and tourism propensities underpinned by high income and free time	High	Medium
Full nest	Children become key preoccupation. Leisure and tourism must meet children's requirements. Costs per person important	Medium	Low
Empty nest	Children have left home. Opportunities for leisure and tourism increase. Exotic destinations and meaning of life sought	High	Medium
Old age	May lack partner, may suffer from infirmity. Safer leisure and travel pursuits sought, package holidays popular	Low	High

(a)

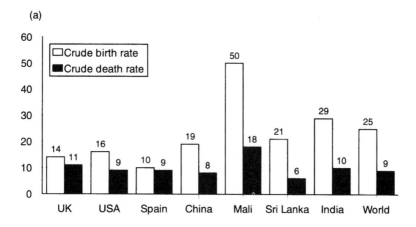

(b)

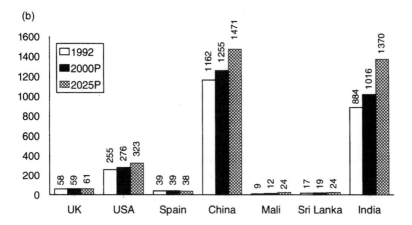

(c)

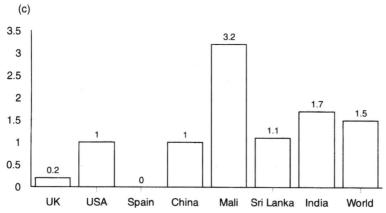

Figure 10.1 Population growth for selected countries. (a) Crude birth and death rates (per thousand per year 1992); (b) total populations in millions (P = projections); (c) average percentage yearly population growth (projection: 1992–2000).

Table 10.3   UK population: changes in regional populations, 1991–1996

Region	Growth (%)
North-east	−0.1
Yorkshire and Humberside	1.1
East Midlands	2.6
Eastern	2.8
South-east	
Greater London	2.7
Rest of south-east	2.8
South-west	2.6
West Midlands	1.0
North-west	0.1
Wales	1.0
Scotland	0.4
Northern Ireland	3.9

Source: Adapted from Office for National Statistics: *Regional Trends*.

Geographic and occupational distribution of the population

The UK population is mainly urban. Only 20 per cent of the population of England lives in the country, whilst the majority of the population lives in the major conurbations such as London, the West Midlands, South-east Lancashire, West Yorkshire and Merseyside. However the population is not static and Table 10.3 shows the major population migrations of recent years.

Some of the key trends that emerge are depopulation of city centres (in London there has been a population drift towards the outer commuter belt of the home counties), migration into the South-east, East Anglia and the South-west, and depopulation of Scotland.

Predicting the future population

There are some population predictions that are unlikely to be subject to much error. For example, predictions about the number of persons retiring, or entering higher education, in the next 10 years are fairly predictable since the people concerned are already born.

Predictions about future population totals have to make assumptions about the factors underlying population change. The birth rate has been stable for the UK in recent years but this cannot be guaranteed. The death rate could be reduced by discoveries which inhibit ageing, or might increase in the face of war or disease. Free movement of labour within the EC makes migration less predictable.

Lifestyles

J. K. Galbraith drew attention many years ago to the paradox of private affluence and public squalor. This was a description of society in the USA where many individuals were becoming richer and richer and yet public facilities were becoming run down. New York illustrates this point graphically. In the short walk along 42nd Street, the chic and stretched limo symbols of Broadway are soon replaced by the nightmare scenes of poverty in the Transit Authority terminal.

UK society has become increasingly polarized in the last two decades. Figure 10.2 illustrates how the rich increased their share of national income whilst the share of the poor declined in the Thatcher years. Unemployment, in particular, has led to the emergence of an 'underclass' in UK society. Thus the leisure and tourism demands of the rich have become ever more sophisticated, whilst access to the poor is ever more limited.

On the other hand, by 1990, two-thirds of households were owner-occupiers. The increase in home ownership has encouraged the growth of

Table 10.4 UK television viewing by social class (hours/week)

Social class	1986	1991	1994
AB	20	19	22
C1	23	24	22
C2	26	27	26
DE	34	32	29
All persons	27	26	25

Source: PSI: *Cultural Trends.*

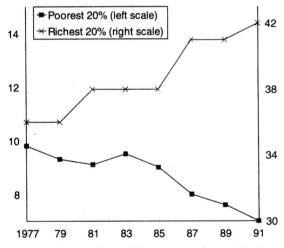

Figure 10.2 Percentage of total disposable income, adjusted for household size.
Source: *Guardian.*

home-improvement leisure activities such as DIY and gardening. Television continues to exert a big influence on people's lives and 98 per cent of households have television sets. The total hours of television viewing have changed very little over the last 10 years, as shown in Table 10.4. There is, however, a marked division between social classes in their viewing habits.

By 1999 over half of households had access to a car and the extension of the motorway network has extended the distance that can be reached within 3 hours of home. Out-of-town shopping and browsing has become a key leisure pursuit. Visitor attractions have benefited from increased mobility, and some parts of the countryside are becoming overwhelmed by their urban visitors.

Culture and attitudes

Culture refers to the dominant beliefs, values and attitudes of society, or a subgrouping in society. Changing beliefs, values and attitudes affect the way in which people perceive, demand and use leisure and tourism products, for example:

- The mass availability of visual and music media has led to a large upward revision of what is ordinary. This leads to an ever-desperate search for the extraordinary in leisure and tourism pursuits.
- Culture is organic. For example, materialism has replaced religion; feminism has made inroads into sexism; hedonism has become a dominant form of social behaviour. Leisure and tourism accommodate these changes with Sunday betting, women-only swimming sessions, and sex tourism in Bangkok.
- The population is becoming less culturally homogeneous and more culturally fragmented. Subcultures have particular leisure and tourism demands.
- Advertising is promoting leisure and tourism fantasies.
- Crime is increasing, as is fear of crime.
- Women have become more significant in leisure and tourism provision and Exhibit 10.4 explores the attitudes and lifestyles of young, single employed women.

Review of key terms

- Political power = the ability to influence events.
- Scenario planning = developing plans to cope with different views of future.
- The Queen's speech = the government's parliamentary agenda for the coming year.
- Crude birth rate = number of births per thousand population.
- Ageing population = average age of population increasing.

Exhibit 10.4   Women with attitude

The Centre for Micro-social Change at the University of Essex has used information from the British Household Panel Study to explore the attitudes and lifestyles of single women between the ages of 25 and 44 in professional and managerial occupations. Between 1966 and 1996 the percentage of women of working age in employment rose from 42.2 per cent to 67 per cent and women form a growing percentage of the rise in numbers of single-person households. These are forecast to rise by 3.4 million between 1996 and 2016. The Household Panel Study is based on a national sample of more than 5500 households. Findings include that single professional women aged 25 to 44:

- Lead active social lives. They regularly go to the cinema and theatre and maintain frequent contact with friends.
- Have a high propensity to engage in weekly active sports. (66 per cent compared with less than 50 per cent of other women).
- Tend to be satisfied with their social lives.(72 per cent to compared with only 50 per cent of other women.
- Are less concerned about the environment. (50 per cent fewer express anxiety about the ozone layer than other women).
- Are less likely to own video recorders, dishwashers and microwave ovens.
- Are more likely to eat out rather than buy convenience food.
- Have greater concerns about health.
- Own fewer PCs (only 16 per cent compared with 55 per cent of others).

Visiting Professor Richard Scase and researcher Jonathan Scales conclude: 'The number of single professional and managerial women aged 25 to 44 is rapidly increasing and their work patterns and lifestyles will have a growing impact on demands for leisure, retailing and housing. Their attitudes are likely to affect the nature of corporate cultures and political debate and the issues that concern them are very different from those that have preoccupied traditional feminism.'

Source: Research findings from The Centre for Micro-social Change at the University of Essex.

Data questions

Task 10.1   *Pressure groups and precious species*

SSSI stands for site of special scientific interest. These are designated sites which are afforded special protection because of their significance to wildlife and rare species. The Countryside and Wildlife Act of 1981 makes it an offence to damage or destroy SSSIs.

But a recent report by the RSPB (Royal Society for the Protection of Birds) records 2256 cases of accidental or deliberate damage recorded in the past six years. Because of this the RSPB has launched a campaign to get tougher wildlife laws introduced. It wants improved legislation to stop deterioration of SSSIs. The RSPB points particularly to events which occur outside of the SSSI boundaries such as excess use of fertilizers, waste and sewage disposal, water abstraction and construction which can lead to a negative impact on the SSSIs. It points to that fact that birds, which are a useful indicator of the health of the environment, are in steady decline.

Chief executive of the RSPB, Graham Wynne, said 'Serious flaws in our wildlife laws have led to many of our finest nature sites being destroyed, damaged or neglected. Unless wildlife law and funding policy are reformed, our natural heritage will slowly bleed to death, and even more animals and plants will become rarities or even disappear. Our report is a powerful indictment of the current wildlife law and policy and their failure to conserve and manage our most precious places for wildlife. The government should act now to ensure parliamentary time in the next session for a bill to reform wildlife legislation.' The RSPB boasts 1 million members which it plans to mobilize to lobby for new legislation.

Source: RSPB press release.

Questions

1 What is a pressure group?
2 What other pressure groups exist in the leisure and tourism sector? What are their aims and methods? What opportunities and threats do they pose for the leisure sector?
3 What is the relationship between a pressure group, a political party, the government and the law?
4 What would be opportunities and threats to the leisure sector of a change in the law as advocated by the RSPB? What other interest groups might oppose the RSPB's plans?
5 To what extent has pressure group activity changed the political environment in the leisure and tourism sector?

Task 10.2   Grey expectations

Whilst global greening is still in its infancy, global greying gathers momentum. Almost everywhere in the world, from Japan to Taiwan, in Singapore, western Europe and the USA, populations are getting older.

In the western European OECD countries, the population of over-65s will grow from a figure of 50 million in 1990 to over 70 million by 2030 – a rise of 40 per cent. With the number of people of working age falling there will be only roughly three workers per retiree compared with five at present. Within these countries, the effects of ageing will be felt most acutely in Germany, with ageing in the UK being more moderate.

Since these predictions can be made with some certainty, we ought to look to the possible consequences: tax and benefit systems may need reviewing. Savings and investment patterns may alter. There will certainly be changes in demand. The market research group Mintel has identified 'third-age consumers' as a significant and distinctive market for leisure, holidays and health care. Another commentator, Ms Frankie Cadwell of a New York advertising firm, Cadwell Davies Partners, expresses surprise that European companies have been much slower to address the needs of this market than their US counterparts. Her firm specializes in selling to the over-50s.

Finally, older populations may be less innovative, more conservative, and have a less adaptive labour force. If this is so, there may be some shift in competitive advantage towards those newly industrializing economies where the average age is lower, such as China, Brazil and India.

Source: Author, from news cuttings.

Questions

1 To what extent is it true that population trends can be predicted with certainty?
2 'Economists predict that demographic restructuring could alter patterns of consumption, production, employment, savings, investment and innovation.' Use these headings to predict how a named leisure or tourism organization might be affected by demographic change.
3 Why might ageing lead to a competitive disadvantage, and which countries are likely to be affected by this?

Task 10.3 Rock around the clock?

The UK, having recently moved to seven days a week shopping may top this up with seven nights too as it moves towards the 24-hour society. Already 300 000 people work at nights and this is forecast to increase to over 750 000 by 2010. Both Oxford and Bradford market themselves as 24-Hour Cities with a focus on their pubs and clubs. Recent trends include:

● All-night TV and radio stations.
● 365-day/24-hour telephone banking services.
● Night opening of some supermarkets.
● Internet shopping with no closing times.
● Round-the-clock share dealing via London, Tokyo and New York.

A report from the Future Foundation, argues that the 24-hour society can be a liberating experience which will enable us to balance work and leisure. It says: 'At the moment, we constantly categorize time: work time, free time, leisure time, quality time, time spent alone, time wasted. All these categories compete with each other and add to the pressures of living. By removing artificial time constraints – the pub closing at 11 pm, the shop closing at 6 pm, the post office opening at 9 am – individuals are free to allocate time as they see fit. The 24-hour society enables us to regain a broader sense of time. In that regard it is a social revolution of epic proportions.'

Questions

1 What evidence is there for a shift towards a 24-hour society?
2 Consumers in the leisure sector are sometimes categorized by their poverty or richness in terms of time and money. Which of these are most likely to benefit from a 24-hour society?

3 Evaluate the opportunities and threats posed by a 24-hour society to organizations in the:
- Hotel sector.
- Transport sector.
- Entertainment sector.
- Fitness sector.
- Sport sector.
- Tourism sector.

Short questions

1 Distinguish between a manifesto, the Queen's speech, a White Paper and a law.
2 What effects might the the 1998 Working Time Directive and the 1999 Minimum Wage Act have on the leisure and tourism sector
3 How might the 1994 Royal Commission on Environmental Pollution affect organizations in the leisure and tourism sector?
4 What changes have occurred to the operating environment of ticket touts?
5 Why is the population of the UK ageing? What are the consequences of this for leisure and tourism organizations?
6 How are changes in lifestyles and attitudes affecting leisure and tourism?

References

Pleasure, leisure and jobs, The Business of Tourism, Cabinet Office, (1988) HMSO.
HMSO (1988) *Broadcasting in the 1990s.*
Mason, D (1987) *Expounding the Arts*, Adam Smith Institute.

Websites of interest

Political parties around the world http://www.psr.keele.ac.uk/parties.htm
Political parties around the world   http://www.agora.stm.it/politic/
The UK Labour Party   www.labour.org.uk
The UK Conservative Party   www.tory.org.uk
The UK Liberal Party   www.libparty.demon.co.uk
Adam Smith Institute   http://www.adamsmith.org.uk
Learning help in economics and business studies   http://www.bized.ac.uk

11 The technological environment and opportunities and threats analysis

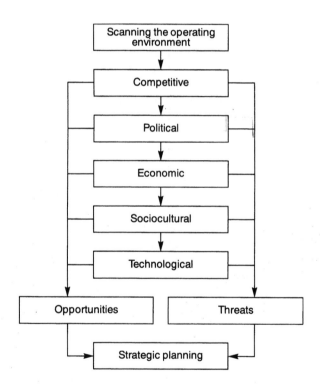

Objectives

First, this chapter concludes PEST analysis by considering the extent and impact of the continuing technological revolution.

Second, this chapter introduces the concept of opportunities and threats analysis. This acts as a summary of the points made in Chapters 8–11. It also provides a useful tool for organizations to identify the key changes in their operating environment and thus acts as a sound basis for reviewing the appropriateness of the organization's strategy.

By studying this chapter students should be able to:

● define the scope of the technological environment
● identify information sources for analysing the technological environment
● identify technological opportunities and threats to leisure and tourism organizations
● conduct an audit of an organization's operating environment
● conduct an opportunities and threats analysis

The technological environment

Technological change offers two key opportunities for leisure and tourism organizations. First it can lead to cost reductions. The long-run average cost curve (LRAC) is constructed on the assumption that technology remains constant, and thus improved production technology will cause the long-run average cost curve of an organization to fall, as illustrated in Figure 11.1. LRAC1 represents the original long-run average cost curve. The use of improved production technology enables the curve to shift downwards to LRAC2. Average costs of producing level of output $0C$ now fall from $0A$ to $0B$.

Second, technology can provide new products and markets. Both of these routes can lead to an improvement in an organization's competitive edge, and can be the basis of price-based or differentiation strategies. However, technological change also poses threats where existing products become obsolete in the face of new developments. Technological change is being delivered mainly at present by the increased processing power of micro-computers, the provision of high capacity datalinks and the fall in price of hardware and software. Silicon chip developments lead to faster data processing. Fibre optics and digital technology mean that data can be

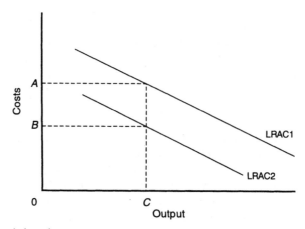

Figure 11.1 Shifting long-run average cost curve (LRAC).

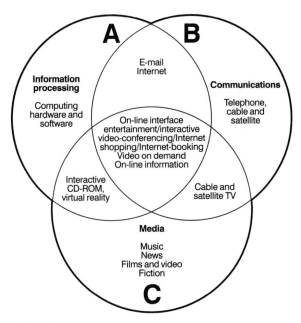

Figure 11.2 Multimedia.

quickly transmitted globally at low cost, and these hardware developments mean that software of ever-increasing sophistication can be developed.

Multimedia is one of the key developments of the 1990s. It is illustrated in Figure 11.2.

Thus at a simple level an organization's computer network on its own can perform word processing, accounting and other functions (circle A). Linked to other computers via datalink services it can access reservation systems and provide E-mail and Internet conferencing (circles A + B). Linked to other media, at the simplest level text, images and video clips can be incorporated into software programs (circles A + C). At the most sophisticated level virtual reality can be set up. Linking PCs and media sources through datalinks provides access to the whole repertoire of computer applications (circles A + B + C). This includes, for example, video on demand, and Internet shopping which enables goods to be chosen at home and delivered to your door. Home booking allows access to central reservation and booking systems from home, with the possibility of video clips of resorts and hotels.

Exhibit 11.1 describes how computer technology is paving the way to ticketless travel.

Technological impacts may be analysed in the following areas:

● hospitality
● tourism
● leisure

Exhibit 11.1   No more 'tickets please'

Almost 50 per cent of passengers flying in the USA now fly ticketless. Travel agents and airlines can book a passenger on to a flight using electronic ticketing without issuing a physical ticket. When a passenger books a flight all that happens is that a reservation is made in the airline's computer system. The system can save large sums in airlines costs and helps passengers too. Passengers identify themselves at check-in by their passport or credit card.

United Airlines is at the forefront of ticketless travel development, whilst Lufthansa leads the way in Europe and Cathay Pacific in the Far East. However, the system does have its critics and a United spokesperson admitted that some travel agents were worried about computer ticketing in case business was lost as passengers cut out the agent and booked direct with the airline. But he added, 'Agents will find their paperwork greatly reduced, and that they save a lot of money by not having to bike or express-post tickets to customers.'

Meanwhile, British Airways is developing Internet booking and its website allows passengers in over 50 countries to book and pay for tickets anywhere on the airline's network. BA's head of global distribution, Roger Flynn, looks to future developments which will involve smart cards and palm or iris-reading identification machines.

BA has also introduced automatic ticket machines at its major airports. These allow passengers to use a credit card to buy a ticket at a machine where they use a touchscreen to select a seat. A boarding pass is printed out in under a minute.

Source: The author.

Hospitality

Showcases such as Hotech, the exhibition for suppliers of hotel technology, provide a good insight into innovations affecting the hospitality industry. Current developments include the following.

First links into central reservation systems are important so that hotels can capture reservations generated from distant terminals. Most travel agents use one of the central reservation systems such as SABRE or Amadeus to book air travel, car hire and accommodation, and access to these systems represents an important marketing tool. For the future, a system that automatically rebooks accommodation to deal with air delays and missed connections is a possibility.

Second, there has been considerable progress in accounting packages. In management accounting, yield management packages are an important tool enabling hotels to maximize revenue by adjusting rates to best-fit changing market conditions. Yield management packages are able to compare likely demand with actual demand and capacity and suggest rates accordingly. In financial accounting, packages enable financial reporting to take place speedily and efficiently.

Check-in time can be minimized by using credit card readers to automate registration and issue a high-technology key which can even be a credit card itself. High-technology keys reduce the possibility of theft since codes may be changed frequently at minimal cost. It is possible for a reservation system to use its database to provide personalized services such as provision of a particular newspaper. Computerized reservation systems can also reduce check-out time to a minimum.

Other computer-assisted management systems range from energy management systems to conference management systems and computer-intelligent buildings. A computer-intelligent building means that most of the functions of the building are computer-assisted, and so, for example, room cleaning schedules can be computer-generated from information from guests' smart keys, pay rolling can be generated from reading employees' time sheets which themselves are based on electronic monitoring, and a wide range of on-screen services are available in rooms.

Exhibit 11.2 shows how technology has been used to cut costs, enabling some French hotels to pursue an effective price-based strategy.

The conference industry illustrates possible opportunities and threats posed by new technology. A recent study found that 36 per cent of hotel room sales was made to conference delegates, and there has been growth in the number of centres with capacities for in excess of 1000 delegates. However, firms such as Xerox are increasingly turning to video-conferencing as a way of reducing travel and hospitality costs, and saving expensive executive time. Some hotels are responding to this challenge and the Hilton National group for example has introduced video-conferencing in its key conference venues.

However, with the growth of multimedia technologies it is possible that more conferencing will in future be office- or home-based, utilizing PCs. It

---

Exhibit 11.2   Hi-tech hotels are revolutionizing budget accommodation in France – Rob Davidson

You're driving through France and decide to stop for the night. The question is: how do you break your journey without breaking the bank? The answer is the budget hotel where a clean, quiet room for up to three people sharing costs from £15 a night.

How are overheads kept so low? Most cost-trimming is achieved by reducing services to a bare minimum. Hi-tech, manpower-saving devices also help to cut costs. A good example is automatic check-ins, which are placed at entrances for use when reception areas are unattended. *La Réception Automatique* works like a cash machine: you insert a credit card and 'converse' with the facility (in French, English or German) about the room you want, how long you plan to stay and whether you want breakfast. The machine then debits your card and issues a key and room number.

French technology is also applied in the automatic cleaning systems installed in the showers and lavatories of the hotels. Every time the facility is used, a powerful spray of a water–disinfectant mix ensures that it is left spotless for the next user.

The labour-saving devices and basic services mean that budget hotels can be run by just two people plus cleaning staff.

Source: *The Independent.*

Exhibit 11.3   The future is virtually here – David Bowen

It is 2008 and you are going into a meeting with your bosses. They are in San Francisco and Bavaria; you are in your house in the Scottish Highlands. You sit down in your office, put on a pair of dark glasses and a glove – both linked by wire to the computer on your desk. You find yourself in an electronic 'room', with a table and chairs. You look round to see your American boss – or rather his hologram – sitting next to you. A moment later the German appears, and the meeting starts. Using your glove you can pass electronic documents around the room – a disembodied hand appears in front of you, to mimic your movements. This is a virtual conference.

In the multimedia world, we are told, we will be able to shop, play, learn and even make love while sitting alone in the house. The virtual conference is a three-dimensional (3D) computer graphic, transmitted by telephone. Combined with 3D spectacles it tricks the brain into believing that it is inside an electronically created room.

Computers sufficiently powerful to digitalize have become available. A CD can store the equivalent of two digitalized editions of the *Encyclopaedia Britannica*. So all we need is the 'information superhighway', a telephone line with the capacity to carry all this information. The present copper phone wire can carry only voice and a limited amount of text and data. Replace it with fibreoptic cable and its capacity increases 250 000 times over. The entire contents of Oxford's Bodleian Library could be transmitted in 42 seconds.

Source: *Independent on Sunday*.

is possible to access video clips of speakers via point-and-click menus and organize discussion groups with video or e-mail links. Similarly, questions can be collected over the conference period and feedback made available on menus. Conferencing has become more flexible and personalized as participants can choose speakers, discussion groups and questions of direct relevance to themselves, and indeed can browse and move between areas with ease. The implications of such a move would be a shift in conference spending away from airlines, hotels, and local hospitality providers towards the providers of datalinks and other hardware and software companies. Exhibit 11.3 describes a possible video-conference of the future.

Travel and tourism

Technological changes in transportation are likely to be extensions of existing technologies in the form of larger jumbo jets, and faster trains for travel. Additionally some shortages of air space may be relieved by using information technology to create smaller air tunnels than the existing air corridors.

Booking and reservation systems are likely to become more sophisticated, globalized and more widely available. The main distribution channels currently are Worldspan, SABRE, Amadeus and Galileo and there have been some disputes between the systems providers and the service providers over charges.

The early entry of American Airlines into computerized reservation systems has given it a competitive advantage in its SABRE system which now generates more profits than the airline operations. Multimedia is filtering into computerized reservation systems and SABREVISION now adds pictures and video images of destinations to information about price and availability.

Exhibit 11.4   Internet travel on line for expansion

In 1994 under the heading 'Computers: meagre catch on the travel lines', the *Independent* newspaper reviewed the impact of PCs on travel bookings. It quoted one travel expert who commented 'On-line services are great tools for finding schedules and fares but they usually lack the ability to book the absolutely last available seat on a plane.' It found a limited market and concluded that 'A bargain fortnight in Benidorm courtesy of the home computer is probably still a few years away.'

By 1999 things had changed considerably. The Internet was well established, both physically and in the mind of suppliers and consumers. Connections were faster and navigation tools better. As more households become connected to the Internet, so it is becoming a more important source for travel bookings and information. For example, travel guides are available on the net. The Lonely Planet website (www.lonelyplanet.com) reported over 63 million hits per month in January 1999. As well as providing standard information, it also posts recent feedback on destinations. Rob Flyn, the site manager said, 'The site is becoming like a daily paper offering today's news for tomorrow's traveller'. Destinations also run their own websites providing details for sightseeing, and links with accommodation and restaurants.

Yellow Pages (www.yell.co.uk) has a travel facility which offers flights, accommodation, car hire and holidays. One of its key attractions is the posting of around 75 000 late deals which are updated every 30 minutes. The site started as a travel information facility and developed into an on-line booking service. One part of its offering is an airline ticket auction. This is a system that posts last-minute airline tickets on the web and invites bids from potential customers, with the tickets being allocated to the highest bidders.

On-line travel booking offers costs savings to suppliers and information benefits to consumers. Consumers also get quicker access to booking on a well-designed site and can avoid long waits on hold that characterize some telephone booking services. Suppliers are keen to move towards more Internet bookings and Delta Air Lines introduced a $2 surcharge on non-Internet bookings. However, it abandoned this after criticism from US travel agents (1999). easyJet, the UK budget airline offers a £1 reduction each way on seats booked via its website (www.easyJet.com).

Booking sophisticated tourism services such as holidays may continue to provide a future for traditional travel agents who have specialized training and can put together complex itineraries. But for straightforward services such as airline seats, hotel reservations, and seats for major entertainment, on-line booking is likely to make substantial inroads into the high street agent's business in the foreseeable future.

Source: The author, 1999.

The increasing use of the Internet may pose some threats to travel agents. Use of NetScape Navigator and Internet Explorer to access the web makes home use straightforward and SABRE is now available via the Compuserve network to home-based PCs. The Windows environment means that it can be used instantly, whereas travel agents had to undergo a half-day training to use the pre-Windows system.

Exhibit 11.4 records that the impact of the Internet on booking services had grown substantially between 1994 and 1999.

Exhibit 11.5   Sex comes on-line

1994: *Virtual Valerie* was the cutting edge of technology for porn – a CD ROM game where 'Val obeys the user's every command'.

1999: Karlin Lillington of the *Guardian* gives an update on the technological progress of porn: 'Not even the defence industry capitalizes on new technical developments as swiftly, and with as much innovation and payback, as the pornographers. They buy the best equipment, use some of the best Internet service companies in the business to give them ultra-fast connections directly to the Internet's backbone, and are always eager to test the newest applications – anything to push images as fast as possible to the paying punters at the end of the mouse. From web video to live chat, on-line credit card transactions to image compression technologies, the on-line sex industry usually got there first and pioneered the format. As a result, the Internet has made silicone as ubiquitous as silicon. Sex is the web's killer application.

An IT applications engineer notes that pornography is one of the key industries involved in the purchase of computer equipment. The economics of porn provide the motive for state-of-the-art expertise to provide competitive advantage. A third of web users surveyed reported that they had accessed a sex site. These billions of hits generate subscriptions and sales. For example a Los Angeles-based website called Danni's Hard Drive had a gross turnover of $2.7 million in 1997 rising to around $3.5 million in 1998. The site averages 5 million hits a day and has established a client base of over 22 000 paying subscribers. Access costs $14.95 per month which gains entry to photos, videos and six live real-time acts.

Industry analysts Forrester Research estimate that pornography produced $137 million for US websites in 1997, and $185 million in 1998. Forrester predicts that by 2001 revenue will have risen to $366 million. This makes pornography third in Internet sales after computers and travel. *Inter@ctive*, a magazine for the web industry, estimates that the supply of adult sites for 1997 was about 10 000.

The Hot & Heavy site boasts 'the hottest 3D virtual reality sex online', and entices its customers to 'use your mouse to move the hottest girls/couples in 3D'. But what of the future?

2002?: Programmers predict that cybersex will take on new dimensions with developments in 'teledildonics'. Here cybersex moves from visual interaction nearer to virtual sex where visual interaction is merged with sensation.

2008?: One cybersex futurologist predicts 'the ability to get and give virtual satisfaction through sensory interactivity'. This would involve donning a helmet to enter a virtual world and a suit to receive and transmits touch sensations. In fact a German research group have already produced a prototype of a full-body sensory suit for virtual sex.

Source: The author 1999.

Leisure

The multimedia revolution offers the prospect of sophisticated home-based leisure and enhancement of attractions away from home.

In the home, video on demand may spell the demise of the video rental store. Digitized movies will be stored in distant databases which can be accessed via a menu and decoding system using cable.

Interactive games which started life on floppy disks are able to exploit the extra speed and memory of CD-ROM technology. Exhibit 11.5 illustrates the development of interactive porn.

Currently, the ultimate development goal of computer games appears to be virtual reality. Virtual reality, or cyberspace as it is sometimes called, is an extension of the technology of the flight simulator. It enables participants to enter a computer-generated three-dimensional environment and interact with the environment. Headsets, data gloves and data suits are the passport to this cyberworld where participants can travel from scene to scene and interact with cyber people and cyber objects.

Virtual reality is also likely to affect leisure away from home. Sega has developed theme parks in Japan with interactive attractions which will let people shoot and steer their way through adventures. Disney utilizes virtual reality in its heritage theme park in Washington DC so that visitors can experience life as a civil war soldier, or as a slave. The future interpretation of heritage may well rely less on exhibits in glass cases and more on participation and interaction with virtual artefacts and virtual historical figures. Exhibit 11.6 explores the world of virtual theatre.

Exhibit 11.6   Three hedgehogs pay out?

Kunick, the leisure operator reported pre-tax profits for the half-year to the end of March 1998 of £4.8 million. This represented an 11.5 per cent rise over the same period for 1997.

Kunick is a supplier and operator of fruit machines and part of its development strategy has been to upgrade this product to reflect changes in technology. To do this it has entered into a joint venture with Sega. The idea is to capture Sega's experience in high-tech and Internet amusement products and breathe a new lease of life into a product which has undergone little change.

The new machines will be networked to a central computer. They will include a range of different amusements which the user can select from an on-screen menu. Russell Smith, chief executive of Kunick, explains: 'They will be multiple-game machines. They will also be easier to update – we will be able to introduce new twists.' The new machines also offer benefits from the point of view of maintenance since they can be monitored for faults by the central computer.

Source: The author, 1999.

Opportunities and threats analysis

An opportunities and threats analysis examines an organization's operating environment. The operating environment can be audited using the framework established in the previous chapters and this is illustrated in Table 11.1.

Once the key opportunities and threats have been established for an organization, its strategic plan can be updated to show how opportunities can be exploited and threats can be countered. Table 11.2 considers the main opportunities and threats facing BA in 1994.

Review of key terms

- Fibreoptics = high-capacity data transmission lines using optical fibre rather than copper wire.
- CRS = computerized reservation system, such as SABRE or Amadeus.
- Multimedia = combination of media sources (e.g. video), computing and communications.
- Computer-intelligent building = building use monitored and controlled by computer (e.g. security, temperature, staff location, room use).
- Digitalization = transforming images and sound to digital code for ease of storage and transmission.
- NetScape Navigator and Internet Explorer = Windows-based operating systems for Internet use.
- Internet provider = company which provides Internet access to PC user.
- Networked computers = computers linked to other computers.
- Interactive = user response encouraged and allowed.
- Virtual reality = computer-generated three-dimensional environment for user interaction.
- Cyberspace = virtual reality environment.

Table 11.1   Opportunities and threats analysis

Environment	*Opportunities*	*Threats*
Competitive		
Threat of entrants		
Power of buyers		
Power of suppliers		
Threat of substitutes		
Competitive rivalry		
PEST		
Political		
Economic		
Sociocultural		
Technological		

Table 11.2   Opportunities and threats analysis for British Airways 2000

Environment	Opportunities	Threats
Competitive		
Threat of entrants	● Limited slots available at Heathrow ● Introduction of 'GO' – own no-frills airline	● Debonair, Ryanair, easyJet ● Competition from other European gateways
Power of buyers		● Overcapacity on transatlantic routes
Power of suppliers		● BAA monopoly of main UK airports ● Limited competition between aircraft and engine manufacturers ● Costs of non-BA CRS
Threat of substitutes	● Poor performance of UK rail companies Road congestion	● TGV in Europe ● Eurostar routes to Paris and Brussels
PEST		
Political	● EC rules forbidding subsidies to airlines of member states	● Monopoly investigations into mergers and alliances ● Environmental lobby against pollution ● Continuing uncertainty over extra terminal at Heathrow
Economic	● Currency fluctuations ● Robust domestic, EU and US economies ● Low costs of aviation fuel	● Currency fluctuations ● Recession in Japan, Economic difficulties in Asia, South America and Russia ● Taxes on air travel
Sociocultural	● Move towards multiple holidays each year	
Technological	● Larger aircraft ● On-line booking ● Improved yield management systems	● Overcrowding of airspace ● Millennium bug

Data questions

Task 11.1   Segaworld, London – Queue: what a torture, by John Tribe

'*Welcome to the next generation of futuractive theme parks*', and what better place for an indoor park than in the middle of a city which is wet and cold for at least half of the year. We '*take the rocket escalator to another dimension*' and it feels good – the steep, long escalator ride to the apex of the Trocadero centre excites the senses. We are on the threshold of '*a galaxy of futuristic experiences in one world*'.

Breathless with anticipation we are delivered into what must be the first themed area – 'Receptionland'. Our first encounter with *Segapeople* is with a man who wants to take our photo. Hmm, we dodge round him, puzzle about what to do, where to go. This *futuristic* world is strangely signless. But look – the queue has not been abolished in this brave new world – and an ordinary kind of sign says its going to be 45 minutes. This must be the place to start.

The kids – there are twelve of them in our party – just cannot wait to encounter the 'Beast in Darkness'. They push and crane their necks round every corner. Eventually we reach its 'lair'. Well it's dark but I must say not terribly beastly. We just wander round corridors, regaled by the occasional *roar* through some speakers and pass a few video screens showing *a beast* going about its daily routines. Then – oh dear, this is so scary – the floor becomes *uneven. Oooh! Aaah!*. Funnily enough the next bit had us all leap out of our skins – a *Segaperson* jumped out on us from around a corner. An old trick, but a good one (and what turned out to be the most exciting moment of the day).

He put us on a ride. Now the kids were scared again. Where were they going? They fought to be with an adult. As our cart set off I recalled my first themepark experience – The Black Hole at Disneyland, California, some 20 years ago. When that cart shot off into the dark, I could only scream out involuntary oaths as it hurtled round its impossible track. It was pure sensation, exhilaration, entertainment.

But the cart in *the beast's lair* just trundled. The commentary said something like '*the beast has escaped its going to get you*'. I felt oddly safe . . . but I hadn't figured on the special effects. The back of my seat took on a life of its own. Almost as if *a beast was trying to get at me*. But my sweatglands were not activated, my pulse missed not a beat, my adrenaline pump failed to kick in. Matthew, aged 8¾, yawned. And that was *The Beast in Darkness*.

Points

Futuricity: 1970s
Beastliness 1/10
Pulse rate: 72 beats per minute
Screamometer: 0 decibels

We skirted *The Combat Zone*, an arcade full of slot machines and arrived at our next queue for *Aqua Planet*. *Aqua Planet* was worth the 45-minute wait. We were strapped into seats, and plunged headlong into a breathless journey. It *was* virtually real. Things jumped out from the screen, we ducked instinctively to avoid collisions. The illusion worked. It was old technology – 3D plastic specs, and tilting seats – but as the brochure brags '*try telling your brain it's not real*'.

Points

Excitement: 7/10
Fun: 8/10

We pass another hanger of slot machines – *Race Track* – down a floor to *Space Mission*. Unfortunately it's *mission impossible* due to maintenance problems.

Points

Length of kid's faces: very long
Robustness of Ride: 0/10 (it is only 5 weeks old)

Just in case you're getting slot machine withdrawal symptoms another huge suite looms into view – *Flight Deck*.

Down another level – we try to join the queue for *Ghost Hunt*. It's just malfunctioned so we have to wait 5 minutes to join the queue. The queue, once reached is long, hot, boring and slow moving. You *'try telling your brain it's not* real' but this is no virtual queue. Over and above the malfunction, *Ghost Hunt* has technical problems. It's only working at half capacity. Still a *Segaperson* hands out free tickets to our kids to make up for the wait. Nice touch I think. What can they do with them? *'They can redeem them at the concession – you need 25 points minimum for a SegaPencil'*. The kids count their tickets – they have 10 each.

Ghost Hunt is bizarre. You get in another cart on another train. You trundle round. Targets appear in front of you. You try to shoot them down. Its just like a regular amusement arcade machine, only its put on a cart. Weird.

Points

What was the point?

We spill out of *'Ghost Hunt'* to a now familiar vista – another sea of slot machines – called *'The* Carnival'. We spot the next ride – *'The House of Grandish'*. The queue is posted as 30 minutes. It hardly moves. As we near the front, the reason becomes clear. This ride is shoebox sized. It takes 4 people at a time. Each session takes $4\frac{1}{2}$ minutes. As we crawl to the front of the queue, Segaworld is suddenly revealed to me as a glitzy con-trick.

'We anticipate that a true Segaworld experience will take four hours', so we arrived at 2.00 pm for a 6.00 pm departure. It is now 4.30, a *Segaperson* tells me that queues are over an hour downstairs, so we are going to miss out on three out of eight rides.

The floor manager is summoned. *Virtual tough-luck-mate. Shouldn't come at a busy time.* As prickly as *Sonic the Hedgehog*.

I ask to see the *Segaboss*. Paul Smith, Operations Manager arrives. *Yes it's very busy, but we are nowhere near our fire certificate capacity. We are the victims of our own success. If you've got a complaint write in on Monday.*

Some victim, some success. It is us, the customer, who are the victims. While *Segaworld* counts the money, we stand in queues. Well I have got a complaint – three as it happens.

Complaint number 1 is that you are sold something that is not there. There is not the capacity in the rides to satisfy the visitor admissions. But you've paid your money upfront. Its like paying in advance to get into a supermarket and finding the shelves empty. Every now and again there is a delivery of bread – but you won't all get some.

Complaint number two is that the rides are a side-show – the main space is devoted to paying slot machines – acres of them. So in effect you pay £12 admission to a fancy amusement arcade.

And complaint number three is that the future has sadly not arrived. The rides are unimaginative, largely old tech. This is not how I understand interactive virtual reality. There is little total immersion (except in Space Mission, but even here the graphics are poor quality). You are not in control of anything. Interactivity is confined to mindlessly bashing a *fire* button. You do not make choices, you do not interact with other people, you follow a set path. It all lacks sophistication.

To be brutally frank, the games on my PC, the movie *Independence Day*, beat *Segaworld* hands down. Or as Louisa (age 12) put it, the best ride of the day was on the Bakerloo line train to get there.

Source: *The Times*, 14 December 1996.

Questions

1 Analyse the opportunities and threats which led to the opening of Segaworld.
2 What type of leisure activity is Segaworld and how did its opening of affect the competitive environment in this sector?
3 Account for the criticisms of Segaworld.
4 The author notes of Segaworld that 'sadly the future has not yet arrived'. What was meant by this statement and to what extent has virtual leisure replaced other forms of leisure?

Task 11.2   Fast forward to the future: video on demand

Dial a pizza? Half an hour later a spotty boy weaves down your street on an old Honda moped. Dial a video? Perhaps a similar scene springs to mind. A fleet of battered Hondas, panniers full of cassettes.

Not if BT have their way.

From today in BT's pilot area you can have VOD, or video-on-demand. To use the system you need a set-top decoder, a remote control device and of course a telephone line. Choose VOD from the remote control and a menu appears on the screen. You're now on-line to the VOD film database. You can browse through a comprehensive range of video titles, request a synopsis of the movie, a cast list or the running time.

Tap in a few more commands and the video of your choice is downloaded to your decoder. You can choose to watch the film now or later on. The problem of the popular new release always out on rental on the night you want to take it out from the local video store is digitally solved. The trials being conducted at present also allow you to choose a range of TV shows including sports, children's programmes, soaps and comedy.

Steve Main, BT's Director of Visual and Broad-Casting Services, explained that the company will charge between £1 and £3 per film to compete head-on with video rental stores, for whom a nationwide VOD system poses a serious threat.

But why BT's sudden interest in films? Competition from cable TV and Mercury means that BT is forced to innovate to keep its market share in a fast-changing environment and if BT fails to capture the emerging VOD market, it will be lost to competitors. So whilst the cable operators are offering telephone services in competition with BT, BT is fighting back by offering entertainment via its telephone lines.

However, VOD technology doesn't stop at the movies. Its scope is enormous and could include home shopping, news services, specialist services, banking and reservation services.

In fact holidays on demand are already possible in the BT pilot programme. Menus allow you to browse through various locations, seeing short video clips of the scenery, hotel facilities and local leisure pursuits. If you like what you see you can make an instant reservation, choosing your dates, your hotels and your airport of departure.

Source: The author, from news cuttings (1994).

Questions

1 What are the constituent parts of VOD technology?
2 What is the likely impact of VOD technology for the leisure and tourism sector?
3 This article was written in 1994. Evaluate the success of VOD since this pilot scheme.
4 What other specialized leisure or tourism services could use VOD technology?

Task 11.3   Cybersky's the limit?

● 1994: If you need to buy a book you'll have to visit a bookshop or telephone one that does mail order.
● 1995: Amazon.com started the Internet market in book sales.

- 1997: Amazon becomes the third largest bookseller in the USA, as sales reach $148 million.
- 1998: WH Smith (UK) acquires for £9.4 million bookshop.co.uk, Europe's largest on-line retail site, selling more than 1.4 million book titles and 50 000 CDs, videos and computer games. This is seen by analysts as a defensive/offensive move against Amazon as well as a way to capture a growing market. In 1997 Internet sales in the UK were worth about £200 000, and are forecast to increase to £800 000 by 2000.

Analysts say that the growth of on-line sales is not necessarily at the expense of high street booksellers – but rather that it is generating extra sales. The reasons for this are several. First, on-line bookstores offer substantial discounts which can be as high as 40 per cent. Second, interactive screens entice potential purchasers with lists of bestsellers, recommendations tailored to personal interests, reviews of books extracts, and interviews with the authors.

On-line selling costs are cheaper not only because of cheaper premises costs and lower staff costs but also because of minimal stock costs – Internet bookstores only take the stock when a customer has ordered a book. The publishing houses are already moving towards smaller print runs and this could lead eventually printing on demand which would further reduce costs of returns and holding stocks.

However despite all these benefits Internet bookstores are still not making profits: In 1997, Amazon reported losses of $28.6 million. But, investors are clearly optimistic about the future since the price of Internet shares, including Amazon, have risen sharply.

Questions

1 What are the benefits of on-line sales to consumers and retailers?
2 What areas should be audited when conducting an opportunities and threats analysis?
3 Conduct an opportunities and threats analysis on a named booksellers that operates high street outlets.
4 Evaluate the impact of on-line sales elsewhere in the leisure and tourism sector.

Task 11.4   Prospects for Eurocamp?

Eurocamp is a UK-based organization which offers a number of holiday brands:

1 Eurocamp: Self-drive camping and mobile home holidays in France, Italy and nine other European countries.
2 Keycamp: Mobile home and tent holidays in France and seven other European countries

3 Sunsites: Camping and mobile-holidays in France and three other European countries
4 Eurocamp independent: European camp-site reservation service for customers with their own caravan, tent or motor home
5 Sites abroad: Budget 'no-frills' camp site reservation service offered by Eurocamp Independent
6 Superbreak: Hotel short breaks throughout the UK
7 Goldenrail: Hotel short breaks with emphasis on rail-inclusive packages.
8 Luxury hotel collection: A unique selection of Britain's finest hotels. Elegant accommodation, fine cuisine and outstanding hospitality
9 Family breaks: A selection of hotels with locations and amenities particularly suited to family short breaks.
10 Eurovillages: Holiday villages and centres in France, Italy, Spain, Holland and Germany.

Question

Conduct an opportunities and threats analysis on Eurocamp. (You may wish to visit the Eurocamp website: www.eurocamp.co.uk/corporate2/pages.)

Short questions

1 How do fibreoptics and digital technology allow home access to computerized reservation systems?
2 Explain how video-conferencing makes use of multimedia technology.
3 Distinguish between reality and virtual reality and explain the importance of the latter to the leisure industry.
4 What are the elements of an opportunities and threats analysis?
5 What is the purpose of an opportunities and threats analysis?
6 Is home-based reservation an opportunity or a threat?

Websites of interest

Leisure opportunities: daily news   www.leisureopportunities.co.uk
Learning help in economics and business studies   http://www.bized.ac.uk

Part Three
Investing in Leisure and Tourism

12 Investment appraisal in the private sector

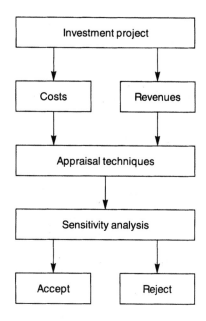

Objectives

With hindsight it is not difficult to analyse the factors that have made some investment projects in the leisure and tourism sector such successes and others such dismal failures. The failures include films (*Raise the Titanic*), transport systems (Virgin Rail) and electronic games (Sega Saturn). The successes include projects as diverse as films (*Titanic*), visitor attractions (Port Aventura), and electronic games (Sony PlayStation).

However, at the planning stage, it is much more difficult to forecast the success of investments, largely because of the uncertainty surrounding the future. This chapter seeks to define the meaning of investment, consider how potential investment projects are appraised and stress the shortcomings of quantitative techniques.

By studying this chapter students will be able to:

- define and distinguish between different types of investment
- analyse the factors which affect an investment decision
- utilize techniques for investment appraisal
- understand the uncertainty surrounding investment appraisal
- analyse the effects of investment on the economy
- evaluate government policy with regard to investment

Definition and examples

In general usage people use the term 'investment' to include bank and building society deposits and the purchase of stocks and shares. Economists are more specific in their use of the term. Investment may be defined as expenditure on capital goods and working capital.

Capital goods can be contrasted with consumer goods. The latter are produced because of the direct satisfaction they yield (e.g. food, CDs, clothes), whilst the former are produced because they improve efficiency of production. Fixed capital goods therefore consist of buildings, plant and machinery, and in the leisure and tourism sector examples include hotel buildings, computer reservation and booking systems, aircraft, and golf-ball making machinery. The total expenditure on such items is recorded as 'gross domestic fixed capital formation' in government statistics.

Working capital consists of stocks of raw materials, semi-manufactured goods and manufactured goods which have not yet been sold. Manufacturers monitor stocks of unsold products closely and these tend to be the key signals in a market economy to reduce or increase production. Working capital is an essential part of production, although modern 'just-in-time' production techniques have reduced the need for large stocks of raw materials and components to be held in factories. Expenditure on these items is recorded in government statistics as 'increase in stocks and work in progress'. Table 12.1 illustrates recent data for the UK showing gross domestic fixed capital formation.

It can be seen that gross fixed capital formation increased in the period 1987 to 1989, fell in 1990 and did not recover its 1988 level until 1995. It has steadily risen between 1993 and 1998.

Figure 12.1 shows the value of new investment projects in the leisure and tourism sector. It shows a similar picture to the total investment figures, reaching a peak in 1989 and falling in the following period, and demonstrates the effects of recession on investment.

Investment can also be divided into gross investment and net investment. Gross investment includes all investment, including that which is for replacement of worn-out machinery, whilst net investment only includes investment that adds to a country's capital stock.

Net investment = gross investment – depreciation

Table 12.1 UK investment 1987–1993 (£m at constant 1995 prices)

Year	Gross domestic fixed capital formation
1987	100 520
1988	115 362
1989	122 158
1990	119 368
1991	109 000
1992	108 246
1993	109 127
1994	107 042
1995	116 360
1996	122 042
1997	129 645
1998*	135 104

* Estimate
Source: Adapted from Office for National Statistics: *Monthly Digest of Statistics*.

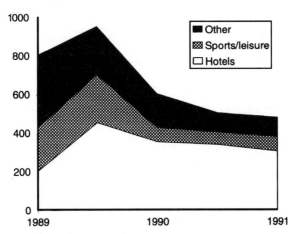

Figure 12.1 Value of new leisure and tourism investment projects commenced in England (£m). *Source*: various.

Factors affecting investment

Investment in the private sector is undertaken to increase profitability. Since we assume that the motive of private sector organizations is the maximization of profits, such organizations will seek to invest in those projects which yield the highest return.

Exhibit 12.1   Holiday Inn: Europe

The UK brewery and leisure group Bass plc has announced new investment plans for extending its Holiday Inn hotels into Europe.

Its chosen strategy is to expand mainly by franchising, and to extend its presence in the budget market. The vehicle for this is the Holiday Inn Express concept aimed at price-conscious travellers.

By avoiding costly city-centre sites and concentrating instead on roadside locations, the investment cost to franchisees is expected to range between £28 000 and £30 000 per room and rooms are likely to cost an average of £35 a night.

Both of these figures are substantially less than those associated with standard Holiday Inns.

Source: The author.

Investment projects will incur planning, construction and running costs and yield revenue when in operation. Thus the profitability of an investment project can be analysed by investigating its costs and revenue. Exhibit 12.1 gives a rough idea of the costs and revenue for a hotel development.

Cost of investment

The main costs of an investment will be:

● planning costs
● costs of capital goods
● cost of financing investment
● running costs of the investment

Planning costs

The planning costs of an investment include consultancy costs for technical feasibility, market research, competitor scanning, financial appraisal and overall project planning. For large-scale projects, planning costs can be considerable and add to the overall project timetable. The British Airports Authority (BAA) has been planning a substantial investment in a new passenger terminal – terminal 5 – at Heathrow Airport. Table 12.2 shows the original timetable for the project as envisaged in 1992. It can be seen that the planning, consultation and enquiry phase represents an equivalent 5-year period to the construction phase, doubling the project timetable to 10 years.

Exhibit 12.2 shows that by 1999, the project was already 4 years behind schedule.

Table 12.2 Terminal 5 timetable

Year	Projected stage
1992	Local consultations
1992	Submission of planning application
1994	Start of public planning inquiry
1995	End of public planning inquiry
1997	Government decision expected *Subject to planning approval being granted*
1997	Start of construction
2001	Completion of phase 1 construction
2002	Opening of phase 1
2016	Terminal reaches maximum capacity

Source: BAA (1992).

Exhibit 12.2   High costs of terminal failure

1999: If things had gone according to plan, BAA's Terminal 5 (T5) would by now be a busy construction site of cranes, half-completed buildings, and road links. The fact that the site is still occupied by the Perry Oaks Sludge Works demonstrates how far the project has slipped behind schedule. The year 2001 was to have seen the completion of phase 1 of the project, but it will now be the year when the government gives its final decision on whether the project is allowed to go ahead. This will push back the opening of phase 1 from 2002 to 2006, if the project is allowed.

The main delay to the project has been the public enquiry which in the event has taken 3 years to hear the evidence of the BAA, local authorities, environmental campaigners and other interest groups. The overall project has an estimated cost of Euros 2.6 billion. But the delays to the project mean that the planning and preparation costs, which have to be paid even if the project is eventually rejected, have now reached Euros 360 million. These costs have been needed to pay for legal teams at the public enquiry, design costs of the building and the cost of land purchase.

BAA insists that Terminal 5 is needed to maintain Heathrow's competitive edge against rival European hubs such as Amsterdam, Frankfurt and Paris. The new terminal would allow passenger numbers to rise from 58 million per year to 80 million. Anti-T5 groups argue that the project would bring about unacceptable levels of congestion and pollution to a densely populated area of West London.

Source: The author, from press reports 1999.

Costs of capital goods

The capital costs of an investment are the costs of buildings, plant and machinery. In some cases these are known costs, since there is a market in commonly purchased capital goods such as computer systems, vehicles and standard buildings. For more complex investments capital costs can only be estimated in the planning stage and for large construction projects, estimates of costs are notoriously unreliable. The original estimate for building and equipping the Channel Tunnel was £5bn but by 1993 the figure had been revised to £10bn. Such escalations in costs are typical of large construction projects. In the case of the Channel Tunnel, factors such as price increases in materials, increased wages, unforeseen technical difficulties in boring the tunnel, specification changes to improve safety, and legal disputes over costs between Eurotunnel and the construction company Trans-Manche Link (TML) have all added to the increased costs.

Cost of financing investment

Finance for investment projects may be found internally out of a company's profits, or externally from the capital markets, for example, through banks or share issues.

External funding by loans carries costs in terms of interest rates that have to paid for the duration of a loan. These interest rates may be fixed or variable. External funding by share issue incurs issue costs but the costs of funding (i.e. the dividend payments to shareholders) are then tied into future profits.

It might appear that internally generated funds do not carry any special costs, since a company does not have to pay interest on its own funds. However there is an opportunity cost of using internal funds. That is the cost in terms of other uses to which the funds could have been put. A company could put funds on deposit in the money markets and gain interest on such deposits. Thus even where internal funds are used for investment, a notional interest rate will be used to represent their opportunity cost. In general, higher interest rates will act as a disincentive to investment.

Running costs of the investment

The running costs of an investment will include all the other costs of operating the project. These include labour costs, maintenance costs and raw material costs. New technology which reduces running and production costs can be an important cause of investment.

Revenue from investment

Total revenue from sales resulting from an investment project can be calculated by multiplying the selling price by the quantity sold and thus the main factors affecting the revenue obtained from an investment are:

● price of output
● quantity of output sold
● other factors

Price of output

The price of the output of an investment project will largely depend on demand and the competition in the market under consideration. This is discussed fully in Chapter 6, and in general the less competition, the more power a supplier will have to set price. Where a monopoly or near monopoly exists, price can be producer-determined (but quantity sold will reflect demand). However, potential competitors will move quickly to produce near substitutes where possible, particularly if a premium price is being charged. Where a few producers exist in a market (oligopoly or monopolistic competition), the impact of a new entrant will change the actions of those already in the market and thus lead to unpredictability. In a perfectly competitive market prices will be driven down to reflect the lowest average costs in the industry.

Thus, although a company may have market intelligence about current prices in the market where its investment is to take place, any estimate of prices in future years is likely to be very uncertain. Channel Tunnel prices, for example, have changed considerably between the planning stage and the present. This reflects the changing marketing strategies of competing ferry and airline companies.

Quantity of output sold

Quantity sold will be closely related to price charged. However it will also be related to factors including consumers' income, competitive prices and advertising. Figure 12.2 shows forecasts of passenger demand for airports in

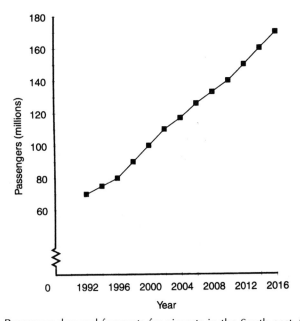

Figure 12.2   Passenger demand forecasts for airports in the South-east. Source: BAA.

the South-east of England. These are part of the feasibility study for London Heathrow's Terminal 5. Clearly there are a range of factors, for example environmental pressures, taxes, fuel costs, which might cause the forecasts to be wrong.

Other factors

Government policy may affect the revenue that derives from an investment project in several ways. First, government taxation policy may affect prices (VAT), or spending power (income tax) or profits (corporation tax). Second government legislation may affect the demand for goods, and finally monopolies and mergers legislation may have an impact upon prices that can be charged.

Expectations play a key part in investment decisions. Expectations reflect views about how successful the economy will be in future years. Where investors have a pessimistic view about the future economy they will generally defer investment decisions.

Property development is a prominent feature of much leisure and tourism investment. Whilst rental income is a part of the anticipated revenue from such developments, capital appreciation can also be an important factor. Thus, such developments are often sensitive to expectations about future prices of property.

Above all, the factors surrounding an investment decision are subject to a great deal of uncertainty. Few of the factors have known values. Current interest rates are known, and where an investment obtains funds at fixed rates, this provides a predictable element. However, where funds are obtained at variable interest rates, considerable uncertainty will exist. Similar uncertainty surrounds the final costs of complex capital projects, price of output and demand for the final good or service. These are all subject to changes in the competitive and political, economic, socio-cultural and technological (PEST) environments.

Appraisal techniques

Having identified the factors affecting the profitability of an investment, these can be used in a variety of quantitative methods to aid decision making. Investment appraisal reports may appear very authoritative, neatly summarizing projects in figures. However in view of the uncertainties discussed in the previous section, care should be taken to examine the assumption on which appraisals are made. The main appraisal techniques are:

- payback method
- average rate of return
- net present value
- internal rate of return

Payback method

This method compares investment projects by measuring the length of time it takes to repay the original investment from the revenues earned. It therefore favours projects which have the earliest payback. The key problems with this method are first that earnings that an investment may make after the payback period are not taken into account, and second revenues are not discounted so earnings within the payback period are given equal weight irrespective of the year they appear in. On the other hand, the sooner the payback, the less a project will be subject to uncertainties, and some companies may see speed of return as a priority over total return. Table 12.3 shows an example of this method and it can be seen that in this example the payback period is 3 years, when the cumulative cash flow reaches zero.

Average rate of return

This method calculates the total earnings from an investment and divides this by the number of years of the project's life. This figure is then expressed as a percentage of the capital costs of the project. For example, if an investment project had a total cost of £100 000 and earned a total of £50 000 over 5 years, the annual earnings would be £10 000, which represents an annual average rate of return of £10 000/£100 000 or 10 per cent on the capital employed. This method also fails to discount future earnings.

Net present value

The net present value method takes into account the fact that future earnings have a lower value than current earnings. For example, £100 today could be invested at a rate of interest of 10 per cent to give £110 in a year's time. Working this backwards, £100 in a year's time is only worth £90.91 today at a rate of interest of 10 per cent. In other words, it has been discounted at a rate of 10 per cent to find its present discounted value. Discount tables exist to assist such calculations but there is also a formula for calculating present discounted value (PDV):

$$PDV = R_t/(1 + i)^t$$

where R = return, t = year and i = rate of interest or discount rate (expressed as decimal).

Table 12.3 Payback method of investment appraisal (£m)

Year	0	1	2	3	4
Costs	2.4	0.4	0.4	0.4	0.2
Revenue	0	1.0	1.2	1.4	1.4
Cash flow	−2.4	0.6	0.8	1.0	1.2
Cumulative cash flow	−2.4	−1.8	−1.0	0.0	1.2

Table 12.4   Discounted cash flow method of investment appraisal (£m)

Year	0	1	2	3	4
Net revenue		2.0	5.0	6.0	6.0
Present discounted value of net revenues		1.82	4.13	4.5	4.1

Note: Discount rate = 10 per cent.

Row 2 of Table 12.4 shows the net revenues of a project with an initial capital cost of £16 m in years 1–4, and row 3 shows these figures discounted to their present values using a discount rate of 10 per cent.

The net unadjusted revenues sum to £19 m and thus the project appears to show a net surplus of £3 m. However, the net present value technique compares costs and revenues discounted to their net present values. The total net revenue falls to £14.55 m when discounted to present value, and the project shows the following net present value:

Costs at present value	£16.00 m
Revenue at present value	£14.55 m
Net present value	−£1.45 m

This negative figure indicates an unprofitable investment.

Internal rate of return

The internal rate of return method also uses discounted cash flow. It calculates the discount rate that would equate the net present value of future earnings of an investment to its initial cost. This rate is called the internal rate of return. An investment will be profitable if its internal rate of return exceeds the rate of interest that has to be paid for borrowing funds for the investment, allowing a margin for risk. A feasibility study into a fixed channel link by Coopers and Lybrand and Setec Economie in 1979 concluded that the internal rate of return on the project would be between 11 and 18 per cent.

When comparing investment projects those with the highest internal rate of return will be selected.

Changes in the level of investment

Changes in the level of investment will be caused by changes in the costs and predicted revenues of investments. These factors are summarized in Table 12.5.

The fall in investment in 1990 shown in Table 12.1 and Figure 12.1 can be attributed to high interest rates making the cost of borrowing funds to invest

Table 12.5   Factors causing changes in investment

	Investment conditions	
	Good	*Poor*
Rate of interest	Low	High
Capital costs predictable?	Yes	No
Project duration	Short	Long
Price of output	Predictable	Uncertain
Market for product	Rising	Uncertain
Competition in proposed market	Limited	Competitive
Political stability	Stable	Unstable
Expectations about economy	Optimistic	Pessimistic
Sensitivity of project to shocks	Low	High
Spare capacity	Low	High

high, falling consumers' expenditure, and poor expectations about the economy in the medium term. Falling demand leaves machinery under-utilized and thus there is little need for new machinery.

The accelerator principle

Investment activity in economies tends to be volatile, that is subject to considerable fluctuations. One of the explanations of this is the accelerator principle.

When demand for consumer goods and services is relatively stable in an economy, much of the demand for capital goods will take the form of replacing worn-out plant and machinery. However, if demand for final goods rises and there is no spare capacity in an industry, then new machinery will have to be purchased. Thus the demand for capital goods will significantly increase to include new machines as well as replacement machines. Similarly, if the demand for final goods in an economy falls, firms will find they have over-capacity and too many machines. They will reduce the stock of machines to the new lower levels needed by not replacing worn out machines, so the demand for capital goods will fall. Thus a rise in the demand for final goods will cause an accelerated rise in the demand for capital goods, and a fall in the demand for final goods will cause an accelerated fall in the demand for capital goods. The accelerator theory helps to explain the sudden fall in investment in 1990, in response to a fall in consumer demand.

Risk and sensitivity analysis

Sensitivity analysis is a technique for incorporating risk assessment in investment appraisal. It works by highlighting the key assumptions upon which investment appraisal figures were based. For example, revenue forecasts for an investment might be based upon:

- sales of 100 000 units per year
- market growth of 3 per cent per year
- price of £3 per unit
- exchange rate of £1 = $1.5

Sensitivity analysis would calculate the effects on an investment appraisal of changes in these assumptions. Such analysis would demonstrate the effects of, for example:

- sales of 80 000 units per year
- market growth of 1 per cent per year
- price of £2.50 per unit
- exchange rate of £1 = $1.75

and thus illustrate a project's sensitivity to a variety of scenarios.

Sources of funds

The main sources of funds for private sector investment include:

- retained profits
- new share issues (see Chapter 2)
- loans
- government assistance (see Chapter 13)

Government policy

In general, right-wing governments interfere as little as possible in free markets, while left-wing governments are often prepared to offer financial assistance where a project provides employment in areas of high unemployment, or where there are wider community benefits. Exhibit 12.3 illustrates government funding for an urban-renewal project.

Review of key terms

- Investment = expenditure on capital goods and working capital.
- Fixed capital = durable capital goods such as buildings and machinery.
- Working capital = finance of work in progress such as raw material stocks, partially finished and unsold goods.

Exhibit 12.3   City Challenge: a neat stroke

City Challenge, the state-funded body responsible for urban renewal projects, has provided £195 000 towards an eight-lane swimming pool that was opened in April at Spitalfields in central London.

The 13-acre site, formerly a fruit and vegetable market, was bought by developers who had planned a large housing and commercial complex but were blown off course by the recession.

The pool represents an interim use for the site which might otherwise remain derelict in a part of London with few local amenities and many social difficulties.

Source: The author, 1994.

- Net investment = gross investment – depreciation.
- Payback method = appraisal technique to see how quickly an investment repays its costs.
- Average rate of return = appraisal technique where the average annual returns are expressed as a percentage of the original capital costs.
- Net present value = appraisal technique where all future revenues are recalculated to their present value so that a comparison can be made with the project costs.
- Internal rate of return = the rate of return of a project on capital employed, calculated by finding the rate that discounts future earnings to equal the capital costs.
- Accelerator theory = explanation why changes in consumer demand lead to larger changes in demand for investment goods.
- Sensitivity analysis = investigation of sensitivity of an investment project to changes in forecasts.

Data questions

Task 12.1

Shares: flights of fantasy – Quentin Lumsden

One of the intriguing aspects of Euro Disneyland is that it is so difficult to value the shares. The stockbrokers SG Warburg has done projections, discounting back the stream of future earnings, to a figure from which it concludes the shares are fair value – and a hold – at the current 1650 p. One number that stands out is the population of the catchment area for Euro Disneyland – some 400 million people. The projections on which many people have done their sums is that there will be 11 million visitors in the first year, rising gently thereafter. But if revenues grow more strongly than expected, the impact on profits will be dramatic because the costs are largely fixed. If there are 1 million more visitors than expected, or ticket prices in future years are 10 per cent higher than budgeted, or if visitors spend an extra pound more than expected on food and merchandise, then profitability will rise at a meteoric rate.

The reasonable conclusion is that Euro Disneyland has a considerable capacity to provide investors with favourable surprises.

Source: *Independent on Sunday*, 22 March 1992 (adapted).

Will Mickey turn his back on Euro flop?

The tragic tale of Euro Disneyland has dragged on since the Paris-based theme park opened its gates in April 1992. The fairy tale turned horror story is entering a new and crucial chapter. The figures are awesome; the park last year lost £607 m. Euro Disney's share prices went into free fall following news of the losses last November and are currently trading around the 400 p mark.

Source: *Observer*, 6 March 1994 (adapted).

Questions

1 What is meant by 'discounting back the stream of future earnings'? Why is this done?
2 The first article was written just before the opening of Euro Disneyland. What factors would the writer have taken into account when evaluating Euro Disney's potential profitability? Which of these factors were certainties?
3 What do the two articles demonstrate about investment appraisal?
4 Evaluate the Disneyland Paris (Euro Disneyland) investment project in the light of its performance to date.

Task 12.2   Reverberations from the Asian economic crisis

The domino effect of the slump in the Asian economies was demonstrated in 1998 by the sacking of 760 staff of Hong Kong's Cathay Pacific Airways. This represented about 5 per cent of its total workforce of 15 000.

Speaking in 1998, David Turnbull, managing director of Cathay Pacific, said 'Just six months ago I would never have thought we would be forced to resort to such painful measures.' The cuts are the most dramatic in the history of Cathay Pacific and follow a recent announcement to reduce the workforce in building maintenance and other services by 550. Mr Turnbull underlined the urgency of the crisis by his comments on December 1997 figures for the airline which he described as 'truly appalling' when turnover fell by more than 25 per cent. The airline reported that 1997 had been a very bad year and that the prospects for 1998 showed few signs for improvement.

Other airlines operating in the region have been similarly affected. Philippine Airlines has an order for 15 new aircraft which were scheduled to be delivered in 1998 – this contract has been put under review. The Australian airline Qantas, has reduced its services to Indonesia, Thailand and Malaysia. Similarly, Garuda, the state-owned airline of Indonesia has been unable to meet a payment for planes leased from Airbus.

The worry in Europe and America is that as airlines hit by the Asian economic crisis seek to reduce capacity this will have a severe knock-on effect leading to cuts in the production of aircraft – particularly by Boeing and Airbus. However, a spokesperson from British Aerospace was confident that a contract to supply 20 Hawk jets to Indonesia would survive the economic crisis.

Source: The author, 1999.

Questions

1 What is the accelerator principle? Explain its relevance and mechanism using this article.
2 What determines the demand for aircraft? Is this demand likely to be stable? How does the globalization of the economy affect the sales of aircraft?
3 The article suggests that 1998 would also be a difficult year for airlines. By reference to the data in Task 9.1, evaluate the likely prospects for investment in aircraft in 1998 and 1999, supplementing your answer with more recent data if possible.

Task 12.3   City: black hole – Jeremy Warner

There was a depressing familiarity about last week's news that Eurotunnel has lost another round of its battle to keep the lid on the costs of the Channel Tunnel. Unless it can reverse the order on appeal, Eurotunnel is going to have to pay the Channel Tunnel contractors a lot more to complete the project than previously thought – making yet another refinancing of the venture look almost inevitable.

You don't need much experience of the construction industry to know that in all building projects the customer inevitably ends up paying considerably more than anticipated. At the risk of embarrassing Warburg Securities, however, I am going to quote from a City circular issued by the firm as part of the marketing effort for Eurotunnel shares when they were first sold to the public in the Autumn of 1987. 'We believe,' the circular said, 'the balance of probability is that Eurotunnel will be completed both on time – May 1993 – and to budget.' The projected cost of the Channel Tunnel was then £4.8 bn. After numerous upgradings, that figure had risen to more than £8 bn by last November. It's a racing certainty that by the time the tunnel opens (late, naturally) the final tally is not going to be far south of £10 bn – or roughly double the original estimate.

So were investors and bankers conned? Sir Alastair Morton, chief executive, and all the others involved in raising finance for Eurotunnel, no doubt were convinced that what they were saying was true. A part of this was to boast how the contracts had been deliberately designed to thwart the contractor's natural tendency to inflate his price. It's all proved so much hogwash and one suspects that deep down everyone must have guessed there wasn't a hope in hell of bringing the project in on budget. The imperative was to make sure it was built, a noble enough aim in itself, but hardly the first priority of the investor. It's possible the tunnel will still yield an adequate return, but it's looking increasingly less likely.

The inflated cost of the tunnel is only part of the problem. The greater imponderable is revenues once the system is up and running. It's hard to see why Eurotunnel's revenue predictions should be any more believable than its estimate of costs.

Source: *Independent on Sunday*, 5 April 1992.

Questions

1 What would be an 'adequate return' for the channel tunnel project? How would this be calculated?
2 Why are construction costs difficult to predict?
3 What impact does the late opening of the channel tunnel have on profit forecasts?
4 Why is this article sceptical about revenue predictions?
5 Evaluate the success of the Channel Tunnel.

Task 12.4   Port Aventura: trying not to be a black hole

There are black holes and there are black holes. The one is a successful ride at Alton Towers. The other is the financial mess that EuroDisney got itself into. EuroDismal as named by its critics, now renamed Disneyland, Paris, down but not yet out.

The Disney fiasco seems perhaps a strange backdrop against which to launch Port Aventura, Europe's second biggest theme park, near Salou on the Mediterranean coast of Spain, due to open in April 1995.

In fact the Tussauds group, owners of Alton Towers (and owned by Pearson, *the Financial Times*/Penguin books/Thames TV conglomerate), has been negotiating to become the theme park's largest shareholder and operating manager.

'Just because EuroDisney has got problems, it doesn't mean that major theme parks in Europe are bound to fail,' says Ms Rebecca Winnington-Ingram, a leisure industry analyst with Morgan Stanley. And of course she is right. Perhaps it is the success of Alton Towers in England that has tempted the Tussauds group into this £200 m Spanish venture.

There are key differences between Port Aventura and EuroDisney, not least of which is the scale of the projects: Disneyland, Paris attracts 11 million visitors a year, but Port Aventura is forecasting 2.7 million in its first year rising to 5 million. Port Aventura is only open for 156 days a year under summer skies (when more than 15 million summer tourists are within easy reach), where Disneyland, Paris is open all year under much more threatening northerly skies.

Port Aventura has also avoided some of Disneyland, Paris's vast fixed costs by concentrating on the theme park and not investing in the accommodation side. Ray Barret, a Tussauds director, offers the following analysis: 'Euro-Disney got its theme park right and what went wrong was its inability to fill its [six] hotels.' The Mediterranean strip in which Port Aventura operates includes large resorts such as Benidorm and has an abundance of hotels already in existence.

The two parks also have a different gearing for their royalty, management and consultancy charges. The Walt Disney Corporation took a massive 31.5 per cent of EuroDisney's operating income from its opening date. Similar charges payable from Port Aventura to Busch Entertainment (the park's designers) and to Tussauds (its managers) start at 12.4 per cent of operating income and are set to fall to 10.4 per cent by 1998.

Source: The author, adapted from press cuttings, January 1995.

Questions

1 Why is Port Aventura likely to be more of a successful investment project than Euro-Disney?
2 Identify four key factors that might be used in conducting a sensitivity analysis on this investment and evaluate their possible impact.
3 Evaluate the success of Port Aventura.

Short questions

1 Distinguish between net investment and gross investment.
2 How important is the rate of interest in affecting the decision to invest in a project?
3 Distinguish between the short-term and long-term effects of investment to an economy.
4 Evaluate the payback method of investment appraisal.
5 What is a project's internal rate of return?
6 Distinguish between working capital and fixed capital.
7 Why is sensitivity analysis used?

Websites of interest

UK share prices   http://www.moneyworld.co.uk/stocks/
Railtrack, www.railtrack.co.uk
British Airways: investor information
   http://www.british-airways.com/inside/ir/index.shtml

Granada Group plc   http://www.granada.co.uk
Marriott International   http://www.marriott.com
McDonald's Corp.   http://www.mcdonalds.com
Nintendo of America Inc.   http://www.nintendo.com
Scottish and Newcastle, plc   http://www.scottish-newcastle.com
Sony Corporation   http://www.sony.com
Time Warner Corporation   http://www.timewarner.com
Trump Hotels and Casinos Resorts Inc   http://www.trump.com
Wilson Sporting Goods Co.   http://www.wilsonsports.com/
Virgin Atlantic   http://www.bized.ac.uk/compfact/vaa/vaa/index.htm
Learning help in economics and business studies
    http://www.bized.ac.com

13 Investment and the public sector

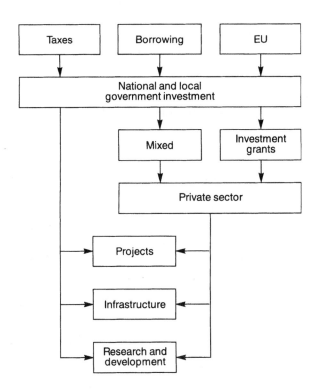

Objectives

The Thatcher revolution caused a fundamental rethink of public investment in the UK as the government sought to 'roll back the frontiers of the state'. As of 1999, the Labour government has maintained a similar stance. Opponents of public sector investment pointed to previous symbols of policy failure such as Concorde as representing the worst aspects of public sector investment – consuming ever-increasing sums of taxpayers' money and never achieving viable commercial sales. Thus Mrs Thatcher was adamant that the Channel Tunnel would be built using private funds or not at all. And so it was.

Yet the Channel Tunnel project also demonstrates the shortcomings of such a policy. The French rail link has been upgraded using public funds, resulting in a fast, efficient journey form Paris to the tunnel at around 185 mph. However, Eurostar trains have to brake sharply to around 60 mph when they enter the British rail link to Waterloo. Lack of private or public funding has meant the track has not been upgraded, and is now unlikely to match the French link before the year 2005.

By studying this chapter students will be able to:

- identify the sources of public sector investment
- identify different types of public sector investment
- describe different methods of public sector investment
- appraise public sector investment projects
- identify public sector incentives for private sector investment
- identify sources of funds for public sector investment

Sources, types, methods and aims of public sector investment

Sources

Public sector investment can be financed from different sources. At the supranational level, the EU is a key source, particularly through the European Regional Development Fund. At the national level, government channels leisure and tourism investment through public corporations, quangos such as the Sports Council and government departments such as the Department of Culture, Media and Sport. Local government is the other major source of public sector investment.

Types

Public sector investment may also be classified according to type. First public sector investment may be in buildings and land, for example parks, leisure centres and museums. Second public sector investment includes plant and machinery such as playground apparatus, computerized booking systems and canal lock equipment. Third public sector investment may be made in infrastructure.

Infrastructure, or social overhead capital, is the construction needed to support economic development, for example, roads, railways and airports, water and sewerage, power and telecommunications. Public investment on infrastructure has been relatively higher in France than that in the UK and exhibit 13.1 reports on the completion of a cornerstone in French public investment strategy.

Infrastructure development is a key part of tourism destination development as it has to precede specific project development such as hotels, leisure sites and restaurants.

Finally public sector investment may be spent on research and development, as illustrated in exhibit 13.2.

Exhibit 13.1   'The train arriving at runway 3 . . .'

Passengers landing at Charles de Gaulle airport used to be faced by a messy onward journey into France. Now, a TGV high-speed station has been opened. The £300 m glass and steel construction links four methods of transport: air, road, *métro* and high-speed rail. The TGV route is able to bypass Paris so that passengers can for example be in Lyons within 2 hours without having to change trains.

Announced by the French government in 1987, the project was co-funded between French Railways (SNCF) and Aéroports de Paris (ADP). Further development of the site is to include banks, restaurants, shops and a Sheraton hotel.

Source: The author, from news cuttings, November 1994.

Exhibit 13.2   Framework programme 5: EU-funded research and development in the new millennium

The fifth framework programme has a budget of Euros 15 billion and offers a strategic plan for the EU's research and development over a five-year period from 1999. Edith Cresson, the European Commissioner in charge of research and innovation, explained that the new programme is radically different from the previous one. 'We are moving from research based on performance for its own sake to research which focuses on the social and economic problems which face society today.'

The programme is divided into five thematic areas most of which include possible tourism and leisure. These are:

1 Quality of life and management of living resources.
2 User-friendly information society.
3 Competitive and sustainable growth.
4 Energy, environment and sustainable development.
5 Human potential and the socio-economic base.

R&D projects in leisure and tourism which have been funded by EU funds include

● ESCAPE – project to investigate pollution of coastal waters.
● A project to restore the stonework of European historic buildings by using laser techniques.
● TOURFOR – a project to use environmental management systems to limit environmental damage of tourism and recreation in forest areas.
● BRAIN – a project to develop mathematical models to improve soundproofing in aircraft cabins.

Source: The author, from *RTD information*.

Methods and aims

The main methods of public sector investment are first via projects which are wholly public sector-financed, second via projects which are jointly financed by the public and private sectors and finally via projects which are private sector investments but which are eligible for public sector investment incentive grants.

The aims of public sector investment include provision of goods and services which have significant public benefits, but which might not be profitable enough to attract private sector investment. Public sector investment may also be focused on projects aimed at the economic development or regeneration of a particular area. Exhibit 13.3 reports on the contribution of mixed public and private sector investment in the arts to the economy of Edinburgh.

Investment appraisal in the public sector

Cost–benefit analysis

Investment appraisal for private sector projects is relatively straightforward, as described in the previous chapter. If a project yields the required return on capital employed then the investment will go ahead.

The different nature of the public sector makes investment appraisal more complex in this sector.

Some parts of the public sector are run on private sector lines. In these cases an investment is required to earn a specified rate of return on capital employed and thus the investment decision is fairly clear-cut.

However, many public sector investments are made for reasons of wider public benefits and thus private sector methods of appraisal are inappropriate. In such cases cost–benefit analysis provides a more useful method of project appraisal. Cost–benefit analysis is described in detail in

---

Exhibit 13.3   Lights up for Edinburgh's new theatre

In 1992 Lothian and Edinburgh Enterprise Limited – part of the Scottish Development Board – backed a £21 m project to turn a bingo hall into a theatre. It is a mixed investment where £6.6 m has come from the private sector and no revenue subsidy will be needed in its operation. The result is a multi-use theatre with the largest stage in the UK.

The theatre represents a major project in Edinburgh's economic revival. It is estimated that 16 000 extra tourists will be attracted to the city, boosting the city's tourism income by £7 m to £257 m.

Source: The author, from news cuttings.

Table 13.1 Cost–Benefit analysis of canal restoration scheme

Costs	Benefits
Private costs Construction costs of project, e.g. ● Materials ● Labour ● Professional fees	*Private benefits* Revenue from project, e.g. ● Craft licences and charges ● Fishing licences ● Rentals from renovated buildings
Social costs Inconvenience costs to local residents of construction	*Social benefits* Drownings avoided through improved canal safety New jobs created by project Improved aesthetics of area

Chapter 19; however its essential details are that all the costs and benefits of a project are identified and weighed up, including social as well as private ones.

Table 13.1 shows an example of possible private and social costs and benefits for a canal restoration scheme.

Private sector investment appraisal of such a scheme would calculate the private costs of the project, and the private benefits. These would be discounted to net present value (as explained in Chapter 12) and since the private costs would almost certainly exceed the private benefits, the investment would not proceed.

However, cost–benefit analysis would analyse the wider costs and benefits. Some extra costs such as noise and congestion associated with the construction phase might be identified. Social benefits of the scheme would include lives saved through improved canal safety, greater public well-being caused by improved aesthetics from the project, and the effects on the local economy of new industries and employment attracted to the area because of the project. The total figures would be subjected to discounting to calculate net present value and it might well be the case that total public and private benefits would exceed costs. Thus there may well be an argument for public sector investment in the project.

Other factors affecting public investment

Whilst cost–benefit analysis is used for appraising some major public sector investment projects, its use is far from widespread. Public sector investment decisions are often determined by the priorities of the political party in power at a national or local level. Decisions will also be affected by interest group activity, and the general economic environment. Public expenditure at a local level has come under increasing direct and indirect control from central government since 1979.

Task 13.2 of the data questions at the end of this chapter illustrates how a move to the left in the Labour party on Birmingham council led to a reversal of its public investment policy. 'City boosterism' had been the philosophy behind a massive investment in leisure, sports and arts facilities, designed to bring visitors and jobs to an area suffering from the effects of de-industrialization. The new leadership has returned to a more conventional policy of investment in schools and housing.

Investment incentives for tourism and leisure projects

Areas of the UK which have high areas of unemployment are designated assisted areas, and the government uses incentives to attract firms and jobs to such areas. These include:

- Regional selective assistance. This is a discretionary grant based on the number of jobs that will be created and the capital costs of the project.
- European Regional Development Fund. This provides grants of up to 50 per cent for job-creating projects and projects to develop infrastructure.
- Regional enterprise grants. These encourage the growth of small businesses.

Exhibit 13.4 describes the steps taken by the European Commission to improve transport links in Europe, and the limited funding it has at its disposal.

Investment incentives are also available for some urban areas and are implemented through the following schemes:

- Enterprise zones. These small designated areas of acute industrial decline have simplified planning rules and 100 per cent allowances against corporation tax for expenditure on buildings.
- Urban development corporations. These have considerable powers to clear and develop derelict sites and encourage private sector investment.
- English Partnerships. This agency has inherited a large portfolio of factories, workshops and offices managed by English Estates.
- City Challenge. This is a Department of the Environment initiative to encourage local authorities to bid for funds for projects to improve inner-city areas.

Finally the Training and Enterprise Councils (TECs) can offer assistance in recruiting and training staff.

Exhibit 13.5 reports on public sector support for investment projects in leisure and tourism.

Exhibit 13.4 Trans-european networks

Piece by piece, the transport system for Europe is dropping into place and 1998 saw the opening of Europe's longest suspension bridge, a 10-mile road and rail link between Denmark and Sweden. The link is part of a Euro 400 billion project called TENs or Trans-European Networks planned up to 2010.

But with EU funding for this network limited to Euros 5 billion between 1998 and 2003, the Transport Commissioner, Mr Neil Kinnock, describes the role of the EU as one of pump priming, rather than full underwriter of costs. So EU expenditure is primarily targeted at feasibility and planning studies and securing funds from other sources.

These sources include the governments of EU member states and lenders such as the European Investment Bank and the European Investment Fund. Mr Kinnock has also stressed a greater role for private sector funding, saying, 'we know that the conventional source of infrastructure investment – the public sector – is not going to be able to meet all the costs'.

By 2015 the TEN plan will improve rapid road and rail links across the EU and into the new member states of eastern Europe. The key TENs scheduled for completion by 2005 include:

- The Madrid–Barcelona–Montpellier high-speed rail link, connecting to the TGV network (Euros 16 billion).
- The Paris–Luxembourg–Strasbourg–Mannheim high-speed rail link (Euros 4.5 billion).
- The London–Paris–Brussels–Amsterdam–Cologne high-speed rail link (Euros 19 billion).
- The Greek motorway network (Euros 10 billion).

Source: The author, 1999.

Exhibit 13.5 Leisure: public sector investment initiatives in 1999

The following examples shows support from a number of different public sector sources for leisure and tourism investment projects:

- Somerset District Council has opened a visitor centre on the River Parrett at Langport with financial help from the Rural Development Corporation.
- Tourism in Thanet has won funds from the European Regional Development Fund, and the UK Government Single Regeneration budget to support investment in local hotels and attractions.
- The Imperial War Museum is to build a 6000 square foot site in Manchester with a budget of £28.5 million. This is a mixed private sector/public sector initiative with £12.5 million coming from the private sector (Peel Holdings), £8.2 million from the European Regional Development Fund, and £2.5 million each from English Partnerships, Trafford Council and the Imperial War Museum.
- The Manchester Museum, the Manchester City Art Gallery and the Manchester Museum of Science and Industry share a £4.5 million grant from the European Regional Development Fund.

Source: The Author, 1999.

Sources of funds

Sources of funds for public investment include:

- operating profits
- taxation
- borrowing
- the national lottery

Operating profits, taxation and borrowing

Operating profits are rare in public sector organizations since, as discussed in Chapter 2, they are run for motives other than profit. Thus public sector investment is mainly financed from taxation receipts and government borrowing. This is a key reason why public sector investment is often under attack, particularly from the Treasury.

First opportunity costs are immediately apparent. Thus the opportunity cost of more public investment is higher taxes, or less government expenditure elsewhere, as illustrated in Figure 13.1.

The circle represents total government spending and no increases in taxes or government borrowing are assumed. An increase in public sector investment from *A0B* to *A0C* can only be accommodated by a fall in other government expenditure of *B0C*. Alternatively, it is assumed below that other government expenditure remains unchanged. In this case an increase in public sector investment from *XY* to *XZ* can only be financed through an increase in taxes or government borrowing of *YZ*.

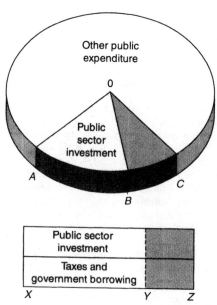

Figure 13.1   Opportunity cost of public sector investment.

Second, when the economy is performing badly, investment is often a target of government policy. If government borrowing is running too high, cutting social security payments or pensions has readily identifiable victims. Cutting investment generally results only in some improvement not taking place and therefore its consequences are more blurred.

The National Lottery

Whilst public spending is generally being squeezed by the Treasury, leisure and tourism is a key beneficiary of the National Lottery. Twenty-eight per cent of the lottery revenue (estimated at £5 billion annually 1998–2002) goes to five major causes, four of which will benefit leisure and tourism. These are charities, the arts, sports, national heritage and the Millennium Fund.

Projects in the arts which have benefited from the National Lottery include first, the South Bank arts complex in London. The National Theatre has recently completed a major refurbishment of its foyer area with the help of lottery funds. Second, the lottery has provided investment funds for the Tate Gallery's proposed new Bankside museum for modern art. The estimated cost of conversion of a disused power station in east London for this project is estimated at £80 m. The English National Opera is also seeking funds to renovate the London Coliseum.

The Sports Council has set up a lottery board to distribute its share of funds. Projects of between £5000 and £5 m can be considered for a grant of up to 65 per cent. Large projects include a new national stadium and local council sports facilities.

The National Heritage memorial fund has responsibility for channelling funds into areas such as museum collections, historic buildings and monuments, landscapes, libraries and industrial heritage.

Other examples of contributions of lottery funding to leisure and tourism investment projects include the following which were announced in 1999:

- The Natural History Museum Earth Galleries (£6 million from Heritage Lottery Fund).
- National Trust renovation of Paul McCartney's Teenage Liverpool home ((£47 500 from Heritage Lottery Fund).
- Redevelopment of Royal Naval Museum, Portsmouth (Heritage Lottery Fund).
- The National Space Science Centre, Leicester (£23 million from the Millennium Commission).

The public sector investment debate

Public investment has been subject to considerable debate during the Thatcher revolution and beyond. The Thatcher government took a stance against public investment based on the following arguments:

1 The public sector is not a good interpreter of people's wants and thus often invests in 'white elephants'.
2 The public sector is not good at ensuring efficient use of funds and tends to allow waste.
3 Public sector investment causes an increase in taxation or public borrowing.
4 Public sector investment 'crowds out' private sector investment.

The Thatcher government therefore removed a large slice of investment from the public sector through its privatization programme. It then concentrated its efforts on creating an 'enterprise economy' which it hoped would stimulate private sector investment by reducing income and corporation tax and making the labour market more flexible.

The arguments favouring public sector investment are:

1 There is insufficient incentive for the private sector to invest in public goods (see Chapter 7).
2 The private sector underinvests in goods which have mainly social benefits.

Thus, where the market is used as the main determinant of investment, infrastructure projects with important public and merit angles will tend to be overlooked, despite the fact that the future capacity of the economy may depend on them. This has led to calls to distinguish between capital spending and current spending in PSBR figures, since the former will involve future benefits.

Review of key terms

- Infrastructure = construction needed to support economic development.
- Cost–benefit analysis = full analysis of public and private costs and benefits of project.
- Net present value = discounting money paid at a future date to its present value.
- 'City boosterism' = investment in projects to regenerate city centres in economic decline.
- Assisted areas = areas of country eligible for government investment grants.
- Regional selective assistance = grant to attract job-creating projects.
- European Regional Development Fund = EU fund for projects and infrastructure to bring jobs to designated areas.
- Regional enterprise grants = grants to promote small businesses in assisted areas.
- Enterprise zones = designated areas of acute industrial decline having simplified planning rules and incentives expenditure on buildings.
- TECs = Training and Enterprise Councils.

Data questions

Task 13.1   *Canals and the superhighway*

No – its not that the UK's network of canals is about to take the loads off the roads. Its just a brilliant piece of lateral thinking that is all part of British Waterway's (BW) search for additional revenue. The result – a creative fusion of the old and the new. Starting in Scotland, optical fibre cables are being laid along canal networks to meet the growing demand for data communications.

BW itself reflects an odd mixture of the old and new. At its centre is a network of partially derelict canals and navigable rivers, most of which are some 200 years old. But its chief executive, Mr Brian Dice, brought with him modern management techniques honed over 25 years of working in the private sector at Cadbury Schweppes.

Private sector? But surely BW was itself privatized in the 1980s along with, amongst others, BT, BA and BAA. Apparently not. BW is still responsible to the Department of the Environment and privatization was ruled out because of its continuing need for public subsidy.

But BW has not been immune to the harsh winds of economic reality and the Treasury has cut its annual funding over the past 10 years by around 25 per cent to an annual figure of £50 m.

Brian Dice has sought to mitigate these cuts. 'I made it a priority that we stop whingeing and concentrate our efforts elsewhere, on the European Regional Development Fund, on central government's City Challenge and derelict land grant schemes and on local authorities and development corporations. The redevelopment of Sheffield canal basin, for example, uses all those sources. We are also keeping leisure fees, for the 1 million boaters and anglers on our canals, marginally ahead of inflation. Freight traffic, principally on the navigable waterways of northern England, also enhances our revenues, although no one is going to put computers on a barge. We have to exploit the honeypot sites and have more income under our own control. The transformation of Gloucester Docks, which now houses the National Waterways Museum, shows what can be done with local authority and private sector involvement. We are seeking similar partners for other undeveloped sites,' he explains.

However, the Treasury prefers BW to sell off surplus sites for private sector development, rather than participate in joint ventures which might involve exposure to financial risk.

The canal network was overlooked for years, and despite recent renovations such as the Kennet–Avon canal in Wiltshire, has a huge and urgent backlog of expensive repairs to lock gates, leaking channels and aqueducts. Although it still carries some freight, its main future lies more as a source of recreation for boaters, anglers, walkers, cyclists and nature-lovers. Nor should its contribution to the country's industrial heritage be overlooked.

But whilst people may agree on the importance of conservation and preservation in the current climate of environmental concern, the question as to how it is to be paid for remains unsolved.

Source: The author, from press cuttings.

Questions

1 What are the sources of investment funds for BW?
2 What sources of funds would be available to a privatized BW?
3 Compare the methods of determining the amount of investment in canals under private sector and public sector ownership.
4 Consider how the canal networks might appear by the year 2010, under private and public sector ownership.

Task 13.2   Rattled of Symphony Hall: Birmingham's bid for new greatness included balletic endeavour, Olympic attempts and brave new temples of culture. Then the city council changed its tune – Nick Cohen

When Simon Rattle raised his baton on 15 April 1991 to lead the City of Birmingham Symphony Orchestra into the first chords of Stravinsky's *Firebird*, the idea that a funding crisis could bring the most acclaimed conductor in the country close to resigning would have seemed preposterous.

At the opening night of the Birmingham Symphony Hall the evidence of the city's bold, almost reckless commitment to economic regeneration through the spending of millions on culture, tourism and service industries could not have been more obvious to the 2200 guests. The symphony hall, everyone agreed, was one of the finest in the world. Labour-controlled Birmingham City Council had, with the support of local Conservatives, uncomplainingly paid the bulk of the £30 m cost. No expense had been spared.

Next door, in Centenary Square, a £150 m convention centre, which was confidently expected to attract business tourists from around the world, was all but complete. Behind the centre a new 13 000-seat indoor athletics stadium which, city planners assured the voters, would help make Birmingham the UK sporting capital, was ready to receive athletes.

The policy of growth through prestige developments was outlined in a council development plan published shortly after the hall opened. 'To a large degree the prosperity of the whole city will depend on the city centre,' it said. 'Entertainment, culture, leisure and recreation have an increasingly valuable role. Indeed, [they] represent the very essence of a large metropolitan international centre.' In the seventies, the essence of Birmingham was making things people wanted to buy. But the recession of the early eighties wiped out 110 000 jobs in a city of 1 million people. In desperation at first, then with an increasingly evangelical conviction, Birmingham's councillors turned to American models of urban regeneration pioneered in the rust-belt cities of Baltimore and Detroit. Civic boosterism is the jargon label – the belief that eye-catching developments in the city centre could replace the lost manufacturing jobs by attracting high-spending tourists, conventioning businessmen and sports fans.

There were early warning signs that the policy was not working. Two Olympic bids failed in the eighties and a Super Prix car race collapsed. But it seemed almost bad taste at the time to mention these setbacks as the right-wing

Labour council and their allies in business and the council bureaucracy exuberantly proclaimed that Birmingham 'was ready to compete with Barcelona and Lyon's'.

Birmingham's boosterism in the eighties has been followed by a profound shift in the city away from prestige projects to a kind of left-wing, back-to-basics policy. Last year, Theresa Stewart, a 63-year-old grandmother and veteran left-winger, beat the right-wing candidates for the Labour leadership on a policy of stopping the search for prestige. Ever since, there has been a changed atmosphere in the city. Education, housing, social services were the priority, not tourists, theatre-goers and conventions. 'For 10 years I was told the council was developing municipal socialism,' she said after winning office. 'It's been more like municipal stupidity.' Ed Smith, the orchestra's general manager, recognizes the shift in emphasis. 'Not a day goes by without money worries,' he said. Other attractions are also in trouble.

Councillor Stewart has said she would 'not spend £10 on another Olympic bid'.

Stand outside the gleaming concert hall and strike out in any direction and in 15 minutes you will hit Birmingham's inner city – a ring of misery running clockwise from Handsworth through New Town, Aston, Small Heath and Sparkbrook to Ladywood. The statistics give a prosaic idea of the poverty. In the nine inner-Birmingham wards, 31 per cent of adults are out of work. Almost four out of 10 of the city's population receive state benefits. In the New Town district, to take just one example, the number of single-parent families is three times the national average and two out of three residents do not have a single O-level or GCSE. If the symphony hall, convention centre and the rest were really to be the source of regeneration, then these are the people who should have benefited from the trickle-down effect. They have not. Most of the jobs created were menial, part-time and low-paid. The council recognized the problem and devised a training programme to prepare the unemployed for full-time work in the convention centre. The result was pitiable. Just 19 inner-city residents got jobs. More significantly, money was diverted from the core services the poor depend on to fund the building boom. An analysis by the University of Central England (formerly Birmingham Polytechnic) estimated that £123 m was taken from Birmingham City Council's housing budget and that spending on school buildings fell by 60 per cent while the lavish city centre developments were being built. Most notoriously of all, the council took more and more from the budget for education, leaving Birmingham with some of the worst schools in the country. In 1991 Birmingham was spending £46 m less than the amount recommended by central government. Birmingham city centre may look marvellous, but it is a gleaming heart surrounded by a decaying body. Councillor Stewart cannot knock down the convention centre, much as she may like to, and the symphony hall and indoor arena will remain. But it is clear that from now on the council's priorities will be housing and education. An extra £43 m will be pumped into schools this year and the money will have to come from somewhere.

Source: The Independent, 9 March 1994 (adapted).

Questions

1 What was the economic rationale behind 'city boosterism'?
2 What factors would you take into account in conducting a cost-benefit analysis on investment in 'city boosterism'?
3 What factors caused a change in Birmingham's investment strategy?
4 What were the opportunity costs of 'city boosterism' in Birmingham?

Task 13.3   Public spaces: lost Victorian heritage

1832: The Whig government conceives the idea of 'public walks'.

1837: Joseph Hume MP tables a parliamentary motion calling for the provision of open spaces to be financed from the public purse for the enjoyment of the public.

1840: The Arboretum in Rosehill, Derby, is opened to fanfares and fireworks. Joseph Strutt commends the park as offering local workers 'the opportunity of enjoying, with their families, exercise and recreation in the fresh air and in public walks and grounds'. The Arboretum is planted with 913 types of trees and shrubs and more than 100 types of rose.

1979: Mrs Thatcher comes to power. Public sector spending cut.

1998: Patrick Weir of the *Guardian* surveys the sorry state of the park. He reports: 'The Lodge House, at the Rosehill Street entrance, serves bleak notice of what lies beyond: a crumbling, boarded up edifice, it would look more at home on a Hammer Horror set. Once in the park, signs of decay are all too evident. Public monuments are in disrepair, the bandstand is burned down, statues are missing and the centrepiece fountain is fenced off. Trees remain untrimmed, while graffiti, litter and dog dirt scar the environment. Gangs congregating at night render the park even less inviting.'

1999: Derby City Council awaits the result of a bid to the Heritage Lottery for £3 millions. The council has made provision to access an initial £200 000 of lottery funds by providing £43 000 in matched funds, but it is not confident of finding the next tranche of £750 000 necessary to release the rest of the lottery's £3 millions.

Steve Jardine, of the DERBYES! Campaign, hopes that residents, local businesses and grant-providing trusts can help. He said: 'The council can't do everything. People must be more proactive. It's a case of priorities and how much we value our parks. They are the lungs of the city, and, as recognized by the Victorians, areas where people can relax and play.'

Source: The author based on article in the *Guardian*.

Questions

1 What differing government attitudes to public sector investment does this article demonstrate?
2 What are the arguments for and against leaving provision of parks and gardens to the private sector?

3 Given the shortage of local council funds – suggest ways in which improvements in this park could be financed.
4 Explain the meaning of the terms *opportunity cost, crowding out, merit goods* and *public goods* in relation to this article.

Task 13.4   Three trains and a bridge

Railtrack, UK: Railtrack, the privatized owner of the UK rail infrastructure, announced in 1998 plans to spend £17 billion over the next decade on investment in the railways. Sir Robert Horton, Railtrack's chairman described Railtrack's plan as 'a blueprint to regenerate the railways'.

However, other commentators saw the proposed investment in a different light. The rail regulator Mr John Swift criticized Railtrack for a failure to invest adequately in the industry and announced he would be carrying out a detailed investigation into the sufficiency of Railtrack's plan. He said of Railtrack: 'Its statement contains very few commitments to deliver significant improvements across the rail network which passengers can recognize. I therefore intend to find out from train operators and funders of the railway whether Railtrack's statement meets their reasonable needs as required by its licence. I must be satisfied that Railtrack has sought to identify these requirements and reflect them in practical plans to improve the railway.'

Mr David Bertram, chairman of the central rail users' consultative committee, added to the criticisms saying: 'We had hoped for something more ambitious. The £4 million a day due to be spent by Railtrack may well not be sufficient, and the easing of congestion at many key points is only at the planning stage, with no firm dates yet'.

The London Underground, UK: The London Underground is to remain in public ownership but will receive a substantial injection of private finance. It is to benefit from a £7 billion programme of private-sector investment to be carried out over 15 years. Future plans for the Underground had included privatization but the government has opted for a private-public partnership.

Skye bridge, UK: Skye bridge spans the sea between the Isle of Skye and the Scottish mainland and was built under the private finance initiative (PFI). Under this programme public schemes are funded by private money. A private-sector consortia designed, built and financed the bridge. and shouldered risks such as construction delays. In return the government entered into a contract to pay for yearly use of the bridge.

The Madrid–Seville high-speed train, Spain: The Spanish Ministry of Transport paid for the pts 450 bn construction costs of the high speed train from Madrid to Seville which opened in 1992. It has been such a success that it later authorized the construction of the extension from Madrid to the French frontier to link with the TVE system. This should be completed by 2003.

Source: The author, 1999.

Questions

1 What different types of investment are demonstrated in this article?
2 In each case what is the main determinant of the level of investment?

3 What are the benefits and drawbacks of investment in transport schemes under regimes of:
- Private sector
- Private/public sector partnerships
- Public sector?

4 What factors would be taken into account in a cost–benefit analysis of the Madrid–Seville high-speed train?

Short questions

1 Under what circumstances would investment grants be available for the construction of a theme park?
2 What is cost–benefit analysis and why is it sometimes difficult to calculate?
3 Compare the sources of funds for public investment projects with sources available in the private sector.
4 What specific leisure and tourism projects might benefit from the national lottery?
5 Compare the factors determining an investment decision in the public sector with those in the private sector.

Websites of interest

English Sports Council   http://www.english.sports.gov.uk/
Forestry Commission   http://www.forestry.gov.uk/
Help for National Lottery Bids   www.havering.gov.uk/decs/lottery.htm
Department for Culture, Media and Sport   http://www.culture.gov.uk
British Tourist Authority   www.visitbritain.com
Railtrack   www.railtrack.co.uk
Learning help in economics and business studies   http://bized.ac.uk

Part Four
Leisure and Tourism Impacts on the National Economy

14   *Leisure and tourism: income, employment and inflation*

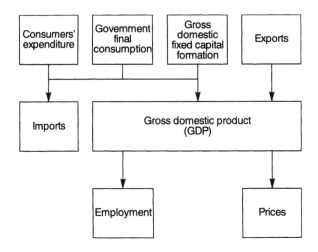

Objectives

Chapter 9 looked at the effects of the economic environment on leisure and tourism organizations. The aim of this chapter is to examine the other side of this question, and ask how the leisure and tourism sector contributes to the general level of economic activity. In particular it will examine the contribution of leisure and tourism to national output, national income and national expenditure, to the level of employment and consider the question of inflation. The issue of economic growth will be covered in Chapter 15, and international impact of leisure and tourism will be addressed in Chapter 16.

By studying this chapter students should be able to:

- distinguish between microeconomics and macroeconomics
- measure the total level of economic activity in an economy
- distinguish between changes in real and money GNP
- measure the contribution of leisure and tourism to GNP
- understand the contribution of leisure and tourism to employment
- utilize simple economic models of the macroeconomy

- understand and apply the multiplier principle
- measure inflation in the leisure and tourism sector
- interpret government policy in this area

GNP and the level of leisure and tourism activity

Macroeconomics

Chapter 2–7 dealt mainly with microeconomic issues. These were issues concerning the actions of individuals (demand) and firms (supply) and their interaction to determine prices in specific markets (e.g. the market for television sets, the market for air travel).

Chapters 14–16 look mainly at macroeconomic issues. These are issues that affect the whole economy. Macroeconomics deals with aggregates. Thus it adds together the spending of individuals to calculate consumers' expenditure, or aggregate demand. It adds together the output of individual organizations to measure national output or product. Similarly, the general price level and rate of inflation are investigated rather than prices in individual markets.

A simple macroeconomic model

Figure 14.1 illustrates a simple model of the national economy.

The economy is divided into two sectors, households and firms. Households own factors of production whilst firms utilize factors of production to produce goods and services. It is assumed in this initial model that all the output of firms is sold, and all income is spent. Additionally, there is no government activity, no savings or investment, and no international trade.

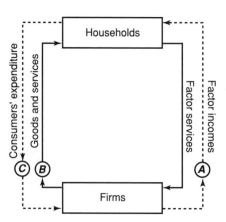

Figure 14.1   The circular flow of income

There are two flows in this system. First, 'real' flows are designated by unbroken lines. These represent the flow of factors of production (land, labour and capital) from households to firms, and the flow of goods and services, made from these factors of production, from firms to households. Second, 'money' flows are designated by broken lines. These represent factor rewards and payments for goods and services. For example, if a member of a household works for a firm it supplies the factor of labour and receives the reward of wages in payment. This payment can then be used to purchase goods and services from firms.

In this simple model of the economy firms buy factors of production to make goods and services, and households sell factors of production to buy goods and services. The model can be used to illustrate the concept of national income. National income is a measure of the total level of economic activity which takes place in an economy over a year. In Figure 14.1, if the total flow of money at point *A* was measured over a year, this would represent the level of national income. The same picture can be viewed from different angles. The total value of goods and services passing point *B* over a year would represent national output or national product, and the total amount of expenditure passing point *C* over a year would represent national expenditure. This gives an important accounting identity:

National income = national product = national expenditure

GNP and its measurement

The key rule in deciding how an item should be treated for national income calculation is whether it represents income earned by, or output (or expenditure on that output) produced by, UK factors of production. The three methods of measuring GDP are described in outline below.

Income method

In this method incomes are added up. Stock appreciation (the increase in the value of firms' stocks due to inflation over the year) is deducted since no increase in output has actually occurred because of this. A residual error figure is included since there will be discrepancies between each of the methods due to statistical collection errors:

    Incomes from employment
+ Incomes from profits
+ Incomes from rents, etc.
− Stock appreciation
− Residual error
= *Gross domestic product*

Expenditure method

Here total spending on final output under different headings is measured. Some goods will be semifinished or finished but not yet sold, so these are added as 'increase in stocks and works in progress'. Exported goods have been produced in the UK but not bought here, so their value is added. Imports have been bought in the UK but not produced here, so their value is deducted. Finally, taxes artificially inflate prices and subsidies undervalue the underlying production costs, so these are deducted and added respectively to move from market prices to factor costs. Once again a residual error is included.

  Consumers' expenditure
+ Government final consumption
+ Gross domestic fixed capital formation
+ Value of increase in stocks and works in progress
+ Exports of goods and services
− Imports of goods and services
− Residual error
= *Gross domestic product (at market prices)*
− Expenditure taxes
+ Subsidies
= *Gross domestic product (at factor cost)*

Output method

Outputs of different sectors of the economy are valued, taking care to avoid double-counting. This occurs where the output of one industry is the input to another. Double-counting can be avoided by measuring the value of final, rather than intermediate output.

+ Value of outputs from different sectors of economy
= *Gross domestic product*

From GDP to national income

Gross domestic product values the flow of goods and services produced in the UK. Some income arises from investments and possessions owned abroad, and thus an adjustment for net property income from abroad is made to GDP to calculate GNP. Finally, some investment spending occurs to replace worn-out machinery. Net national product (NNP) or national income deducts this amount (capital depreciation). These final calculations are summarized below:

  Gross domestic product
+ Net property income from abroad
= *Gross national product*
− Capital consumption
= *Net national product (national income)*

Real and money national income

When national income figures are compared over two different time periods, the effects of inflation can be misleading. Money national income or national income at current prices includes the effects of inflation. Real

Table 14.1 Average household expenditure 1996–97 (£ per week)

Category	£	£
Housing	49.10	
Fuel and power	13.35	
Food and non-alcoholic drinks	55.15	
Restaurant and café meals		*7.81*
Take-away meals eaten at home		*2.43*
Alcoholic drink	12.41	
Tobacco	6.07	
Clothing and footwear	18.27	
Household goods	26.74	
Pets and pet food		*2.78*
Household services	16.63	
Telephone		*5.46*
Personal goods and services	11.64	
Motoring	41.20	
Fares and other travel costs	7.45	
Air and other travel and transport		*3.51*
Bicycles, boats, purchase and repair		*1.25*
Leisure goods	15.17	
Books, maps, diaries		*1.14*
Newspapers		*2.01*
Magazines and periodicals		*0.84*
TVs, videos, computers and audio equipment		*6.08*
Sports and camping equipment		*0.66*
Toys and hobbies		*1.61*
Photography and camcorders		*0.94*
Horticultural goods, plants, flowers		*1.89*
Leisure services	33.95	
Cinema and theatre		*0.87*
Sports admissions and subscriptions		*2.19*
TV, video and satellite rental, TV licences		*3.26*
Miscellaneous entertainment		*1.04*
Educational and training expenses		*4.55*
Holidays in UK		*2.41*
Holidays abroad		*7.45*
Other incidental holiday expenses		*3.37*
Gambling payments		*3.82*
Cash gifts, donations		*5.00*
Miscellaneous	2.21	
Leisure items		**72.36**
All expenditure groups	**309.07**	

Source: Adapted from Office for National Statistics: *Family Spending, A Report on the 1996–97 Family Expenditure Survey.*

national income or national income at constant prices has had the effects of inflation removed.

Leisure and tourism contribution to GNP

Table 14.1 gives an indication of the importance of the leisure and tourism sector to the UK economy. From the data it can be seen that nearly 24 per cent of average expenditure in 1996 to 1997 was on leisure items. Table 14.1 shows the difficulties in defining leisure. The Office for National Statistics has two categories – leisure goods and leisure services. Some other leisure items have also been highlighted, and clearly some aspects of 'motoring' and 'clothing and footwear' will include leisure expenditure.

Care needs to be exercised in interpreting the contribution of leisure to national income using Table 14.1 alone. The exhibit records UK household expenditure, but as the earlier section on GNP calculation explained, exports of leisure goods and services need to be added to this figure and imports deducted. Imported services are clearly an important part of holiday expenditure. Similarly, some leisure activity does not involve an activity which is bought and sold in the market. Neither informal sports games nor DIY labour are measured in GNP statistics because of this, although both result in services enjoyed or value added.

Leisure and tourism employment

The demand for labour is a derived demand. Labour is demanded when a good or service is demanded. Employment in the leisure and tourism sector is thus directly related to expenditure on goods and services provided by the sector. Figure 14.2 shows the possible outcomes of leisure and tourism spending.

Some expenditure will be on imported goods or services and will therefore create employment overseas. UK leisure and tourism goods and

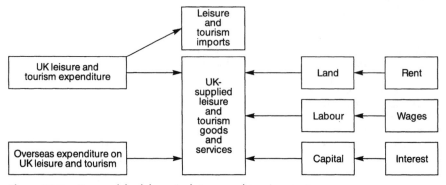

Figure 14.2 Demand for labour in leisure and tourism sector.

services will be supplied as a result of domestic expenditure and exports. The resulting derived demand for labour will also depend upon the price of labour relative to other factors of production and the possible technical mix of factors of production able to provide the goods or services. For example, if the price of labour rises, producers will attempt to use more machinery (capital) where this is technically possible.

Sector employment

Table 14.2 shows recent employment trends in leisure and tourism service industries.

Table 14.3 shows the total number employed and unemployed during the same period.

The general employment picture shown in Table 14.3 is one of rising employment (and falling unemployment) in response to the boom in the economy in the late 1980s, with employment prospects worsening again towards 1992 as a result of the recession and a fall in consumers' expenditure. The total employment in leisure and tourism services recorded in Table 14.2 mirrors this national trend, but within the data, numbers employed in libraries, museums, galleries, sports and other recreational services have

Table 14.2 Employment in leisure and tourism service industries (GB) in thousands)

	1990	1995	1996	1997
Hotels and other tourist accommodation	289	293	307	311
Restaurants, cafés, etc.	302	319	333	356
Public houses, bars and clubs	446	396	391	369
Travel agencies/Tour operators	72	79	83	75
Libraries, museums, galleries and other cultural activities	72	73	74	71
Sports and other recreational activities	290	298	312	297
Total	1471	1459	1499	1419

Source: Adapted from Office for National Statistics, *Labour Market Trends.*

Table 14.3 UK employed and unemployed (millions)

	1990	1991	1992	1993	1994	1995	1996	1997	1998*	1999
Employees in employment	22.9	22.3	21.8	21.6	21.5	21.9	22.3	22.8	23.2	
Unemployed	1.6	2.3	2.8	2.9	2.6	2.3	2.1	1.6	1.4	

Source: Adapted from Office for National Statistics, *Economic Trends.*
*Estimated

Table 14.4   Employees by sector in the UK (thousands)

	1985	1987	1989	1991	1993	1995
Manufacturing sector	5002	4815	4851	4319	3913	4026
Service sector	14 428	14 897	15 929	16 187	16 180	16 606
Paper, printing, publishing and recording media	463	459	472	462	445	465
Hotels and restaurants	1004	1009	1176	1209	1162	1230

Source: Adapted from Office for National Statistics, *Labour Market Trends*.

increased despite the recession of the early 1990s. The figures also show that unemployment has been a persistent feature of the UK economy in recent years, with unemployment not dipping below 1.4 million.

It is more difficult to extract employment in leisure manufacturing from published data, as many of the industrial classifications used by the Department of Employment include leisure and non-leisure items.

Table 14.4 shows the employment totals for the services and manufacturers sectors in the UK, with specific data for paper, printing, publishing and recording media, and hotels and restaurants.

Whereas employment in the services sector has grown in importance, manufacturing employment in the UK has shown a long-term decline. This is caused by two factors. First, technological progress enables productivity increases in manufacturing and thus the ratio of labour input to output declines. Second, manufacturing has been subject to intense competition from overseas where low labour costs in particular result in increased import penetration in UK markets. This is known as deindustrialization.

Wages

Wages in any particular labour market will be determined by the demand and supply of labour. The supply of labour to some parts of the leisure and tourism (for example, hotels and catering) sector is largely unskilled and this exerts a downward pressure on wages. This is illustrated in Table 14.5 which

Table 14.5   Average gross weekly earnings (GB, 1998) (£)

Industry	Manual	Non-manual
Manufacturing	330	454
Hotels and restaurants	199	335
Financial intermediation	373	522
Education	256	420

Source: Adapted from Office for National Statistics, *Labour Market Trends*.

shows the total wage costs per hour of selected industries. The costs shown include all employer costs (training and national insurance, for example) and thus are roughly 20 per cent higher than wages received.

Leisure and tourism multipliers

The analysis of data in the previous sections has looked at tourism and leisure contributions to national income and the economy at a single point in time. This is termed as 'static' analysis. However, consideration of Figure 14.1 shows that tourism and leisure expenditure, like any other form of expenditure, also has 'dynamic' effects due to the circular flow of income and expenditure in the economy. The initial effects of expenditure will generate income but there will be further effects as that income generates expenditure and so on.

Figure 14.3 illustrates the circular flow of income and expenditure derived from Figure 14.1. Assume now that there is an investment into this closed system of £100 000 on a new leisure complex. Firms will hire factors of production to the value of £100 000 and therefore national income, measured at point *A*, will rise by £100 000. However, the effects of the investment do not stop there. The workers who earned money from building the complex will spend their money in shops and bars, etc. Thus the incomes of shop and bar owners will rise. They in turn will spend their incomes. In other words, a circular flow of income and expenditure will take place. The investment expenditure sets in motion a dynamic process, and the total extra income passing point *A* will exceed the initial £100 000. This is known as the multiplier effect.

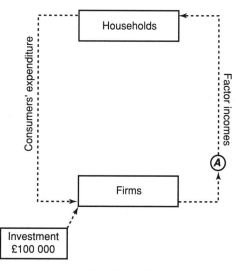

Figure 14.3 Investment and the circular flow of income.

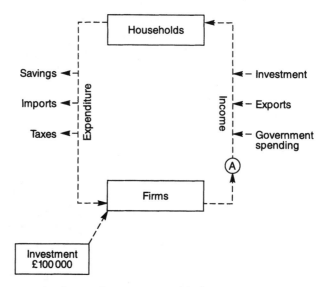

Figure 14.4 Circular flow with injections and leakages.

In the closed system illustrated by Figure 14.3, the effect would be perpetual and infinite, with the extra expenditure circulating round and round the system. In the real world however there are points at which money can leave and enter the system. This is illustrated in Figure 14.4.

The key leakages or withdrawals from the economy are savings, imports and taxes. Savings represents funds retained by households and firms. Imports result in expenditure flowing overseas, and taxes represent money taken out of the circular flow of income by the government in the form of income tax, VAT and corporation tax, for example.

On the other hand there are also injections or flows into the circular flow of income. These are investment, exports resulting in money from overseas entering the circular flow, and government spending including for example pensions and unemployment benefit. Clearly there are often strong relationships between specific leakages and injections. To keep the model simple, injections and leakages are located neatly around the system but in reality they occur in many different places.

The existence of leakages means that money is flowing out of the economy during each cycle. So, in the example of the £100 000 investment in a leisure complex, perhaps £10 000 might be saved by workers, £5000 spend on imported goods, and £10 000 taken in taxation. Thus the initial effect on national income measured at point A in Figure 14.4 is £100 000. Out of this, £25 000 will be lost in leakages from the economy, leaving £75 000 to recirculate, adding another £75 000 to national income at point A. This process then continues, but with each cycle becoming smaller. It should be seen that the size of the multiplier effect will depend upon the amount of the original injection under examination and the leakages from the economy.

The Keynesian multiplier

The Keynesian multiplier can now be formally analysed. The multiplier (k) shows the amount by which a change in expenditure (ΔEXP) in an economy leads to a change in national income (ΔY):

$$\Delta EXP \times k = \Delta Y$$

Thus if an increase in investment on a leisure complex of £100 000 led to a final increase in national income of £400 000, then the multiplier would have a value of 4.

The multiplier can be illustrated by reference to Table 14.6 and Figure 14.5.

Investment in the leisure complex of £100 000 is made and national income at point A is raised by £100 000. In round 2, leakages consist of £10 000 in savings, £10 000 in taxes and £5 000 in imports, leaving £75 000 in domestic expenditure to recirculate round the circular flow. An extra £75 000 is therefore added to national income at point A. In round 3 leakages consist of £7 500 in savings, £7500 in taxes and £3750 in imports, leaving £56 250 in domestic expenditure. This process continues, and the leakages reduce the value of extra domestic expenditure and national income at every round. In fact, the extra amounts of national income tend towards zero. If the additions to national income in column 6, for years $1 - n$ (where n = the year in which the effect has dwindled to near zero) were added up, they would sum to £400 000, thus giving a value for the multiplier of 4.

There is also a formula for calculating the multiplier:

$$k = 1/MPL$$

where MPL = the marginal propensity to leak (the proportion of extra income that leaks out of the economy).

Table 14.6 Multiplier rounds

Round	ΔS	ΔT	ΔM	ΔEXP	ΔY
1				100 000	100 000
2	10 000	10 000	5 000	75 000	75 000
3	7 500	7 500	3 750	56 250	56 250
4	5 625	5 625	2 812.50	42 187.50	42 187.50
5	4 218.75	4 218.75	2 109.36	31 640.63	31 640.63
6	3 164.06	3 164.06	1 582.03	23 730.47	23 730.47
7	2 373.05	2 373.05	1 186.52	17 797.85	17 797.85
8	1 779.76	1 779.76	889.89	13 348.39	13 348.39
9 – n	$\cdots$	$\cdots$	$\cdots$	$\cdots$	$\cdots$
Total				400 000	400 000

Note: Rounds $9 - n$ represent the remaining multiplier rounds. S = Savings; T = taxes; M = imports; EXP = expenditure; Y = income; Δ = change in.

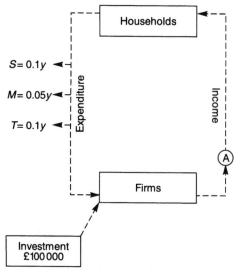

Figure 14.5   The multiplier round. S = Savings; M = imports; T = taxes; Y = income.

$$MPL = MPS + MPM + MPT$$

where MPS = marginal propensity to save (the proportion of extra income saved), MPM = marginal propensity to spend on imports (the proportion of extra income spent on imports) and MPT = marginal propensity to be taxed (the proportion of extra income taken in taxes.

In the above example, $MPS = 0.1Y$, $MPM = 0.05Y$ and $MPT = 0.1Y$, where Y = income. Therefore:

$$k = 1/(0.1 + 0.05 + 0.1)$$
$$k = 1/0.25$$
$$k = 4$$

Tourism multipliers

Considerable research has been done into the impact of tourism and leisure expenditure using multiplier techniques. The aim is to assess impact on incomes, output and employment at national, regional and local levels. This is clearly an important issue for governments in assessing the contribution of such developments to economic activity. The main multipliers developed for impact analysis are:

- the output multiplier
- the income multiplier
- the employment multiplier
- the government revenue multiplier

Table 14.7   Multiplier and expenditure impacts

Value of multiplier	Leakages from the economy	Impact of expenditure on income
High	Low	High
Low	High	Low

Taking the case of the tourism income multiplier (TIM), values vary according to leakages, as summarized in Table 14.7, and actual results include Canada (TIM = 2.5), UK (TIM = 1.8), Iceland (TIM = 0.6) and Edinburgh (TIM = 0.4).

Exhibit 14.1 discusses tourism multipliers in Scotland.

Leisure and tourism inflation

Inflation can be defined as a rise in the general level of prices or a fall in the purchasing power of money. It is measured by the retail price index (RPI). If one country has a faster rate of inflation than that of other countries, it can cause a decline in international competitiveness. This is likely to affect firms producing leisure products for the export market, and countries which rely on tourism. It is less likely to affect firms in leisure services since customers rarely have the option to seek lower prices overseas for these.

Constructing a tourism destination price index

It is possible to construct a tourism destination price index (TDPI) using a similar methodology to that used to construct the general RPI. Table 14.8

Exhibit 14.1   Small is beautiful

The Scottish Office has been studying the relationship between size of tourism establishments and effects on local income and spending. Its findings are that smaller organizations are more beneficial to local economies because the centralized buying activities of large organizations take spending out of the local area.

The Scottish Tourism Multiplier Study on Edinburgh made the following findings. In 1990, it is estimated that domestic and overseas tourists spent £276m in Edinburgh. For every £1000 spent by UK-resident tourists in Edinburgh, approximately £346 in income is generated locally and £127 in income is generated in the rest of Scotland. It takes about £27 000 of spending by domestic tourists to create one new job in the city.

Source: Scottish Office.

Table 14.8   Tourism price index, example (pesetas)

Item	Weight (W)	1996		1997		1998	
		Price (P)	P × W	Price (P)	P × W	Price (P)	P × W
Babycham (25 cl)	0.4	200	80	220	88	250	100
Beer (0.5 l)	4.0	190	760	195	780	200	800
Three-course meal	11.6	800	9280	880	10 208	950	11 020
. . .	. . .	. . .	. . .	. . .	. . .	. . .	. . .
. . .	. . .	. . .	. . .	. . .	. . .	. . .	. . .
Total			50 107		52 612		56 119
Index multiple				0.0019957291			
Index			100		105		112

Notes: Item = row 1, column 1; the dots in rows 6 and 7 denote the rest of the basket of goods.

gives an example of such an index. The steps are as follows (with rows and columns referring to Table 14.8):

- First it is necessary to define the population for whom the index is intended. This might be a specific index for golfers or skiers.
- Next an expenditure survey must be conducted to establish the spending patterns of the target population, ensuring that a representative sample of the target population is surveyed.
- From this two important findings should emerge – first a 'basket of goods' (and services) that lists the items bought by tourists can be compiled (column 1), and second the relative importance of each item can be gauged from the expenditure survey and each item given a weighting accordingly. For example, if an expenditure survey in Magaluf, Majorca showed 10 times more beer to be consumed than Babycham, then beer would be assigned a weighting 10 times more than that for Babycham (column 2). Thus if beer and Babycham both rose in price by 20 per cent, the effect of Babycham on the TDPI would be less than the beer effect.
- A survey of the prices of the basket of goods is then conducted (column 3).
- Expenditure on each item is determined by multiplying its price by its weighting (column 4).
- The total expenditure on the basket of goods is recorded (row 8).
- This amount is then converted to a index number with base 100, by using a multiplier (row 9), and this becomes the base year reading. (For example, if the expenditure total is £50, a multiplier of 2 is needed to convert the result to 100.)
- The basket of goods is priced at regular intervals (columns 5 and 7), with expenditure totals (row 8) being converted to an index number (row 10) using the multiplier established in the base year (row 9).

Table 14.9   *Tourism price index (exchange rate-adjusted)*

	1996	1997	1998
Total (Pts)	50 107	52 612	56 119
£1 = ? Pesetas	198	240	251
Total (£s)	253.06	219.22	223.53
Index multiple		0.39516	
Index	100	86.54	88.33

The index resulting from this exercise (Table 14.8) gives a picture of tourism inflation in the local currency. It is possible to adjust the index to reflect exchange rate conditions in different countries. Thus, whilst Table 14.8 measures tourism inflation for a Spanish visitor to a Spanish destination, Table 14.9 shows how the index can be adapted for a British visitor.

Table 14.9 uses the expenditure data from row 8 of Table 14.8. This is then converted to an equivalent in the currency under consideration (sterling in this example). A new index multiple is calculated to convert the raw expenditure figure to an index number with base 100. Comparison of the two tables shows the importance of considering exchange rate fluctuations when comparing prices between tourist destinations.

It must be remembered that any tourism price index represents an average picture, and individuals will be affected differently according to their particular expenditure patterns. Care must also be exercised in the collecting of data. There must be consistency of sources, otherwise the index will be distorted by changes in prices which result for example by moving from a local store to a supermarket.

Table 14.10 shows the relative sterling prices of commonly consumed leisure goods and services in different countries.

Table 14.11 shows some of the components of the RPI for the UK. It can be seen that inflation in the travel and leisure sector as a whole has been similar

Table 14.10   *International price comparison for leisure goods and services, 1998 (£)*

	UK	USA	Italy	Germany	France	Denmark
Compact disc	13.38	9.56	12.14	11.08	13.08	11.84
Paperback book	5.94	4.22	6.17	5.40	3.53	8.11
Cinema ticket	4.45	4.44	4.07	4.13	4.70	4.62
22-inch colour TV	387.46	201.19	375.23	307.96	351.46	501.83
Radio cassette recorder	49.99	34.67	51.49	50.52	57.48	60.18
Restaurant dinner	19.99	16.78	17.38	17.69	17.28	21.17
Drink at bar	3.29	3.29	2.58	4.20	4.90	5.59

Notes: Restaurant dinner for one, bar drink is double measure of spirits.
Source: Adapted from ECA International.

Table 14.11   UK retail price indices (January 1987 = 100)

	July 1994	July 1998	July 2000
All items	144	163	
Travel and leisure	146	164	
Audiovisual goods	75	56	
Tapes and discs	113	120	
Toys, photographic and sport goods	121	119	
Books and newspapers	159	187	
Gardening products	141	142	
Television licences and rentals	118	130	
Entertainment and other recreation	193	232	

Source: Adapted from Office for National Statistics, *Labour Market Trends*.

to that of the general level of inflation. However, within the sector audiovisual equipment prices have actually fallen whilst entertainment and other recreation prices have shown steep rises.

Government policy

Income and employment

Governments throughout the world see leisure and tourism as a source of employment, particularly where structural changes in the economy have led to job losses, as exhibit 14.2 shows.

Government policies to promote employment may include the following:

Demand management

Where there is unemployment throughout the economy, some economists advocate government stimulation of aggregate demand so as to induce more production and thus employment. Aggregate demand may be stimulated through tax cuts, increased government spending and interest rate cuts. The major drawback to such a policy is its tendency to encourage inflation.

Export-led policies

Overseas expenditure on leisure and tourism products can contribute to employment. Government policy here includes expenditure on the BTA which promotes the UK overseas and thus overseas demand for UK leisure and tourism services.

A low exchange rate also assists exports of services and leisure goods.

Exhibit 14.2   Artistic revival for Cill Rialaig

Cill Rialaig is a deserted village on the western fringes of Europe in County Kerry, Ireland. It never really recovered from the nineteenth century potato famine and the last inhabitants left in the 1950s. Plans for economic regeneration are being made based on the model of St Ives in Cornwall, England. It is hoped to encourage a community of artists and to build a £1 million art gallery, modelled on Cornwall's Tate.

Visiting artists are encouraged by a policy of rent-free accommodation and renovation of buildings is being helped by artists donating a finished picture to the project which is sold in the newly built local arts centre.

Mr O'Connell is typical of those who have found employment through the scheme. He works at the Arts Centre making picture frames. This is part of a government-sponsored back-to-work scheme for the long-term unemployed. He hopes to become self-employed when the government scheme runs out.

An application has been made to the Tourist Board, Arts Council and Ministry of Arts for funds to finance an international art gallery in nearby Waterville to attract major touring exhibitions more visitors. Local doctor Derry Gibson supports the scheme saying, 'We went through the eighties with everyone emigrating. Post offices and garda stations were closing. It was a very depressing time. An idea like this could revitalize the place and bring families back. We don't want hordes of campers and caravans, but if people could come and enjoy the peace and quiet and mix that with a bit of culture it would hold them in the area instead of them just passing through.'

Source: The author from article in the *Guardian*, 1998.

Wages and conditions of employment

The Conservative government had a policy of 'flexible labour markets'. The Conservative government view was that high wages, complex labour laws and unionization act as a disincentive to employers to create jobs. To this end wages councils which enforce minimum wages were abolished, and the UK opted out of EU labour laws, including paternity leave for fathers. A succession of laws curbing trade union activity was passed in the 1980s. The Labour government, elected in 1997, has introduced a minimum wage and has brought UK labour laws in line with that of the EU.

Project assistance

The government also considers direct assistance with projects on an individual basis, particularly where a project can be shown to bring employment to areas of high unemployment. There was for example considerable competition between France and the UK over inducements offered to lure EuroDisney to each country. The EU also has a regional fund which can be a source of financial assistance.

Inflation

Governments of countries with comparatively high rates of inflation may utilize counter-inflationary policy. However it is important first to diagnose the cause of inflation.

Causes of inflation

The causes of inflation can be divided into the categories of cost-push, demand-pull, monetary, taxation and expectations.

Cost-push inflation occurs when increased production costs are passed on as price rises. These can include first wage increases which outstrip productivity increases. Second increased raw material prices can be important. If raw materials are imported, a fall in the exchange rate can increase their local currency price.

Demand-pull inflation tends to occur when an economy is growing too fast. It arises because the aggregate demand in the economy exceeds the aggregate supply in the economy and therefore prices are bid up. Labour for example may become scarce, putting an upward pressure on wages.

Too rapid an increase in the money supply of an economy can cause an increase on consumer credit which can stimulate demand-pull inflation and accommodate cost-push inflation.

Increases in indirect taxes such as VAT will have an effect on prices, whilst if people expect inflation to rise, they will often seek to protect their living standards by higher wage demands. These of course will then cause the very inflation that people are seeking to avoid.

Counter inflationary policy

Government counter inflationary policy will affect the economic environment of leisure and tourism organizations.

Cost-push inflation may be tackled by a high exchange rate policy. Whilst this may be good for tackling inflation, it makes firms' exports less competitive.

Wage rises may be tackled by government-imposed incomes policy to curb pay increases. This may cause a deterioration in industrial relations.

Deflationary policy may be used to tackle demand-pull inflation. This may entail increasing interest rates to curb consumer borrowing, or increased taxes to reduce consumer spending. Either way, whilst inflation may be tackled, firms will suffer a general contraction in demand.

High interest rates are sometimes also used to curb overexpansion of the money supply by reducing the demand for borrowing.

Review of key terms

- Macroeconomics = the study of the national economy.
- National income = a measure of the total level of economic activity which takes place in an economy over a year.

- GDP = gross domestic product.
- GNP = gross national product.
- NNP = net national product (national income).
- Money national income = national income calculated at current prices.
- Real national income = national income calculated at constant prices (inflationary element removed).
- Tourism income multiplier (TIM) = exaggerated effect of a change in tourism expenditure on an area's income.
- TDPI = tourism destination price index.
- Basket of goods = typical items bought by a defined group.
- Cost-push inflation = inflation caused by changes in input prices.
- Demand-pull inflation = inflation caused by excess of aggregate demand over aggregate supply.
- Demand management = government policy to influence total demand in an economy.

Data questions

Task 14.1

Table 14.12 shows retail price indices for selected countries.

Table 14.12 Retail price indices (1990 = 100)

	1993	1994	1995	1996	1997	1998*
United Kingdom	116	119	122	125	128	131
Germany	111	114	116	117	119	121
Italy	116	121	128	132	135	138
United States	110	113	116	119	122	123
Japan	106	106	106	106	108	108
Canada	110	110	113	115	117	118

*Estimate.
Source: Adapted from Office for National Statistics, *Labour Market.*

Questions

1 If entrance to Disneyland cost $20 in 1990, and its price has kept pace with inflation, what would a ticket cost in 1998?
2 Why might the retail price index for a country not be a good guide to tourism prices?
3 What other information would you seek before deciding on which countries might be good or bad value to visit?

4 Account for the differing rates of inflation between countries.
5 Why is the Italian rate of inflation likely to fall to German levels post-1999?

Task 14.2   Local reflections on the Channel Tunnel

The Channel Tunnel is dug, equipped and running. How does local opinion see its effects?

John Ovenden, Labour leader, and Allison Wainman, Liberal Democrat leader on Kent County Council, made a joint statement reflecting on possible impacts, on the official tunnel opening.

'For Kent, the tunnel is a mixed blessing. There is no doubt that many people in Kent have paid and will continue to pay a high price in terms of the environmental effect of the project.

'Equally, traditional cross-channel operators, who provide many jobs for Kent people, face a real challenge, although there is every sign that they are responding positively.

'However, we are determined to maximize the benefits for Kent of the tunnel. By opening up transport corridors at the heart of Europe, it represents an opportunity too good to be missed at a time when the country is well-placed to take advantage. For too long, parts of the county have been in the economic doldrums.'

It is certainly true that Kent has had its fair share of economic misery in recent years. Agricultural employment in the county, renowned for hop growing and orchards, has suffered a steady long-term decline in the face of mechanization. It is easy to forget that Kent once had a coal industry which closed in the face of cheap imports in the 1980s. Defence cuts and the peace dividend have been responsible for the decline of Chatham whose prosperity has rested on its naval dockyards. Such is the level of unemployment in north and east Kent that they have gained assisted-area status. Thanet is eligible for assistance from the EU on account of its 17 per cent unemployment rate.

Consultants estimate that nearly 2000 jobs will have been created by the Channel Tunnel by 1996. However, it is also estimated that about 15 000 people are employed in jobs related to port activities in Kent and that a net loss of 3000 of these jobs will result from the impact of the tunnel on ferry services by 1996.

More difficult to estimate is the employment effects of the tunnel on the tourism industry. The county is second only to London as a destination for overseas visitors, who spent £132 m in 1992. It is likely that the tunnel will boost this figure.

Source: The author, from news cuttings, 6 May 1994.

Questions

1 What general employment conditions are described in the article for Kent?
2 Describe the employment effects of the Channel Tunnel using the following headings:

(a) Direct (employment provided by the project itself)
(b) Displacement (employment lost because of the project's effects)
(c) Indirect (employment gained or lost by the project's effects)
3 What are the likely mulitplier effects on Kent of:
(a) the construction phase of the tunnel?
(b) the operation phase of the tunnel?

Task 14.3

Table 14.13 shows consumers' expenditure on selected leisure items.

Questions

1 What is the significance of the term 'at 1990 market prices'?
2 How would these figures need to be adapted if they were used to help compile GNP?
3 To what extent are such figures on expenditure a guide to changes in the level of employment in each of the areas?

Table 14.13   Consumers' expenditure at 1990 market prices (£m)

	1986	1988	1990	1992	1994	1996	1998
Radio, television and other durable goods	2957	4195	4729	5324	6418	8210	
TV and video hire charges, licence fees and repairs	3145	3197	3204	2991	3127	3009	
Sports goods, toys, games and camping equipment	2506	2838	3443	3398	3881	4397	
Betting and gaming	2924	3124	3116	2914	3292	5083	
Newspapers and magazines	3197	3219	3286	2964	3109	2898	

Source: Adapted from Office for National Statistics, *Annual Abstract of Statistics*.

Task 14.4   The death of inflation?

The Centre for Economics and Business Research (CEBR) issued a forecast in December 1998 that the UK economy will move into a period of 'negative inflation'. It has warned that by 2002 retail prices will be falling by about 0.2 per cent per year. This would reverse the postwar trend of inflation that accelerated in the 1970s after sharp rises in oil prices and an intense period of wage-price spirals. Much behaviour in the economy has been based on expectations of continued inflation. This includes investment in property and a readiness to use credit for the purchase of goods. Chief executive of CEBR, Professor Douglas McWilliams, said: 'This will be a new world for most people working today. In the future we will no longer be able to think in terms of the annual wage and price increases.'

Negative inflation will result if oil and commodity prices continue to fall, if world trade is hit by recessions in major economies, and if companies are left with large stocks of unsold goods. Janice Clark, an economist with CEBR, predicts that once negative inflation starts, a prolonged cycle of falling prices may follow. Producers are likely to want to compensate for reduced prices by reducing wages and this will enable prices to fall further but also reduce demand putting further downward pressure on prices.

Some of the consequences of negative inflation may include:

- A fall in interest rates (CEBR expect these to fall to 2.4 per cent by 2002).
- Pay cuts.
- Consumers delaying purchases in the hope of lower prices.
- A collapse in property prices.
- A 1930s style period of depression.

Source: The author, from reports from The Centre for Economics and Business Research.

Questions

1 How accurate was this forecast? Discuss reasons for this
2 What is the difference between a recession and negative inflation?
3 'Negative inflation – opportunity or threat to the leisure industry?' Discuss with reference to the ways in which opportunities could be exploited and threats successfully managed.

Short questions

1 Distinguish between changes in money and real GNP.
2 What are the main leakages and injections into the circular flow of income?
3 What is meant by the tourism income multiplier and what determines its size?
4 Outline the main steps involved in constructing a tourism price index.
5 What recent government polices have (a) encouraged; (b) discouraged employment in the leisure and tourism sector?

Websites of interest

USA: statistics   http://www.stat-usa.gov/
New Zealand: statistics   http://www.stats.govt.nz/statsweb.nsf

Australian Bureau of Statistics   http://www.abs.gov.au
Brazil: statistics   http://www.ibge.gov.br
Canada: statistics   http://www.statcan.ca
Office for National Statistics   http://www.emap.com
World Bank   http://www.worldbank.org
International Monetary Fund   http://www.imf.org
Learning help in economics and business studies   http://bized.ac.uk

15   Leisure and tourism and economic growth

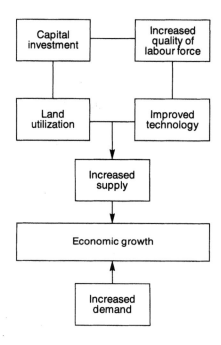

Objectives

The objective of this chapter is to examine how leisure and tourism can contribute to the long-term growth of economies. First general aspects of economic growth will be discussed. Second case studies will demonstrate how leisure and tourism have contributed to economic growth in developed countries such as France, Japan and Spain.

Third, the special problems of growth and development in less developed countries will be examined. Case studies of China and Vietnam will be used to illustrate the role of leisure and tourism in such development. There is clearly much further scope for tourism development in less developed countries which had only about a quarter share of world tourism receipts in the 1990s.

Issues surrounding the costs of economic growth and development will be examined in Chapters 18 and 19.

By studying this chapter students should be able to:

● define and explain economic growth
● review critically the concept of economic growth
● understand the determinants of economic growth
● evaluate appropriate growth strategies for developed and developing countries
● evaluate the contribution of the leisure and tourism sector to growth

Meaning and measurement of economic growth

Meaning and measurement

Economic growth is defined as the increase in real output per capita of a country. There are thus three elements involved in its measurement. First the change in output of an economy needs to be measured. The most commonly

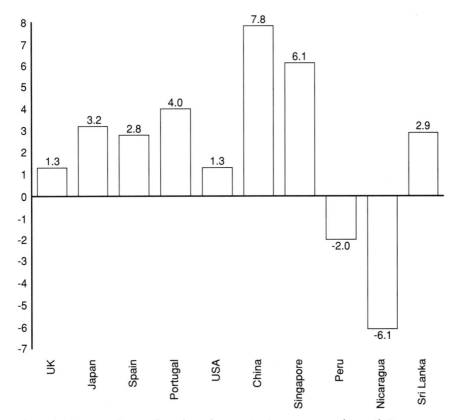

Figure 15.1 Growth rates for selected countries (average annual growth in gross national product per capita (1985–1994)

used measure of output is GNP. However, as explained in Chapter 14, money GNP, or GNP at current prices, can overestimate changes in a country's output. This is because they include increases due to higher prices as well as higher output. Therefore real GNP figures are used to calculate growth. Second, the GNP figures need to be adapted to take account of increases in population. Dividing real GNP by the population gives real GNP per capita. Figure 15.1 illustrates some comparative data for international growth rates.

It can be seen that the economy of China has exhibited remarkable growth of over 7 per cent per annum, due largely to its economic reforms which have allowed foreign investment and private enterprise. However it is control of population growth (1.2 per cent per annum) that has enabled high per capita economic growth. On the other hand, relatively high population growth in Peru (1.9 per cent per annum) has meant that per capita economic growth has been negative.

Problems of measurement

Figure 15.2 records per capita GNP data for various countries and demonstrates the huge international inequalities that are apparent.

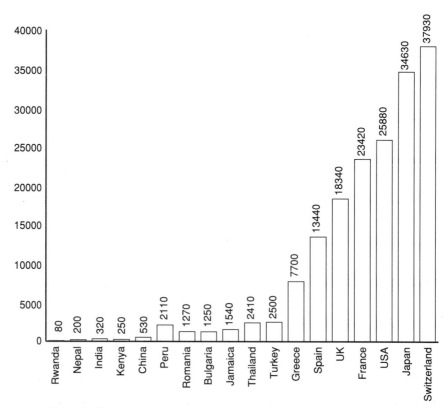

Figure 15.2   Dollar gross national product per capita for selected countries (1994)

However, there are several problems involved in the measurement of GNP and thus economic growth. First there are the problems associated with collecting national income data, as discussed in Chapter 14. Data collection is a particular problem in countries which do not have a highly developed statistical branch of government. Less developed countries also have a bigger subsistence sector where goods and services are produced for self-consumption and therefore do not enter the market or appear on national income statistics. Second, in making international comparisons, country information measured in local currency is generally converted to dollar units. Thus some apparent changes in growth may in fact stem from currency movements against the dollar. Third, over a period of time the labour force may work fewer hours in a week. GNP figures do not reflect this and they may therefore underestimate some aspects of economic improvement. Fourth, GNP per capita figures are an average. They may disguise the fact that there are large differences in incomes of the population, or that some sectors of the community may actually be becoming poorer. Finally, economic activity which contributes to GNP has some unwanted side-effects in the form of pollution. GNP information takes no account of these, a matter which is discussed more fully in Chapters 18 and 19.

Rationale for growth

The rationale for the pursuit of growth is that people become better off in an economic sense. There are more goods and services produced to meet people's material wants. This may result in some combination of more employment, more public services, less taxes, more leisure time or more consumption. How the benefits of growth are actually distributed depends on the workings of the economic system and government policy.

In less developed countries the results of economic growth are generally much more profound, bringing social and environmental changes with material prosperity. Distribution of benefits is often less even. 'Those with land to sell, housing to rent, hotels to run, and labour, goods and services to sell favour it. The landless poor are generally less impressed'.

The causes of economic growth

Economic growth is promoted by an increase in the quality or quantity of inputs into the economy. It can therefore be examined under the headings of land, labour, capital and technology.

Land

Different countries have not only differing amounts of land but also different types of land. Resources may include mineral and agricultural ones, and in the leisure and tourism sector, climate, scenery, coasts and countryside are important resources. It is by the exploitation of such resources that countries can use their comparative advantage against other possible tourist destinations. The success of the French tourism industry is largely dependent on the country's natural endowments which allow skiing and beach and countryside leisure developments. Similarly, specific land resources can be identified as attractions for other destinations, including:

- Nepal: Everest
- Caribbean: Coral Reef, climate
- USA: Grand Canyon, Niagara Falls, Death Valley
- Kenya: game parks
- The Gambia: beaches and climate

Labour

The labour force can be analysed in terms of its quantity and quality. The importance of the quantity of the labour force depends largely upon its relationship with other factors of production, land and capital. Where labour is a scarce factor of production, growth may be achieved by increasing the supply of labour, for example by encouraging immigration. However in many economies labour is in overabundant supply. This means that the productivity of labour is low. This is particularly true in less developed countries in the agricultural sector where land is overcrowded. On the other hand the low wages that result from an abundant labour force can in some cases be a source of economic growth. Wages in China, for example, are very low by international standards, and this has partially accounted for the inflow of foreign investment and the growth of China's industrial sector. The production of leisure goods such as audio equipment and toys is an important part of this industrial growth.

It is the quality of the labour force that is important in increasing productivity and improvements in quality stem from education and training programmes. Education and training can take place in both the public and private sector. In the UK, the government funds most general education and much vocational education, whilst industry often invests in specific training.

Exhibit 15.1 shows how the UK education system has responded to the growing demands of the leisure and tourism industries.

The government has set up a system of vocational qualifications (national vocational qualifications or NVQs and general national vocational qualifications or GNVQs) to complement A-level provision and established education and training targets for the year 2000 which include:

- 50 per cent of school-leavers to attain NVQ level III, GNVQ advanced level or 2 A-levels
- 50 per cent of the employed workforce to attain NVQ level III, GNVQ advanced level or 2 A-levels
- 30 per cent of school-leavers to enter higher education

Exhibit 15.1   Courses for horses

Education and training for leisure and tourism is as diversified and dynamic as the sector itself. Further education can provide job-specific National Vocational Qualifications (NVQs) and more general, sector-based, General National Vocational Qualifications (GNVQs). For example, Brent Farnworth, 16, works in Heathcote's Brasserie in Preston. He is studying for NVQs at levels 2 and 3 at Heathcote's School of Excellence in Manchester on a day-release basis. This allows him to combine practical experience with organized training for a recognized qualification.

Gavin Bates, 17, is a trainee footballer at Preston North End Football Club and volunteer instructor at an outdoor pursuits centre. He attends college for one day a week for an Advanced GNVQ in leisure and tourism.

In higher education a recent report has shown that applications to traditional academic courses such as the physical sciences and humanities have dropped by up to 20 per cent since 1995 but that vocational courses are becoming more popular. There are now over 65 institutions offering degrees in Tourism, which can be combined with a variety of options such as languages and business studies. As well as tourism there are courses in Leisure Management, Golf Course Management, Football, Rugby and Popular Music.

Coventry University offers a degree in Equine Studies. Mike Wells, a spokesperson for Coventry, explains: 'We've now had five cohorts of graduates going out into the market, and their employment prospects are excellent. Our students are of a very high calibre. It's not about teaching them to ride horses, but is an academic course that will stand them in good stead whatever career they choose.'

Source: The author, 1999.

For leisure and tourism education and training, this has meant:

- the rationalization of training qualifications under NVQs. These are available, for example, in sport and recreation (coaching adults) or (facility operations) and travel services (guiding services)
- the introduction of GNVQs in leisure and tourism
- the expansion of degree and HND programmes in leisure and tourism

Finally it is different cultural aspects of countries' populations that is an important motivation for tourism.

Capital

Capital, in the form of plant and machinery, results from investment and distinction must be made between gross investment and net investment. Net investment refers just to investment which increases a nation's capital stock and therefore does not include replacement investment.

Net investment = gross investment – depreciation

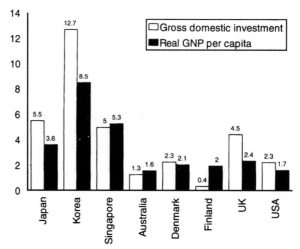

Figure 15.3 Investment and growth in selected countries (percentage annual average growth 1980–1992).

Investment in new plant, machines and other capital enables labour productivity and GNP to rise. This can be an important source of economic growth for developing countries as labour moves from a relatively unmechanized agricultural sector to a mechanized industrial sector. Figure 15.3 records data for changes in investment and economic growth for selected countries. Since this chapter is showing that there are a range of contributors to economic growth, it is clearly not possible to make direct correlations between rates of investment and rates of growth. However it can be noted that Japan, Singapore and Korea have recorded relatively high levels of investment and growth, in contrast to Australia, Denmark and Finland.

The quality of investment is also an important issue. Investment in inappropriate machinery will have little effect on productivity and growth.

Investment in infrastructure is important to develop industry in the leisure and tourism sector. This includes airports, ports and motorways, which allow access.

A nation's cultural heritage includes investments made in previous generations and preserved for enjoyment today. For example, a third dimension to France's tourism attraction is its rich and well-preserved historical built environment. Other examples of cultural heritage capital include:

- China: the Great Wall, the Forbidden City
- Rome: the Sistine Chapel, the Coliseum
- Egypt: the Pyramids
- Peru: Macchu Picchu

Technology

Improved technology can increase growth by reducing production costs and creating new products for the market. The leisure products industry has particularly benefited from new product technology with camcorders, personal stereos, CDs, PCs and the electronic games market.

Exhibit 15.2 demonstrates the potential of technology to change the frontiers of tourism.

Exhibit 15.2   Space tourism

As the search for the exotic becomes more difficult on earth, attention has turned to space to satisfy the demands of the most adventurous tourists. Buzz Aldrin a former Apollo astronaut, is one of a number of people employed to develop and promote space tourism.

A Japanese firm is developing plans for a hotel on the moon and a firm of architects, Wimberly Arson Tong & Goo, are planning a hotel in space which is scheduled to be orbiting 200 miles above the earth by 2017.

A UK firm called Space Adventures are already accepting deposits for space flights. It is estimated that the flights will cost around £60 000, and a deposit of £4000 secures a place on the waiting list.

Source: The author, 1999.

Promoting growth

Growth-promotion policies tend to split into those that require government intervention and those that rely on liberalizing the free market.

Intervention

Interventionists believe the government should play a key role in funding appropriate education and training, and investing in infrastructure. They also note that the volatility of interest rates and exchange rates in the free market inhibits growth and so argue that government should manage the economy to provide a stable environment.

Government intervention can also promote balanced growth where aggregate demand expands at a similar rate to aggregate supply, thereby avoiding the problems of inflation or unemployment associated with unbalanced growth.

Free market

The free market approach blames government intervention for lower growth. It is claimed that government spending programmes 'crowd out' funds, leaving less available and at higher interest rates for the private sector. Similarly, it is claimed that high taxes act as a disincentive for firms to invest. Supporters of market liberalization argue that profit is the best incentive for investment and that the price mechanism will ensure that investment and other resources are attracted to high-growth areas of the economy. Such policies are often referred to as 'supply side' policies.

BA is used as an example to illustrate the improved economic performance that can be obtained when an organization is privatized and freed from government control.

Leisure and tourism development in developed countries

The following case studies illustrate the role of different factors in the economic growth of Spain, France and Japan.

Leisure and tourism development in Spain

Leisure and tourism development has clearly made an important contribution to raising Spain's GNP per capita to levels approaching its EU partners.

Table 15.1 shows the rapid growth of international tourist arrivals to Spain since World War II.

The rapid growth of Spain's tourism industry can be attributed to a number of causes. First its natural resources – particularly of coastline, beaches and climate. However many countries enjoy similar natural features but have not enjoyed such growth. It is Spain's proximity to the fast-growing economies of western Europe that provided the demand, with tourists from the UK, Germany and France being the most numerous. Accessibility in terms of air transport and motorway developments has also played a part. The success of tourism in Spain has itself stimulated investment whilst earlier investment was often subsidized by overseas aid. For example, German investment in Gran Canaria was encouraged by the German government as a result of the 1968 Strauss Act which granted tax concessions for investments in underdeveloped countries. To these factors must be added the low wage costs which have enabled Spain to compete successfully with France and the active encouragement of government.

Table 15.1 International tourist arrivals to Spain (millions)

1955	1960	1965	1970	1975	1980	1985	1990	1996
2.5	6.1	14.3	24.1	30.1	38.0	43.2	52.0	61.8

Source: Adapted from World Tourism Organization, Compendium of Tourism Statistics.

There is a government ministry with direct responsibility for tourism, the Ministry of Transport, Tourism and Communications, and tourism has been represented at ministerial level in Spain since 1951. It has provided direct investment (for example in the *paradores* – the chain of state-run hotels often using renovated buildings of historical interest), as well as subsidies and infrastructure improvements (for example to develop ski resorts). The government also funds the Institute of Tourism of Spain which promotes Spain abroad. Since joining the EU in 1986, Spain has benefited from European Regional Development Fund grants for infrastructure, particularly for providing better road access in the northern coastal region.

Tourism expenditure contributes more than 10 per cent to Spain's GDP and contributes to 11 per cent of total employment. Spain's projected balance of tourism payments for 1995 was US$21161.

The main problems that have arisen from Spain's reliance on tourism are first its dependence on economic prosperity in countries such as the UK, Germany and France. Recessions in those countries in the early 1980s and early 1990s caused tourism expenditure to fall in Spain. Second, tourism employment tends to be low-skilled and seasonal, and finally the dash for tourism growth in the 1960s and 1970s caused environmental degradation which threatens the continued prosperity of some of the earlier resort developments. However, if the late 1990s, tourism in Spain had recovered in line with the economics of Europe, and there have been successful programmes to rescue resorts such as Benidorm, Torremolinos and Magaluf from earlier planning mistakes.

Leisure and tourism development in France

Leisure and tourism is central to French economic prosperity. France is the world's most popular international tourist destination and it runs a healthy surplus on its tourism balance of payments, as illustrated by Table 15.2. France has a diverse and well-balanced tourism industry. Winter sports tourism attracted between 1.5 and 2 million arrivals in 1997 excluding day trips. Disneyland Paris is now the leading short-break destination in Europe and visitors have risen from 9.8 million in 1991 to 11.7 million in 1996. The Eiffel Tower attracted 5.5 million visitors in 1996. However, the capacity of tourism capacity to France has only risen slightly from 17.163 million beds

Table 15.2 International arrivals and tourism balance of payments for France

	1991	*1994*
Tourist arrivals (thousands)	118 584	131 907
Tourism balance of payments (US$m)	8 692	11 199

Source: Adapted from World Tourism Organization, Compendium of Tourism Statistics

in 1994 to 17.307 million in 1997 (all accommodation including hotels and campsites).

As well as being the premier international destination, France is the premier destination for its own residents. Tourism in France accounted for about FF565 billion of expenditure in 1997, representing around 7 per cent of GNP and 9.7 per cent of total employment, but 56 per cent of this expenditure was by French domestic tourism. One reason for this is that, in contrast to Japanese workers, French workers receive a minimum of 5 weeks' paid leave and this represents considerable potential domestic demand.

As well as tourism services, France exports leisure goods – particularly skiing and camping equipment, and has domestic air and ferry capacity in the form of Air France and Brittany Ferries. The latter was set up specifically to promote tourism to Brittany so as to promote that region's economic development.

The demand for tourist facilities stimulates considerable private investment in hotels and other provision, but there is also a history of state encouragement. In terms of infrastructure, for example, France has a well-developed system of roads and railways. Recent investment in the high speed train (TGV) has resulted in links between Paris and Lyons, Lille, Nantes and Bordeaux.

The Maison de France, mainly financed from public funds, was set up in 1987 to promote French tourism products. It is estimated that every franc spent by the Maison de France generates FF100 in tourism receipts and its main activities include information, advertising, sales promotion and public relations. Maison de France has 33 offices abroad, but government funding fell from 72 per cent in 1987 to 38 per cent in 1997.

There have been two major government-assisted regional development schemes based on tourism. First the Languedoc-Roussillon project. This was supported by more than FF6bn of state funding and commenced in 1963. It stimulated private investment and increased tourist visits to the area from 500 000 in 1964 to over 3.5 million by the late 1980s and it has been estimated that 30 000 new jobs were created in the region between 1965 and 1980. The second government initiative was the Aquitaine scheme which planned a big increase in tourism capacity on the Atlantic coast south of La Rochelle.

Leisure and tourism development in Japan

Japan's postwar economic development was largely driven by the export of manufactured goods. These included a comprehensive range of leisure goods. Indeed, it was the quality and innovative nature of much of these products that made them so successful. The product list includes recreational cars and motor cycles, jet-skis, audio and video equipment, sports equipment and musical instruments.

Following the wave of manufacturing investment there has been a movement towards investment in leisure projects. This has been encouraged by the government with the passing of the Comprehensive Resort

Region Provision Act in 1987 which provides tax relief and infrastructure support for resort construction projects. One of the aims of this is to create more balance in Japan's growth. Japanese economic growth has relied heavily on exports and these are subject to external factors such as overseas recessions and exchange rate movements. Investment in domestic leisure provision stimulates domestic demand and provides development in rural areas. Projects have included golf courses, ski facilities, marinas and amusement parks along with hotel and infrastructure development.

Ironically, Japanese workers have generally elected not to take the benefits of economic growth in increased leisure time. Their working year is around 200 hours more than in comparable industrialized countries.

Japan's persistent surplus on the current account of its balance of payments (US$131bn in 1993) accounts for two other important features in its leisure and tourism activities. First Japan runs the world's biggest tourism account deficit, with tourism expenditure overseas exceeding tourism receipts by U$35 566m in 1995. Second Japan is very active in overseas investment. Some of this has involved aid to developing countries (for example, loans for resort infrastructure in Thailand). The majority is in the form of private investment. It is estimated for example that Japanese companies own 150 golf courses overseas.

In contrast to many developing countries, Japan is able to build on its strong economic base. High GNP enables high savings which can finance more investment which further contributes to GNP. However, in 1998 Japan suffered from a severe economic recession with GNP declining by 2.6 per cent.

Economic growth in developing countries

Stages of development

The World Bank divides economies into the following categories:

- low-income economies (e.g. Mali, India, Nepal)
- lower middle-income economies (e.g. Peru, Turkey, Jamaica)
- upper middle-income countries (e.g. Brazil, Greece, Poland)
- high-income oil-exporters (e.g. Kuwait)
- industrial market economies (e.g. UK, USA, France)

The main basis for placing countries in these categories is GNP per capita and the low- and middle-income countries represent various stages of economic development and growth. There are a number of explanations for the low incomes of countries and several strategies for promoting economic growth. For some of these countries, promotion of the leisure and tourism sector will be an appropriate strategy.

Characteristics

The low standards of living enjoyed by less developed countries (LDCs) are characterized not just by low per capita GNP but by a range of other indicators. These include high levels of mortality, and low levels of literacy, medical care and food consumption. The economic circumstances of LDCs vary widely but barriers to economic growth in LDCs may include:

- high population growth (leading to over-population of land and low productivity)
- low incomes, leading to low savings, leading to low investment, leading to low incomes (low rate of capital formation)
- undeveloped financial sector to recirculate savings
- low levels of training and education
- few resources
- dependence on raw material exports
- employment centred on the agricultural sector of economy
- traditional (non-entrepreneurial) culture
- foreign currency shortages
- poor terms of trade (exports cheap, imports expensive)
- international debt

Development strategies

Strategies to promote faster economic growth in LDCs generally involve investment in the agricultural, manufacturing or service sectors of the economy in order to improve labour productivity. This then raises the two key considerations for development. First, given the low rates of GNP per head, where will investment funds be obtained from? Second, what specific projects are most appropriate?

The main sources of investment funds are:

- domestic savings (but these are often low because of low incomes)
- government investment funded through taxes or borrowing
- private foreign investment
- overseas aid

The main strategies for development include:

- import substitution (producing goods that are currently imported)
- export-led growth (producing goods and services where a local cost or other advantage can be established) – leisure and tourism can be important elements in this strategy
- population control
- education and training projects
- infrastructure projects

These strategies may take place under a planning environment which can be either market- or government-led.

However the history of development projects includes a number of projects that have been inappropriate for the circumstances of the particular developing country. This particularly applies to technologies which require expert foreign management and costly imports, and projects which are labour-saving in countries with high unemployment.

The following case studies show the contribution of the leisure and tourism sector to economic development in China and Vietnam, illustrating different development strategies.

Leisure and tourism development in China

The characteristics of the Chinese economy are atypical of many developing countries, yet its population of over 1 billion and rapid rate of development will ensure its growing importance over the next few decades. It is atypical first because of its communist government and second because, despite its low per capita GNP and large agricultural sector, it has relatively high literacy, low mortality rates, and its economic growth has recently been spectacular, averaging 7.8 per cent between 1985 and 1994 and exceeding 10 per cent in 1994. Its population growth is slowing rapidly with a one-child policy. Some of these features are illustrated in Table 15.3, which compares China with India.

China is a good example of how leisure goods and tourism services are being mobilized as part of a general development strategy. Table 15.4 shows the growth in tourism receipts over the past few years.

Tourism is expanding first because of China's open-door policy, which has replaced a long period of mistrust of foreigners and barriers to tourism. Second, China is rich in cultural capital, and third, its low-wage economy makes tourism relatively cheap.

However, investment in infrastructure and accommodation is crucial to tourism development and to counter the low level of investment associated with its low per capita GNP, China has encouraged private foreign investment in the form of joint ventures. This has been important in the

Table 15.3 Development indicators for China and India

Country	GNP per capita ($)		Life prospect at birth (years)		Under-5 mortality per 1000	
Year	1965	1995	1960	1995	1960	1995
India	90	320	47	62	282	116
China	85	530	43	69	203	42

Notes: GDP = gross domestic product; NA = not available.
Sources: various.

Table 15.4   China's tourism receipts and expenditure (US$m)

	1985	1990	1995
Tourism receipts	979	2212	8733
Tourism expenditure	314	470	368

Sources: *World Travel and Tourism Review,* CAB International, Oxford (Ritchie, J.R.B. and Hawkins, D., eds). World Tourism Organization, *Compendium of Tourism Statistics.*

accommodation sector for the development of hotels. In Beijing, for example, the Hotel Beijing-Toronto was financed with Canadian capital, is run by Japanese management and profits are shared with China.

China's growth is fuelled primarily by its growth in exports. Here China exploits its international advantage in wage costs. Exports cover a range of goods and include audio equipment, toys and sports goods from the leisure sector.

The movement of labour from China's agricultural sector to the manufacturing and service sector has enabled labour productivity to increase.

Tourism in Vietnam

In 1975, the communist government of Vietnam emerged victorious from a long war with the USA. Vietnam entered a period of centrally planned economic development and international isolation, limiting its trade and tourism exchanges to those with the former USSR and its allies.

A change in direction was heralded in 1986 when strict central planning was relaxed in favour of free enterprise. Additionally the period of international isolation finished as restrictions on foreign investment and ownership were lifted.

Tourism was a key beneficiary of this change in policy direction. Vietnam is well endowed in may of the basic tourism factors of production – unspoiled beaches, interesting landscapes, and cultural heritage. To this can be added a cheap and plentiful labour supply. After 1986, capital, the missing ingredient for economic development, was now eagerly supplied by foreign investors. Between 1988 and 1995, almost $2 billion was invested in over 100 hotel projects including those involving multinational hotel chains such as the Hyatt and Marriot (USA) Omni (Hong Kong) and Hotel Metropole (France). Tourism to Vietnam boomed with arrivals rising from 300 000 in 1991 to over 1.3 million by 1995. By 1995, tourism earnings were estimated at over $400 million making a contribution of over 10 per cent to Vietnam's GNP.

There are two major problems facing Vietnam in its progress towards economic growth. First is the problem of foreign debt. Vietnam owes over

$26 billion in foreign debt and the World Bank classifies Vietnam as a severely indebted low-income country. This hampers the development process as Vietnam has to use a high proportion of its national income to repay interest and capital on its foreign debt.

The second problem is one of multinational ownership. The lack of domestic capital has mean that much of Vietnamese investment in tourism has been supplied by multinational corporations. This enables tourism capacity to grow in the short run faster than otherwise might be the case. But multinational investment means that the multiplier effect of tourism to Vietnam is reduced with a high proportion of tourism expenditure being exported back to shareholders of the multinationals in the form of profits.

Both of these factors limit the ability of low-income countries such as Vietnam to take the full benefits of the expansion of tourism.

Review of key terms

- Economic growth = the increase in real output per capita.
- Per capita = per person.
- Net investment = gross investment – depreciation.
- Productivity = output per employee.
- NVQs = national vocational qualifications.
- GNVQs = general national vocational qualifications.
- LDC = less developed country.
- Import substitution = producing goods that are currently imported.
- Infrastructure = social capital such as roads and railways.
- Joint venture = overseas and domestic investment partnership.

Data questions

Task 15.1 *World travel and tourism council report on Brazil*

Brazil offers an unenviable mixture of contrasts for tourists.

On the one hand, the Rio Carnival when, as the Journey Latin America (JLA) brochure describes, 'Brazilians let go – over-eating, over-drinking, over-dressing, overundressing: over-indulgence in just about everything. 1994 bookings for carnival week are well up on last year according to tour operators.

Brazil boasts equatorial rainforest, most of the length of the Amazon river, and the Iguassu Falls, said to be more spectacular than Niagara and more panoramic than Victoria.

On the other hand Brazil is equally famous for its death squads, for its violence and for its street children.

A JLA spokesperson illustrates the contrasts, saying, 'We brief our groups when they arrive in Brazil and tell them to be careful, and not to wear lots of jewellery or carry video cameras. Outside Rio, it is much more relaxed and there are stunning areas of jungle, popular with wild-life watchers. There is not really a problem with making arrangements, but the *mañana* syndrome is still there – the feeling that everything will happen, in time.'

A recently published World Travel and Tourism Council (WTTC) report suggests that Brazil's enormous untapped tourism potential could create wealth, jobs and a way out of the poverty the country suffers through lack of economic development.

The report catalogues some of Brazil's current economic difficulties such as hyperinflation, unemployment and international debt, but concludes that tourism could provide the country's biggest source of employment.

Currently, Brazil is largely undeveloped as a package destination and a successful tourism-development strategy, says the WTTC report will depend on the injection of massive investment funds by the government.

Some parts of the tourist infrastructure are partially in place. Hotel room rates, for example, are competitive with those of other destinations in the Caribbean. Sanitation, roads and airports however all need considerable investment to provide extra capacity and the level of standards expected by international tourists. The WTTC report points out that investment in these areas will benefit tourist and locals alike.

Above all, the WTTC suggests an urgent need for a national travel and tourism policy in Brazil. This should contain, it states, partnership ventures between the public and private sectors, a plan to remove the bureaucratic barriers to entry which deters foreign visitors, and an effective strategy to market the country internationally.

Source: The author, from WTTC report, January 1994.

Questions

1 How should investment in tourism in Brazil be tackled to ensure a maximum impact on local unemployment?
2 What infrastructure investment needs to take place to develop tourism and where is such investment likely to stem from?
3 What current economic problems facing Brazil inhibit growth?
4 What arguments are there for and against government investment in tourism?
5 How does '*mañana* syndrome' relate to growth?

Task 15.2   *Tourism and economic development in India*

Tourism can provide an important route for economic growth in India. It has been estimated that international tourism has an income multiplier of 0.93, which suggests that a large proportion of spending by international tourists is retained in the country. The effects on employment are also significant.

Estimates here suggest that an increase in international tourism expenditure of Rs 1 million results in the creation of 173 new jobs.

But tourism to India has shown only modest growth in recent years. Arrivals have risen from 1.28 million in 1981 to 2.12 million in 1995. However, when set against the expansion of tourism at the global level, it can be seen that India's share of tourism has in fact fallen. So whilst in 1981 tourist arrivals to India represented 0.44 per cent of total world arrivals of 288.8 million, by 1995 world arrivals had risen to 563.6 million and India's share of these arrivals had fallen to 0.38 per cent. The same picture of relative decline can be traced through data for tourism receipts. In 1981, India's share of world tourism receipts stood at 1.14 per cent. This figure had fallen to 0.69 per cent by 1995. It is also noted that the tourism performance of India compares unfavourably with its neighbours in the region – particularly Hong Kong, Thailand and Singapore.

The main reasons proposed for India's poor relative performance is that tourism has had a low priority in the government's national development plans. The fact that India was largely closed to inward investment until the 1990s is cited as one key problem inhibiting development of a tourism infrastructure. An inappropriate civil aviation policy is cited as another major problem area. Attention has also been drawn to areas such as marketing, and manpower development, nether of which have been given sufficient support by the government.

Suggestions for improving India's performance in international tourism include the following:

1 Greater power and financial resources to the Department of Tourism to coordinate tourism development policy.
2 Policies to improve the level of investment in tourism infrastructure (both private and public sectors).
3 Development of a more competitive and liberalized civil aviation sector.

Source: The author, based on: Raguraman, K. (1998), Troubled passage to India, *Tourism Management*, **19**(6), pp. 533–543

Questions

1 What factors inhibit economic growth in India?
2 Why has India's share of international tourism declined?
3 Distinguish between an income and employment multiplier. Suggest reasons why these multipliers are relatively high for India.
4 What factors determine the level of public sector and private sector investment in India?
5 Evaluate the case for and against encouraging greater foreign private sector investment in India.
6 Evaluate the case for and against greater public sector planning of tourism in India.

Task 15.3   Cool Britannia: Leisure, tourism and economic growth in the UK

Refer to Table 15.1 and any other relevant data.

Questions

1 What is economic growth and why is it prized?
2 Examine the significance of leisure and tourism as a contributor to economic growth in the UK.
3 Examine the strengths and weaknesses of the leisure and tourism sector in terms of its underlying factors of production of:
   ● Land
   ● Labour
   ● Capital
   ● Technology
4 How can the public and the private sectors contribute to the growth of the leisure and tourism sector? Evaluate the relative merits of private versus public sector contributions.

Task 15.4   Development of sustainable rural tourism in Bulgaria

The following are extracts from Ilieva's (1998) SWOT (strengths, weaknesses, opportunities, threats) analysis of the potential for rural tourism in Bulgaria:

Strengths:

● Natural and anthropological potential.

Weaknesses:

● Superstructure – in many cases facilities do not meet the requirements of the modern tourist.
● Infrastructure – an outdated traffic and telecommunications systems.

Opportunities:

● National advertising budget-financial resources for national tourist advertising.
● Educational programmes – there are five higher education institutions and many colleges where tourism students are being taught.

Threats:

● Macroeconomic frame – The slow pace of reforms, the unstable economic, political and legal situation . . . hamper the development of tourism.

Source: Ilieva, L. (1998) Development of sustainable rural tourism in Bulgaria. In D. Hall and L. O'Hanlon, *Rural Tourism Management: Sustainable Options Conference Proceedings*, SAC, Ayr.

Questions

1 What other factors affecting Bulgaria should be included in a SWOT analysis?
2 Evaluate the potential for tourism to contribute to Bulgaria's rural economic development in view of its strengths, weaknesses, opportunities and threats.

Short questions

1 What is real GNP per capita?
2 What are the key determinants of economic growth?
3 What is balanced growth?
4 What factors led to the importance of leisure and tourism in the economies of France and Spain?
5 What are the advantages and problems of joint ventures for the Chinese economy?
6 Why is China successful in exporting toys?
7 Compare private foreign investment with government investment in a hotel as alternative development strategies.

Websites of interest

USA: statistics   http://www.stat-usa.gov/
New Zealand: statistics   http://www.stats.govt.nz/statsweb.nsf
Australian Bureau of Statistics   http://www.abs.gov.au
Brazil: statistics   http://www.ibge.gov.br
Canada: statistics   http://www.statcan.ca
World Bank   http://www.worldbank.org
International Monetary Fund   http://www.imf.org
Learning help in economics and business
studies   http://www.bized.ac.uk

Part Five
International Aspects of Leisure and Tourism

16 Leisure and tourism: the balance of payments and exchange rates

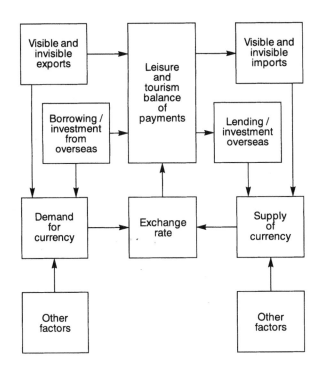

Objectives

As well as measuring the contribution of the leisure and tourism sector to the level of national income we can consider its contribution at the international level to a country's balance of payments. The balance of payments records export earnings and import expenditure.

Exchange rates are an important part of the picture. The exchange rate of a country's currency is inextricably linked with the balance of payments. Changes in a country's balance of payments may cause changes in the demand and supply for its currency and thus movements in its exchange rate. These currency movements may subsequently cause changes in the patterns of exports and imports which can cause feed-back to the balance of payments.

The balance of payments is also one of the key macroeconomic variables which government policy-makers monitor closely. If the balance of payments should move into an unsustainable deficit, government policy would be changed to address the problem, causing repercussions throughout the rest of the economy.

After studying this chapter students will be able to:

- understand the balance of payments accounts
- analyse the contribution of the leisure and tourism sector to net export earnings
- describe and explain comparative data for balance of payments accounts
- understand the significance of exchange rates to leisure and tourism organizations
- distinguish between spot and forward rates of exchange
- analyse exchange rate movements
- understand government and EC policy in trade and international payments

Trade and trading blocs

The EU continues to liberalize trade within community countries. The Single European Act, which came into effect in 1992, defines the single market as 'an area without internal frontiers in which the free movement of goods, persons, services and capital is ensured in accordance with the provisions of this Treaty'.

Some of the specific outcomes of this act which impinge on the leisure and tourism sector include the dismantling of EU internal border checks (some exceptions remain), and more competition in air and shipping services.

On 1 January 1999 eleven EU countries fixed the exchange rate between their currencies in a landmark step towards fall introduction of the Euro in 2002.

The balance of payments

The balance of payments is an account which shows a country's financial transactions with the rest of the world. It records inflows and outflows of currency. It is divided into three parts – the current account, net transactions in UK assets and liabilities, and the balancing item. The main difference between these parts is that the current account measures the value of goods and services traded, whilst the net transactions in UK assets and liabilities measures flows of capital, for example loans, and investments. The balancing

Table 16.1   UK balance of payments (£m)

	1995	*1996*	*1999*
Current account			
Visible trade	−11 582	−12 598	
Invisible trade	7910	12 163	
Current balance	−3672	−435	
Transactions in UK assets and liabilities			
Transactions in assets	−118 844	−219 293	
Transactions in liabilities	120 524	217 095	
Net transactions	1680	−2198	
Balancing item	1992	2633	

Source: Adapted from Office for National Statistics, *Economic Trends*.

item is an error term which arises from compiling the data from a diverse range of surveys. Table 16.1 shows recent balance of payments data.

The balance of payments account always balances in an accounting sense. Every expenditure of foreign currency must be offset be a receipt, otherwise the expenditure could not take place. For poorer countries (as with poorer people), this means that expenditure (on imports) cannot exceed earnings (from exports) because they simply run out of (foreign) currency.

However for countries with a developed financial sector, current import expenditure may exceed current export income. This can be financed, perhaps by borrowings, or perhaps by selling assets. In such a case, although the account would balance in an accounting sense, it would show structural imbalance. This is because such a position could not be sustainable over a long period. Sources of borrowing would dry up and there is only a finite stock of assets to be sold. The implications of such a structural deficit are discussed below in the section on government policy.

In the balance of payments account for 1996 shown in Table 16.1, it can be seen that the three parts of the balance of payments sum to zero:

$$-435 - 2198 + 2633 = 0$$

The current account

The current account records payments for trade in goods and services and is thus divided into two parts – visible and invisible trade.

Visibles

Visibles represents exports and imports in goods and is divided into the following sections:

- food, beverages and tobacco
- basic materials

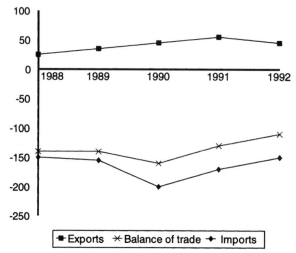

Figure 16.1   Value of foreign trade in sports footwear (£m). *Source*: Adapted from CSO; *The Pink Book 1994.*

● fuels
● semimanufactures
● manufacture
● others

The leisure sector is represented in this part of the account, for example, by trade in alcoholic beverages, electrical goods and sports equipment and sports wear. Figure 16.1 shows the balance of trade in sports footwear, whilst Table 16.2 shows the UK total visible trade balance over recent years.

The information for sports footwear demonstrates similar characteristics to that for UK visible trade as a whole. First it exhibits a deficit, with imports exceeding imports. This has been caused by uncompetitive UK exchange rates (although this is less evident since sterling's exit from the ERM in 1992), and cheap overseas production costs – particularly labour costs. Countries such as South Korea, Indonesia and the Philippines, for example, account for more than 50 per cent of the value of imports for trainers.

Table 16.2   UK visible trade balance (£m)

	1989	1990	1991	1992	1993	1994	1995	1996	1997	1998*	1999
Visible trade	−24 683	−18 809	−10 284	−13 104	−13 394	−10 527	−11 724	−13 086	−11 792	−17 209	

*Estimate.
Source: Adapted from Office for National Statistics, *Economic Trends.*

Second the information shows the deficit peaking in 1989–1990. This demonstrates the relationship between growth in the economy as a whole and the balance of payments. During the late 1980s the UK experienced a period of rapid growth followed by a sharp recession. For the UK there is a strong link between economic growth and import demand.

Invisibles

Invisibles records the trade in services or intangibles under the following headings:

- government
- sea transport
- civil aviation
- travel
- financial and other services
- interest, profits and dividends
- private transfers

The key items of relevance to the leisure and tourism sector are civil aviation and travel. Also significant are interest, profit and dividends, which records payments relating to overseas business investments. For example, profits returned to the French-owned Brittany Ferries from its activities in the UK would represent an invisible trading debit under this section. Table 16.3 records data for overseas travel and tourism earnings and expenditure. This covers goods and services provided to UK residents during trips of less than 1 year in overseas countries (and vice versa) but excludes transport. The data are based upon international passenger surveys.

The value of tourism earnings depends not just upon the number of visitors but also their average expenditure.

Exhibit 16.1 underlines the significance of this point.

Table 16.4 shows invisible trade for civil aviation and total UK invisibles.

Table 16.3 Overseas tourism: UK earnings and expenditure at current prices (£m)

Item	1993	1994	1995	1996	1997	1998*	1999	2000
Credits (visitors to UK)	9487	9786	11763	12290	12244	12815		
Debits (UK visits abroad)	12972	14365	15386	16223	16931	18950		
Net UK earnings	−3485	−4579	−3629	−3933	−4689	−6145		

*Estimate.
Source: Office for National Statistics, *Monthly Digest of Statistics*.

Table 16.4   Net UK earnings from civil aviation and total services at current prices (£m)

Activity	1989	1990	1991	1992	1993	1994	1995	1996
Civil aviation	−528	−295	−384	−536	−269	−708	−458	−725
Invisible balance	3361	3689	3564	4950	5516	4776	6877	7142

Notes: NA = Not available.
Source: Office for National Statistics, *UK Balance of Payments*.

Exhibit 16.1   They came, they saw . . . but didn't spend much

The following extract from the *International Tourism Reports* comments on East European tourists to Paris:
'Paris has long represented a dream destination for many East Europeans. When they were suddenly free to travel after so many years of isolation from the western world it was natural that the French capital would be their first goal. It should nevertheless be pointed out that most East Europeans travelling to France in the early 1990s slept in their coaches travelling to and from and at their destinations and took much of their food with them. As a result their contribution to the country's international tourism receipts was minimal.'

Source: *International Tourism Reports*, 1998, Vol. 3, Travel and Tourism Intelligence, London.

Exhibit 16.2   Football kicks off into the red

From 1998 the UK Office for National Statistics will include football transfer market dealings in the balance of payments statistics. This is largely due to the big increase in value of international signings to premiership clubs which are in excess of £70 million for 1998. They will either be included as erratic items if clubs record them as intangible assets or invisibles if they are treated as providers of a service.

Official figure for the 1998 balance of payments showed an overall deficit of around £2 billion on the current account, largely due to the strength of the pound making imports more competitive and the Asian crisis suppressing demand for UK exports. The inclusion of football transfers will add to the deficit given a net excess in value of imports over exports of footballers.

Reporting for the *Guardian* newspaper, Mark Atkinson and Mark Milner said, 'The level of recent deals is equivalent to the UK's annual imports from Trinidad (Aston Villa got Dwight Yorke cheap when they bought him from there for £120,000 nine years ago) or double the annual imports of lemons. Given the performances of some signings from abroad, that is enough said about lemons.'

Source: The author based on report in the *Guardian*, 1998.

Table 16.5 International tourism balance of payments

Country	1991	1993	1995	1997	1999
USA	14 635	17 162	15 282		
France	9 054	10 728	11 199		
Spain	14 582	15 006	21 161		
UK	−4 539	−5 027	−5 167		
Germany	−20 703	−27 162	−36 454		
Japan	−20 549	−23 303	−33 566		
China	2334	1886	5045		
Turkey	2062	3025	4045		
Australia	237	555	2496		
New Zealand	83	243	886		
Thailand	2657	2923	4292		

Source: Adapted from World Tourism Organization, *Compendium of Tourism Statistics*.

It can be seen from Tables 16.3 and 16.4 that invisibles as a whole contribute to net earnings of foreign currency for the UK, albeit on a downward trend. Civil aviation shows a small, variable deficit, and tourism shows a net outflow of foreign currency for the UK, a trend which is growing.

Exhibit 16.2 shows how football signings add to the UK balance of payments deficit.

Tourism is a net earner to the balance of payments of some countries and Table 16.5 shows some of the main net tourism surplus and deficit countries.

Exhibit 16.3   Tourism key to Cuban economic recovery

Cuba's GNP fell by around 35 per cent between 1989 and 1993 mainly as a result of the ending of its special relationship with the former Soviet bloc. In 1989 the top four export earners for Cuba were sugar, nickel, shellfish and tobacco. However, by 1994, sugar exports were in decline having been hit by a combination of poor harvests and the loss of guaranteed prices in the USSR.

Tourism, for many years spurned by the Castro government, has proved to be a source of economic recovery. Presenting the 1997 budget, Mr José Luis Rodriguez said that a lack of foreign currency was the biggest obstacle to sustained economic growth. Exports had increased by 33 per cent in 1996 headed by tourism which had surpassed sugar as the main export earner. But imports had risen by a similar amount leading to a trade deficit of over $1.2 billion. He said that prospects for continued success in export earnings from tourism and nickel were good.

Source: The author, from press cuttings.

France and Spain boast large tourism surpluses, and tourism surpluses are rising rapidly for Turkey (1985 = $1108 m), and China (1985 = $665 m). On the other hand, Germany and Japan both have significant deficits in their tourism payments accounts, and, as shown earlier, the UK has a steadily deteriorating deficit. Exhibit 16.3 shows how important tourism is to countries with general balance of payments problems.

Net transactions in assets and liabilities

Whilst the current account of the balance of payments records the export and import of goods and services, this part of the account deals mainly with movements of capital. It is divided into transactions in external assets and transactions in external liabilities. Such capital movements can be considered under the headings of investment, lending and borrowing, and official reserves activity.

Investment

This can be further subdivided into direct investment and portfolio investment. Direct investment is the direct purchase of firms or land or buildings abroad. Portfolio investment is the purchase of securities or shares abroad. Such activity leads to an outflow of funds, but a potential future inflow of profits or dividends under invisibles in the current account. Conversely, disinvestment or overseas inward investment causes an inflow of capital.

The transaction featured in exhibit 16.4 would lead to an outflow under the net transactions in assets and liabilities heading of the UK balance of payments and a corresponding inflow in the French balance of payments.

Lending and borrowing

This records international loans. A loan to an overseas company will lead to an outflow of capital but future inflows of interest payments in the invisible part of the current account.

Exhibit 16.4   Forte wins £230 m battle for Meridien hotel group

Forte yesterday won control of the four-star Meridien hotel chain, as Air France, its majority owner, announced that it would sell its 57.3 per cent Meridien stake to the British group.

Forte, owner of 853 hotels worldwide, will take control of the 58 hotels in the Meridien chain for a cash payment of FF1.09 bn.

Source: Guardian, 15 September 1994 (adapted).

Official reserves activity

Government use of official reserves of foreign currencies is recorded here. An increase in reserves leads to a corresponding outflow of capital from the balance of payments account.

The balance of leisure and tourism payments

The complex effects of leisure and tourism activities on a country's balance of payments are illustrated in Table 16.6 by an example of international currency flows associated with Disneyland Paris.

Table 16.6 illustrates many of the issues surrounding leisure and tourism contributions to foreign currency earnings on the balance of payments.

Table 16.6   The balance of Disneyland Paris payments for France

	Exports/credits	Imports/debits
Current account		
Visible trade	Exports of Disneyland Paris merchandise	Purchase of overseas equipment
		Merchandise imported from USA and Far East for sale
		Imported foods for catering
Invisible trade	Admission charges paid by overseas residents	Royalties and management fees paid to US parent company
	Souvenirs bought by overseas residents	Dividends paid to overseas shareholders
	Meals bought by overseas residents	Interest paid on loans to overseas banks
		Overseas marketing
		Private transfers by overseas workers employed
Transactions in assets and liabilities		
Investment in France by overseas residents	Direct investment from the US parent company of 49% of Disneyland Paris	Sales of Disneyland Paris shares by overseas residents to French residents
	Purchase of Disneyland Paris shares by overseas residents	
Investment overseas by French residents		
Banking transactions	Borrowings from overseas banks	Capital repayments to overseas banks

Potential earnings can be diminished in several ways. First, consider the element of overseas ownership. The greater the share of overseas ownership, the more profits are exported in the form of dividends to overseas shareholders. Second the role of overseas banks is significant. A high initial loan from foreign banks results in significant capital and interest repayments flowing overseas. Third, the degree of import content of goods sold must be considered. Tourists buying Disney *Dumbo* video tapes are making more of a contribution to the US balance of payments than the French one. Fourth some projects employ a high proportion of foreign nationals who repatriate some of their earnings. Finally the construction of a project may entail the use of overseas contractors and importation of equipment.

Trends and comparisons

UK balance of payments

Table 16.7 shows recent changes in the totals and components of the UK balance of payments.

The current balance recorded a record deficit in 1989 of nearly £23 bn, largely reflecting the boom in the UK economy of the late 1980s. Even during the recession the current balance remained in deficit, falling to £8 bn in 1991. The invisible trade balance improved strongly in the late 1980s, with the result that the current balance has moved towards more of an equilibrium position over the medium term.

Table 16.7   The UK balance of payments (£m)

Year	Current account			Net transactions in UK assets and liabilities	Balancing item
	Visible trade	*Invisible trade*	*Current balance*		
1987	−11 582	6599	−4983	7026	−2043
1988	−21 480	4863	−16 617	10 352	6265
1989	−24 683	2171	−22 512	19 415	3097
1990	−18 809	541	−18 262	10 960	7308
1991	−10 284	2632	−7652	6728	924
1992	−13 406	2867	−10 539	7098	3441
1993	−13 680	2799	−10 881	12 142	−1261
1994	−10 527	10 359	−168	−5745	5913
1995	−11 582	7910	−3672	1680	1992
1996	−12 598	12 163	−435	−2198	2633
1997	−11 792	19 798	8006	−8112	106
1998*	−17 209	18 608	−1404	11 412	−10008
1999					

Source: Adapted from Office for National Statistics, *Economic Trends* and *Monthly Digest of Statistics*.
*Estimate

Government policy

In the short term a balance of payments deficit on current account is not necessarily a problem. It can be offset by borrowing from overseas, or overseas direct or portfolio investment into the UK. There are, however, limits to borrowing and the selling of UK assets abroad, and so an acute long-term current account deficit will require government intervention. This may take the form of:

● devaluation or currency depreciation
● deflation
● protectionism

Each of these will affect leisure and tourism organizations.

Devaluation or currency depreciation

This is a policy of allowing a country's currency to fall in value or depreciate under a system of floating exchange rates, or moving to a lower rate under a fixed exchange rate system. The aim is to stimulate exports by making their foreign currency price cheaper and to curb imports by increasing their sterling price. An example of the effects of devaluation is shown later in Table 16.8.

Success of the policy will depend upon demand elasticities. For example, devaluation will only increase total foreign currency earnings from exports if demand is elastic, so that the fall in the foreign currency price per unit is compensated for by a larger proportionate rise in demand.

Deflation

A deflationary policy involves the government reducing spending power in the economy. The rationale is that, since imports form a significant proportion of consumer expenditure, a reduction in spending power will in turn reduce imports. Figure 16.2 shows the relationship between imports and the overall level of consumer spending in an economy.

Table 16.8 The effects of currency movements on prices

		Local currency price	Purchase price: £1 = 10 FF	Purchase price: £1 = 8 FF
Visible import	Rossignol skis	1000 FF	£100	£125
Invisible import	Apartment for week in Val d'Isère	2000 FF	£200	£250
Visible export	Litre of Scotch whiskey (before tax)	£5	50 FF	40 FF
Invisible export	Night at Heathrow hotel	£50	500 FF	400 FF

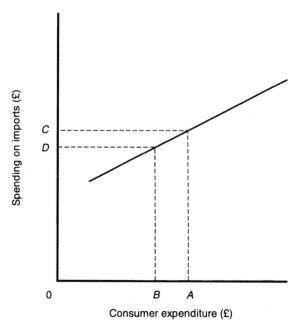

Figure 16.2   The effects of deflationary policy on export spending.

Deflation is achieved through increasing interest rates or increasing taxes. If deflationary policy reduced consumer expenditure from 0*A* to 0*B*, then import spending would fall from 0*C* to 0*D*.

The effects of deflationary policies of the early 1990s on the imports of sports footwear can be noted from Figure 16.1, where it can be seen that imports fell considerably.

Protectionism.

This entails direct controls on imported goods, including taxes on imports (tariffs) and limits on import volumes and values. The threat of retaliation and the rules of international treaties such as the EU and GATT (the General Agreement on Tariffs and Trade, which exists to reduce protectionism) make protectionism a difficult option.

Exchange rates

Significance of exchange rates

The exchange rate is the price of one currency expressed in terms of another currency. Exchange rates are important to leisure and tourism organizations for a number of reasons. Firms selling or manufacturing goods in the UK may import either the finished good or the raw materials to make the finished good. For example, ski equipment is mainly imported and a fall in the value of sterling against the currency of the exporting country will mean a rise in the sterling cost of equipment. The purchase of tourism facilities abroad is classed as an invisible import and so a fall in the value of sterling will increase the sterling price of such facilities.

A fall in the value of sterling will however reduce the foreign currency price of UK visible exports such as Scotch whiskey and invisible exports, including inbound tourism.

Table 16.8 shows the effects of a fall in the value of sterling from £1 = 10 FF to £1 = 8 FF. Notice that the UK price of imports rises whilst the foreign currency price of exports falls.

The conclusion from Table 16.8 is that organizations selling imported goods and services may favour a higher exchange rate, whereas those exporting goods and services may favour a lower one. Exhibit 16.5 links a fall in the value of the rand to tourism growth in South Africa.

Exhibit 16.5   Rand continues to fall

The South African rand fell by more than 5 per cent in one day in 1998, after speculators started to sell the currency in large amounts. This followed the realization that intervention to support the rand on the foreign exchange markets was being financed from South Africa's own limited foreign exchange reserves rather than by the USA and Britain. The clear signal was that the rand would fall further – prompting the rash of sales. Here speculators sell in order to repurchase in the future at a lower price.

While the continued weakness of the rand is good for exports in general and for tourism in particular it makes imports more expensive and can therefore lead to a worsening balance of payments in the short term. This is because it can take some time for consumers to adjust their spending patterns as prices change.

Source: The author, 1999.

Above all, stability of the exchange rate is crucial for organizations whose operations involve significant foreign currency transactions. It was very difficult for firms to engage in transatlantic business in the early 1980s for example when the exchange rate fluctuated between £1 = $2.40 and £1 = $1.10.

Determination of floating exchange rates

A floating exchange rate is one which is determined in the market without government intervention. This has been the case for the UK since 1972, with the exception of the period October 1990 to September 1992, when sterling was part of the exchange rate mechanism (ERM) of the European monetary system (EMS). The exchange rate is determined, like most prices, by the forces of demand and supply. On the foreign exchange markets sterling is demanded by holders of foreign currency wishing to buy sterling and sterling is supplied by holders of sterling wishing to buy foreign currency. Using the Deutschmark (DM) to stand for all foreign currencies, we can identify the main determinants of the demand for and supply of sterling as follows:

Demand for sterling (supply of DM)

● demand for UK visible exports
● demand for UK invisible exports
● demand for funds for direct and portfolio investment in the UK
● demand for funds for overseas deposits in sterling bank accounts
● speculation
● government intervention

Supply of sterling (demand for DM)

● demand for German visible exports
● demand for German invisible exports
● demand for funds for direct and portfolio investment in Germany
● deposits for funds for deposits in DM bank accounts
● speculation
● government intervention

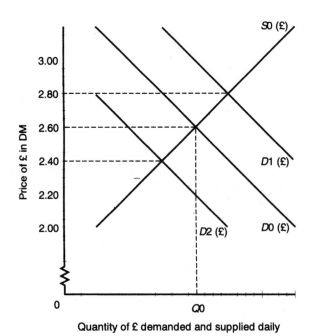

Figure 16.3   The price of sterling in Deutschmarks. See text for details.

Figure 16.3 shows typical demand and supply curves for sterling against the DM.

The demand for pounds is represented by the demand curve D0, and S0 shows the supply of pounds. The equilibrium exchange rate is at £1 = DM2.60, where the number of pounds being offered on the foreign exchange market is equal to the number of pounds demanded (0Q0). Should any of the determinants of the demand or supply of sterling change, the demand and/or supply curves will shift position and a new equilibrium price will be achieved.

The price of sterling will rise if the demand curve for sterling shifts to the right. In Figure 16.3 a shift of the demand curve from D0 to D1 causes the exchange rate to rise to DM2.80. This could be caused for example by a significant increase in the value of UK exports, or a rise in UK interest rates causing foreign currency holders to switch their deposits into sterling accounts to earn higher interest rates. A leftward shift of the supply curve for sterling would have a similar effect on the exchange rate.

The price of sterling will fall if the demand curve for sterling shifts to the left. In Figure 16.3 a shift of the demand curve from D0 to D2 causes the exchange rate to fall to DM2.40. This could be caused for example by a significant fall in the value of UK exports, or a fall in UK interest rates causing foreign currency holders to switch their deposits out of sterling accounts to earn higher interest rates abroad. A rightward shift of the supply curve for sterling would have a similar effect on the exchange rate.

Determination of fixed exchange rates

In October 1990 the UK entered the ERM of the EMS. This was a system designed to maintain a fixed rate of exchange between currencies of EU member states to assist intracommunity trade. The UK joined at a rate of £1 = DM2.95. To allow some flexibility in the system, most currencies were allowed to fluctuate within a band of ±3 per cent, although sterling was allowed to operate within a wide band of ±6 per cent. Figure 16.4 shows the main features of the system.

Notice that a trading ceiling is drawn at £1 = DM3.13, which is 6 per cent above the central rate of £1 = DM2.95, and similarly a floor is drawn at £1 = DM2.77. The factors which affect demand and supply are the same as those identified in the previous section and within the ± 6 per cent band the exchange rate is determined as if in a free market.

However, should trading conditions move the rate of exchange outside of its permitted band, the government is committed to take steps to return the exchange rate within the band. In the event, the pound was forced to withdraw from the ERM in September 1992 due to over-whelming speculative pressures.

One of the difficulties of membership of the ERM was that interest rates were the main policy instrument available to the government to

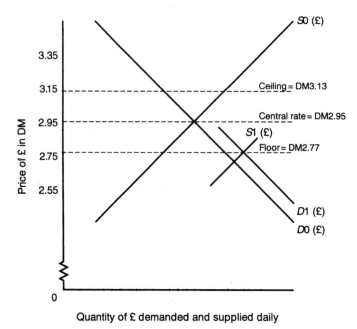

Figure 16.4   The exchange rate under the exchange rate mechanism.

maintain the exchange rate and sudden changes in interest rates were detrimental to the economic environment in which firms operate (see Chapter 9) and the level of investment (see Chapter 12).

The Euro

The UK's bad experience with the ERM was a key reason for it staying on the sidelines when eleven EU countries fixed their exchange rates on 1 January 1999 in the final preparations for the introduction of the Euro – a single European currency. Table 16.9 shows the fixed exchange rates of the eleven founder members together with rates of the Euro against the pound and dollar both of which are still market-determined and therefore still float against the Euro.

The Euro is introduced fully in 2002. The development of the Euro can be traced back to the acceptance of the Delors report on monetary union in 1989. The Maastricht Treaty, signed in 1992, laid the foundations for the Euro and set the economic conditions necessary for member states to join. These were known as the convergence criteria. In 1994, the European Monetary Institute was set up. This is the institution that has the responsibility for the introduction and the managing of the Euro. In effect it is a European central bank. The introduction of the Euro was held up because too few countries had met economic convergence criteria, but by 1998, the eleven founder members had all met the criteria.

Table 16.9 Euro exchange rates

Currency	1 Euro buys
Deutschemark	1.9
French franc	6.56
Italian lire	1936
Spanish peseta	166
Portuguese escudo	200
Finnish markka	5.95
Irish punt	0.788
Dutch guilder	2.20
Austrian schilling	13.76
Belgian franc	40.34
Luxembourg franc	40.34
UK pound	0.704
US dollar	1.17

Trends

Table 16.10 traces recent changes in key exchange rates against sterling.

It is possible to discern relative stability for sterling in the EC exchange, markets brought about by ERM membership, between 1990 and 1992. Thereafter movements in sterling are more pronounced, with particularly large changes registering against the French franc and the Deutschmark.

Forecasting exchange rates is notoriously difficult. The value of the Euro fell from 1 Euro = £0.70 in January 1999 to £0.64 in March 1999. However, predictions had been that the Euro would increase in value. *The Guardian* (14 December 1998) said 'The practical problem is how to prevent the euro term becoming too strong too early.'

Spot and forward foreign exchange markets

The spot market is the immediate market in foreign currency and represents the current market rate. Payment is made today and the transaction takes

Table 16.10 Selected exchange rates against sterling

	1993	1994	1995	1996	1997	1998*	1995
US dollar	1.50	1.53	1.58	1.56	1.64	1.65	
Deutschmark	2.48	2.48	2.26	2.35	2.84	2.95	
French franc	8.51	8.49	7.87	7.99	9.56	9.91	
Peseta	191	204	197	198	240	251	
Drachma	344	371	365	376	447	501	
Italian lire	2360	2467	2571	2408	2789	2915	

*Estimate.
Source: Adapted from Office for National Statistics: *Financial Statistics*.

place today at today's rate. There is a margin making dealers' selling prices slightly more than buying prices.

However some organizations seek protection from exchange rate fluctuations, particularly if they need to quote for contract prices involving a large foreign currency consideration. The forward market exists to satisfy demand for a guaranteed future exchange rate. Payment is made today but the transaction is made in the future (e.g. 3 months) at a rate agreed today.

Government policy

The government faces a dilemma in its exchange rate policy as in many other policy areas. A lower exchange rate for sterling makes export prices competitive and discourages imports, whilst a high exchange rate, by cutting import prices, helps to combat inflation. Between the late 1980s and 1992, policy was to encourage a high rate of exchange to counter inflation, but after 1992, post-ERM, the exchange rate was allowed to fall, improving the UK international competitiveness.

Policy instruments to affect the exchange rate consist of interest rates and direct buying and selling by the Bank of England. Raising interest rates will generally increase the demand for sterling as currency is moved from overseas banks to UK banks to benefit from higher interest rates.

EU policy regarding exchange rates remains that of eventual European Monetary Union (EMU) – with the Euro as the common European currency. The UK government decided to remain outside the first group of eleven countries that introduced the Euro. It has decided on a referendum to determine policy with regard to joining the Euro, but has promised swift action to join if the results of the referendum are in favour of joining. The Conservative opposition party opposes joining the Euro.

Review of key terms

- Balance of payments = record of one country's financial transactions with the rest of the world.
- Exchange rate = price of one currency in terms of another.
- Current account = value of trade in goods and services.
- Net transactions in UK assets and liabilities = record of international movements of capital.
- Balancing item = error term.
- Visible trade = trade in goods.
- Invisible trade = trade in services.
- Devaluation or currency depreciation = movement to a lower exchange rate.
- Deflationary policy = government policy to reduce economic activity.
- Protectionism = policy to control imports
- GATT = General Agreement on Tariffs and Trade (tariff-reducing treaty).

- Floating exchange rate = one which is determined in the market without government intervention.
- ERM = Exchange Rate Mechanism.
- EMS = European Monetary System.
- Fixed exchange rate = constant rate of exchange maintained by market intervention.
- Spot market = the immediate market in foreign currency.
- Forward market = futures market for currency.
- EMI = European Monetary Institute.

Data questions

Task 16.1

Table 16.11 shows inward and outward tourism receipts. The figures have been collected by the Office for National Statistics.

Table 16.11 Overseas tourism spending in UK/British tourism spending overseas at current prices (£m)

Year	Overseas tourism spending in UK	British tourism spending overseas
1987	6260	7280
1988	6184	8216
1989	6945	9357
1990	7748	9886
1991	7386	9951
1992	7891	11243
1993	9487	12972
1994	9786	14365
1995	11763	15386
1996	12369	16310

Source: Adapted from Office for National Statistics, *Annual Abstract of Statistics*.

Questions

1 Comment on the changes shown in the data.
2 Calculate the net tourism surplus/deficit for 1994 and 1995.
3 How are forecasts made?
4 What are the benefits and problems of forecasts?
5 What policies could be used to counter the UK's balance of tourism trade deficit?

Task 16.2   Twenty Euros for a can of Coke? You must be kidding

The eleven European Member States of Austria, Belgium, Finland, France, Germany, Ireland, Italy, Luxembourg, Netherlands, Portugal and Spain are all in the first wave of the Euro zone. On 1 January 1999 exchange rates between their currencies were fixed and the Euro became legal currency. However, it is only from 1 January 2002 that Euro notes and coins will replace those of domestic currencies and all transactions will use the Euro. During a short transition period there will be a dual circulation of both Euro and national bank notes and coins. After that period, only Euro bank notes and coins are legal tender and the process of changeover to the Euro will have been complete. It is estimated that 12 billion Euro bank notes and some 50 billion Euro coins will have to be produced before 1 January 2002, when the Euro notes and coins will start circulating.

The agreement of European Monetary Union (EMU) was ratified by the Treaty of Maastricht and the Exchange Rate Mechanism (ERM) provided a practical rehearsal. The European Central Bank in Frankfurt was established in 1998 to regulate the new currency.

Jacque Santer, the former President of the European Commission, cited the following benefits of the Euro in a speech in Chicago in May 1998:

1 '... The future Euro zone is roughly comparable in size and economic weight to the United States. It will have nearly 300 million inhabitants, and account for almost 20 per cent of the world GDP and of world trade, comparable to the United States.'
2 '... The Euro zone will have a high degree of stability. The European Central Bank, whose independence has constitutional rank, will guarantee price stability, defined in operation terms as inflation between 0 and 2 per cent.'
3 '... It will continue to spur economic growth, and will therefore indirectly stimulate job creation.'
4 '... The Euro will also have a profound microeconomic effect on the functioning of Europe's internal market. By removing transaction costs and completely eliminating currency fluctuations and currency risk, trade, investment and travel in the Euro zone will be greatly facilitated, and prices driven downwards through greater competition.
5 '... In the financial sector, the potentially positive impact of the Euro is especially large.'
6 '... The big unknown is the Euro's international impact. Will it become a truly international currency, performing the role of the unit of account, means of payment and reserve currency.'

Willem Buiter, Professor of International Macroeconomics at the University of Cambridge, gave a more measured support for the Euro at a speech in London in December 1998.

'EMU will succeed in generating greater Euroland-wide prosperity than would have been likely under any alternative monetary arrangement. As regards macroeconomic stability it will make a modest positive contribution, provided the national countries redesign their automatic fiscal stabilizers to generate more strongly anti-cyclical deficits. Lower transaction costs and greater price transparency will help complete the single market, limit price discrimination and other restrictive practices. These are worthy and worthwhile gains, but it is unlikely to add up to a hill of beans.'

Those opposed to EMU draw attention to the following questions:

- Would joining EMU create better conditions for firms making long-term decisions to invest in an EMU country?
- How would being part of the single currency affect trade?
- Are business cycles compatible so that those economies in the EMU zone can prosper under a single Euro interest rate?
- If economic problems or currency problems do emerge, is there sufficient flexibility to deal with them.
- Will joining the EMU help to promote higher growth, stability and a lasting increase in jobs.

Sources:
The European Commission (website: http://europa.eu.int/euro/html/)
The Bank of England (website: http://www.bankofengland.co.uk)
Newspapers: The *Guardian* and *The Daily Telegraph*.

Questions

1 Explain the meaning and importance of the following terms to a named leisure or tourism organization: *macroeconomic stability, single Euro interest rate, anti-cyclical deficits, restrictive practices.*
2 Evaluate the impact of the Euro on consumers of leisure and tourism goods and services.
3 Evaluate the impact of the Euro on producers of leisure and tourism goods and services.
4 Evaluate the decision of the UK and Denmark to opt out of the initial Euro zone.

Task 16.3   Greek tourism: past, present and future

Greece, like many other tourism destinations, suffered two poor seasons in the early 1990s. The culprit is not hard to find. The recession which gripped Europe and the USA with rising unemployment and high interest rates cut deeply into consumer spending and non-essentials such as holidays were inevitably hit hardest.

The forecast for 1994 is promising and the Greek government and travel trade agree that over 10 million tourists will visit the country this summer. Tourism's significance to the Greek economy is illustrated by some key statistics. The population of Greece is 10 million. According to official figures, 1993's 9.4 million tourists boosted Greece's balance of payments by $3.5 bn –

a useful contribution to a country which ran a total current balance of payments deficit of around $6 bn.

But further probing of the data gives cause for concern. Per capita spending by tourists is one of the lowest for any tourist destination. The shortness of the season is also seen as a problem, running from May to mid-September.

Many of the hotels in Greece are in the two- or three-star category, family-run and over 25 years old. This puts them in a poor bargaining position with the European tour operators who insist on low costs. They also find themselves in competition with up to a million unlicensed beds. The householders who let out these extra beds pay no taxes and can offer low prices for tourists. Market conditions, then, keep accommodation prices depressed.

A favoured strategy to raise per capita spending and boost tourism foreign exchange is to take the tourism product upmarket. The construction of seven new casinos is the centrepiece of the new thinking. The government is providing incentives for new hotel construction and modernization, with funds also available for the development of golf courses, conference centres and marinas.

Source: the author, from news cuttings, June 1994.

Questions

1 Detail the factors affecting the level of tourism receipts in Greece.
2 Which of these factors have helped growth in tourism receipts and which have hindered such growth?
3 What policies can encourage an increase in per capita tourist spending, and what are the dangers of such policies?
4 Evaluate the contribution of tourism to the Greek balance of payments since 1994.
5 Why has Greece not entered the initial round of the Euro? What are the consequences of this for tourism in Greece?

Short questions

1 Illustrate which parts of the balance of payments account are affected by the activities of a named organization in the leisure and tourism sector.
2 Under what circumstances would a fall in the value of the drachma (a) increase and (b) decrease earnings of sterling for Greece?
3 How might persistent current account deficits affect organizations in the leisure and tourism sector?
4 Explain how a fall in the value of sterling would affect three different organizations in the leisure and tourism sector.
5 Explain what factors have caused fluctuations in the sterling exchange rate over the past year.

Websites of interest

USA: statistics   http://www.stat-usa.gov/
New Zealand: statistics   http://www.stats.govt.nz/statsweb.nsf
Australian Bureau of Statistics   http://www.abs.gov.au
Brazil: statistics   http://www.ibge.gov.br
Canada: statistics   http://www.statcan.ca
The Euro (EU site)   http://europa.eu.int/euro/
Euro help for firms   http://www.euro.gov.uk/
Learning help in economics and business studies   http://bized.ac.uk

17 Multinational enterprises

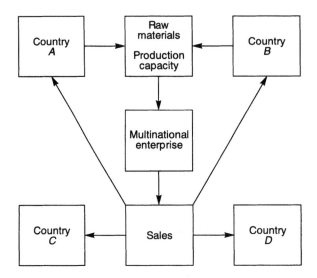

Objectives

A significant trend in the 1980s and 1990s is the globalization of the economic environment. This means that goods and services are increasingly being produced and sold across national economic boundaries. This chapter investigates the rise of the multinational enterprise (MNE) and analyses the motives for multinational operations as well as the effects of MNEs on consumers, parent countries and host countries. It also considers the relationship between MNEs and governments in parent and host economies. The significance of MNEs cannot be underestimated since it has been estimated that the 200 largest MNEs have a combined sales equal to about one-third of the world's GDP.

By studying this chapter students should be able to:

- explain the meaning of an MNE
- understand the motives for extending operations overseas
- analyse the effects of MNEs
- evaluate government policy relating to MNEs

Meaning and extent of multinational enterprise

An MNE is one which has production or service capacity located in more than one country. The MNE has a headquarters in a parent country and extends its operations into one or more host countries. The headquarter countries for many of the key MNEs in travel and tourism are the USA, the UK, France, Germany, Japan and Hong Kong.

The main ways in which multinational operations are extended are by investment in new or 'greenfield' capacity, by taking an equity stake in a foreign company (i.e. buying up shares) or by operating a franchise or alliance with a foreign company.

Airtours plc is a good example of an MNE intent on globalizing its operations as illustrated in Exhibit 17.1

Motives for going multinational

The general motive for companies going multinational is profit maximization. In this respect investment overseas can be viewed in a similar way to any investment. The criterion for profit maximization for an investment is that the rate of return should be better than other possible uses for the capital that is to be employed. The rate of return will be related to the cost

---

Exhibit 17.1   Airtours spreads its wings

Airtours is a multinational group with operations in seventeen countries on three continents, and over 20 000 employees. As we travel towards the year 2000, we are already the world's number one provider of air-inclusive holidays, with over 8 million passengers last year. Our current asset base includes thirty-six aircraft flying our passengers around the world, twenty-six resort properties, a fleet of eleven cruise ships, including associates, sailing the Mediterranean and Caribbean Seas and 825 retail shops selling an innovative range of travel services.

- In October 1997 the company acquired a beach-front development in Bahia Feliz, Gran Canaria.
- In late 1997 the company acquired the shares of Sun International NV which establishes the company's presence in the Belgian, Dutch and French tour operating markets.
- Overseas expansion also continued . . . with the acquisition in May 1998 of a 29.03% interest in Frosch Touristik GmbH, a major tour operator in Germany.
- Summer 1998 has also seen the . . . Group's first venture into Eastern Europe.
- The company has also expanded into Ireland and south-eastern USA following the acquisition of Panorama Holiday Group . . .

Source: Airtours Annual Report and Accounts, 1998.

of, and the revenue derived from, the investment. Thus motives for overseas investment will include cost reductions or increased sales resulting from production or service provision overseas.

Companies involved in manufacturing leisure as well as other goods now have much weaker ties with any particular region or national economy. The increase in international trade has made the market place more competitive and companies much more aware of the need for achieving price leadership or adding value to their products in order to achieve market share and profitability. Thus firms are more ready to transfer production to another location should circumstances favour this.

Service sector companies that wish to extend their services to overseas markets generally have little option other than to invest in capacity overseas.

Specific motives for multinational expansion can include the following:

- lower labour costs
- lower other costs
- exploiting 'national diamonds'
- marketing advantages
- scale economies, integration and competition
- extension of product life cycles
- tariff avoidance
- incentives in host economies

Labour costs

In order to achieve price leadership, firms are constantly attempting to lower their costs below those of their rivals. One of the key factor costs that can be reduced by globalization is labour costs. Countries such as China, Malaysia, Singapore and Thailand are popular destinations for production plants for MNEs because of their cheap labour rates. As well as cheap rates, labour and health and safety legislation is much less onerous on organizations in these countries. Union power is also very limited. Thus in the audio products industry, Motorola, a Swiss company, has an assembly plant in China for some of its car stereo range which it sells in the UK. Similarly, the Japanese Sony company has products assembled in Malaysia. It is not uncommon for UK publishers to have books printed in Singapore and Hong Kong.

A similar trend towards investment in tourism destinations can be observed with countries such as Turkey offering lower wage rates than those found in Spain and France.

Other costs

MNEs have access to international capital markets, so local interest rates are rarely a consideration. Land costs and planning regulations, though, can be an important factor, particularly in 'greenfield' developments. The rate of exchange between the parent and the host economy will also be significant.

'National diamonds'

Porter (1990) investigated the source of different countries' competitive advantage in the production of goods and services. He suggested an important factor which he calls the 'national diamond' effect. Why should the Japanese for example be so competitive in the production of cars when they have few local raw materials and relatively high wages? Porter's answer is that intense competition and demanding consumers in the home market are key factors which cause firms to improve technology, quality and marketing. In other words, the product is polished and reworked into a national diamond. This then enables such companies to compete successfully in overseas markets where local products are comparatively uncompetitive since they have not been similarly honed.

Marketing advantages

Some companies have an internationally renowned corporate image which can be exploited by extending operations overseas. Examples here include Holiday Inn (hotels), McDonalds (fast food) and Disney (entertainment). The name is important for two reasons. First it guarantees a standard. This may encourage use, for example, by tourists in foreign destinations who may want their hotel room to represent 'a slice of home', or who are sceptical about using unknown hotels. Second, foreign branded names, particularly US ones, are popular status symbols in some less developed countries. The queues around McDonalds in Beijing and Moscow are testimony to this.

Scale economies, integration and competition

Multinational expansion may be a way of extending profits through vertical integration. For example, tour operators and airlines invest in accommodation overseas to extend their profits.

Similarly, a strong incentive for horizontal integration may be the reduction in competition that occurs from buying foreign competitors. There are also considerable economies of scale to be achieved through transnational ownership. Economies of scale are discussed more fully in Chapter 5, and include bulk purchasing, advertising economies and utilization of specialist inputs from different geographical areas.

Extension of product life cycles

Product life cycle refers to the different stages in the marketing of a product. Products which have reached the mature end of their product life cycle in thier initial market and are thus suffering a decline in sales may be revived by launching them in overseas markets – particularly in less developed economies.

Tariff avoidance

Where the exports of a country are affected by tariffs, companies affected may elect to set up production within the tariff area. This is perhaps one of the reasons why the UK has attracted so much investment from Japanese MNEs in the past decade. Such companies can thereby market freely into the EC without tariff barriers.

Incentives in host economies

Investment and running cost can often be reduced by operating overseas and taking advantage of government incentive packages.

Multinational enterprises in leisure and tourism

Air travel

There is a growing tendency for global strategies in major airline companies. The two main directions to this strategy are horizontal globalization and diversification.

Horizontal globalization involves extending service networks worldwide. The motives for this include the general benefits of horizontal integration as discussed in Chapter 5, but increased market share is clearly a key motive.

Whilst BA's turnover is highest in Europe there is significant potential growth in passengers in the Americas, Southern and Pacific regions. Hence BA's global strategy has involved investment in foreign airlines to provide global representation and extend BA's passenger base. An added advantage is that linked airlines practise code sharing. Under code sharing, connecting flights of an airline group can share a common flight number. So a passenger flying from the UK to Perth, Australia will see the flight as one BA flight number rather than a BA flight and a Qantas transfer.

Exhibit 17.2 records the announcement of British Airways 'Oneworld' alliance.

Figure 17.1 shows some of the major airline partnerships.

There is also an incentive for airlines to diversify into complementary activities. The logic behind this is that the airlines have customers who are likely to require related travel services – primarily car hire and accommodation. Thus it is not uncommon for airlines to have alliances with or equity stake in or ownership of car hire companies and hotel operators.

Exhibit 17.2   Oneworld

British Airways announced its new global partnership in 1998. BA's Oneworld is an alliance between British Airways, American Airlines, Canadian Airlines International, Cathy Pacific and Qantas. The heart of this alliance is a 'code-sharing' agreement where one airline sells a ticket on another carrier's flight, but issues a ticket carrying its own two-letter code. Oneworld is taking its activities further by joint marketing activities and the pooling of the frequent-flyer programmes of its members. Such agreements help airlines to extend their marketing and fill empty seats.

The popularity of alliances is the fact that there are financial and political difficulties which face airlines attempting traditional take-overs and mergers. Alliances allow airlines many of the benefits of merger without the related problems.

The main advantage is to establish a global network where passengers can be sold tickets in any part of the world to travel between any airports in the world. This helps to reduce passenger wastage when customers are forced to change carriers to reach destinations outside the network of their initial carrier.

Oneworld employs 220 000 staff and serves 632 destinations in 138 countries. It operates 1524 aircraft, accounts for an aircraft departure on average every 14 seconds and carries 174 million passengers each year.

Source: The author, 1999.

British Airways, American Airlines, Canadian Airlines International, Cathy Pacific and Qantas

United Airlines, SAS, Lufthansa, Thai Airways, Air Canada and Varig

Delta, Sabena, Austrian Airlines and Swissair

Northwest Airlines, KLM and Alitalia

Figure 17.1   World airline partnerships.

Shipping

Ferry and cruise operations tend to be multinational in their operations. Many UK, US and Scandinavian cruise companies operate in the Caribbean. Typically such ships are registered not in the country of their parent firm but in countries which offer flags of convenience, such as Panama and the Bahamas. In doing this, shipping companies can benefit from less stringent shipping regulations and lower taxes. The crewing of such ships is often provided from low-wage countries to cut costs, whilst the officers tend to be recruited from parent countries. Purchases of ship's stores and refittings can be done in ports which offer lowest costs.

Hotels and hospitality

Major MNEs in the hotel sector include US corporations such as Starwood, Patriot and Marriot International and UK companies such as Forte, Granada and Bass. Bass has expanded significantly into a global hotel presence since the late 1980s. It bought the Holiday Inn chain outside North America in 1988 and the remainder in 1990 and in 1998 it paid nearly £1.8 billion for the InterContinental hotels chain. This added 117 hotels with 44 000 rooms and a handful of mid-range Forum hotels to its global hotel portfolio.

Globalization is able to bring important cost savings to hotel chains. For example Bass should be able to develop a single reservations system covering both Holiday Inns and InterContinental. MNE hotels are able to exploit their international brand names and can often take advantage of cheap land prices at an early stage of the development of a tourist destination.

The Compass Group is a major UK-based food services MNE. It employs over 170 000 employees working in more than fifty countries around the world. It has developed its own brands such as Upper Crust, Café Select and Franks and also operates under other franchises such as Burger King, Pizza Hut and Harry Ramsdens. Table 17.1 shows the global spread of its turnover and profit and Table 17.2 shows some of its global activities. The company's

Table 17.1   Turnover and profit by geographical area (1998)

Area	Turnover (£m)	Profit (£m)
UK	746	54
North America	1394	61
Europe and rest of world	2073	102

Source: Compass Group, Annual Report 1998.

Table 17.2   Compass Group: global activities

Global Business Division	Contracts in 46 airports in 14 countries, including GDG (Paris), Dresden, Chek Lap Kok (Hong Kong), and Lanzarote
Eurest Inflight Services	Inflight meals for the Mediterranean charter and world-wide holiday market
Austria	Café Silberkammer and Café Nautilus
Restaurant Associates (US)	Contracts for catering at US Tennis Open and Ryder Cup; Metropolitan Museum of Modern Art
France	Catering contracts for Gare du Nord and Gare du Metz stations and Eurotunnel at Coquelles.

Source: Compass Group, Annual Report 1998.

vision statement is 'To be the highest quality and most profitable owner and operator of the world's top foodservice businesses'.

Leisure goods

BTR plc is a UK industrial conglomerate company which owns the Dunlop, Slazenger, Carlton and Maxfli sporting goods brands. It has recently commissioned a new factory in the Philippines to supply tennis balls to the North American and Far East markets. It is therefore able to combine cheap sourcing of goods from less developed countries with high-priced branded sales in developed countries' markets. Pro-Kennex, the world's largest manufacturer of rackets, also sources much of its products from low-wage economics and has been manufacturing in Taiwan since the 1960s. Wilson Sporting Goods, a leading supplier of golf and rackets to the UK market, is owned by the Amer Group, a Finnish company.

Leisure services

Wembley plc is known mainly for its ownership of Wembley stadium, but it also has multinational interests which exploit its stadium management skills. It won the contract to manage the Hong Kong stadium which opened in March 1994. The contract is operated through Wembley International (Hong Kong) Ltd for the period to March 2004 with a further 5-year option. It also engages in international consultancy. Recent activities include design projects for Le Grand Stade, near Paris, for the new national stadium for the 1998 World Cup, and the stadium for the 1998 Commonwealth Games in Kuala Lumpur, Malaysia.

Effects of multinationals on host economies

The effects of MNEs on host economies are mixed. The main benefits can include:

- extra investment and related effects
- technology and skills transfer

However some of the problems that can arise from MNE activities include:

- leakages from the economy
- prices and bargaining power
- exporting of externalities
- threat to local competition
- power to pull out
- enclaves and dual development
- resource grabbing

Benefits of multinationals to host country

Extra investment

The key benefit to host economies is the introduction of new investment. Such investment will represent investment which is extra to that which a host economy is able to generate itself and is important because capital tends to be scarce in developing countries and such capital shortages can retard economic development. The effects of such investment will be the primary effects (resulting from construction of facilities, etc.) and the secondary effects (resulting from running of the facilities). As discussed in Chapter 14, the investment will give rise to extra income and growth in the economy and the associated benefits in terms of employment and foreign currency earnings.

Technology and skills transfer

It may be that the use of skilled labour and advanced technology introduced to an area by MNEs transfers to the local economy by way of demonstration effects. This depends partly upon the training and level of skilled employment offered by the MNE.

Problems of multinationals for host country

Leakages from the economy

MNE investment in an economy will generally generate more leakages than investment funded locally. This is because MNEs will remit profits to the parent company, often employ more foreign staff and sometimes use more imported inputs.

Prices and bargaining power

MNEs who represent monopoly or near-monopoly purchasers of a local input (for example, hotel rooms) will be able to negotiate low prices with suppliers and thus reduce the impact of foreign expenditure in a local host area.

Exporting of externalities

It is sometimes alleged that the reaction of MNEs to environmental pressures and legislation in parent countries is to set up overseas in order to avoid extra compliance costs. In this view, externalities of production are simply exported, often to less developed countries which are sometimes keen to accept such externalities in order to retain international competitiveness.

Threat to local competition

The low-cost, high-technology and high-quality goods and services associated with MNEs may make it difficult for new local firms to enter the industry. This is illustrated in Figure 17.2.

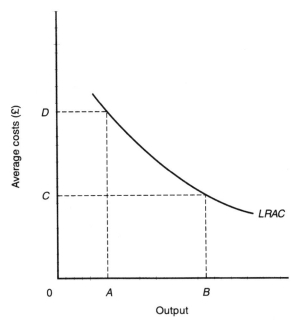

Figure 17.2   Costs for MNEs and local firms. *LRAC* = Long-run average cost curve.

LRAC represents a typical long-run average cost curve associated with the production of a particular product. It is downward-sloping, reflecting the considerable economies of scale that are derived from large-scale production. Because of its size and international buying power, an MNE is likely to enjoy low average costs of 0*C* at a large global level of output 0*B*. New domestic firms trying to enter the market will face higher average costs of 0*D* associated with their small size 0*A*, and thus find it difficult to compete.

Power to pull out

MNEs, like other private sector organizations, seek to maximize profits. They are therefore constantly monitoring the environment to exploit changes in international costs or demand patterns. They thus have no particular loyalty to an area and can pull out, taking with them foreign expenditure (in the case of tour operators) or employment (in the case of manufacturers).

Enclaves and dual development

One possible result of MNE investment is that a development will be exclusively for foreigners and exclude local people. For example, the Coral Resort owned by a Japanese company on the island of Cebu in the Philippines is guarded by armed security personnel and the beach area is only accessible to Coral Resort guests. Exclusive developments such as these are termed enclaves.

Resource grabbing

Local resource prices in developing countries (particularly land) are often low in international terms, and developing countries are generally short of capital and foreign exchange. MNEs tend to have ready access to capital and thus are granted planning permission. One result of this is that MNEs may purchase large areas of land relatively cheaply. This resource is then lost to local exploitation which might be appropriate at a future stage of a country's development. At a Japanese golf course development in the Philippines it was calculated that 150 hectares of land were bought for 150 million yen, a fraction of land prices in Japan, and that the development would yield 600 million yen of income by recruiting just 300 members out of an eventual target of 1600 members.

Government policy and multinationals

Governments view the activities of MNEs with mixed feelings, on the one hand attempting to encourage them and the increased income, employment and foreign exchange earnings they can bring, but on the other hand conscious of less attractive characteristics.

Government assistance for multinationals

Because of the potential benefits to a host economy, governments often offer incentive packages to MNEs to attract their projects. For example, initial estimates for Disneyland Paris suggested that the project would create 18 000 jobs in the construction phase and 12 000 jobs in the operating phase as well as earning US$700 m in foreign currency each year. Because of this there was considerable competition between the governments of France, the UK and Spain to provide the most attractive incentive package to attract Disneyland and enable their national economies to benefit from its effects. In the event the French government provided a comprehensive infrastructure package including new roads and rail connections. It assisted Disneyland Paris with land purchase, provided a loan at preferential interest rates and gave planning permission for future linked developments.

Government resistance to multinationals

Competitive threat

In some cases governments may think that MNE expansion in their country may pose a danger to domestic companies and thus may attempt to limit MNE expansion, as exhibit 17.3 illustrates.

Power and accountability

Another government concern regarding MNEs is that of their power and accountability. Some MNEs have turnovers that exceed the GNPs of smaller economies, and this can make some governments feel impotent in terms of policy. Similarly, MNEs, through their substantial resources, can exert considerable powers lobbying governments to protect and promote their interests. In some cases the nature of a MNE's product or service can be threatening to governments. This is particularly so in media services. News Corporation has worldwide ownership of newspaper titles as well as world satellite television interests. News Corporation is thus able to exert a considerable influence on public opinion.

Transfer pricing and tax losses

Because MNEs conduct business across national frontiers, they can often rearrange their accounts to minimize their tax position. This is known as transfer pricing. Transfer pricing takes advantage of different rates of corporation tax in different countries. Assume there are two countries. Country *A* has corporation tax of 40 per cent and country B has corporation tax of 20 per cent. It will clearly pay an MNE that operates across countries *A* and *B* to ensure that most of its profits are earned in country *B* and thus pay a smaller amount of tax. It does this by adjusting the internal prices of goods traded within the company.

For example, if it imports raw materials for its manufacturing plant in country *A* from its plant in country *B*, it can charge itself an artificially high

---

Exhibit 17.3 Virgin Protests

Virgin Atlantic has protested strongly to the competition authorities about the British Airways Oneworld alliance, despite having its own agreement with Continental Airlines, British Midlands, Malaysian and Ansett. It argues that these mega-alliances are formed to squeeze out smaller independent airlines and will lead to less competition. This view is supported by travel agents Hogg Robinson who note that there is no evidence that the new alliances have brought down prices or raised service standards.

Source: The author, 1999.

price for these materials. In doing so it will make high profits in country *B* but pay the lower rate of 20 per cent corporation tax on them. The results of this will mean that profits on finished goods sold in country *A* will have been lowered due to the high import charges, thus payments of high corporation tax (40 per cent) in country *A* are minimized. This means that more profits are retained across the MNE's international operations and that country *A* loses tax revenue.

Review of key terms

- Globalization = organization of a firm's production and sales on a worldwide basis.
- Multinational enterprise (MNE) = one which has production or service capacity located in more than one country.
- Parent country = base country of MNE.
- Host country = country in which MNE is operating.
- Greenfield development = new investment on a new site.
- National diamond = product or service for which a country has built a world reputation.
- Product life cycle = stages in marketing of product from growth to maturity and decline.
- Tariff barriers = taxes on goods imported into a geographic area (e.g. the EU).
- Code sharing = packaging of interconnecting flights of linked airlines into one flight code.
- Demonstration effect = method by which skills and technology are transferred to a host economy by participation of local labour.
- Enclave = local MNE development which is isolated from the main host economy.
- Resource grabbing = MNE utilizing of host country's resources which prevents later domestic utilization.
- Transfer pricing = adjusting the prices of goods traded internally within MNEs to minimize tax.

Data questions

Task 17.1   Bass plc and hotel globalization

1993: Holiday Inn Worldwide (owned by Bass) has more than 1770 hotels and 338 000 guest rooms making it the single largest hotel brand in the world. Throughout 1993, 159 hotels were added and joint venture agreements signed in Mexico, Indonesia, and India, with development agreements in Germany and South Africa.

Approximately 90 per cent of Holiday Inn hotels are owned by franchisees. Hotel owners select the Holiday Inn name because they want the global marketing power of the strongest brand name in the hotel industry. They want the most advanced hotel reservation system to deliver the maximum number of room nights. Over the past year, a global sales force has been established to market hotel rooms to multinational corporations, travel agents and tour operators. Holiday Inn is the industry leader in provision of regular on-site training to staff. Holiday Inn Worldwide believes that its brand strength, enhanced by the investment in the systems described above, will enable it to increase significantly over the next five years the number of hotels flying the Holiday Inn flag.

Source: The 1993 Annual Report of Bass plc.

1999: In February 1998 Bass paid around £1.8 billion for the InterContinental hotels (ICH) chain, adding 117 hotels and 44 000 rooms to its hotel portfolio. This was just one example of a number of large international hotel deals which included the $1 billion purchase of Ramada Hotels (Renaissance) by the US Marriott International owners of the Ritz-Carlton hotel chain. Eric Pfeffer president of Cendent's hotels division commented, 'Globalization is the name of the game'. The move towards globalization is driven by economies of scale, marketing benefits and the good growth prospects for international tourism. With its acquisition of ICH, Bass has achieved good coverage across price ranges and is able to offer four-star hotels in addition to its mid-market Holiday Inns. It also adds to its geographic coverage in Europe and Asia.

Source: Press reports, 1999.

Questions

1 Why did Bass plc acquire Holiday Inn Worldwide and InterContinental hotels?
2 Why does Holiday Inn Worldwide use franchising rather than direct ownership to expand its international operations?
3 What are the benefits to Bass plc of multinational expansion in hotels?
4 What are the main benefits and problems to the Indian government of the Holiday Inn joint venture agreement?
5 What factors limit the globalization of hotel provision?

Task 17.2   *Rock around the world*

1998 saw the first global album chart compiled by the London-based Media Research and Information Bureau for CNN International. The album charts from 37 countries are used to compile the global chart. It is in effect a chart of charts and weightings are used to determine the position according to market share. At world number one is James Horner's original soundtrack for the film *Titanic*, with sales of more than 20 million. *Titanic* is typical of the increasing trend towards the global corporate leisure product. First, the film, then the soundtrack, then the exhibition – the making of *Titanic*. Each supports and extends the life of the other and each leads to their own series of spin-offs.

The world chart is dominated by Anglo-American artists but non-mainstream British groups – Massive Attack and Garbage – are in the top 10. The German group Modern Talking, and Denmark's Aqua also feature:

The World Top 10 albums:

1 Titanic – *Original Soundtrack*
2 Madonna – *Ray Of Light*
3 Celine Dion – *Let's Talk About Love*
4 Massive Attack – *Mezzanine*
5 Savage Garden – *Savage Garden*
6 Garbage – *Version 2.0*
7 Simply Red – *Blue*
8 Modern Talking – *Back For Good*
9 Lenny Kravitz – *Five*
10 Aqua – *Aquarium*

Billboard magazine has compiled a European chart, which shows similar trends to the global chart. Simply Red are number one, Madonna is number two, and the soundtrack from *Titanic* is at number four.

The European top 10 albums:

1 Simply Red – *Blue*
2 Madonna – *Ray Of Light*
3 Modern Talking – *Back For Good*
4 Titanic – *Original Soundtrack*
5 Massive Attack – *Mezzanine*
6 Celine Dion – *Let's Talk About Love*
7 Lenny Kravitz – *Five*
8 Die Aerzde – *13*
9 Boyzone – *Where We Belong*
10 Garbage – *Version 2.0*

Film soundtracks also feature heavily in the US album chart, and the influence of TV also shows with *Songs From Ally McBeal*, at number eight.

US top 10 albums:

1 City of Angels – *Original Soundtrack*
2 Godzilla – *Original Soundtrack*
3 DMX – *It's Dark And Hell It's Hot*
4 Garth Brooks – *The Limited Series*
5 Backstreet Boys – *Backstreet Boys*
6 Dave Matthews Band – *Before These Crowded Streets*
7 Sparkle – *Sparkle*...
8 Vonda Shepherd – *Songs From Ally McBeal*
9 Shania Twain – *Come On Over*
10 Titanic – *Original Soundtrack*

Questions

1 How is the music business likely to respond to the growing global market for music?
2 What is meant by the 'global corporate leisure product'? Why is this kind of product attractive to MNEs?
3 What benefits arise from the globalization of music?
4 What are the drawbacks of the globalization of music?

Task 17.3   *Developments in Zanzibar*

Zanzibar is an idyllic island off the east coast of Africa. In Nungwi villagers use rough red planks to make dhow boats and live on a harvest of mangos, almonds, coconuts, cloves and citrus fruit, and by netting fish from the Indian Ocean. Its future looks set to for radical change with a significant tourism development planned.

The UK-owned East Africa Development Company is coordinating a massive $4 billion investment proposal in northern Zanzibar on the Nungwi peninsula. The East Africa Development Company (EADC) has been granted a 49-year lease renewable for another 49 years for $1 a year to develop the peninsula. As part of the deal, the government has taken a 26 per cent stake in the venture. Forte Meridien, the UK-based hotel group, is one of several UK companies which are partners in the proposals which will become East Africa's biggest holiday resort. The scale of the proposals include a harbour for cruise ships, fourteen luxury hotels, holiday villas, three golf courses and a world trade convention centre. The Nungwi scheme will be one of the world's biggest building projects.

The benefits to the multinational companies involved are clear. Zanzibar is a destination with a good year-round climate, land prices are cheap, and so is labour. There is also the prospect of a greenfield site on a large scale. There are also potential benefits to local people in terms of higher-paid jobs and better living conditions if clean water and electricity are introduced. Nungwi village recently suffered an outbreak of cholera when raw sewage contaminated its well.

But Sue Wheat, writing in the *Guardian*, is keen to point out the strong counter-arguments against this development. She notes that although 20 000 people currently live on the site, the plans make no mention of them and suggest that the area is uninhabited.

Sue Wheat poses some other key questions raised by the development of the site:

1 Water rationing is currently the norm in this area. How will the development affect water supplies?
2 How will local needs and environment issues be tackled?
3 Where will the 20 000 residents go?
4 Will any jobs created be suitable for the largely fishing and farming communities?

5 Will the resort use local produce and benefit local farmers or will it import foodstuffs to cater for visitor tastes?

Patricia Barnett director of the pressure group Tourism Concern, is sceptical whether benefits promised to local people will materialize and is campaigning to protect Nungwi.

Source: The author from press reports, 1998, 1999.

Question

Evaluate the costs and benefits of the Nungwi development to:

● The host country.
● The local host community.
● The East Africa Development Company.
● Forte Meridian.

Task 17.4   U.S. Consumers give Adidas, Reebok and Nike the boot

The 1990s were a period in which Adidas, Reebok and Nike consolidated their positions as global market leaders in sports goods. Demand seemed insatiable and fuelled high prices. Supply was outsourced to take advantage of labour rates in less-developed economies – at one stage Nike was employing Asian workers at around 50p a day. The companies were able to exploit this difference in global economic conditions and produce in cheap markets and ship the goods to sell in expensive ones. Profits rose.

But in 1998 the gravy train was derailed and US sports retailers found themselves overstocked and forced to reduce prices to shift unsold stock. Analysts blame the fact that the brands have become too common along with bad publicity arising from stories of exploitation of workers in poorer countries for the slump in sales. This caused a shareholder panic about the global state of the market. Fears for the survival of trainer footwear caused heavy falls in the shares of sportswear manufacturers and retailers.

But in the UK the markets are holding up. The sports market in footwear is worth £850 million and clothing is worth £ 1.4 billion with both showing signs of growth. This is reflected in improved share prices.

The US overstocking problems have been attributed to the over-optimism of manufacturers who over-supplied the market. The US problems are also seen as a shift in consumer tastes away from big brand sportswear. This has led Nike to review its advertising campaigns and Reebok to reassess its image. Part of Nike's problem has been global saturation of its brand which is now seen worn by parents and children, rich and poor, and in just about every country in the world. In a change of strategy Nike has cut spending on sponsorship and US advertising. The company aims to makes the Nike brand less obvious, and so relaunch it as an object of desire, rather than the commonplace.

PR director for Reebok, Dave Fogelson said: 'We have cut back on sponsorship of teams because we need a more balanced approach, placing emphasis on outdoor marketing in order to help establish what we represent. We all followed the successful model of the Nike Air Jordans, and in terms of that we created a monster by focusing on the player rather than the shoe. We need to be smarter about marketing our brand.' Adidas has recently acquired the French ski and golf-wear group Salomon in an effort to diversify into the winter sports market.

Source: The author, 1999.

Questions

1 What is transfer pricing and how can MNEs benefit from it?
2 What are the other main opportunities available for these trainer footware companies as MNEs?
3 What are the main threats facing these trainer companies as MNEs?
4 Evaluate the economic benefits and disadvantages faced by governments which host MNE operations.

Short questions

1 What MNEs exist in the leisure goods, leisure services and tourism sectors of the economy? What makes these companies MNEs?
2 Why and how are airlines 'going global'?
3 Using a named overseas project of an MNE, evaluate:
   (a) the benefits of the project to the host country
   (b) the problems of the project to the host country
   (c) the benefits of the project to the MNE
4 What is meant by transfer pricing?
5 Why do MNEs invest from and to the UK?

Reference

Porter, M. (1990) *The Competitive Advantage of Nations*, Macmillan.

Websites of interest

Granada Group plc   http://www.granada.co.uk
Marriott International   http://www.marriott.com
McDonald's Corp.   http://www.mcdonalds.com

Nintendo of America Inc.   http://www.nintendo.com
Scottish and Newcastle plc   http://www.scottish-newcastle.com
Sony Corporation   http://www.sony.com
Time Warner Corporation   http://www.timewarner.com
Trump Hotels & Casinos Resorts Inc.   http://www.trump.com
Wilson Sporting Goods Co.   http://www.wilsonsports.com/
Virgin Atlantic   http://www.bized.ac.uk/compfact/vaa/index.htm
Learning help in economics and business studies   http://www.bized.ac.uk

Part Six
Leisure and Tourism and Environmental Issues

18 Environmental impacts of leisure and tourism

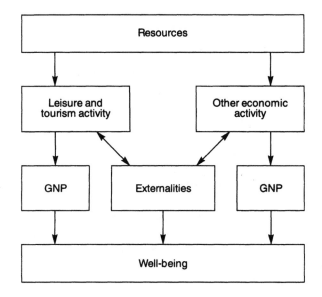

Objectives

Chapters 14–16 examined the contribution of leisure and tourism to countries' national economies. Traditionally, economic analysis has measured impacts in terms of readily measurable variables such as employment, balance of payments and GNP. The objective of this chapter however is to examine the issues raised by environmental economics.

Environmental economics involves a wider view of the impact of economic development and growth, taking into account well-being rather than just measuring how much richer people become in monetary terms. Issues such as global warming, acid rain and resource depletion have been highlighted as threats to economic growth and even to the future of our species, and critiques and techniques developed by environmental economists can be readily used in the leisure and tourism sector.

First, questions can be raised about the validity of focusing measures of success solely on the uncritical use of GNP data. Second, environmental accounting techniques seek to include a wide rage of considerations when considering the cost and benefits of particular projects. These include effects on the natural and built environment, as well as raw material and waste product issues.

When subjected to environmental scrutiny, the leisure and tourism sector can display examples of previously unaccounted overall benefits as well as costs. Additionally, as well as being the perpetrator of negative environmental effects, the sector is sometimes the victim of environmental pollution caused elsewhere.

After studying this chapter students will be able to:

- distinguish between growth in GNP and growth in well-being
- distinguish between renewable and non-renewable resources (sources) and analyse the use of such resources
- understand the significance of waste disposal capacity (sinks) to the economy
- analyse the effects of the existence of open-access resources on resource use
- identify the existence of externalities and their contribution to well-being

Economic growth and well-being

Chapter 15 considered the contribution of the leisure and tourism sector to economic growth. Economic growth was measured by examining changes in real GNP per capita. Environmental economists point out that such figures may give a misleading impression about improvements in economic well-being for the following reasons:

- The environmental costs of producing goods and services which appear in GNP are not always accounted for.
- The distribution of the benefits of economic growth is not always even.
- GNP figures may include 'defensive' expenditure.
- The destruction of the natural environment is not shown.

Exhibit 18.1 demonstrates some of these concepts in relation to the development of an airport.

The discussion in exhibit 18.1 shows the need for caution in equating growth in GNP with growth in well-being. Indeed, some economists have argued that when a wider view of economics growth is taken, the costs may exceed the benefits. Such analysis has caused the questioning of policies which lead to fastest economic growth without regard to the wider consequences and some environmental economists have called for a halt or limit to economic growth.

The New Economics Foundation has produced an Index of Sustainable Economic Welfare (ISEW) as an alternative measure of economic progress to

---

Exhibit 18.1   Development and well-being

The building and the running of an airport will add to GNP in terms of expenditure on building materials, fixtures and fittings, roads and access, staffing and consumables. However local residents will suffer from increased noise and atmospheric pollution as well as traffic congestion – none of these costs will appear in GNP data.

Whilst some local residents may benefit in terms of job opportunities, gainers and losers are often different people. The main gainers from the development are the shareholders of the airport company, airlines and tour operators, employees, and travellers themselves. Local residents are likely to form only a small fraction of these categories and so the benefits of such growth will be unevenly shared. GNP per capita figures only show average effects of growth.

Because of the extra noise, some residents will buy double glazing, more petrol will be used because of traffic congestion, and roofing contractors will gain more work because of vortex effects of aircraft (the tendency of aircraft engine thrust to cause intense patches of air currents which remove roof tiles). This is defensive expenditure. It is expenditure made to try to combat some of the ill-effects of the development. It does not leave anyone better off than before the development, but it contributes to GNP data, exaggerating the apparent benefits of the development.

Finally the development will involve loss of the natural environment. This represents the loss of an amenity to some people in terms of views or tranquility or open space, but again this loss fails to register in GNP data.

---

that of GDP. It argues that while in 1997 GDP in the UK was over one and a half times higher than that in 1972, 'during the same period violent crime has quadrupled, the incidence of asthma has tripled, the number of workless households has tripled, car traffic has almost doubled and concentrations of climate changing gases in the atmosphere have grown to perilous levels'. The ISEW adjusts GDP accounts to take account of a wider understanding of welfare. Its five main adjustments are:

1 Defensive expenditure (spending to offset social environmental costs) are deducted.
2 An allowance is made for long-term environmental damage.
3 Net investment is included.
4 Changes in the distribution of income are valorized to reflect the higher marginal utility derived by extra income earned by poorer people.
5 A value for household labour is included.

Comparisons between changes in GDP and the ISEW over time are striking. Whilst per capita GDP grew at an annual average of 2 per cent between 1950 and 1966 the ISEW only grew by an annual average of 0.6 per cent. But in recent years the indices have actually moved in different directions. Between 1990 and 1996 whilst per capita GDP has risen by an annual average of 1.1 per cent, per capita ISEW has actually fallen by an annual average of 1.3 per cent.

Externalities

The notion of externalities has already been briefly discussed in Chapter 7. Externalities are those costs or benefits arising from production or consumption of goods and services which are not reflected in market prices. Because of this there is little incentive for firms to curb external costs, since they do not have to pay for them. Externalities can be divided into the following categories:

- Production on production. This is where one firm's external costs interfere with the operation of another firm, e.g. noise from discos and clubs which creates a noise nuisance to hotel residents.
- Production on consumption. This is where industrial externalities affect individuals' consumption of a good or service, e.g. aircraft noise affects people trying to listen to music; increase in crime levels in resorts; visual pollution of hotels, caravans and car parks affects enjoyment of landscape.
- Consumption on production. This occurs when for example external costs of consuming a good or service interfere with a firm's production process, e.g. traffic jams caused by a leisure park cause transport delays to local firms.
- Consumption on consumption. This is where the external effects of an individual's consumption of a good or service affect the well-being of another consumer, e.g. holiday-makers destroying coral reef, congestion around a football stadium causing inconvenience to other people.

Figure 18.1 shows how firms tend to over-produce goods and services which are subject to externalities.

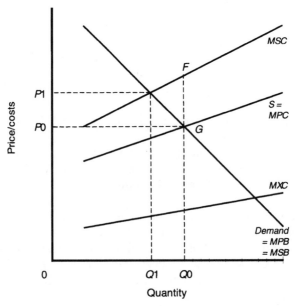

Figure 18.1   External costs, private costs and optimium output. See text for details.

Demand curve D shows the marginal private benefit of consuming the good and, assuming there are no external benefits, it also represents the marginal social benefit. It shows how much consumers are willing to pay for extra units of output. Supply curve S shows the marginal private costs of production, i.e. costs per extra unit of output.

Producers will wish to expand their output to $0Q0$ since the price they receive from extra units of production will exceed the costs of extra units of production up to that point. Beyond that point the extra costs of producing each good will exceed the price received for it. Thus $0Q0$ represents the optimal market level of production.

Curve MXC represents marginal external costs, perhaps because of noise or other pollution effects. Adding MXC to MPC generates the marginal social cost curve MSC. Notice that now we include external costs, i.e. previously unpriced environmental resources, the level of output $0Q0$ is no longer optimal, since marginal social costs exceed marginal social benefits by the amount FG. A reduction in output to $0Q1$ where $MSC = MSB$ would need to take place to provide the optimal social level of production.

The case of sewage discharges into the sea illustrates this point. Whilst there is little marginal private cost to the water companies for pumping sewage into the sea, it represents a loss of well-being to people who want to use the sea. There is a considerable marginal external cost which takes the form of cleaning costs to surf equipment, medical costs to treat infections and loss of earnings caused by sickness. These are readily quantifiable costs to which must be added the general unpleasantness of contact with sewage. Exhibit 18.2 considers some of the externalities posed by tourism development in Greece.

It demonstrates the fine balance that has to be achieved in tourism development, with over-development causing degradation of the place itself, which can threaten future demand and prosperity.

Another consequence that may stem from such development is that price inflation and property prices may rise, making it increasingly difficult for

---

Exhibit 18.2   Tourism curse visited on this blessed Aegean isle

The Greek island of Amorgos is rugged, barren and beautiful.

But things are changing fast since locals can now make more money through tourism in 2 months than they could otherwise make in a year.

The tourism boom is taking its environmental toll. There are growing problems with water, sewage and rubbish, although officials are reluctant to acknowledge them.

'If we're careful we'll be all right. Our only real problem is plastic water bottles,' says Mr Vekris, a local mayor. 'You know the quality of our lives has really improved with tourism'.

And indeed it has. It has meant washing machines and colour televisions for local inhabitants, but these are luxuries that will ultimately be at the expense of Amorgos.

Source: *Guardian*, 6 September 1994 (adapted).

those not participating in the development, and thus benefiting from rising wages and profits, to remain in the area. This effect is termed economic dualism and occurs where a traditional and a growing sector of the economy exist side by side. The growing sector may increasingly threaten the traditional sector and participants in the traditional sector may only be able to access limited parts of the growing sector.

It is also possible to identify less obvious, distant, external costs of tourism and leisure developments. For large-scale resort developments, for example, consideration can be given to the sources of raw materials for building and the subsequent effect of quarrying for stone or forest depletion for timber.

Use of resources

Environmental economics distinguishes between two types of resources. Non-renewable resources are those which have a fixed supply. Once they have been used up there will be none left for future generations. Renewable resources are those which are capable of being replenished.

Non-renewable resources

Landscapes, views, open spaces and tranquillity represent non-renewable resources in the leisure and tourism sector. They are used up by general economic development as well as by leisure and tourism development itself. An important consideration concerning the use of non-renewable resources is the rate of depletion and hence the level of resources bequeathed to future generations.

The urgency of this problem can be illustrated as follows: Economic development uses up such resources. It also generates increases in incomes and leisure time and thus the demand for such resources. Thus we have the prospect of dwindling natural resources having to provide for increasing demands and thus degeneration occurring at a quickening pace.

Renewable resources

An important renewable resource for large-scale tourism development in some parts of the world is water. Large-scale development requires considerable resources of fresh water. It is here that the technique of impact assessment is important. Forecasts need to be made of water use against water renewal, although in some circumstances the latter may be supplemented by water diversion schemes. If water is obtained from underground aquifers, these will eventually run dry or be subjected to salt or other pollution if the rate of extraction exceeds the rate of replenishment.

This problem is compounded by the free access problem, where it is not in anyone's interests to preserve water if everyone is drawing it from the same source.

Exhibit 18.3   Calls for brake on mountain biking – Nicholas Schoon

The government is pondering whether restrictions on mountain bikes may be necessary because their growing popularity is damaging some of the nation's best scenery.

This week a report to be published by the Council for the Protection of Rural England will highlight mountain biking as one of the ways in which unrestricted countryside leisure and tourism are increasingly harming the environment. The cyclists often use footpaths, although the law says they should be restricted to bridle ways and byways. The broad, highgrip tyres they use are stripping out vegetation and leaving deep, muddy furrows.

Walkers and ramblers complain that they are irritated and frightened by mountain bikes that pass them at speed. Some regard the bicycles as an inappropriate, unnatural leisure pursuit in cherished landscapes such as the 11 national parks of England and Wales.

Source: Independent, 9 May 1994 (adapted).

Resources such as footpaths and public parks also have a renewable resource element to them. If the rate of wear of footpaths for example exceeds the rate of regeneration of protective vegetation, degradation will occur, as illustrated in Exhibit 18.3.

One of the reasons for such overuse and degradation is that the use of footpaths and public parks is free to the user. In markets where prices prevail, price is an important factor in rationing the demand for scarce resources. Consumers economize on use so as to conserve their limited money income. Where price is zero, there is no incentive to economize. The

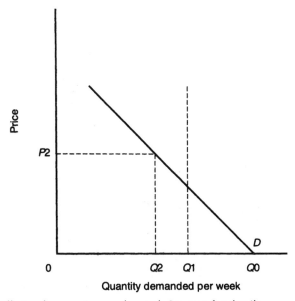

Figure 18.2   Effects of zero price on demand. See text for details.

use of unmetered water illustrates this point. For example, many people leave the tap on when they are cleaning their teeth, using a couple of pints of water where only half a cupful is needed since there is no incentive to economize on use. Figure 18.2 shows the economics behind this.

Curve D represents the demand curve for the use of a footpath. As price falls, demand rises. At price $P2$ demand would be $Q2$. If zero price is charged, demand rises to $0Q0$. For some paths this may result in usage which exceeds the limits where the resource can regenerate itself. If $0Q1$ represents the point of use beyond which regeneration cannot take place, then $Q1Q0$ represents use which causes degeneration of the resource at zero price.

The macroeconomy and waste

Figure 18.3 recalls the simple circular flow of income model used earlier to underpin introductory macroeconomic analysis.

Factors of production are purchased by firms from households and combined to produce goods and services which are then sold to households. Household expenditure is financed from the income derived from selling factors of production to firms. Additionally there are leakages from the system in the form of taxes, savings and imports, as well as injections into the system of government spending, investment and exports.

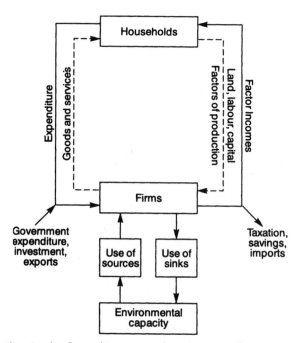

Figure 18.3 The circular flow of income and environmental capacity.

However, in its simple form, the model fails to illustrate some key points about the relationship of the economy to the environment. In particular it fails to show the production of waste materials (use of sinks) and the using-up of resources (use of sources). In fact the production of waste materials is partially covered by the model and partially not. Exhibit 18.4 illustrates this point.

The article is about Newquay in Cornwall, UK, whose population of 100 000 is swollen by up to a million summer visitors. A key product of the tourism industry is sewage. This waste is collected and partially treated by South West Water, and this activity is picked up by traditional economics in the simple circular flow diagram as the use of factors of production to perform a service. However the raw sewage that is discharged directly into the sea represents the use of a waste sink and the simple circular flow model does not reflect this.

The circular flow model can show an increase in economic growth caused by tourism – increased expenditure, generating increased incomes which in turn allow increased expenditure – without highlighting a significant threat to such growth in terms of pollution effects. The use of the waste sink is free to South West Water and thus there is little incentive for it to amend its behaviour. There is, though, clearly a limit to the capacity of the sea to assimilate this waste. Where this assimilative capacity is exceeded, degradation of the sea occurs.

Environmental economics seeks to make the link between economic production – in this case tourism – on the one hand, and the production of and the ability of the ecosystem to absorb waste on the other. It further seeks to amend economic models to incorporate this relationship so that such economic development can take place without causing feedback which would threaten economic development, or cause an unacceptable level of pollution.

Thus Figure 18.3 adds an environmental dimension to the simple circular flow model to highlight that production uses sources and sinks and that the environment has a limited capacity to meet these demands.

Exhibit 18.4   Surfing in the sewers

'I've just come back from a surf. The water quality wasn't too bad today because the wind was blowing offshore and the tide was going out. When the wind blows on to the shore and when the tide is high you still get the occasional pad or condom floating by.'

The surfers are far from happy. And it's not hard to see why. A quick walk on to the headland and you notice the air begins to smell rich, sweet and vile. A brown slick drifts out to sea off the point. Tucked away beneath the cliffs is its source – the same old sewage outflow pipe, pumping out output all day long.

Source: *Guardian*, 5 August 1994 (adapted).

Open access and overuse

There is a particular problem posed by open access to resources. The sea is an example of an open-access resource. It does not have a clear owner and therefore it is difficult to exert property rights over it – for example, preventing waste dumping. Because of this there is little incentive to reduce outflows into the sea.

The problem becomes more difficult with seas such as the Mediterranean. The Mediterranean coastline is shared by a number of countries. If one country should decide to reduce outflows of sewage into the sea, it will still suffer the ill-effects of the outflows from other countries who might even think that there is now more capacity for their sewage.

Exhibit 18.5 goes beneath the sea to record the destruction of an open-access resource.

Environmental effects of other sectors on the leisure and tourism sector

The general environmental concerns of global warming, ozone depletion, acid rain and atmospheric pollution each have impacts on the leisure and tourism sector.

Exhibit 18.5   Reefs under threat

It took thousands of years to create the majestic coral reefs that lie under the earth's oceans. These vast limestone structures have been laid over the centuries by reef-building corals. They are home to a huge diversity of plants and over 200 species of fish.

The Great Barrier Reef, off the coast of Australia extends for some 2000 kilometres and is a magnet for scuba divers. The Belize Barrier Reef stretches for some 250 kilometres off the coast of Belize in central America.

But the reefs are under threat from industry, from agriculture and from tourism. Industrial fishing techniques using dynamite can blow up the fragile polyps that create the reefs. Rain forest clearance smothers the Belize Reef as thickly polluted run-off flows out of the rivers into the oceans.

Meanwhile, the tourism trade is set to kill one of its golden gooses. Whilst some boat operators practise good conservation methods and coach and cajole their clients to respect the coral, the growing size of the tourist tide threatens reef preservation. Boatloads of inexperienced snorkellers and divers regularly inflict unintentional damage, by touching sensitive polyps or smashing coral branches with a kick of a flipper.

But not all the damage is accidental. Some boat operators let their anchors drop on the reefs – the damage is evident by the clouds of debris thrown up. And some tourists seem unable to resist taking home just one small momento ('that won't make any difference'). For those who don't make the dive themselves there are plenty of willing hands – and souvenir shops in reef resorts are often full of rare shells and coral curios.

Source: The author, from press cuttings, January 1995.

The early 1990s for example witnessed successive years of poor snow conditions in European ski resorts. Global warming would clearly have an impact on the height of snow cover, thus putting low-level resorts out of business and shortening the length of the ski season. For example, a weather forecasting model at the UK Hadley Centre for Climate Prediction and Research predicts a 3°C increase in UK average temperatures between 1998 and 2100. This is based on estimated outputs and effects of greenhouse gases. The results are bad news for the Scottish ski industry since more of the precipitation that falls in Scotland will be in the form of rain rather than snow. Exhibit 18.6 demonstrates alarming possible effects of global warming.

Carbon dioxide emissions, the main source of which is fossil-fuel burning, are the main contributor to global warming. Some commentators have predicted an increase in the average surface temperature of the earth of between 2 and 5°C over the next hundred years if carbon dioxide emissions double over the same period.

However not only are the physics and the chemistry of this calculation fraught with uncertainty, but so are the economics. It is difficult to predict the rate of economic growth and the subsequent demand for fossil-fuel burning for energy provision. Also there is a time lag between the emission of greenhouse gases and the effect on global warming.

Exhibit 18.6 'Paradise' islands unite against sea-level threat: alarm over global warming – Geoffrey Lean

Fakaofu Atoll, the main island of the watery territory of Tokelau, has just one of the world's 400 million automobiles and it is making a lonely contribution to the island's impending extinction.

Tokelau, a group of islands administered by New Zealand – just 12 square kilometres of land in more than 250 000 square kilometres of Pacific Ocean – is expected, literally, to be wiped off the map by pollution. So are six other scattered strings of atolls, including similar dependencies and independent nations, among them the 1196-island state of the Maldives in the Indian Ocean.

As carbon dioxide emitted by fuel burned in the world's cars, homes and industries heats up the climate, many scientists believe that the seas will rise and eventually drown such low-lying islands.

Though small may be beautiful, however, it is also vulnerable. These islands' water supplies are usually limited and are increasingly being depleted by the tourism on which at least half their economies depend. Tourism increases pollution – only one-tenth of the sewage produced by the 20 million people who visit the Caribbean each year receives any kind of treatment. Increasingly dirty seas and oil spills imperil economies.

But the greatest threat of all comes from global warming. The highest point on the main island of Kiribas, in the Pacific Ocean, is 2 foot above sea level; and scientists' best estimate is that the seas will rise higher than this over the next century.

Source: Independent on Sunday, 13 March 1994 (adapted).

Exhibit 18.7   Lights, camera, destruction

Twentieth-Century Fox, searching for a location to film Alex Garland's best-selling novel, *The Beach*, chose Maya Bay on Phi Phi Ley island, situated off southern Thailand. The film stars Leonardo DiCaprio and Tilda Swinton. However, Maya Bay's natural state of scrub bushes did not quite fit the imagination of the producer of the film, Andrew Macdonald. He wanted coconut trees and long clear views over sand and sea and gained permission from the Thai forestry department to give the beach a makeover. The government added its blessing to the project saying that the film would benefit the economy by promoting Thailand.

However, John Vidal reported in *The Observer* that 'More than half of the level section of the beach has now been dug up and the sand dunes broken up. Hundreds of holes have been dug, destroying the roots of plants that hold the dunes together.' The actions of the film unit have attracted the attentions of local environmental groups. They staged a demonstration on the beach wearing DiCaprio masks and protested that the damage caused by digging up plants was damaging the ecosystem and would lead to beach erosion.

Ozone depletion may also affect the leisure and tourism sector. The ozone layer is a layer of gas around the earth which protects it from ultra-violet radiation from the sun. Recent thinning of the ozone layer has been attributed to use of CFCs – chlorofluorocarbons – which have been used in the manufacture of spray cans and refrigerators. The main harmful effects of ozone depletion are to increase the danger of skin cancer after exposure to the sun. Clearly this may affect the demand for holidays based around sunbathing.

Acid rain is the term given to acidic deposits caused mainly by the emission of sulphur dioxide into the atmosphere by industry. Its main effects in the leisure and tourism sector include:

- corrosion of buildings (particularly the stonework found on cathedrals)
- damage to trees (making forest areas less attractive to tourism)
- pollution of rivers and lakes

The external effects of specific industrial developments can also have an impact on the leisure and tourism sector.

Exhibit 18.7 illustrates the effects of the film industry on the tourism sector.

Positive environmental effects of leisure and tourism

Although much of the environmental debate focuses on the detrimental effects of economic development, there are also benefits which can be noted. The inflow of foreign tourists to London for example sustains a breadth of

---

Exhibit 18.8   Deforestation: The tourism alternative

In 1990 about 11 000 square kilometres of Amazonian rainforest were cleared and by 1995, that figure had jumped to more than 29 000 square kilometres. The latter represents an area equivalent to over 6 million football fields. The forest is being subjected to a series of developments which involve its wholesale destruction. These include industrial-scale agriculture schemes, cattle ranching and tropical timber cutting. To support these schemes there have been forest highway projects, energy distribution schemes and resettlement programmes.

The environmental consequences of this destruction are threefold. First, the Amazon rainforest is home to Amerindian settlements. Second, it contains almost 50 per cent of the world's terrestrial species and is a crucial site for maintaining biodiversity. The Amazon rainforest also plays an important role in the global carbon and water cycles. Trees are essential in reducing carbon dioxide levels in the atmosphere and about one-fifth of the earth's fresh water flows down the river Amazon. Meanwhile, carbon emissions from slash-and-burn clearance programmes add to global warming.

Nigel Sizer, a senior associate with the World Resources Institute and José Goldemberg who has an environment portfolio in the Brazilian government, suggest alternative uses of the forest to prevent its destruction, emphasizing the role leisure and tourism can play: 'Brazil is receiving hundreds of millions of dollars in international assistance administered by the World Bank to reduce deforestation. More careful use of these G-7 funds could go a long way towards combating the crisis . . . Investments could be made in alternative development, such as community forestry, non-timber products, education and tourism, instead of subsidizing rainforest destruction'.

Source: The Author, 1999.

---

theatres that could not be supported by the indigenous population. The existence of tourism in remote rural areas can make the difference between local shops remaining profitable, and therefore open, or not. Similarly the income and interest derived from tourists help to preserve heritage sites, contributing to restoration and upkeep. National parks and forest provide not only facilities for tourism but also preserve habitats for flora and fauna.

Exhibit 18.8 illustrates the potential for tourism to counter global deforestation.

Review of key terms

● Environmental economics = analysis of human well-being as well as the flow of money in the economy.
● Defensive GNP expenditure = expenditure that takes place to defend or protect one party from the external effects of the activities of another (e.g. double glazing as a defence from noise pollution).

- Externalities = those costs or benefits arising from production or consumption of goods and services which are not reflected in market prices.
- ISEW = Index of Sustainable Economic Welfare.
- Non-renewable resources = those which have a fixed supply.
- Renewable resources = those which are capable of being replenished.
- Waste sink = part of the environment where waste products are deposited.
- Assimilative capacity = ability of sink to absorb waste.

Data questions

Task 18.1   Cashing in on a hole in the sky: David Nicholson-Lord argues that green economics should replace Adam Smith

The adage that every cloud has a silver lining is even truer now that the sun is shining. This month saw the start of an alliance between Boots and the Cancer Research Campaign to promote 'sensible sun behaviour'. The benefits for the Cancer Research Campaign are obvious: extra money for research. But what's in it for Boots?

Here's a clue. There are five 'play safe in the sun' guidelines and at least three involve buying something: sunhats, sunglasses, suncream. Who sells sunglasses? Why, Boots does – in fact it is offering customers discounts if they trade in their old ones. Boots also sells suncream. The lucrative sun-protection market is worth £110 m and Boots has about 47 per cent of it.

The hidden factor in all this is the gap in the ozone layer opening up 20 miles above our heads and letting in carcinogenic radiation. Skin cancer rates in the UK are double those of 20 years ago, and although lazing on foreign beaches is still largely to blame, the ozone factor is catching up fast. In the USA alone, accelerating ozone loss could cause an extra 200 000 skin-cancer deaths over the next 50 years. Profit margins on suncreams are about 50 per cent and the market is growing at around 4 per cent a year. Suncreams with a high protection factor make up 70 per cent of it. From a purely business perspective, holes in the ozone layer are exceptionally good news.

There is another, more serious angle to this. When the Treasury does its sums, that portion of the £110 m sun-protection market arising from worries about ultraviolet radiation will be added to GNP and will count as economic growth. Thanks to the hole in the ozone layer and the skin cancer epidemic, we will all be that little bit richer. As a way of measuring progress, this is clearly a nonsense, since the quality of our lives will undoubtedly be poorer.

Fortunately, some economists are developing a better way of assessing growth. Later this year the New Economics Foundation, a group of 'green' economists, will produce the UK's first index of sustainable welfare, a form of alternative GNP measuring progress since the fifties, not only in income but in areas such as health, education, diet and environmental quality. These developments signify that the environmental movement is evolving a coherent critique of conventional economic theory which includes a response to the accelerating pace of planetary degradation – global warming in particular.

The global free market emerges as one of the villains. To a generation nourished on the idea that unlimited free trade is a good thing, this may be hard to accept. It rests on the assumptions that, first, cash relationships are invading and destroying areas of community life in which they have no place; and second, far from being a benevolent 'invisible hand' – Adam Smith's phrase – the market is blind to the environmental and social destruction it causes. Hence the global cash economy is a game that only the rich and powerful can win.

Which brings us back to Boots and the GNP. In the postwar era, GNP has been transmuted from being a purely statistical tool into a national political goal. Unscrambling it promises to be an exercise both cathartic and revelatory. An index of sustainable economic welfare developed in the USA, for example, shows that while the sum total of economic activity, measuring both 'good' and 'bad' expenditure, has continued to increase, improvements in welfare levelled off in the late sixties and since 1979 have declined.

In other words, we have lots more suncream, sunglasses and sunhats – but we can't really enjoy the sunshine any more.

Source: *The Independent*: 31 May 1993 (adapted).

Questions

1 'Thanks to the hole in the ozone layer . . . we will all be that little bit richer.'
   (a) Explain what is meant by this.
   (b) Explain why 'this is clearly a nonsense'.
2 'The environmental movement is evolving a coherent critique of conventional economic theory.' Explain the meaning of this statement.
3 Explain what economic 'goods' and 'bads' derive from leisure and tourism economic activities.
4 Should green economics replace Adam Smith?
5 Distinguish between GDP and ISEW using this article.

Task 18.2   Tourist overcrowding spoils enjoyment of historic venue: Chester approaches saturation point – David Nicholson-Lord

So many tourists are crowding into Chester, one of Britain's oldest and most beautiful cities, that they are spoiling it for each other, according to the first 'environmental capacity' study by a local authority.

The study, to be published next month, highlights the dilemma faced by many historic towns where visitor numbers are nearing saturation point. It examines pedestrian densities in the city using a test of psychological 'comfort' developed by an American academic.

According to the English Historic Towns Forum, centres such as Cambridge, York and Canterbury are struggling to cope with pollution, congestion and growing tensions between residents and visitors. Some towns are now trying to discourage visitors. The Chester study examined walking speeds, traffic flows and pedestrian numbers and found widespread evidence of tension caused by the 'competing demands for the limited street space in the heart of the city'. In much of the historic centre, pedestrian comfort was 'below acceptable levels', it said. 'In the most critical locations, [the] tension is strained beyond capacity.' The crowding was 'detracting from any pleasure of being in this historically rich environment'.

Chester, a city of 119 000, has an estimated 2–3 million visitors a year, most of whom crowd into a narrow centre inside the Roman walls. A spokesman for the city said pedestrian pressures were sometimes 'uncomfortable', adding: 'We are looking at what development Chester can sustain without further erosion of the fabric and the historic centre.' Pedestrianisation and new bus routes are being considered.

In a new guide for historic towns, the forum, and the English Tourist Board, urge them to adopt 'visitor management plans'. Stephen Mills, head of development at the board, said many places felt they had too many visitors 'but you can't stop people coming – therefore you need to manage them in order to survive'.

In Cambridge, however, the council has refused to promote the town. One theme suggested – but not adopted – was the 'Great Cambridge stay away day', with the slogan: 'Cambridge is full – we don't want you.'

York, according to the forum, has reached a ceiling on visitors.

Bourton-on-the-Water, the most visited village in the Cotswolds, also 'suffers intensely from congestion and other problems'. In Bath, residents had turned hosepipes on open-top tourist buses.

Source: *The Independent*, 31 May 1994.

Questions

1 What are externalities?
2 Classify the leisure and tourism-related externalities into:
   (a) production on production
   (b) production on consumption
   (c) consumption on consumption
   (d) consumption on production
3 What are the economic causes of 'crowding [that is] detracting from any pleasure of being in this historically rich environment [of Chester]'.

Task 18.3   Fasten your seatbelts and prepare for unsustainable take-off

The Heathrow Association for the Control of Aircraft Noise (HACAN) has recently published data from a number of sources about the effects that airports have on their local environment. These include:

● Sedative use increases by 8 per cent in areas affected by aircraft noise.
● Fourteen per cent more anti-asthma drugs are consumed by people living within 10 kilometres of an airport.

- Transport 2000 calculates that every return air ticket generates an average of four car journeys.
- Dr Meyer Hillman, a transport specialist, has shown that every passenger on a return flight to Florida is responsible for a discharge of 1.8 tonnes of carbon dioxide.
- The Intergovernmental Panel on Climate Change is expected to show that aircraft emissions are responsible for about 10 per cent of the world's carbon dioxide production.
- Mortality rates are near Los Angeles Airport are 5 per cent higher than in quieter places.
- The reading ability of 12–14-year-olds who attend schools under flight paths is reduced by 23 per cent.
- Children exposed to aircraft noise are more likely to develop anxiety disorders.
- Airport expansion means more noise and less countryside.
- CO_2 emissions are forecast to increase by 500 per cent by 2100.
- High-altitude carbon emissions from aircraft are less likely to be reabsorbed by forests or oceans than other emissions, and are therefore more serious threats to the greenhouse effect
- Sulphur dioxide emissions from aircraft on the polar routes contribute to ozone depletion.

Source: HACAN.

Questions

1 What externalities are associated with air travel?
2 Assess the impact of air travel on renewable and non-renewable resources
3 Are the quiet skies an example of open access over-use ?
4 What evidence is there to suggest that the market equilibrium of air traffic exceeds the optimum social equilibrium?
5 How should GDP figures be adjusted to take account of the externalities of air travel?

Short questions

1 What additions and what subtractions would environmental economists like to see with regard to GNP figures?
2 Distinguish between the four types of externalities.
3 What unpriced externalities arise from the:
   (a) location of a football stadium?
   (b) building of the channel tunnel?
   (c) development of a lakeside campsite?
4 Under what circumstances are renewable resources exhaustible?
5 What environmental problems arise from open-access resources?

Websites of interest

New Economics Foundation
  http://sosig.ac.uk/neweconomics/newecon.html
Tourism Concern   http://www.gn.apc.org/tourismconcern/
Friends of the Earth   www.foe.co.uk
Surfers against Sewage   www.sas.org.uk
United National Environmental Programme –
  Tourism   http://www.unepie.org/tourism/home.html
British Airways: Environment Report
  http://www.british-airways.com/inside/comm/environ/environ.shtml
Learning help in economics and business studies   http://www.bized.ac.uk

19 Sustainability and 'green' leisure and tourism

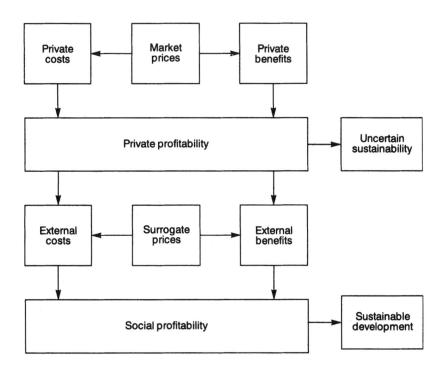

Objectives

Chapter 18 examined the environmental impacts of the leisure and tourism sector. It considered ways in which the market failed to signal long-term problems of resource depletion, waste production and disposal, and other unpriced externalities. It highlighted the distinction between what was most profitable for firms and what was most profitable for society as a whole. It chronicled a wealth of evidence of undesirable results if the market was left to dictate future developments without any regard for wider environmental considerations.

This chapter examines strategies for utilizing environmental economic analysis to enable development of the leisure and tourism sector to take place with due regard to possible side-effects. The aim of such analysis is to prevent the side-effects of development causing socially unacceptable damage to the environment or indeed to stifle the very developments themselves.

By studying this chapter students will be able to:

- understand the limitations of the price mechanism in allocating resources in respect of environmental considerations
- explain the meaning of sustainable development
- utilize the concept of cost-benefit analysis to determine the value of a project to society as a whole
- evaluate a variety of methods to impute value to unpriced externalities
- evaluate different policy instruments for encouraging sustainability and environmental consideration
- understand the range of influences on environmental policy

The price mechanism and the environment

The market economy does in fact have an in-built tendency to conserve resources. In the model where competing firms seek to maximize their profits, since profit is defined as total revenue minus total costs, there is a constant pressure to economize on resources and hence minimize costs. Exhibit 19.1 is a transcript of a report on the Radio 4 Today Programme which shows this principle in action.

However the current market price of resources is not always an accurate measure of its true cost. This is particularly the case for unpriced open-access resources such as the sea. Chapter 18 explored the fact that, whilst the costs of sewage pumping into the sea were minimal for water companies, considerable pollution costs are incurred by other users of the sea. Similarly the loss of landscape and views caused by tourism destination development is not apparent in the profit and loss accounts of the organizations involved. Equally the price mechanism does not give due regard to the future. Overexploitation of non-renewable resources such as coastline, countryside, rivers and mountains may leave future generations materially worse off than the current population. These considerations mean that the market often leads to overproduction and overdevelopment of projects where there are considerable unpriced externalities.

Meaning of sustainable development

There is considerable debate about the precise definition of sustainable development. It should also be noted that several levels of sustainability may be considered. At the widest level, sustainability of world economic development embraces those planet-threatening issues of global warming,

---

Exhibit 19.1   Costs of green business a lie

Sue MacGregor: Now, a book published this week appears to knock on its head the old adage that it costs business the earth to protect the environment: the authors of the book say the opposite is often the case. Roger Harabin reports on a news story that seems almost too good to be true.

First woman: This is your room, sir.

Roger Harabin: Hotels gobble power, and power pollutes.

First woman: You've got the television over here; over here we've got a mini-bar, fully stocked . . .

Roger Harabin: But one hotel group has switched on to a little-used form of power generation that's cleaner than others. At the Russell Hotel in central London the secret is in the basement. Here under the plush reception rooms is the hotel's very own generating station. In a normal power station the heat from making electricity goes to waste, but the Forte group has installed a system called combined heat and power which pipes the hot water to warm the bedrooms. The manager, Ben Sington, says the savings are enormous.

Ben Sington: When they told me that they were going to give me a machine in this useless piece of space, and give me £6000 worth of savings a year I couldn't believe it, and it's true, it has given me that.

Source: *The Today Programme*, Radio 4, 12 September 1994 (adapted).

---

resource depletion and ozone loss. Sustainability can also be considered at a national economy level, at a regional level, at a tourism destination level and at an individual leisure or tourism project level.

The 1987 *Brundtland Report* for the World Commission on Environment and Development defined sustainability as 'development that meets the needs of the present without compromising the ability of future generations to meet their own needs'. It therefore laid considerable emphasis on what is termed 'intergenerational equity'.

Key elements in this approach to sustainable development are first, the rate of use of renewable and non-renewable resources and maintenance of natural capital. Implicit here is that renewable resources should not be used beyond their regenerative capacities. Additionally, where non-renewable resources are used up, future generations should be compensated by the provision of substitute capital in some form so that, at the minimum, a constant stock of capital is maintained across generations.

The second key element in the *Brundtland Report* is consideration of the effects of development on waste sinks.

Sustainability has also been defined as growth which is not threatened by feedback, for example, pollution, resource depletion or social unrest. This can be related to tourism destination development. In this case sustainability would be that level of development which did not exceed the carrying capacity of the destination and thus cause serious or irreversible changes to the destination. It is development that can sustain itself in the long run.

It is also possible to consider environmental costs and benefits when considering specific projects. This approach considers the total social and private costs against the total private and social benefits of a project with a view to summarizing its total social value, taking into consideration environmental impacts as well as market profitability.

The key principles of sustainability can be summarized as:

● consideration of externalities
● consideration of depletion of non-renewable resources
● tailoring use of renewable resources to their regenerative capacity
● tailoring of economic activity to the carrying capacity of the environment

Since the operation of the free market in its present form does not guarantee the inclusion of the above principles in resource allocation, it follows that the implementation of sustainable development will involve modifications of free market activity. These implementation issues are considered in the remainder of this chapter.

Cost–benefit analysis

Individuals are constantly, if unconsciously, performing private cost–benefit analyses when making purchasing decisions. They compare the costs to themselves of purchasing an item (its price) with the benefits of purchase (the satisfaction they receive). Similarly, firms compare the costs of producing an extra good or service with the benefits (revenue) received from doing so. Cost–benefit analysis makes similar comparisons except that it includes the wider costs and benefits to society as well as those accruing privately to firms and individuals.

For a project or development to be socially acceptable the sum of the benefits to society (including external and private benefits) must exceed the sum of the cost to society (including external and private costs). This may be written as

$$\Sigma B > \Sigma C$$

where Σ means 'the sum of', B = to the benefits to society and C = the costs to society.

A problem arises from using this equation in its raw form. When we measure costs and benefits, some happen immediately, and some happen at some future date. People would prefer to have money today than in the future. This is because £100 today is worth more than a promise of £100 in 10 years since it can earn interest in the intervening period. Therefore future values must be adjusted to give present values. This is known as discounting and the rate used to discount is generally related to the long-term interest rate. The formula for finding a present value is:

$$\frac{B_t}{(1 + r)^t}$$

where B_t = the benefit in year t and r = the discount rate.

Thus incorporating discounting techniques to the formula for social acceptability for projects gives:

$$\frac{B_t}{(1 + r)^t} > \frac{C_t}{(1 + r)^t}$$

where C_t is the benefit in year t.

There is considerable debate amongst environmental economists about the use of discount rates since, if environmental damage resulting from a project results in the distant future, then its effects are minimized in cost–benefit analysis by discounting. It is felt by some that this attributes too little significance to, for example, the potential damage caused by storing nuclear waste.

Pricing the environment

It is relatively straightforward for firms to perform private cost–benefit analysis and determine a profit-maximizing level of output. The costs of inputs are readily available and selling prices can be gauged from scanning the competition, from historical data and, ultimately, are determined in the market. There are thus some firm figures which inform production levels.

However when we move into the arena of external costs and benefits we encounter the problem of missing markets and thus find pricing difficult. We can easily calculate the costs of aircraft use in terms of fuel, staffing and depreciation, but how do we measure the cost of aircraft noise? We clearly need to address this problem if we are to use cost–benefit analysis to determine a level of economic development which maximizes total private and social profitability.

Several methods have been developed by environmental economists to impute value for unpriced goods or services and these are now explained.

Willingness to pay (WTP) method

Here survey techniques are used to find out how much households are willing to pay for the preservation of an environmental asset – for example, a piece of woodland threatened by a road development. The survey can include people who are currently visiting the asset and those who do not visit it but care about it. The total valuation of the asset can then be found by multiplying the average WTP by the number of people who enjoy the asset.

The main difficulty of using the WTP method is whether respondents reply to the hypothetical WTP question in the same way as they would if faced with actual payment.

Hedonistic pricing method (HPM)

Hedonistic pricing values environmental resources by considering their effect on the prices of goods or services that have readily observable market prices. House prices are a convenient yardstick for this exercise.

House prices are affected by a number of factors – condition, number of rooms, central heating, garden size and nearness to transport and shops. They are also affected by environmental factors, for example prices will be depressed by the presence of aircraft noise and increased by the presence of a park. HPM involves the collection of data recording price, and the presence or absence of all the salient determinants of price. Once a price can be established to reflect the non-environmental factors (number of rooms, etc.) then the effects of the environmental factor under analysis (e.g. aircraft noise) can be attributed to variations in the price of houses with otherwise similar characteristics. An imputed cost can then be attributed for aircraft noise nuisance.

Difficulties involved with HPM mainly centre around the large number of differences that occur between houses, and the changes in other factors such as interest rates during data collection.

Travel cost method (TCM)

The assumption behind this method of environmental asset valuation is that there is a relationship between the travel costs that a visitor has incurred to visit a tourism or recreational site and their valuation of that site. The attraction of this method is that travel costs for visitors by car are readily measurable as they consist mainly of petrol costs. A survey records the distance visitors travelled to the site, and technical details about their car. From this, travel costs are calculated. This is then compared to the number of visits the individual makes per year to the site.

Figure 19.1 illustrates a typical scatter diagram which might result from plotting travel costs against number of visits, after adjusting for other factors such as income differences. A typically shaped demand curve $D0$ relates the price of visiting the site (measured by travel costs) to the demand (the number of visits per year). A total value of the site for recreational use can be obtained from this information.

There are however problems which arise in using TCM. First travelling involves use of time which represents an additional cost for many people. Second, some people may arrive on bicycle or on foot and thus register no

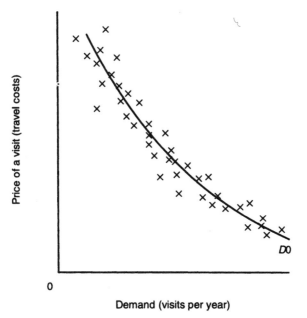

Figure 19.1 Use of travel cost method to construct a demand curve for a tourism/recreational site.

travel cost, even though their actual valuation of the site may be positive. Third, people may combine visiting the site with other activities on the same journey and it is difficult to unscramble the contribution of travel costs to each.

Dose–response method

This valuation method depends upon the availability of data linking the effects of pollution to a response in, for example, human health, or crop production. The effects of sewage pollution in the sea could be measured in terms of medical resources needed to remedy pollution-induced sickness, and loss of earnings.

Replacement cost technique

This might offer a way of measuring some of the environmental effects of acid rain. For example, the cost of restoration of buildings damaged by such pollution could be measured and thus the cost of acid-rain pollution measured.

Mitigation behaviour method

Some pollution effects result in households undertaking defensive expenditure which can be measured in the market. The existence of aircraft noise pollution, for example, may lead households to fit double glazing to mitigate its effects. This defensive expenditure can be summed to find costs incurred from the pollution.

Privatization of free-access resources

Since free-access resources are often overused (for example the sea as a waste sink), privatization of such resources is sometimes advocated. In such a case use of the resources (e.g. sewage disposal) would have to be bought and thus a price would be charged for a hitherto free service. The price would fluctuate, like all market prices, to reflect the demand and supply of the service.

Controlling environmental damage

The first step towards controlling environmental damage and promoting sustainability is understanding the environmental impacts of economic activity, as described in Chapter 18. The next step is the measurement of external costs and benefits in monetary terms, as described in the previous section. This then raises the question of how such information can be used to provide a socially optimum use of resources in the economy (one that considers wider environmental effects than that produced from actions based solely on free market prices).

There are several possible solutions ranging from ownership, to direct regulation and market–based incentives.

Ownership

There is little incentive for an organization in the private sector to consider cost–benefit analysis when appraising a project. It will, instead, attempt to satisfy its shareholders by seeking to maximize profits. However, in principle a public sector organization has an incentive to consider social costs and benefits, since external costs will fall upon the electorate. The actual way in which public sector organizations approach externalities will in practice depend upon the demands of the government.

Voluntary sector organizations may have aims and objectives which encompass consideration of the full social costs and benefits. Exhibit 19.2, describing National Trust conservation work, illustrates this.

Direct regulation

Direct regulation methods, sometimes known as command and control (CAC), involve the government setting environmental standards. These might take the form of water quality standards or planning regulations. They can be divided into preventive controls and retrospective controls. By and large the preventive controls are more effective.

Exhibit 19.2   Issues

As a major conservation charity, the Trust does its utmost to practise what it preaches: it therefore aims to minimise adverse effects of its activities on the environment. Surveys of sewage and farm-waste discharges were largely completed in 1993, and innovative ways of treating waste and of minimising it in the first place are being brought in.

The Trust also committed itself to reducing its energy consumption and to producing full Environmental Impact Assessments for all proposals exploiting renewable energy.

Source: The National Trust; *The Year in Brief 1993–4.*

Planning permission is a preventive control seeking to stop developments that do not meet planning guidelines. Planning guidelines are devised to ensure that developments consider wider environmental issues and impacts. Enforcement is relatively straightforward since building may not commence without the necessary permission. This type of control is criticized for its bureaucratic nature and the extra costs that are generated.

Retrospective controls include the setting of environmental control targets, after the externality-producing project has been commissioned. These include limits to aircraft and other noise, and water quality levels. Litter laws and penalties also fall under this category. Critics argue that such control methods themselves use considerable resources in monitoring and policing the limits, and that non-compliance rates can be high. Figure 19.2 in the next section compares their effectiveness with green taxes.

Market-based incentives

The idea behind market-based incentives is to incorporate externalities into existing market prices so as to cause producers to adapt their behaviour accordingly. It follows the polluter pays principle (PPP) adopted by the OECD in 1972 as its key economic instrument for environmental policy.

The key to PPP is the adjustment of market prices so that firms pay the full and true costs of externalities or environmental degradation. Thus, instead of the environment being separate and external to the free market, the two are integrated, and market prices signal not just private costs and benefits but full social costs and benefits.

The main ways of implementing the PPP include deposit-refund schemes, marketable permits, product charges and emission charges.

Deposit-refund schemes

This is a scheme for encouraging recycling, as in bottle deposits, or in minimizing dumping, as in supermarket trolley schemes. If you dump your trolley you lose your deposit.

Marketable permits

Permits are issued allowing a given level of pollution. For example, the total number of noise units for aircraft could be stipulated for a particular airport. These permits are then tradable. Supporters of this system stress its flexibility. Some aircraft operators can reduce noise pollution more cheaply than others. They can do so and sell permits to those who find it expensive to reduce noise pollution. Thus the total amount of pollution is limited, but how it is achieved is likely to involve flexibility and lowest costs.

Product charges

This involves charges on goods or services which cause externalities in production, use or disposal. One of the economic justifications for taxes on alcohol is to reduce consumption and thus minimize externalities in use (being drunk and disorderly). It is interesting to speculate whether scenes such as those described in exhibit 19.3 are less common in countries such as Norway and Sweden where there are much higher alcohol taxes.

Emission charges

These are taxes on the emission of air, noise, water and solid waste pollution. Figure 19.2 compares the operation of an environmental tax with a direct environmental control.

Exhibit 19.3   Emergency: Britons having fun – Sandra Barwick

It was New Year's Eve, but the mood was not exactly festive in the accident and emergency department of St Thomas's Hospital. 'We don't normally have vomit bowls laid out at reception,' sighed the assistant director, Susan White, 'but those are what we are going to need.' The first casualty arrived, at 11.25, prone on his trolley, visible only in patches: large hairy legs, a pair of immobile trainers, some vomit-speckled hair. 'He's had a combination of beer, champagne and something else,' said the ambulanceman, deadpan. 'We think he's Spanish.' A faint cry of 'Waaaa-aaaa' came from the trolley as it was wheeled away.

At midnight, the chimes of Big Ben came over the television. In they came, one after the other, bound to their trolleys. Almost all were men in their late teens or early 20s, in dirty jeans over which they had vomited. Outside the minor surgeries department a line of men sat or lay: punchmarks embedded on their cheeks, bottles broken on their heads, noses broken, lips cut. One had been bitten, one had had a cigarette stubbed out on his eye.

'Happy New Year,' the ambulancemen said with ironic detachment to their prone charges.

Source: The Independent, 2 January 1993 (adapted).

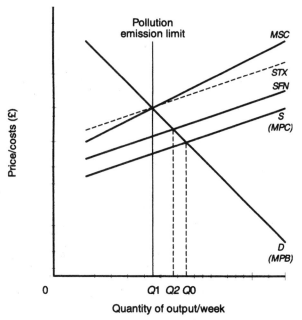

Figure 19.2 Comparison of taxation and direct environmental control. See text for details.

D represents the demand curve and marginal private benefit for a product. *S* represents the supply curve and marginal private costs of production. Profit-maximizing firms will continue to produce where the price paid for extra sales (indicated by the demand curve) is greater than the extra costs of production (marginal private cost). They will thus produce a level of output of 0Q0.

However, in this example, production causes pollution, and external costs. Adding these to marginal private costs generates the marginal social cost curve *MSC*. The socially optimum level of output is now found at 0Q1 since production should be increased at all points where marginal private benefit (MPB; indicated by how much consumers are willing to pay for extra units of the good) exceeds marginal social cost.

The imposition of a pollution tax is designed to make the firm internalize the previously external costs of pollution and integrate environmental considerations. A pollution tax which raised the marginal private costs curve (*S* or *MPC*) to *STX* would cause the firm's private profit-maximizing level of output to coincide with the social profit-maximizing level of output at 0Q1.

A similar result could be achieved by imposing a pollution emission limit at 0Q1. A system of fines would be needed to enforce such pollution limits. The system of monitoring of standards and imposition of fines is not totally effective, though. If, considering the likelihood and level of fine, the firm's *MPC* were only increased to *SFN*, then the firm would produce a level of output of 0Q2 – thus the system of direct control would be less effective than the system of taxation. It would also incur administrative costs.

In reality, although administrative costs are lower than for direct controls, there are several problems in setting an environmental tax. These include imputing monetary value to pollution costs, long-term pollution costs and the relating of pollution levels to output levels.

A further criticism of environmental taxes and environmental charging is their regressive nature, in that their effects will hit the poor proportionately more than the rich. In theory this problem might be addressed by compensating the poor by income tax adjustments.

Green consumers

Leisure and tourism consumers themselves have power to change the environmental effects of goods and services by purchasing those which are environmentally friendly. In order to do this they first need raised consciousness about the environmental effects of their purchases. Special-interest groups such as Friends of the Earth are an important source of consumer education in this respect.

Second consumers need more information supplied with goods and services about their environmental effects. Such 'ecolabelling' has gained ground in areas such as detergents but has yet to be widely adopted in key leisure and tourism products.

The power of the individual is also spreading from the high street to the stock exchange as ethical investors ask questions about environmental impacts when considering share purchases.

Policy shapers

Government environmental policy and thus its deployment of direct controls and market-based incentives is informed by a wide range of sources. The government itself will have a general political agenda which it wishes to pursue. Its own government departments, particularly the Department of Heritage, the Department of Transport, Regions and the Environment, are an important source of ideas. Publicly funded quangos such as the Sports Council, English Heritage and the Countryside Commission add to the picture. The leisure and tourism industry itself will lobby government either via individual firms or through trade associations such as the British Hospitality Association. Finally there is a range of voluntary associations and interest groups which generally focus on a particular issue. Examples include Tourism Concern, the Council for the Protection of Rural England and the Ramblers Association.

Firms' environmental policies

Increasingly, individual firms are appointing environmental managers, compiling environmental policies and conducting environmental audits and action plans. There are several motives for this. First, anticipation of

Exhibit 19.4   World Travel and Tourism Council environmental guidelines

Environmental improvement programs should be systematic and comprehensive. They should aim to:

- identity and continue to reduce environmental impact, paying particular attention to new projects
- pay due regard to environmental concerns in design, planning, construction and implementation
- be sensitive to conservation of environmentally protected or threatened areas, species and scenic aesthetics, achieving landscape enhancement where possible
- practice energy conservation
- reduce and recycle waste
- practice fresh-water management and control sewage disposal
- control and diminish air emissions and pollutants
- monitor, control, and reduce noise levels
- control and reduce environmentally unfriendly products, such as asbestos, CFCs, pesticides and toxic, corrosive, infectious, explosive or flammable materials
- respect and support historic or religious objects and sites
- exercise due regard for the interests of local populations, including their history, traditions and culture and future development
- consider environmental issues as a key factor in the overall development of travel and tourism destinations

Source: World Travel and Tourism Environmental Research Centre, 1994.

government controls may save money in the long run or even preclude their need. Second environmental action leads to savings on input costs. Finally an improved market image may result.

Leadership in this area has come from the CBI and the World Travel and Tourism Council (WTTC), both of which have published guidelines. The key WTTC guidelines are listed in exhibit 19.4.

Organizations such as BA produce a regular environmental report setting and monitoring targets for:

- noise
- emissions
- waste
- congestion
- tourism and conservation

Finally, environmental impact assessment (EIA) has become an EU requirement for some projects.

Review of key terms

- Sustainable development = development which can endure over the long run.
- Intergenerational equity = ensuring future generations do not inherit less capital than the current one.
- Natural capital = raw materials and the natural environment.
- Regenerative capacity = limit to harvesting of renewable resource whilst maintaining stock level.
- Cost–benefit analysis = comparison of full social costs and benefits of a project.
- Discounting = adjusting future monetary values to present monetary values.
- Willingness to pay (WTP) method = discovery of what people would be prepared to pay for a currently unpriced resource.
- Hedonistic pricing method (HPM) = imputing a price for an environmental externality by determining its effect on other prices.
- Travel cost method (TCM) = imputing the value of a site by measuring the cost of travel to it.
- Dose–response method = measuring effects of pollution in monetary terms.
- Replacement cost technique = measuring costs of pollution by calculating restoration costs.
- Mitigation behaviour method = measuring costs of pollution by counting defensive expenditure.
- Command and control (CAC) = direct regulations, e.g. water quality regulations.
- Market-based incentives = adjusting prices to reflect external costs.
- Polluter pays principle (PPP) = polluter pays the full cost of pollution effects.

Data questions

Task 19.1   A real adventure (and so cheap): 'sustainable tourism' gives little back to the Third World – Rupert Gordon-Walker

We wait on a path in the Hinku Valley as another weather-battered group creaks towards us from Mera, one of Nepal's 20 000 ft (about 6000 m) trekking mountains. Their strained, peeling faces contrast with their porters' clear complexions and bored expressions. One scabby Lancastrian in hi-tech gear gasps through windcracked lips, 'It's amazing. But now I'm shattered; I'm emotionally and physically drained.' Another mumbles that he will be back to 'conquer it next time', while 20 over-burdened, under-clad porters rush past, anxious that nothing should interrupt their journey home to the comfort of a wood fire. It is just as well they hurried away, as they might not have cared for the parting words of one of our number. 'They have to learn,' he said. 'They can't keep chopping down trees.' His remarks epitomised one of the chief ambiguities in what has come to be known as 'sustainable tourism' – tourism that, according to its proponents, should do minimal harm to the environment and tries to put something back.

The campaign for 'sustainable tourism' is a branch that sprouted from the 1987 report of the UN-sponsored World Commission on Environment and Development. The report, *Our Common Future*, extends the most recent hand-hold for those who feel, with Ruskin, fear and loathing for the 'plague wind' of industrialization.

Organisations like Tourism Concern, founded in 1988, are in the vanguard of a movement that derides so-called 'eco-tourism' – tourism to wilderness areas – as a marketing gimmick used by travel companies. 'Sustainable tourism', which aspires to put something back into underdeveloped countries, appears to be having little effect.

While World Tourist Organisation figures show a 17 per cent shift towards the Third World as the holiday-maker's preferred destination between 1980 and 1989, this increase has not had the predicted effect. If you ignore unquantifiable 'trickle-down' benefits, the Third World's share of receipts from tourism has actually fallen by 4 per cent.

This paradox is explained by a feature of such tourism that is depressingly evident to anyone who has endured the affronted whine of the professional on sabbatical when 'overcharged' for a taxi trip to the Giza pyramids that costs less than his Tube fare to work. You cannot help suspecting that the campaign for 'sustainable tourism' is little more than a rationalised desire to keep the Third World a cheap place to visit.

It is an inescapable fact that the notion of 'sustainable tourism' is riddled with internal conflicts. Its adherents tend to assume that the interests of the local communities coincide with their own desire to preserve such regions, whereas the local communities might actually prefer their national government's development schemes. It also tends to forget that by trying to preserve the colourful backwardness that supports their image of primitive arcadia, it may also be maintaining hideous levels of poverty and deep social injustices. In other words, 'sustainable tourism' may fail to make either an economic or a moral contribution to the regions it says it wants to help.

In a paper commissioned by the World Wide Fund for Nature called *Beyond the Green Horizon* (1992), Tourism Concern pleads for what we all yearn for when faced with wear and tear on our favourite landscape: the preservation of the status quo through restraint and positive conservation policies. It also insists that local people must determine whether their own backyard should receive visitors at all, and then reap the economic benefits if they do.

The alternative to preservation does not have to be sex tours to Manila, but nor should it be the creation of parks for Western interest groups that designate indigenous communities as 'guardians of nature and local customs'.

Self-indulgence is not the least of the faults of the self-righteous. In Banos, Ecuador, a 25-year-old Australian globe-trekker consults his *Lonely Planet* guide book. He eats muesli in a bed-and-breakfast run by a young ex-advertising couple from London, while New Age music hums from the CD player. He turns to a man who has recommended a cheap local guide for a jungle trip. 'It says he kills animals.' 'He has to, there aren't any cafés out there.' 'I don't care. I'm not impressed.'

Source: *The Independent*, 13 August 1993.

Questions

1 What definition of sustainable tourism is given in the article? How does it compare to the *Brundtland* definition of sustainability? Does the Nepal trek fulfil the conditions for sustainable tourism?
2 Is the chopping down of trees by local sherpas sustainable? If not, why does it occur?
3 'You cannot help suspecting that the campaign for 'sustainable tourism' is little more than a rationalised desire to keep the Third World a cheap place to visit.' Is this a just criticism or misunderstanding of sustainable tourism?
4 What problems of valuation of the natural environment might arise if cost–benefit analysis were used to judge between 'preserving colourful backwardness' of a tourism destination or providing industrial development?

Task 19.2   Environment: under deafening skies

Residents of the tiny village of Longford barely flinch any more. Living within a few hundred yards of one of Heathrow's two runways, they have become accustomed to the deafening roar of transatlantic jumbos as they heave themselves into the skies. Lunchtime conversation under umbrellas outside the White Horse stops involuntarily every few minutes to allow the ear-splitting din to die down. The plane passes, chatter resumes . . . for a moment.

'You get used to it,' the locals shrug philosophically. Many work or have worked at the airport. They have learned to rely for their sanity on the hours of relative peace when Heathrow switches its operations to the south runway. Until then, those at home tend to spend most of the time locked behind double glazing.

It might seem bad now, but with a dramatic increase in the number of passengers forecast by the aviation industry and consequent expansion plans, environmentalists are fearful of what lies ahead. At Heathrow, already the world's busiest international airport, the BAA has lodged a formal planning application for a massive fifth terminal costing £900 m, which will double the airport's annual capacity to nearly 80 million passengers.

Clusters of opposition groups have mushroomed around the country's main airports to fight the expansion plans. The argument they have to counter is the creation of much-needed jobs and the economic shot-in-the-arm which the aviation industry claims they would bring.

Rita Pearce, who has lived in Longford for 23 years and worked for Pan-American at Heathrow for 16, now believes enough is enough. The pollution has already taken its toll on her family's health, she says – she has had pleurisy five times in 2 years and her two daughters have developed asthma – and she believes increased air traffic and the introduction of night flights from October will make life there unbearable. 'It's going to be absolute hell,' she said.

If planning permission for the fifth terminal is granted, in addition to the main terminal building with up to three satellites, there are plans for three giant car parks, with access provided by a new spur road from the M25 spanning the Colne Valley Park, described by Friends of the Earth as a unique river valley in the capital, important for wildlife and recreation. The plans also assume the M25 will be widened to 14 lanes in the Staines area to the south-west. The sewage works, meanwhile, occupying the site of the proposed T5, would have to be shifted on to green belt land to the north-west of the airport.

Families in the area don't believe reassurances that T5 will not require a third runway. A report last week suggested that BA had drawn up plans for a new Heathrow runway to the south of the existing two.

Source: *Guardian*, 23 July 1993 (adapted).

Questions

1 Draw up a list of private and social costs and benefits of the development of T5.
2 In what ways could you attempt to measure the monetary value of the costs and benefits?
3 Under what economic circumstances should the T5 development go ahead?

Task 19.3   Show them the way to go Dome

January 1999's *Transport Retort* (the magazine of Transport 2000) reported on transport plans for the expected 70 000 daily visitors to the Millennium Dome in Greenwich, London. These include a tube link, satellite park-and-ride schemes, and car access only for orange badge holders. The government has promised a car-free event. However it is estimated that 25 per cent of visitors will make part of their journey by car or taxi. This means about one and a half million car journeys assuming two people to a car. Greenwich already suffers from poor air quality – during 1997, ozone, nitrogen dioxide and particulates* were higher than international health guidelines on at least twenty days – and the Dome will make things worse. This is especially serious for the 20 per cent

---

* Particulates are tiny pieces of solid or liquid matter that are small enough to go through natural body filters and penetrate the lungs. They are emitted by exhausts because of incomplete combustion of fuel. Some of the chemicals are carcinogenic (cause cancer).

of children who have asthma and the 10 per cent of adults who are unable to work because of a long-term respiratory illness. Public opinion has forced a reduction in inner-city park-and-ride schemes because they increase local congestion and pollution and arguably contribute to car dependency. However, a 1000-car site is still planned at Woolwich just across the river. In addition, traffic is likely to increase because of the new Sainsbury's (1400-car park) and the Millennium Eco-village (paradoxically including a 1423-car park). Greenwich council admit that many people may try to leave their cars just outside the mile-and-a-half parking exclusion zone.

In the mid-1990s, various organizations devised methodologies for measuring some of the external effects of road transport in the United Kingdom. The figures for air and noise pollution were approximately £20 000 million and £3000 million respectively, congestion costs about £19 000 million and the cost of death and injuries about £3000 m depending on the valuation put on a life.

Transport Retort in July 1998 listed other impacts of road transport including:

- Stress for travellers and residents.
- Loss of green space for roads and parking.
- Worsening health for increasingly car-dependent people (sedentary lifestyles in place of walking and cycling).
- Loss of independent mobility for children, senior citizens and non-car-owners because of deteriorating public transport.

Other external costs include the cost of providing street lighting and the associated light pollution, long term damage to buildings through vibration, and the deaths each year of about one million domestic and wild animals.

Sources: compiled by Nigel North from:
Transport Retort, January 1999, 'Dome Alone'.
Transport Retort, July 1998, diagram 'quantified health effects of traffic are only the tip of the iceberg'.
Blue Print 5, 'The True Costs of Road Transport' Maddison, Pearce *et al.*, (1996) Earthscan.
Royal Commission Report, (1995), *Transport and the Environment*, Oxford University Press.
How Vehicle Pollution Affects our Health, Ashden Trust, 1994.

Questions

1 What are externalities? List the external costs of road transport mentioned in the article.
2 In the estimates of external costs, each of the 3600 lives lost annually is valued at about £700 000. Some international studies argue that this figure should be closer to £2 million. With this new figure calculate the total measured external costs of road transport for the United Kingdom.

3 The special taxation (petrol duty and vehicle excise duty) paid by motorists is estimated at £26 000 million for 1998–1999. Comment on the argument that motorists pay too much tax.
4 The article lists some impacts which are not measured. Suggest ways to attempt to measure those external effects.
5 What practical policies would you suggest to persuade visitors to the Dome to leave their cars at home?

Task 19.4   WTTC environmental guidelines

Refer to WTTC guidelines listed in exhibit 19.4.

Questions

1 What incentives and disincentives are there for firms to adopt these guidelines?
2 Use the guidelines to evaluate critically the environmental friendliness of a named organization in the leisure and tourism sector.

Task 19.5

Table 19.1 illustrates some of the possible economic benefits and costs of leisure and tourism. Critically review the comprehensiveness of the table and use it as a basis to analyse the effects of two leisure or tourism developments.

Table 19.1   Leisure and tourism costs and benefits

Benefits	Costs
Satisfaction of wants	Distortion of local prices
Employment	Satisfaction of some wants at the expense of others
Foreign exchange earnings	Imports
Technology transfer	Congestion
Improved health	Aesthetic degradation
Better understanding of things	Pollution
Regeneration in depressed areas	Resource depletion
Engine for economic growth	Erosion
Source of profit	Loss of natural environment
	Loss of local control of resources

Short questions

1 List the various parties that would wish to influence a named leisure or tourism development and identify their viewpoints.
2 Explain the various ways in which the cost of aircraft noise could be imputed.
3 What is the approximate present value of £100 due in a year's time, if the discount rate is 10 per cent?
4 What are the essential elements of sustainable development?
5 What are the five key stages in cost-benefit analysis?

Websites of interest

Tourfor: Environmental management of leisure in forest areas
    http://www.buckscol.ac.uk/leisure/tourfor/home.htm
British Airways Environmental Report
    http://www.british-airways.com/inside/Comm/environ/environ.shtml
WTTC   www.wttc.org/
Green Globe: A worldwide environmental management and awareness
    programme for the travel and tourism industry
    http://www.greenglobe.org/
EcoNett: links to environmental tourism pages
    (via home page of) www.wttc.org
Tourism Concern   http://www.gn.apc.org/tourismconcern/
Friends of the Earth   www.foe.co.uk
Surfers against Sewage   www.sas.org.uk
United Nations Environmental Programme – tourism
    http://www.unepie.org/tourism/home.htm
Learning help in economics and buisness studies   http://www.bized.ac.uk

Part Seven
Integrated Case Studies

20 Integrated case studies

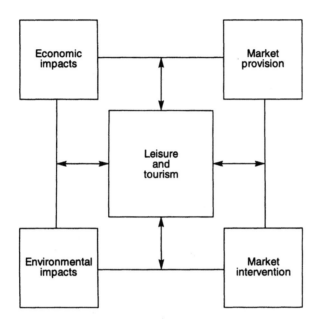

Objectives

The objectives of the case studies in this chapter are to analyse economic features and developments in the leisure and tourism sector which cut across chapter headings. This is shown in Figure 20.1.

Case 1

Is ecotourism sustainable? Costa Rica – too successful for its own good

A three-hour boat trip through a maze of jungle-lined canals takes us from the town of Moín, on the Caribbean coast of Costa Rica, to Tortuguero, 'the turtle region'. As we drift through the sinuous turns of the waterways, our guide points out monkeys, snakes, caimans, mud turtles and dozens of different birds. A real-life amusement park with awesome jungle life! The

	Case 1	Case 2	Case 3	Case 4
CH1	X		X	
CH2		X	X	
CH3		X		
CH4		X		X
CH5		X		
CH6		X	X	
CH7	X	X	X	X
CH8		X		X
CH9		X	X	
CH10		X		
CH11		X		
CH12		X		
CH13			X	
CH14	X	X		X
CH15	X		X	
CH16		X		
CH17	X	X	X	X
CH18	X	X		X
CH19	X	X		X

Figure 20.1   Matrix of chapter subjects in case studies

hamlet of Tortuguero has two churches, three bars, two souvenir shops and is the headquarters of the Caribbean Conservation Corporation (CCC). The organization runs the Tortuguero National History Museum and works with researchers and paying volunteers to monitor sea turtle activity and bird populations. The CCC was active in instigating the creation of Tortuguero National Park to protect the endangered species of sea turtles poached for their shells, meat and eggs – a rumoured aphrodisiac. Our nocturnal visit to witness the fascinating natural ritual of turtle nesting has to be arranged with a certified local guide. No memorabilia pictures allowed since flashlights deter turtles from nesting. Our guide explains: 'Before the park was created in 1973, people used to live by hunting the turtles. Now most locals have some sort of part-time or seasonal job to provide services for tourists and permanent researchers. Some people still resent imposed restrictions on hunting and farming but the new generation has a vested interest in conservation'.

In Tortuguero, we stay at Tortuga Lodge owned by Costa Rica Expeditions, one of the country's most renowned eco-tourism operators. They have installed a solar energy system and water-saving fixtures with the help of a local energy-efficiency expert. The operator also implements a local programme in Tortuguero whereby all the lodges and hotels used in their tours donate a dollar per participant to the local community. The project has helped fund improvements to the school and the installation of a water distribution system. Impressive trip so far. But, mosquitoes are voracious and sharks patrol local waters. The journey back to the Capital, San José, will be by single-engine charter since Tortuguero is inaccessible by road. A 12 kg baggage restriction is imposed for all passengers to ensure safety and to save on costs.

Along with Belize, Costa Rica is the most renowned ecotourism destination of Latin America. International scientists and biologists were the first to take an interest in the country's immense biodiversity and played a significant role in promoting environmental conservation. While Costa Rica covers a mere 0.03 per cent of the planet's surface, it has over 5 per cent of all life forms on earth. Today, 27 per cent of the territory is under some form of protection – either as National Parks, Wildlife Refuges or Biological Reserves. The first ecotourism initiatives launched by private enterprises capitalized on the expanding park system to entice foreign tourists. Tourism arrivals grew at an average annual rate of 15 per cent between 1990 and 1994, well above the global tourism average. In spite of a sharp drop in growth (3 per cent) in 1996, the country, which is roughly the size of Wales, attracts some 792 000 visitors annually. Critics fear that its popularity will lead to its downfall. The new conservation challenge is to control the crowds that flock to the rainforest. 'On national holidays, we've had hundreds of people entering the park' says a ranger at Manuel Antonio Natural Park. 'The noise people make while walking along the paths puts enormous psychological pressure on some animals. We've had to close the area on Mondays to give the animals a rest. Now there's talk of closing it on Tuesdays too.'

In the Monteverde Reserve administrators have set a 100 visitors-a-day ceiling to preserve ecological integrity. Environmentalists have campaigned against paved road access to the protected areas in order to control numbers. Many of the parks require four-wheel drives to reach them and some can only be accessed by boat or on foot. Most parks still lack visitor centres and trails are not always marked. However, in a controversial step in 1994, park entrance fees for foreigners rose from US$1 to an unrealistic US$15 causing uproar among ecotourists. Subsequently the 'Green Pass' was introduced allowing entrance to five national parks at 50 per cent of the official price. 'We've got to focus on the type of visitor we want to attract', adds the ranger. 'Do we really want the day-tripper culture up here? Maybe they'd better stay in their enclaves. Some scientists here would even claim that if so-called ecotourists were really concerned about the rainforest, they'd support conservation organizations from home rather than invading sensitive ecosystems.'

In 1502, on his fourth and last voyage to the New World, Christopher Columbus reached the Caribbean shores of Central America and met natives wearing heavy golden necklaces. Believing he had found the mythical 'Eldorado' he named the area 'Costa Rica', the rich coast. The land, however, did not yield any gold and remained one of the poorest colonies of the Spanish Empire. Introduced in the 1820s, coffee became the main generator of foreign exchange boosting Costa Rica's economic development. Owing to a slump in market prices, coffee export earnings dropped to third place (US$245.4 million) in 1990, overtaken by bananas (US$ 315 million) and tourism (US$ 275 million), in first and second places respectively. Since 1993 tourism has established itself as the largest earner of foreign exchange totalling US$ 688.6 million in 1996, which accounts for 23.4 per cent of all export revenue. Costa Rica may have found its new 'Eldorado'. It is today one of the most prosperous and stable countries of Central America. Tourism receipts represent 8.9 per cent of GDP (1994) and the industry is reported to be the most important sector for employment, generating over 60,000 direct jobs and a similar number of indirect ones.

In spite of increases in export earnings, economic growth fell from 4.5 per cent in 1994 to around 1.5 per cent in 1996. The country is under constant pressure from the International Monetary Fund and the Inter-American Development Bank to reduce its fiscal deficit and repay its foreign debt. The Government response to increase revenues included a 1 per cent levy on company assets, the raising of import tariffs and a 50 per cent rise in the national sales tax – from 10 per cent to 15 per cent. This increase, added to the 5 per cent tax on air transport, the 3 per cent levy on hotel accommodation (to finance the Costa Rican Institute of Tourism) and the 10 per cent service charge, makes the national tourism product an expensive and uncompetitive option.

Battles often rage in Costa Rica over land use. Until the tourism boom deforestation was seen as the means to economic development. Large companies, often foreign multinationals, are still involved in logging tropical rainforests for their precious hardwoods, mining, large-scale cattle raising and the exploitation of banana plantations. The practice of pesticide spraying of bananas constitutes not only a major environmental problem but also a health hazard for plantation workers who are said to suffer from pesticide poisoning. The growth of the population, expected to reach 4 million in 2000, has led to increasing encroachments upon the rainforest for subsistence farming.

Advocates for tourism development argue that its economic significance has prevented further destruction of the forest. 'When tourists visit parks and reserves they are sending positive messages to the government and they are paying for the conservation of Costa Rica's natural and wildlife resources' exclaims our guide from Costa Rica Expeditions. 'We use local businesses whenever possible and invest in the training of local guides. That way the dollars stay in the country and everyone benefits.'

In 1995, at the Berlin Climate Change Summit, Costa Rica's President, José Maria Figueres, took the issue one step further by suggesting, along with other world nations, that industrialized countries should finance conservation projects such as reforestation in developing countries as the cost of saving the planet should be shared by all.

Source: Anne Aichroth

Questions

1 Explain differences in the concepts of ecotourism and sustainable tourism drawing examples from the article. To what extent is ecotourism sustainable?
2 Discuss and evaluate arguments for and against each of the following:
 - The extension of the road system to remote natural reserves.
 - The increase in park entrance fees.
 - The taxation of tourist facilities.
3 Assess the overall costs and benefits of tourism for Costa Rica's economy and environment.
4 What opportunity costs are incurred through agricultural and industrial use of the land?
5 Comment upon the President of Costa Rica's request at the 1995 Climate Change Summit in Berlin.

Case 2

The economic impacts of football

The English Premier league continues to flourish. It had a combined turnover of £464 millions in 1996–1997 and is the richest in the world. Its nearest rival, Italy's Serie A, had a turnover of £377 million. It is growing at a remarkable rate of 37 per cent per annum and average profits per club stand at £4.3 million. The two star performers in the Premiership were Manchester United with a turnover of £88 million followed by Newcastle United with a turnover of £41 million.

Organizations

A number of UK football clubs are now public limited companies and their share prices appear in stock exchange listings. These clubs include

Table 20.1   Financial profile of Manchester United plc, 1993–1997

Year ended 31 July	1993	1994	1995	1996	1997
Turnover £000s	25 177	43 815	60 622	53 316	87 939
Operating profits £000s	7392	10 999	15 649	14 167	26 201
Pre-tax profit £000s	4202	10 776	20 014	15 399	27 577

Source: Annual Company Reports and Account.

Manchester United and Tottenham Hotspur. Public limited company (plc) status means that giving value to shareholders becomes a prime consideration for clubs. The period between 1994 and 1996 was a particularly good one for football share prices when Manchester United's shares rose from £1.30 to £4.80 and Tottenham's from 70p to £4.80. The financial figures for Manchester United, shown in Table 20.1, give some reasons for this rise in share values. Newcastle United was floated on the stock exchange in April 1997. The flotation helped to raise capital to pay for their new 80 000-seater stadium. Although its shares are now quoted on the stock exchange, Sir John Hall and his family still own the majority shareholding in the club through their company, Cameron Hall Developments Ltd.

Elsewhere in Europe, Italian Serie A teams are planning to float, with Lazio favourite to be the first. A number of Dutch, German and Scandinavian clubs are also planning to float and capitalize on the growing popularity of the game.

The soccer business, like any other, is subject to take-overs and mergers. In 1997, Olympic Marseille, one of the top French clubs bought Adidas, the German sports company. In 1998, Rupert Murdoch's News Corporation (owners of BSkyB, a major provider of football TV coverage) made a take-over bid for Manchester United whose share price had fallen to £2.20. This represents a form of vertical integration where the owner of supply channels would also own a service to be supplied. As such the government has to rule whether this is in the public interest. Similar vertical integration has occurred in Mexico where the TV company Televisa owns the America, Necaxa and Atlante football clubs and TV Azteca owns Atletico Morelia and Veracruz. Problems that can arise from these arrangements include manipulation of publicity, arrangements for match times, and using tactics unfavourable to competing clubs.

In addition to this vertical integration there are moves by UK clubs to integrate horizontally with foreign sides. This can create synergies. and achieve economies of scale. Everton, Tranmere Rovers and Manchester City have all invested in Irish clubs. These can then be used to nurture new and young players and make their playing squads broader and more flexible.

Ticket prices

Ticket sales are of prime importance and typically account for 40–50 per cent of a club's revenue. Ticket prices pose an interesting economic problem for clubs: they are governed by the underlying supply of and demand for seats. On the supply side, the necessity for Premiership clubs to move to all-seating stadia as a result of the Taylor Report has in many cases limited supply. The supply curve for seats is totally inelastic at the capacity level of the stadium. Demand for seats is strong owing to the continued high profile of the Premier League. For popular clubs with limited capacity this means that there is often excess demand for tickets. For example, Premier League and FA Cup champions (1997–1998) Arsenal have a maximum capacity of 38 000 at their home ground at Highbury in North London. Their matches are regularly sold out. Indeed their European Champions League (1998–1999) matches which were held at Wembley sold at a capacity of 73 000. This is an indication of potential demand.

Football clubs are unique and therefore competition is limited. Adam Brown, who sits on the government's Football Task Force, argues that 'clubs should each be regarded as monopolies and regulated accordingly'. He adds: 'You can't "buy" Manchester United from anywhere else can you?' There is potential to increase prices so as to equate demand with supply and increase sales revenue. Indeed, average ticket prices in the Premiership rose from £13.25 in 1996 to £15.45 in 1997, an increase of 16.6 per cent during a period when inflation in general was only 3.6 per cent. However, there is still excess demand for tickets at many clubs. Currently the excess demand for Arsenal tickets is managed by membership schemes, first come first served allocation and the operation of ticket touts in the illicit market.

Other income sources

The other major source of income for clubs is from TV sponsorship. Premiership income has been substantially bolstered by income from television deals. A four-year contract with BSkyB worth £693 million was signed in 1997–1998, which provides for extra payments for overseas rights after 1998–1999. At the international level, the rights for the 2002 World Cup TV coverage have been sold by FIFA to a German company for $2.2 billion. Mintel estimate that about 25 per cent of spectators at matches buy a programme at an average price of £1.50. Merchandising and sponsorship also add to income. Manchester United's main sponsors, the electrical goods company Sharp, currently (1999) pay the club £2 million per year. United also has an additional group of eight select sponsors. United seeks to exploit its brand in innovative ways. For example, it has formed a new joint venture company with Countryside Leisure Management to build a 100-bed hotel next to its Old Trafford stadium. The club will receive a fee for every guest.

Catering is not yet well developed in most clubs. The quality of food and drink sold in most grounds is poor with a predominance of burgers, hot dogs and pies sold at stand-up bars in consumer-unfriendly conditions. In 1997–1998, catering is estimated to generate an average revenue of £1.50 per head for 40 per cent of the crowd. The potential for increased revenue here is considerable as supporters currently spend large sums on food and drink before and after matches outside the ground.

Costs

Wage inflation has been notable in the Premier League. Wages rose in 1995–1996 by 34 per cent and again by 35 per cent in 1996–1997. The Bosman ruling that allows players freedom of movement when their contracts have expired has helped to inflate wages and transfer fees for players still under contract stood at £240 million in 1996–1997.

International trade

Football can affect a country's balance of payments on the import side and the export side. In terms of imports, transfers to the English premier league totalled £100 million in 1996–1997 and reached such a value in 1998 that for the first time the Office for National Statistics is to include them in the UK balance of payments accounts. Jaap Stam set the record with a £10.5 million signing from PSV Eindhoven to Manchester United, and overall £70 million of soccer imports took place between June and August of 1998. Table 20.2 records some of the key transfers.

Signing international stars is a key strategy in maintaining performance which in turn improves the export potential of soccer. This is illustrated by the fact that Manchester United is developing plans to exploit its brand globally. It has a target to open 150 United shops around the world before 2002. To achieve its aim its has established a new subsidiary, Manchester United International, and is employing design consultants specializing in leisure brands to plan the stores. Its first shops have already opened at airports in Dublin, Copenhagen and Hong Kong, selling merchandise such as replica kits, memorabilia and videos.

Table 20.2 Premiership signings from overseas, 1998

Player	Signed from	Signed to	Price (£m)
Jaap Stam	PSV Eindhoven	Manchester United	10.5
Pierluigi Casiraghi	Lazio	Chelsea	5.4
Dietmar Hamman	Bayern Munich	Newcastle	5.0
Marcel Desailly	AC Milan	Chelsea	4.6
Jesper Blomqvist	Parma	Manchester United	4.4
Olivier Dacourt	Strasbourg	Everton	3.8
Vegard Heggem	Rosenborg	Liverpool	3.5

Ironically, this expansion programme was launched in 1998 which was a poor year for merchandise sales that were down from £29 million to £24 million. However, the United chairman, Professor Sir Roland Smith, put this down to two short-term problems – the club is about to change its strip and the poor financial situation in Asia has affected exports. He reported that market research carried out by the club had indicated good medium-term prospects for the venture.

Summary of opportunities and threats facing clubs

- Consumer spending on football remains strong.
- Demand for tickets strong at top end of game.
- Virtual fans.
- Season ticket holders.
- Restricted capacities at grounds.
- Take-overs and mergers.
- Secondary revenue: merchandising, catering, etc.
- Players' wages and transfer fees.
- BSkyB rights.
- Divide between premier league and the rest is growing.
- Exploitation of consumers by clubs.
- Importance of financial results for plcs.
- High fixed costs for some clubs.
- Importance of staying at the top.

Sources

Deloitte and Touche (1998), *Annual Review of Football Finance.*
Mintel (1998), *The Football Report.*
Sir Norman Chester Centre for Football Research (1998), *Premier League Survey.*
Colman's Football Food Guide (1998).
Fletcher Research (1998), *How to Make Money out of Football.*
Newspapers: The *Guardian* and *The Times.*

Questions

1 Compile a list of economic impacts of football and comment on their measurement. Are there any negative impacts of football?
2 Discuss the issues surrounding ticket prices for Premiership matches, and evaluate different approaches to pricing and ticket allocation.
3 Conduct an opportunities and threats analysis on a named football club.
4 Evaluate the advantages and disadvantages of the flotation of Newcastle United to its various stakeholders.

5 Use economic analysis to explain wages of footballers compared to those of stewards. Is there an economic case for controlling wages?
6 Prepare a time series chart of share prices for a named club. Account for the movements in share prices.
7 What kind of take-over was the purchase of Olympic Marseille by Adidas? Evaluate the move from the point of view of consumer interests and those of Adidas.
8 What evidence is there to support the view that football clubs are a monopoly? Should this be seen as a problem?

Case 3

Cuba: sun, sand, sex and sea – a sustainable route to rising GNP?

Cuba's centrally planned economy has recently gone through a period of extreme difficulty as illustrated in Figure 20.2, and chronicled by Avella and Mills (1996:56):

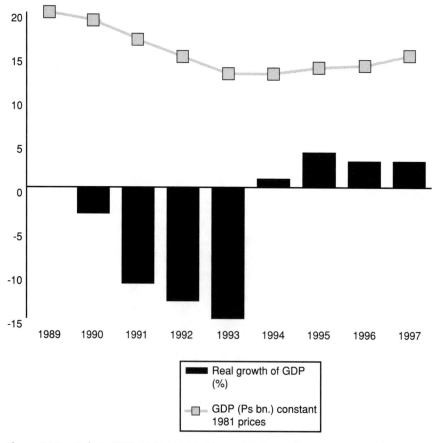

Figure 20.2   Cuba's GDP 1989–1997. *Notes:* 1995 = estimate, 1996 and 1997 = forecasts. *Source:* Economist Intelligence Unit (1996)

The Gross Social Product has declined by 46% in five years because of reduced international trade, particularly in respect of sugar exports . . . The island's factories are producing at only 30% capacity . . .

Most of these difficulties may be traced back to the collapse of the former Soviet Union in 1991 which led to the annual loss of:

. . . US$6 billion in economic aid, $1 billion in military assistance, 10 million tons of oil, and $6 billion worth of imported goods. [Cuba] also lost its major trading partner, and now had to sell its sugar at a fair market value.

Perrottet and Biondi, 1995: 60–1

It is these factors which led Fidel Castro to introduce, in 1990, 'a special period in peacetime', a period of intense economic austerity which still persists. The passing of the Helms-Burton Act in 1996 has added to economic difficulties with a tightening of US-led economic sanctions against Cuba.

Perhaps the most vivid illustration of Cuba's economic collapse was the 1994 *balseros* (rafters) exodus which hit the international headlines. Thousands of *balseros* deployed inner tubes and makeshift rafts in an attempt to find economic salvation in Miami. It is not hard for the visitor to Cuba to see how this 'special period' translates into everyday living. A significant part of the fishing fleet remains in the harbour through lack of fuel. Many houses remain unfinished through lack of building materials. The fabric of the city of Havana is falling apart. The average salary is 170 pesos a month rising to 400 pesos for a teacher and 500 pesos for a doctor. But there is a chronic shortage of basic groceries – from soap and toothpaste to cooking oil, and so the local currency – the peso is virtually worthless. There is little in the peso stores that isn't rationed. The huge motorways that span the island are virtually empty.

Against this backdrop of economic hardship, tourism has emerged as a key source of economic growth and regeneration. Figure 20.3 illustrates tourism's growing importance for foreign currency earnings. While the top four export earners for Cuba in 1989 were sugar, nickel, shellfish and tobacco, by 1994, tourism earnings had surpassed those of sugar which have been hit by a combination of poor harvests and the loss of guaranteed prices in the markets of the former Soviet Union.

Table 20.3 illustrates tourist arrivals between 1990 and 1995. It can be seen that there has been a dramatic growth in tourism arrivals which roughly doubled between 1990 and 1994. The estimated arrivals for 1996 are 930 000 (Casals, 1996), and there are ambitious plans for the future:

The country is not yet satisfied with the growth rate, number of visitors or the amount of businesses, although these are coming close to the projections for the year 2000, when Cuba must receive between 2.3 to 2.5 million tourists, contributing some three billion dollars to the Cuban economy

Casals, 1996: 14

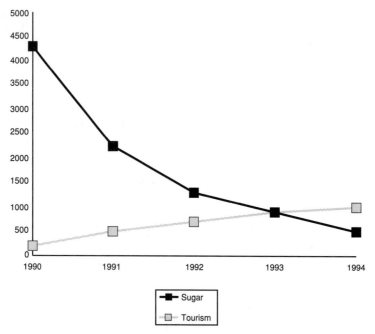

Figure 20.3   Cuba's foreign earnings from sugar and tourism ($ millions). *Note:* 1994 = estimate. *Source:* Economist Intelligence Unit (1995)

Table 20.3   Cuba: tourist arrivals and gross revenue

Year	Tourist arrivals (000s)	Gross revenue % growth	$ million
1990	327	3.8	243
1991	415	26.7	387
1992	455	9.7	567
1993	544	19.5	720
1994	617	13.5	850
1995	738	19.6	1100

Source: Economist Intelligence Unit (1996).

Tourism development and tourism strategy

Cuba's tourism industry currently spans the following types of tourism:

● Medical.
● Cultural and heritage.
● Sex.
● Socialism.
● Beach-resort.

● Conference and business.
● Special interest.

Of these, cultural and heritage and beach resort tourism are the most important, although dollar desperation means that prostitution is endemic and sex tourism permeates many of the categories. Cultural and heritage tourism is focused on the two major sites of Havana and Trinidad. Their attraction is underlined by the fact that Havana was designated by UNESCO in 1982 world cultural heritage status, and Trinidad, a UNESCO world heritage site in 1988.

Cuba has a number of beach resorts including Santa Lucia, Cayo Coco, Guadalavaca, Ancon and Cayo Largo, but its principal beach resort is Varadero. Varadero is a 45 km narrow peninsula with over 20 km of beaches. It is situated on the north of the island, about 80 km east of Havana. Its prime importance in terms of tourism is illustrated by the following:

By 1994 there were over 22 000 . . . tourist quality hotel rooms in the island . . . and by the year 2000, the government plans to have 30 000 hotel rooms in Varadero alone.

Perrotet and Biondi, 1995: 71

So Varadero lies at the heart of tourism development for Cuba. It has benefited from expenditure on infrastructure and boasts its own international airport and good road communications. It parades a range of hotels from the pre-revolutionary Internacional (built in 1950), the Soviet-built Club Atabey, to the 1990s joint venture hotels – the Sol Palmeras, the Melia Varadero and the Melia Las Americanas (all joint ventures with the Spanish company Grupo Sol). Several five-star hotels are currently under construction.

Varadero is then an area where the economic plans of the Cuban authorities, the profit prospects of joint venture companies and the vacation dreams of the tourists meet. There is an clear interdependency between these groups and successful economic development of Varadero depends on both demand and supply side factors. On the supply side the availability of capital to expand capacity and improve resort infrastructure is crucial. Hence the importance of joint ventures, and the potency of the Helms–Burton Act to deter such ventures. Recent reports (Economist Intelligence Unit, 1996) suggest a mixed reaction to Helms–Burton. A $400 million investment from Canadian Wally Berkoff has recently been announced, and Sol Melia intend to retain their Cuban interests. On the other hand two Spanish companies – Paradores Nacionales de Turismo and Hoteles Occidentales – have postponed investment decisions.

Another issue on the supply side, a problem common to socialist countries, is their lack of service culture (Burns, 1995) and consequential difficulties in delivering services to a high quality. Finally on the supply side, Cuban destinations must vie with other Caribbean destinations who are also competing strongly for the tourist dollar. This mix of factors (undeveloped resort infrastructure, uneven service and strong competition) points up the strategy currently being pursued by the Cuban authorities as a low-price/ limited value-added one (Kotler, 1988; Bowman; 1992; Tribe, 1997).

We therefore now turn our attention to the demand side to discover how well this policy is received by tourists. In particular, do they allow for the relatively low price of the destination in their overall evaluation of their holiday experience? Tribe and Snaith (1998) found that in reality holiday-makers do not expect Varadero to be any different from other Caribbean destinations such as Mustique, or Antigua or Barbados. As a result of their high expectations, the product they are offered in resorts such as Varadero is often unsatisfactory for them.

Now this has potentially serious consequences for Cuba's tourism, and general economic policy. Emphasis hitherto has been on beds, beds, beds. This is a narrow supply side policy. It is narrow because the supply-side requires a more general attention to resort development. Tribe and Snaith (1998) suggest that items requiring urgent attention which emerge from their survey are:

- Restaurant provision.
- Bar provision.
- Nightlife provision.
- Shopping facilities.
- Hotel meal provision.
- Prices in Varadero.
- Access to Cuban heritage and culture.
- Industrial pollution.
- Service quality.

Then there is the question of prostitution to which the authorities maintain an ambivalent attitude.

In conclusion, tourism represents a key strand in Cuba's economic renewal but many brochures and NTO materials give a very carefully selected view of Varadero, and significant aspects are left out in the presentation of the destination. This leads to significant critical gaps between expectations and realizations for holidaymakers to Varadero. Current marketing of Varadero is therefore unsustainable, and this threatens the longer-term economic prospects. The routes to sustainable marketing (in the economic sense) are either to upgrade reality towards publicity or to downgrade publicity towards reality.

Thus one route to closing these gaps is to make brochures for Varadero more honest. Although, 'a stone's throw from the beach' is no longer used in brochures to describe treks of more than a kilometre, partial views and accounts of destinations are still common and result in dissatisfaction. The other route is to transform Varadero as a destination. There are already signs of this in Varadero which has embarked upon a programme of five-star hotel construction. But the creation of enclaves within an enclave is not a substitute for balanced development of the resort. Considerable development of infrastructure is required to support the stock of economy hotels.

Questions

1 What economic problems is Cuba facing and to what extent can tourism assist in solving these problems?

2 What are the strengths and weaknesses of Cuba as a holiday destination?

3 What are the opportunities and threats facing Cuba as a holiday destination?

4 'Varadero is then an area where the economic plans of the Cuban authorities, the profit prospects of joint venture companies and the vacation dreams of the tourists meet.' Explain what is meant by this statement and what conflicts exist between these parties.

5 What are the key environmental impacts of tourism to Cuba?

6 Assess the relative merits of a tourism development programme for Cuba based on:
● Central planning.
● Private enterprise.
● Mixed ventures.

7 'Multinational enterprises are the key to Cuban development.' Critically evaluate this statement.

References and suggested further reading

Avella, A. and Mills, A. (1996), Tourism in Cuba in the 1990s: back to the future, *Tourism Management*, **17**(1).

Bowman, C. (1992), Charting competitive strategy. In: Faulkner, D. and Johnson, G. (eds.), *The Challenge of Strategic Management*, London, Kogan Page.

Burns, P. (1996), Hotel management training in Eastern Europe: Challenges for Romania, *Progress in Tourism and Hospitality Research*, **1**(1), pp. 53–62.

Calder, S. and Hatchwell, E. (1993), *Travellers Survival Kit: Cuba*, Oxford, Vacation Work.

Calder, S. and Wheat, S. (1995), Travel: Why do you think they're called operators?, *Independent Newspaper*, 2 September, London.

Casals, R. (1996), Increased participation by foreign capital, *Granma International*, 5 June, p. 14, Havana.

Economist Intelligence Unit (1995), *Country Report: Cuba, Dominican Republic, Haiti, Puerto Rico*, Second Quarter, London, Economist Publications.

Economist Intelligence Unit (1996), *Country Report: Cuba, Dominican Republic, Haiti, Puerto Rico*, Third Quarter, London, Economist Publications.

Hall, D. (1992), Tourism development in Cuba. In: Harrison, D. (ed.), *Tourism and the Less Developed Countries*, London, Belhaven Press.

Hatchwell, E. and Calder, S. (1995), *Cuba in Focus: A guide to the people, politics and culture*, London, Latin America Bureau.

Katz, I. (1995), Travel: Cuba, *Guardian*, London, 1 July, p.42.

Kotler, P. (1988), *Marketing Management*, Hemel Hempstead, Prentice-Hall.

Observer (1994), Game for a fistful of dollars, 26 June.

Perrotet, T. and Biondi, J. (eds.) (1995), *Insight Guides: Cuba*, Hong Kong, APA Publications.

Pollard, J. and Rodriguez, R. (1993), Tourism and Torremolinos, *Tourism Management*, August, pp. 247–58.

Poon, A. (1993), *Tourism, Technology and Competitive Strategies*, Oxford, CAB International.

Ryan, C. (1995), *Researching Tourism Satisfaction*, London, Routledge.

Tribe, J. (1997), *Corporate Strategy for Tourism*, London, International Thomson Business Press.

Tribe, J. and Snaith, T. (1998), From SERVQUAL to HOLSAT; holiday satisfaction in Cuba, *Tourism Management*, **19**(1).

Case 4

Tourism: a taxing business

The following extracts reveal different attitudes to taxes on tourism.

1 Tourism taxation

Taxes on the tourism industry can stifle growth if they are not equitable and applied after careful consultation between fiscal authorities and the tourism sector, according to a report, *Tourism Taxation*, prepared by the WTO. Graham Wason from management consultants Deloitte Touch who prepared the report says 'Governments have realized that taxing tourism is an easy way to gain extra revenue without upsetting their own voters and the industry is very concerned about the upward trend'. He identified 40 different types of taxes levied on the tourism industry throughout the world and noted that tax rates were increasing. 'It is not realistic to say we don't want to be taxed. If we didn't pay taxes there would be no money for improving airports or roads or to invest in necessary social services. but it is important that tourism is not unfairly taxed.'

The report notes that charges for entry and exit visas are among the worst taxes on tourism with some countries such as the Marshall Islands charging $20 to enter the country and another $20 to leave. Consultant Oliver Bennet suggests 'It is much better to encourage people to come into the country and then to tax them on consumption while they are there.' Other problems noted are when governments change taxes without giving tour operators sufficient time to incorporate the changes into their pricing structures.

Euro MP Petrus Cornelissen urged the EU to give tourism priority treatment because of its ability to create new jobs. He particularly criticized plans to scrap duty-free shopping in 1999 which threatened the jobs of 100 000 people employed directly or indirectly in the sector. He said 'Tax-free shops are not just a bonus for travellers, they are a major source of revenue for the airport authorities, enabling airport fees to be kept at lower levels.'

Source: WTO Press Release.

2 Taxing the Seychelles

The government of the Seychelles has imposed a $100 environmental tax on tourists payable on arrival at the airport. The tax is being imposed in order to limit visitor numbers and provide funds for environmental projects. In 1998 about 130 000 tourists a year visited the island and the government wants to encourage an upper limit of 180 000 so as not to overcrowd the beaches. The tax is also part of a strategy to maintain the upmarket image for the island.

Keith Betton of the Association of British Travel Agents thinks that the tax is a bad idea. 'The bottom end of the market is very price sensitive. This could send people to other holiday destinations like Mauritius'.

Source: The *Guardian*.

3 Enough is enough

More than 75 groups in 23 countries are protesting today (6 November 1998) as part of Friends of the Earth Europe's *Right Price for Air Travel* campaign. They are calling on governments and the European Union to introduce a kerosene tax for all flights with the EU as well as emissions-related charges and stricter noise and emissions around airports.

Air travel is the fastest-growing source of greenhouse gas emissions. It is responsible for about 7 per cent of global warming, including 3 per cent of global carbon dioxide emissions. Yet a 50-year-old international agreement means airlines pay no duty on the fuel they use, whereas motorists and long-distance coach operators have to pay over 40 pence per litre. Even train companies pay 3 pence per litre for their diesel. Roger Higman, Friends of the Earth's senior transport campaigner, said: 'Flying is the most polluting form of transport there is. Yet airlines pay no duty on the fuel they use and therefore have little incentive to conserve fuel or control their emissions. The tax exemption gives airlines an unfair advantage over other forms of transport, encouraging people to travel in the least environmentally friendly way. The Chancellor . . . must back European moves to end this loophole by taxing airlines for the fuel they use'.

Source: Friends of the Earth Press Release, 6 November 1998.

4 Different accounts of aircraft pollution

Pat Malone:

- 'Aircraft emissions are not covered by international agreements seeking to limit emissions of greenhouse gases. At the Kyoto environmental summit last year they were specifically exempted because negotiators could not agree on how to pin responsibility on individual nations.'

- 'Aircraft burn 3 per cent of all fossil fuels used on earth, and their turbines produce between 1.5 billion and 2.2 billion tonnes of CO_2 every year.'
- 'Passenger jets may be responsible for as much as 10 per cent of all greenhouse gas emissions – according to some estimates – with their pollution being injected directly into the upper atmosphere as a kind of "intravenous fix" for global warming.'

Source: The *Observer*, 8 November 1998.

Pierre Jeanniot, Director-General, International Air Transport Association:

- 'Allow me to correct some of Pat Malone's assertions on air pollution (*News*, 8 November): "Aircraft produce between 1.5 and 2.2 billion tonnes of CO_2 every year". The true figure is closer to 0.5 billion tonnes, that is, 2.5 per cent of the world total from the burning of fossil fuels.'
- 'Passenger jets may be responsible for as much as 10 per cent of all greenhouse gas (GHG) emissions.' Carbon dioxide emissions from air traffic contribute about 1.5 per cent of man-made annual input to global warming. Cumulative emissions of exhaust gases from air traffic are thought to be around 3 per cent.

Source: Letter to the *Observer*, 22 November 1998.

Questions

1 What kinds of taxes are imposed on tourism?
2 Explain the relationship between demerit goods, merit goods, public goods, taxation and tourism.
3 Why is elasticity of demand an important consideration in setting tax levels.
4 Evaluate the case for scrapping duty free tax concessions.
5 What are the arguments for and against taxation of aviation fuel?
6 What factors should determine the amount of tax imposed on aviation fuel.
7 In what ways could taxes on tourism be used to maximize employment and minimize environmental damage?
8 Compare taxation with other instruments for achieving environmental improvements in the leisure and tourism sector.
9 Why is it important to accurately assess the environmental impacts of air travel? Why do disagreements such as those noted above make life difficult for economists?

Sources and resources

Websites

The following websites offer bibliographic listings in leisure and tourism, and may be useful to those trying to research a specialist area. Websites are notoriously transient, so be aware that some of these may cease to function throughout the life of this book.

University of California Davis: Olympic centennial athletic, sport, recreation
   bibliography project   http://www-nutrition.ucdavis.edu/olympics/
Bibliography: consumer culture and leisure
   http://158.223.1.1/~soa01ds/bibcon.htm
University of Waterloo Electronic Library: recreation and leisure studies
   electronic library   http://www.lib.uwaterloo.ca/discipline/recreation/
University of Houston, Hospitality and Tourism Indexes, Abstracts,
   Bibliographies, and Table of Contents Services
   http://info.lib.uh.edu/indexes/hosp.htm
Bibliography of Economic Impacts of Parks: recreation and tourism
   http://pilot.ms.edu/user/changewe4/bibli.htm
University of Connecticut: a collection of extensive bibliographies on
   various aspects of tourism, sports, and leisure
   http://playlab.uconn.edu/frl.htm
Central Queensland University: leisure and tourism resources
   http://library.syd.cqu.edu.au/tourism.htm
Research and scholarship about leisure and recreation
   http://www.gu.edu.au:81/uls/leis/services/lswp/
Tourism and Hospitality Bibliography
   http://omni.cc.purdue.edu/~alltson/books.htm
St George Campus Library: sport and leisure resources
   http://www.library.unsw.edu.au/~stg/sport.html
Tourism Hospitality and Leisure Journals
   http://omni.cc.purdue.edu/~alltson/journals.htm
University of Buckingham: tourism resources
   http://158.223.1.1/~soa01ds/bibcon.htm

Written materials

Archer, B. (1996), Economic impact analysis, *Annals of Tourism Research*, **23**(3), pp. 704–7.

Archer, B. and Fletcher, J. (1996) The economic impact of tourism in the Seychelles, *Annals of Tourism Research*, **23**(1), pp. 32–47.

Archer, B.H. (1982), The value of multipliers and their policy implications, *Tourism Management*, December, pp. 236–41.

Archer, B.H. (1984), Economic impact: Misleading multipliers, *Annals of Tourism Research*, **11**, pp. 517–18.

Archer, B.H. (1995), Importance of tourism for the economy of Bermuda, *Annals of Tourism Research*, **22**, pp. 918–30.

Archer, B.H. and Owen, C.A. (1971), Toward a tourist regional multiplier, *Regional Studies*, **5**(4), pp. 289–94.

Ashworth, G.J. and Dietvorst, A.G.J. (eds.) (1995), *Tourism and Spatial Transformations: Implications for Policy and Planning*, CAB International.

Ashworth, G.A. and Voogd, H. (1990), *Selling the City*, Wiley.

Barke, M. Towner, J. and Newton, M. (eds.) (1995), *Tourism in Spain*, CAB.

Bergstrom, J.A., Cordell, H.A., Ashley, G.A. and Watson, A.A. (1990), Economic impacts of recreational spending on rural areas: a case study, *Economic Development Quarterly*, **4**(1), pp. 29–39.

Bramham, P., Henry, I., Mommaas, H. and Van der Poel, H. (eds.) (1993), *Leisure Policies in Europe*, CAB International.

Briguglio, L. Butler, R. Harrison, D. Filho, W. (eds.) (1996), *Sustainable Tourism in Islands and Small States: Case Studies*, Pinter.

Briguglio, L., Archer, B., Jafari, J. and Wall, G. (eds.) (1996), *Sustainable Tourism in Islands and Small States: Issues and Policies*, Pinter.

Brown, F. (1998), *Tourism: Blight or Blessing?*, Butterworth-Heinemann.

Bryman, A. (1995), *Disney and his Worlds*, Routledge.

Bull, A. (1995), *The Economics of Travel and Tourism*, Longman.

Burns, P. And Holden, A. (1995), *Tourism: a new perspective*, Prentice-Hall.

Bushnell, R. and Hyle, M. (1985), Computerized models for assessing the economic impact of recreation and tourism. In: Propst, D.A. (ed.), *Assessing the Economic Impacts of Recreation and Tourism*, pp. 46–51 Asheville.

Butler, R., Hall, R. and Jenkins, M. (eds.) (1998), *Tourism and Recreation in Rural Areas*, Wiley.

Byrnes, W.J. (1993), *Management and the Arts*, Focal Press.

Cater, E. and Lowman, G. (1994), *Ecotourism: A Sustainable Option*, Wiley.

Coccossis, H. and Nijkamp, P. (eds.) (1995), *Sustainable Tourism Development*, Ashgate.

Conlin, M. and Baum, T. (eds.) (1995), *Island Tourism: Management Principles and Practice*, Wiley.

Cooke, A. (1994), *Economics of Leisure And Sport*, ITBP.

Cooper, C. and Wanhill, S. (eds.) (1997), *Tourism Development: Environmental and Community Issues*, Wiley.

Cooper, C., Fletcher, J., Gilbert, D., Wanhill, S. and Shepherd, R. (1998), *Tourism: Principles and Practice*, Longman.

Croall, J. (1995), *Preserve or Destroy? Tourism and the Environment*, Caloust Gulbenkian Foundation.

Cullen, P. (1997), *Economics for Hospitality Management*, ITBP.

Cushman, G., Veal, A.A. and Zuzanek, J. (eds.) (1996), *World Leisure Participation: Free Time in the Global Village*, CAB International.

Dardis, R., Derrick, F., Lehfeld, A. and Wolfe, K.A. (1981), Cross section studies of recreation expenditures in the United States, *Journal of Leisure Research*, **13**, pp. 181–94.

Dardis, R., Soberon-Ferrere, H. and Patro, D. (1994), Analysis of leisure expenditures in the United States. *Journal of Leisure Research*, **25**(4), pp. 309–21.

Davidson, R. (1994), *Business Travel*, Longman.

Davidson, R. (1998), *Tourism in Europe*, 2nd ed, Longman.

Davidson, R. and Maitland, R. (1997), *Tourism* Destinations, Hodder and Stoughton.

Dawson, S., Blahna, D. and Keith, J. (1993), Expected and actual regional economic impacts of Great Basin National Park. *Journal of Park and Recreation Administration*, **11**(1), pp. 45–57.

Deegan, J. and Dineen, D.A. (1997), *Tourism Policy and Performance: The Irish Experience*, ITBP.

Department of the Environment (1990), *Tourism and the Inner City*, DOE.

Dickinson, B. and Vladimir, A. (1996), *Selling the Sea: Inside Look at the Cruise Industry*, Wiley.

Doganis, R. (1991), *Flying Off Course: The Economics of International* Airlines, Routledge.

Doganis, R. (1992), *The Airport Business*, Routledge.

Eadington, W.R., and Redman, M. (1991), Economics and tourism, *Annals of Tourism Research*, **18**, pp. 41–56.

Eaton, B. (1996), *European Leisure Business: Strategies for the Future*, Elm.

Elkin, R. and Roberts, R. (1987), Evaluating the human resource (employment) requirements and impacts of tourism developments. In: Ritchie, J.R.B. and Goeldner, C.R., *Travel Tourism and Hospitality Research: A Handbook for Managers*, John Wiley.

Elliot, J. (1997), *Tourism: Politics and Public Sector Management*, Routledge.

English, Donald B.K., Bergstrom, John C. (1994), The conceptual links between recreation site development and regional economic impacts, *Journal of Regional Science*, **34**(4), pp. 599–611.

Fitzgibbon, M. and Kelly, A. (1997), *From Maestro to Manager: Critical Issues in Arts and Culture Management*, Oaktree Press.

Fleming, W.R. and Toepper, L. (1990), Economic impact studies: Relating the positive and negative impacts to tourism development, *Journal of Travel Research*, Summer, pp. 35–42.

Fletcher, J.E. (1989), Input-output analysis and tourism impact studies, *Annals of Tourism Research*, **16**, pp. 514–29.

France, L. (ed.) (1997), *Earthscan Reader in Sustainable Tourism*, Earthscan.

Frechtling, D.C. (1987), Assessing the impacts of travel and tourism – Introduction to travel impact estimation. In: Ritchie, J.R.B. and Goeldner,

C.R., *Travel Tourism and Hospitality Research: A Handbook for Managers*, John Wiley.

Frechtling, D.C. (1987), Assessing the impacts of travel and tourism – Measuring economic benefits. In: Ritchie, J.R.B. and Goeldner, C.R., *Travel Tourism and Hospitality Research: A Handbook for Managers*, John Wiley.

Frechtling, D.C. (1996), *Practical Tourism Forecasting*, Butterworth-Heinemann.

Fujii, E., Khale, M. and Mak, J. (1985), An almost ideal demand system for visitor expenditures, *Journal of Transport Economics and Policy*, **19**(2), pp. 161–71.

Gee, C.Y., Makens, J.C. and Choy, D.J.L. (1997), *The Travel Industry*, Van Nostrand Reinhold.

Gee, C.Y. (ed.) (1997), *International Tourism: A global perspective*, World Tourism Organisation.

Glyptis, S. (ed.) (1993), *Leisure and the Environment: Essays in Honour of Professor J.A. Patmore*, Belhaven Press.

Go, F.M. and Pine, R. (1995), *Globalization Strategy in the Hotel Industry*, Routledge.

Hall, C.M. (1994), *Tourism and Politics: Policy, Power and Place*, Wiley.

Hall, C.M. (1997), *Tourism in the Pacific Rim: Development Impacts and Markets*, 2nd ed, Longman.

Hall, C.M. and Jenkins, J.M. (1995), *Tourism and Public Policy*, ITBP.

Hall, C.M. and Lew, A. (eds.) (1998), *Sustainable Tourism: A Geographical Perspective*, Addison Wesley.

Hall, C.M. and Page, S.J. (1996), *Tourism in the Pacific: Issues and Cases*, ITBP.

Hall, M. (ed.) (1998), *Sustainable Tourism: A Geographical Perspective*, Longman.

Hanlon, P. (1996), *Global Airlines: Competition in a Transnational Industry*, Butterworth-Heinemann.

Harris, R. and Leiper, N. (eds.) (1995), *Sustainable Tourism: An Australian Perspective*, Butterworth-Heinemann.

Harris, R., Heath, N., Toepper, L. and Williams, P. (1998), *Sustainable Tourism: A Global Perspective*, Butterworth-Heinemann.

Harrison, D. (ed.) (1992), *Tourism and the Less Developed Countries*, Wiley.

Harrison, L.C. and Husbands, W. (eds.) (1996), *Practising Responsible Tourism*, Wiley.

Haywood, L. and Butcher T. (1994), *Community Leisure and Recreation: Theory and Practice*, Focal Press.

Holloway, C.J. (1998), *The Business of Tourism*, Longman.

Inkpen, G. (1998), *Information Technology for Travel and Tourism*, 2nd ed. Longman.

Inskeep, E. (1997), *Tourism Planning*, Van Nostrand Reinhold.

Ioannides, D. and Debbage, K.G. (eds.) (1998), *The Economic Geography of the Tourist Industry: A Supply-Side Analysis*, Routledge.

Johnson, P. and Thomas, B. (eds.) (1992), *Choice and Demand in Tourism*, Mansell.

Johnson, P. and Thomas, B. (eds) (1992), *Perspectives on Tourism Policy*, Mansell.

Johnson, R.L. and Moore, E. (1993), Tourism impact estimation, *Annals of Tourism Research*, **20**, pp. 279–88.

Johnson, R.L., Obermiller, F., and Radtke, H. (1989), The economic impact of tourism sales, *Journal of Leisure Research*, **21** (2), pp. 140–54.

Jones, P. and Pizam, A. (eds.) (1993), *The International Hospitality Industry: Organisational and Operational Issues*, Longman.

Knowles, T. (1996), *Corporate Strategy for Hospitality*, Longman.

Kotas, R., Teare, R., Logie, J., Jayawardena, C. and Bowen, J. (eds.) (1996), *The International Hospitality Business*, Cassell.

Kottke, M. (1988), Estimating economic impacts of tourism, *Annals of Tourism Research*, **15**, pp. 122–33.

Krippendorf, J. (1989), *The Holiday Makers: Understanding the Impact of Leisure and Travel*, Butterworth-Heinemann.

Lawson, F. (1998), *Tourism and Recreation Development*, Focal Press.

Lea, J. (1998), *Tourism and Development in the Third World*, Routledge.

Lieber, R. and Allton, D. (1983), Visitor expenditures and the economic impact of public recreation facilities in Illinois. In: Leiber, S. and Fesenmaier, D. (ed.), *Recreation Planning and Management*, pp. 35–64, Venture Publishing.

Lieber, S. and Fesenmaier, D. (1989), Recreation expenditures and opportunity theory: the case of Illinois. *Journal of Leisure Research*, **21** (2), pp. 101–23.

Lockhart, D.G. and Drakakis-Smith, D. (eds.) (1996), *Island Tourism: Trends and Prospects*, Pinter.

Lundberg, D., Stavenga, M. and Krishnamoorthy, M. (1995), *Tourism Economics*, Wiley.

Lundberg, Donald E., Krishnamoorthy, M. and Stavenga, Mink H. (1995), *Tourism Economics*, Wiley.

Mathieson, A. and Wall, G. (1992), *Tourism: Economic, Physical and Social Impacts*, Longman.

McCormack, F. (1994), *Water Based Recreation: Managing Water Resources for Leisure*, Elm.

McNeill, L. (1997), *Travel in the digital age*, Bowerdean Publishing.

Medlik, S. (1994), *The Business of Hotels*, Butterworth-Heinemann.

Middleton, V.T.C. with Hawkins, R. (1998), *Sustainable Tourism: A Marketing Perspective*, Butterworth-Heinemann.

Milne, S.S. (1987), Differential multipliers. *Annals of Tourism Research*, **14**, pp. 499–515.

Mowforth, M. and Munt, I. (1998), *Tourism and Sustainability: New Tourism in the Third World*, Routledge.

National Park Service (1990), *Economic impacts of protecting rivers, trails, and greenway corridors – a resource book*, US Department of the Interior National Park Service, California.

Oppermann, M. (ed.) (1997), *Pacific Rim Tourism*, CAB International.

Oppermann, M. and Chon, K.-S. (1997), *Tourism in Developing Countries*, ITBP.

Page, S. (1994), *Transport for Tourism*, ITBP.

Page, S.A. and Getz, D. (eds.) (1997). *The Business of Rural Tourism: International Perspectives*, ITBP.

Pattullo, P. (1996), *Last Resorts: The Cost of Tourism in the Caribbean*, Cassell.

Peacock, M. (1995), *Information Technology in the Hospitality Industry*, Cassell.

Pearce, D. (1989), *Tourist Development*, Longman.

Poon, A. (1993), *Tourism, Technology and Competitive Strategies*, CAB.

Price, M.F. (ed.) (1996), *People and Tourism in Fragile Environments*, Wiley.

Priestley, G.K., Edwards, J.A. and Coccossis, H. (eds.) (1996), *Sustainable Tourism?: European Experiences*, CAB International.

Propst, D.B. and Gavrilis, D.G. (1987), The role of economic impact assessment procedures, *Recreational fisheries management, Transactions of the American Fisheries Society*, **116**, pp. 450–60.

Ravenscroft, N. (1992), *Recreation Planning and Development*, Macmillan.

Shackley, M. (1996), *Wildlife Tourism*, ITBP.

Shaw, G. and Williams, A. (eds.) (1997), *The Rise and Fall of British Coastal Resorts; Cultural and Economic Perspectives*, Pinter.

Sheldon, P.J. (1997), *Tourism Information Technology*, CAB International.

Sheldon, Pauline J. (1990), A review of tourism expenditure research. In: Cooper, C.P. (ed.), *Progress in tourism, recreation and hospitality management*, Belhaven Press.

Shone, A. (1998), *The Business of Conferences in the Hospitality and Leisure Industries*, Butterworth-Heinemann.

Sinclair, M.T. and Stabler, M.J. (1997), *The Economics of Tourism*, Routledge.

Sinclair, M.T. and Stabler, M.J. (eds) (1991), *The Tourism Industry: An International Analysis*, CAB International.

Spotts, D.M. and Mahoney, E. (1991), Segmenting visitors to a destination region based on the volume of their expenditures, *Journal of Travel Research*, Spring, pp. 24–31.

Stabler, M.J. (ed.) (1997), *Tourism and Sustainability: Principles to Practice*, CAB International.

Swarbrooke, J. and Horner, S. (1998), *Consumer Behaviour in Tourism: An International Perspective*, Butterworth-Heinemann.

Taylor, D., Fletcher, R. and Clabaugh, T. (1993), A comparison of characteristics, regional expenditures, and economic impact of visitors to historical sites with other recreational visitors, *Journal of Travel Research*, **32**(1), pp. 30–5.

Taylor, F. (1993), To hell with paradise, *A history of the Jamaican Tourism Industry*, University of Pittsburgh Press.

Teare, R. and Olsen, M. (eds.) (1992), *International Hospitality Management: Corporate Strategy in Practice*, Longman.

Teare, R., Canziani, B.F. and Brown, G. (eds.) (1997), *Global Directions: New Strategies for Hospitality and Tourism*, Cassell.

Theobald, W. (ed.) (1998), *Global Tourism: The Next Decade*, 2nd ed, Butterworth-Heinemann.

Thomas, R.(ed.) (1996), *The Hospitality Industry, Tourism and Europe*, Cassell.

Torkildsen, G. (1992), *Leisure and Recreation Management*, Spon.

Tribe, J. (1997), *Corporate Strategy for Tourism*, ITBP.

Var, T., and Quayson, J. (1985), The multiplier impact of tourism in the Okanagan, *Annals of Tourism Research*, **12**, pp. 497–514.

Wagner, J.E. (1997), Estimating the economic impacts of tourism, *Annals of Tourism Research*, **24** (3), pp. 592–608.

Wahab, S. and Pigram, J.J. (eds.) (1997), *Tourism, Development and Growth: The Challenge of Sustainability*, Routledge.

Walsh, R.G. (1986), *Recreation Economic Decisions: Comparing Benefits and Costs*, Venture Publishing Inc.

Wanhill, S. (1988), Tourism multipliers under capacity constraints, *Service Industries Journal*, **8**, pp. 137–42.

Weaver, D. (1998), *Ecotourism in the Less Developed World*, CAB International.

Wells, A.T. (1993), *Air Transportation*, ITBP.

Wheatcroft, S. (1994), *Aviation and Tourism Policies: Balancing the Benefits*, ITBP.

Williams, A.M. and Shaw, G. (eds.) (1991), *Tourism and Economic Development: Western European Experiences*, Wiley.

Witt, S.F. and Witt, C.A. (1992), *Modelling and Forecasting Demand in Tourism*, Academic Press.

WTO (1991), *Tourism to the Year 2000: Qualitative Aspects Affecting Global Growth*, World Tourism Organisation, Madrid.

WTO (1993), *Investments and Financing in the Tourism Industry*, World Tourism Organisation, Madrid.

WTO (1994), *GATS Implications for Tourism*, World Tourism Organisation, Madrid.

WTO (1996), *Tourism and New Information* Technologies, World Tourism Organisation, Madrid.

WTO (1996), *Tourism and Environmental Protection*, World Tourism Organisation, Madrid.

WTO (1997), *Agenda 21 for the Travel and Tourism Industry*, World Tourism Organisation, Madrid.

WTO (1997), *Asia Tourism – Towards New Horizons*, World Tourism Organisation, Madrid.

WTO (1997), *Compendium of Tourism Statistics*, World Tourism Organisation, Madrid.

WTO (1997), *Multilateral and Bilateral Sources of Financing for Tourism Development*, World Tourism Organisation, Madrid.

WTO (1997), *Senior Tourism*, World Tourism Organisation, Madrid.

WTO (1997), *Yearbook of Tourism Statistics*, World Tourism Organisation, Madrid.

Yale, P. (1995), *The Business of Tour Operations*, Longman.

Yeoman, I. and Ingold, A. (eds.) (1997), *Yield Management: Strategies for the Service Industries*, Cassell.

Zhou, D., Yanagida, J.F., Chakravorty, U., and Leung, P. (1997), Estimating economic impacts from tourism. *Annals of Tourism Research*, **24**(1), pp. 76–89.

Index